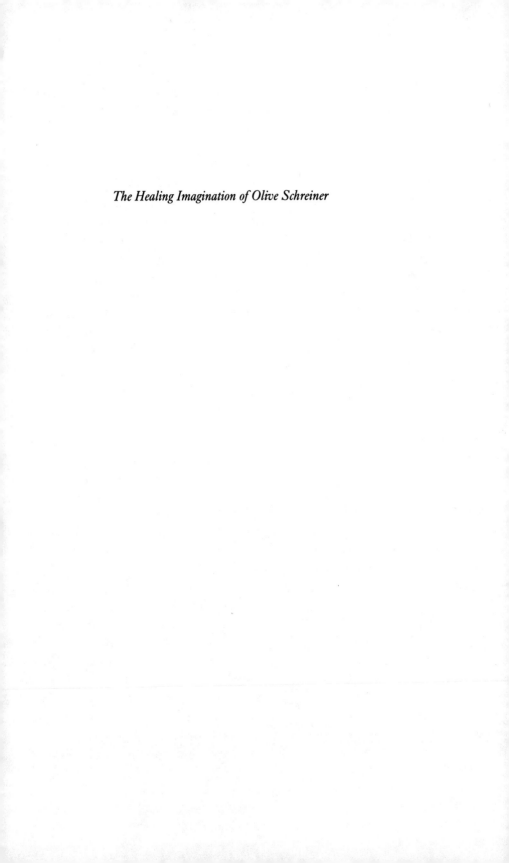

The Healing Imagination of Olive Schreiner

THE HEALING IMAGINATION OF

Olive Schreiner

BEYOND SOUTH AFRICAN COLONIALISM

Joyce Avrech Berkman

The University of Massachusetts Press

Amherst

B
Schreiner

Copyright © 1989 by
The University of Massachusetts Press
All rights reserved
Printed in the United States of America
LC 88-38518
ISBN 0-87023-676-8

Library of Congress Cataloging-in-Publication Data
Berkman, Joyce Avrech.
   The healing imagination of Olive Schreiner : beyond South African
colonialism / Joyce Avrech Berkman
      p.   cm.
   Bibliography: p.
   Includes index.
   ISBN 0–87023–676–8 (alk. paper)
      1. Schreiner, Olive, 1855–1920.   2. Authors, South African—19th
century—Biography.   3. Feminists—South Africa—Biography.
4. Social problems in literature.   5. Colonies in literature.
I. Title.
PR9369.2.S37Z588   1989
823—dc19
[B]   88-38518
                                                          CIP

British Library Cataloguing in Publication data are available.

With joy
I dedicate this book to—

my parents, Lillian and Ben
my siblings, Gloria and Norman
my sons, Jem and Zak
and my husband, Lenny

CONTENTS

ACKNOWLEDGMENTS

THE ROAD CULMINATING in this book has been long, serpentine, and strewn in places with forbidding bramble. At various junctures I thought of turning back, beginning anew, or settling for a few articles. Midway along this trek I completed my monograph, *Olive Schreiner: Feminism on the Frontier* (Montreal: Eden Press, 1979). The preparation of this study both slaked and abetted my desire for further research and reflection upon Schreiner's life and work. Some of the individuals whom I acknowledged in this earlier book continued to play a key role in sustaining my resolve and in assisting me to complete the volume you now have in your hands. During the past decade, other people appeared who provided help at critical milestones. To all of these individuals I am deeply grateful, and I delight in the opportunity to salute them publicly.

The original manuscript for this book was roughly twice its current length. Despite its sprawling character it received rigorous scrutiny from a group of scholars whose shrewd, incisive advice and enthusiasm for it inspired me during the revising process. I am thankful for the generosity of Frank Turner. His affirmation of my thesis and major interpretations, his queries and thoughtful criticism, as well as his list of names of scholars who would be interested in my study, emboldened me at a time when I was feeling discouraged and uncertain about my manuscript's future. Deborah Epstein Nord's sensitive and subtle understanding of my work, evident in her critique of both my unrevised and my revised manuscripts, contributed decisively to its publication. Ann Scott, coauthor with Ruth First of a remarkable biography of Schreiner that presents interpretations of Schreiner at times markedly different from mine, did not hesitate to express her pleasure in my study and save me from some embarrassing errors. Similarly, Bernard Lightman and Dorothy O. Helly's wise and caring criticism of my manuscript pointed out some of its disturbing ambiguities and oversights. Sean Redding, Leonore Noll Hoffmann, and Susan Kent offered excellent suggestions and much support.

Among others who read the entire manuscript, two scholars deserve special recognition. I am much indebted to Harriet Sigerman's detailed and shrewd advice on how to expunge sections of the manuscript with minimal harm and on how to condense and prune unwieldy passages. I am also thankful for her unflagging interest in my professional undertakings. Susan Gardner's role in the evolution of my study was inestimable. First, she was my vital lifeline to South African primary and secondary sources. A combination of the absence of grant support for my work and my psychological and moral ambivalence about traveling to South Africa prevented me from consulting documents directly at their South African loci. Susan not only furnished me with copies of whatever I requested, as well as photographs and postcards of important Schreiner sites, she also alerted me to manuscript and photograph holdings, relevant recent publications, names and addresses of current South African Schreiner scholars, and pertinent South African conferences. Second, as an intellectual comrade, Susan probed in her brilliant letters to me her own and others' analyses of Schreiner's life and fiction, and she provided riveting accounts of contemporary South African politics and society, which endowed South Africa with a specificity and immediacy instrumental to my successful completion of this book.

My book was substantially aided by those who shared their Schreiner research with me or who equipped me with significant primary sources: Karen Smith, David Wolpe, Yaffa Draznin, Joanne Gates, David Staines, Stephen Gray, Cherry Clayton, Jane Marcus, Diane Postlethwaite, Stephen Clingman, Ellen Ziff, Joanne Dobson, Flavia Alaya, Judith Walkowitz, Rita Kissen. I am enormously grateful for the contribution of Betty Fradkin Tetlow whose massive collection of Schreiner sources was indispensable to both my present and my earlier Schreiner studies.

I am happy to credit the following for their permission to consult and quote from sources under copyright: Syfrets Trust and Executor Company for the estate of Olive Schreiner; The Harry Ransom Humanities Research Center at The University of Texas at Austin; Sheffield City Libraries Archives Division; Dr. Muriel Rafdord; and Oliver Schreiner. The staffs of the libraries at the University of Massachusetts, Amherst, Amherst College, and Smith College have gladly provided help whenever I needed it.

Since I doubt whether this book would have appeared without the entrance of the word processor into my life, I thank the contributions of Robert Griffith, who as chairperson of the history department warmly encouraged my scholarship and urged me to acquire computer skills, and Abel Alves, who served as my computer instructor. When Abel was not available, history department secretaries Alice Izer (who typed the initial chapters of my first draft) and Barbara Einfurer rescued me from technological jams.

In preparing this manuscript for publication, Jessie Rodrique revised footnotes for consistency of form and verified their accuracy. Barbara Palmer served as a keenly observant, painstaking, knowledgeable copy editor. It was a pleasure to work with the book's indexer, Susan Huston. Throughout the entire period, from contract arrangements to the book's publication, the editorial staff of the University of Massachusetts Press has cooperated with me in an invariably kindly, enthusiastic, and highly professional manner.

Others who provided assistance or heard me out at special moments were Michael Wolff, Warren Wagar, Martha Ayres, Martha Garland, Sandra Peacock, Ann and Michael Meeropol, "Pat" Murphy, Charles Grench, Alex and Anita Page, Elizabeth Petroff, Eva and Norman Brown, Lee Hoffman, Leonard Thompson, Karen Searcy, Cynthia Eagle Russett, Nina Auerbach, Laura Donaldson, Barbara "Penny" Kanner, Polly Allen, Lissa Greenough, Pat Schneider, Barbara Pridham, and Moira Clingman. I owe my periodic renewal of energy and enduring belief in the importance of my work to many of my students and colleagues in the history and women's studies departments of the University of Massachusetts.

Finally, I turn to the intellectual and emotional munificence of my husband, Leonard Berkman. He was my tireless, passionate, supreme friend along the entire journey, responding closely and critically to every draft of the manuscript. He was my perpetual copy editor and more. He provoked me to rethink my assumptions and arguments, and he sharpened my vision of the book as a whole. Challenging my stylistic choices, he suggested arresting ways to clear away verbal thickets and debris. His excitement for my project and his wholehearted support for feminism in private as well as public relationships eased my juggling of family, civic, and professional responsibilities. Above all, his boundless faith in me enabled me to forge ahead even when I was stumbling left and right. His loving patience set a model for my two sons, Jeremy and Zachary, who have spent their youth with Olive Schreiner as a kind of curious aunt-spirit who annoyed, intrigued, and amused them and who vied with them for my attention. Empathetic with me at every stage of the manuscript, they never asked me to abandon my project and always celebrated news of its progress. Such bountiful love from my husband and sons sustained my confidence and resolve during the dog days of composition.

Joyce Avrech Berkman
February 1989

The Healing Imagination of Olive Schreiner

INTRODUCTION

You, you, yourself must save yourself. From those weak
limbs strike off the fetters; with your strong hands bend
down and heal the wounds your hands have made;
remove the sand about the heavily sunken feet.
When they are healed and free and strong, they, they
and not another, will bear you to the mountains where
you would be.

Olive Schreiner, *From Man to Man*

WHEN OLIVE SCHREINER (1855–1920) was almost thirty years old, a friend inquired whether he might venture her biography. On the brink of her fame as a distinguished British South African author, Schreiner adamantly opposed such a project: "I won't give him any details. I don't want my life written by anyone."[1] She never deviated from this position, modifying it only to the extent that she did not object to people writing about her books. They, not her life, she gave to the world.[2] Set so against potential biographers, she actually took steps to thwart them. Repeatedly, she implored Havelock Ellis, the groundbreaking sexologist with whom she corresponded for many years, to destroy all her letters. Reluctantly, and only in part, he obliged. A voluminous correspondent, she made similar requests of others. And she herself systematically burned letters from others to her. Despite all her efforts, more than four thousand letters survive.[3]

Prominent among Schreiner's objections to a biography was her fear of its possible disregard for her mental and artistic life, given the reading public's preference for literary gossip over serious intellectual concerns. She drew a distinction between what she termed people's "abstract opinions" and their private lives. The eagerness of interviewers to write about the personal and

3

domestic facets of her life galled her since what she most craved was for them to take her ideas, her "large impersonal views," seriously. The trivializing articles of innumerable Victorian women's magazines confirmed her anxieties.[4] To some extent her fear has proven justified. The various biographical treatments of Schreiner focus disproportionately upon dramatic episodes in her personal history at the expense of comparable scrutiny of her writing.[5] I intend to repair that imbalance.

Of course, Schreiner's life experiences bear relevance to any analysis of her "abstract opinions" and artistic activity. What follows is an interpretation of her work as permeated by a unique thematic pattern, one that also characterized her life and its interconnections with the broader social and cultural movements of her time. The pattern emerged in her urge to heal both her own and society's ills and, as a corresponding process, to reconceive the relations between spiritual and material reality. In this striving she ran counter to the dominant Victorian outlook of her peers. For most Victorian Christians the cosmos divided between a literal Heaven and Hell, the saved and the damned, the moral and the immoral, the soul and the body, the transcendental and the mundane. Among Victorian philosophers, idealists sparred against materialists, rational understanding against intuitive knowledge. Likewise, in social relations, the spheres between men and women were sharply differentiated; so too the boundaries between children and adults, black people and white, colonizer and colonized, one social class and another, and, as Michel Foucault and Jeffrey Weeks have pointed out, the morbid and the healthy, the sexually perverse and the sexually normal.[6] The "correct" ordering of these contraries translated into power struggles: Heaven over Hell, mind over body, white over black, men over women, England over its colonies and European rivals, the fit over the unfit, ad nauseam. No wonder military vocabulary peppered mid- and late-Victorian rhetoric. No wonder Sunday school children dutifully committed to memory Baring-Gould's "Onward, Christian Soldiers, Marching as to War" while their parents learned Monsell's "Fight the Good Fight." As Thomas Hughes declaimed in *Tom Brown's School Days*, "After all, what would life be without fighting, I should like to know? From the cradle to the grave, fighting, rightly understood, is the real, highest, honestest business of every son of man."[7] The "muscular Christianity," instilled in paramilitary organizations and elsewhere, fostered the heroic ideal of an enlightened Christian warrior. Theories of the evolution of the species promulgated by Social Darwinists made such warriors indispensable. Marxists, with their portrayal of history as the saga of class struggle, obviously contributed their own rhetoric of conflict.[8] No wonder young Schreiner, out on the

South African veld, wondered "Why did everyone press on everyone and try to make them do what they wanted? Why did the strong always crush the weak? Why did we hate and kill and torture? . . . Why had the world ever been made?"[9]

Apart from the writings of a small band of early- and mid-Victorian intellectuals who sought to "make it whole," Schreiner's revulsion from the binary discourse of her times found little support among those she met or the works she read.[10] Still, she persisted. In place of a military articulation of reality, Schreiner substituted a medical counterpart. In Schreiner's writing the theme of healing recurrently surfaced; to describe various philosophical, political, and social issues, she resorted again and again to medical analogies. In doing so, her prose not only reflected her long-standing ambition to become a doctor (and, once thwarted, a nurse and midwife) but echoed as well the ambition of countless nineteenth-century women in Europe and America.

Late eighteenth- and early nineteenth-century movements to professionalize medicine severely restricted women from exercising their traditional roles as healers. The campaign of mid- and late-nineteenth-century European and American women to enter the medical profession constitutes one of the century's epic dramas. These women were motivated, as was Schreiner, by altruism and self-interest alike. Traditional female desires to serve others, to relieve and prevent suffering, fused with a passion for scientific knowledge about their own and others' bodies, a defiance of gender conventions, and a yearning for independent professional status.[11] Predictably, the more progressive-minded among these women recognized the interdependence of individual and social health and entered political movements for social transformation.[12] Like Schreiner, those women channeled their unrealized medical aspirations into seeking cures for social and political ills.[13]

The approach Schreiner took to individual and social healing relied upon an organic conception of life's structures. Throughout her adult years she studied the symbiotic relations among parts of the body. When examining the body politic, she focused similarly upon the reciprocity of parts. Unlike most nineteenth-century organic theories, which assumed the superiority or centrality of one anatomical feature over another, Schreiner's organicism was decidedly antihierarchical. She insisted that, just as the mind is not superior to the heart or body, healthy social intercourse rests upon equality of races, classes, and sexes. Her paramount concern was how to encourage such equality without creating either a homogeneous community or a pluralistic one limited to a "separate but equal" formulation.

Schreiner's effort to create organic democratic communities that accommodated cultural differences, interaction, and change was essentially a struggle to move beyond South African colonialism. The acceptance of an oppositional and hierarchical ranking of cultures is intrinsic to the institutional arrangements and symbolic structures of colonialism. The colonial mentality interprets human differences, be they ethnic, racial, class, or gender, in terms of self and "other," dominant and subordinate. Schreiner's intent, akin to what the literary scholar Mary Poovey calls the "recuperative program"[14] of current French feminist deconstructionism, was to envision alternatives to the social and symbolic order of oppositional and deferential patterns embedded in colonial Victorian views of human differences. Recognizing, as have many contemporary critics of colonialism, that the assumptions of the dominant culture often reach into the psyches of those dominated and thereby foster degrees of "inner colonization," Schreiner sought to remove all forms of colonial domination, symbolic no less than literal.

Herself a colonizer with relation to non-English Africans, Schreiner, lacking formal education and the cultural advantages of "home," that is, metropolitan England, experienced the prevailing English contempt for the "inferior" colonial, albeit white and British. She suffered, too, from the multiple forms of adult, male, and evangelical Christian domination over a young, skeptical woman. Resisting her own "inner colonization," she strove to liberate herself from the guilt and fear her upbringing instilled. Her marginal, dislocated position within a land replete with ethnic and racial differences made issues of human variety and hierarchy all the more immediate and intense.

In her zeal to repair the ruptures in psyche and society, Schreiner, like many holistic, unitary-minded thinkers today, did not always ponder sufficiently the severity of each rupture. Her aversion to conflict and violence led her at times not only to underestimate how intractable were conflicts between mind and body, emotions and reason, but to downplay as well the wrenching of sex, race, and class antagonisms. Periodically frustrated and disillusioned, she lapsed on occasion into self-pity and despair, as when, late in life, she painted herself "only a broken and untried possibility."[15] Several of her major works remained unfinished or came into print in amputated forms, heightening her sense of fragmented triumph. Poignantly, she introduced *Woman and Labour,* her last published book within her lifetime, with the prediction:

> You will look back at us with astonishment! You will wonder at passionate struggles that accomplished so little; at the, to you, obvious paths to attain our

ends which we did not take; at the intolerable evils before which it will seem to you we sat down passive; at the great truths staring us in the face, which we failed to see; at the truths we grasped at, but could never get our fingers round.[16]

For Schreiner to remain life-affirming, she had to counterbalance her despair through perhaps an undue faith in the possibility of nonviolent, egalitarian social progress. As a result, her writings became unevenly effective in analyzing and offering resolutions to social discord. A comparative weighing of her multifarious efforts to heal will clarify, I hope, the complex interplay between her personal experience and her social and intellectual milieu, wherein and why she faced certain truths with remarkable perspicacity but could never get her "fingers round" others.

In attempting to wrap my "fingers round" Schreiner's life and thought, I have adapted the structure of this book to conform to its analytic axis of her healing imagination. Although I set the biography chapter (Chapter 1) apart from the study of her "large impersonal views," I, unlike Schreiner, discern many connections between dilemmas in her life and tensions in her thought, which I examine in Chapters 2 through 8 along with a scrutiny of her relationship to the dominant and dissenting intellectual, political, and social movements of her time. For my opening chapter, instead of a traditional linear birth-to-death account of her life, a service Ruth First and Ann Scott perform admirably in their full-scale biography of Schreiner, I shall apply a topical approach to explore critically the origins and dynamics of Schreiner's healing endeavors. Chronological sequence will appear within the topical organization only when relevant to explanations of Schreiner's progress in self and societal understanding.[17]

Instead of providing either conventional plot synopses and character profiles for discussions of her fiction (always a frail substitute for reading the work itself) or traditional glosses of her nonfiction, Chapters 2 through 8 delineate and combine motifs, passages, and details from the array of her published works and correspondence to illuminate the ways she dismantled Victorian dichotomies and imagined alternatives. What draws me to Schreiner's fiction is less its literary significance—the concern of most Schreiner critics—than the nature of her fertile intellect as it grappled with perplexing issues and overstepped the boundaries of genre. Through this approach, I can chart hitherto little-studied relationships between her fiction and nonfiction.

The specific ordering of chapters is purposeful: Because Schreiner's social and political thought stemmed from intellectual tendencies, assumptions, and logic rooted in her views on religion, nature, and the evolution of the species, the sequence of chapters follows suit. This sequence seeks to redress the usual imbalance in Schreiner scholarship, which places her identity as a composer of fiction in the foreground. I leave that direct discussion of Schreiner's artistic creativity for the final chapter. I do so as well because issues arising from her aesthetic process, her critical values and literary techniques, offer variations on many of the themes, dissonances, and resolutions introduced in prior chapters. If I can offer an interdisciplinary analysis commensurate with Schreiner's multifaceted writing, I will have found all the fingers with which to cradle her mind.

I

"The dream of my life was to be a doctor"

FROM PHYSICIAN OF THE BODY
TO HEALER OF THE BODY POLITIC

> I wonder if they have medical books at the London
> Library. Sometimes when I can read nothing else I can
> lose myself in the account of a disease and the remedies
> and mode of treatment.
>
> Olive Schreiner to Havelock Ellis, July 28, 1884

IN OLIVE SCHREINER's first published novel, *The Story of an African Farm* (1883), her female protagonist, Lyndall, twice studies herself in a mirror. The first instance happens midway through the novel. Eyes in the mirror lock with her own: "There was a world of assurance in their still depths. So they had looked at her ever since she could remember, when it was but a small child's face above a blue pinafore." Confirming a special lifelong inner relationship with the mirrored eyes, Lyndall muses, "We shall never be quite alone, you and I, . . . We are not afraid; we will help ourselves!" Later in the novel, near death, she props a mirror up against a pillow on her breast and finds comfort in the familiar eyes which for many years had counseled her against fear and promised to fight on her side. Now, even though her fingers stiffen, "The wonderful yearning light was in the eyes still. . . . Then slowly, without a sound, the beautiful eyes closed. The dead face that the glass reflected was a thing of marvelous beauty and tranquility."[1]

The self-affirmation here contrasts sharply with Lyndall's literary prototype, the eponymous protagonist of Schreiner's earlier though posthumously published novel *Undine,* who ricocheted between views of herself as wicked and as misunderstood. Undine's persona came far closer to that of the young Schreiner, who, as a little child gazing in her mirror, "would . . . see the

9

wicked, keen, bright little face look at me, as though it were someone else." Lyndall embodied Schreiner's more self-esteeming later adolescence and adulthood.[2] When by early adolescence her sense of identity was sufficiently formed, Olive Schreiner changed her name. Roughly at the age of fourteen or fifteen she dropped "Emilie," which she had been called since birth (though she was christened Olive Emilie Albertina after her three dead brothers), and opted instead for her rightful "Olive."[3] In adult years, reluctant to yield her maiden name upon marriage, she convinced her husband-to-be, Samuel Cron Cronwright, to adopt as his surname "Cronwright Schreiner" while she remained "Olive Schreiner."[4] Both of these acts, uncommon for her times, conveyed her bold pursuit of self-definition. She would be, in short, her own mistress.

The process of owning herself remained a turbulent lifelong struggle. Schreiner took years to confront her early self-alienation and self-hatred. For years she refused to view herself in a mirror or permit a mirror in her room.[5] Torn between positive and negative self-images, Schreiner had to confront a cluster of issues, chief among which: her drive toward personal and intellectual vitality in the face of nature's malice, most marked in the fatal illness of her beloved younger sister and her painful and crippling asthma; her attempts to fuse intimacy with autonomy, service to others with self-realization; her yearnings for intimate relationships that afforded a seemingly contradictory sexual and psychic rapport; her difficulties in establishing her cultural identity, given her complex colonial situation and her ambivalence toward the culture and politics of Great Britain; and, after her abortive effort to become a doctor, her search for a viable career that could combine her ambitions to write fiction and to heal political and social woes. That she often found these coordinate goals irreconcilable was in large measure a consequence of her being a highly unconventional woman alienated from the dominant social and political structures of her time and, in lesser measure, a function of her specific temperament.

Schreiner's climb toward self-affirmation and the ability to grapple with personal and societal conflicts took place in highly diverse social and cultural milieus. These settings exposed her to multiple languages as well as to the clash of religious, ethnic, and racial identities which enhanced her sense of identity confusion and marginality even as they promoted her cultural alertness, tolerance, and passion to affirm cultural differences and heal the wounds of cultural collision. An introductory thumbnail sketch of the sequence of geographic environments throughout Schreiner's life seems in order here. Her childhood and adolescent quest evolved within various locales of South Africa:[6] from the desolate Cape province frontier site (Wittebergen) of the Wesleyan Native Reserve Mission Station where Schreiner was born on March 24, 1855; to Healdtown, where her family moved when she was six; to Cradock, where from the age of ten to fifteen she lived with her brother Theo and her sister Ettie; to diverse homes of relatives and family friends during her midadolescence (including a stay at New Rush diamond fields); and, in late adolescence, to the abodes of her employers, for whom she worked as a governess. In 1881 Schreiner sailed to England, remaining there until 1889, during all of which time inner struggles sharply intensified and the severity of her asthma spurred frenetic geographical movement within England and trips to the Continent. Returning to South Africa in 1889 and marrying Samuel Cron Cronwright in 1894, she began to strike a balance between increasing success and agonizing setbacks as she neared her life goals. By the time she settled again in England in 1914, residing there until a few months before her death in South Africa during the night of December 10, 1920, she had come to terms with many of the most vexing personal issues in her life, however largely unrealized her dreams for societal wellbeing remained.

Mitigating somewhat the problematic vicissitudes of her life was Schreiner's willingness to voice her personal pain. In the nineteenth century, women were expected "to suffer and be still." As a young adult, Schreiner tried to adhere to this stoic dictum. In her journal entry of November 2, 1880, she wrote, "However bad things are we can endure them in silence and take joy in enduring. . . . Silent endurance that seeks no friend, no helpers." More often, though, Schreiner railed against this self-repression. The context for the stoic quotation above itself suggests her ambivalence, for the sentence preceding it reads: "I am determined to be fearless; let every man speak out from the depths of his heart and take the result coolly." Among her closest adult friends and with her husband she did not curb her expression of pain.[7] Her readiness to deviate from Victorian gender norms on this matter not only enhanced her self-acceptance and honest intimacy but also served as a vital source of her growth as a writer and social reformer, enabling her to feel keenly and communicate eloquently others' sufferings and joys.

Schreiner's desire to lessen human suffering as a doctor arose early: "I can't remember a time when I was so small that it was not there in my heart."[8] Interestingly, her mother and four of her six siblings shared in her dream of a medical career.[9] Ultimately thwarted in her medical ambitions, she would heal through sheer power of pen and tongue. To Havelock Ellis she insisted: "I have always built upon the fact *From Man to Man* will help other people, for it will make men more tender to women . . . make some women more tender to others. . . . it will comfort some women by showing them that others have felt as they do. Do you *long* so too sometimes to lessen the pain and suffering in the world?"[10]

As Schreiner strove to heal herself and society she encountered the classic tension between idealism and realism on both personal and societal planes. She had to judge whether her aspirations for herself and society were feasible and, if so, whether in near or distant future. She had, too, to determine whether the means she chose to promote her various goals were viable for her specifically and for society at large. Despite her debilitating asthmatic condition and persistent frustrations as a social reformer, she generally revealed a vibrant optimism. Indeed, it is the interplay between her keen suffering and resulting suicidal depression and her indomitable joyfulness and appetite for adventure that sparks her finest writing and her correspondence.

Though Schreiner survived a childhood and adolescence replete with physical, emotional, and psychic pain, her confidence, at times naive, in her ability to ease her own and others' suffering reflects the numerous joyful and empowering experiences of her youth. Her particular medley of subjection to and spirited defiance of natural and human oppression underscores the various nineteenth-century impediments to young girls' metamorphoses into self-esteeming, autonomous adults. It epitomizes, too, Schreiner's singular mix of socially approved and idiosyncratic styles of resistance as she offered hearty witness to Victorian belief in the conquering of adversity through individual, even female, willpower.

Schreiner's paramount childhood encounter with the combined barrage of physical, emotional, and psychic pain occurred when, at age nine, she watched the death of her two-year-old infant sister, Ellie. Schreiner regarded Ellie's birth as "The most important event of my childhood" and, in later years, held that "My love for her has shaped all my life." She slept beside the motionless baby until Ellie was buried, after which the nine-year-old mourner sat by her sister's grave for hours brooding over life's significance. This experience of grief and mourning appears in Schreiner's novels as when, in *African Farm*, Lyndall, having lost her baby born out of wedlock, sits on a drizzly day by the baby's grave, unable to depart, rain dripping from her hat and shawl. Once she finally tore herself away, she would go "to bed and . . . not [rise] again from ɪt; never would, the doctor said." Schreiner claimed that Ellie's death was decisive in her lifelong love for women, her total rejection of Christianity, her mystic awareness of the blending of spiritual and material reality, her pacifism and democratic idealism, and her ambition to become a doctor."[11]

Schreiner's grief for Ellie and its fictional translations foreshadowed a tragic event in her adult life: Sixteen hours after a normal birth, she lost what would be her only child, a daughter, delivered on April 30, 1895. Having married in her thirty-ninth year and already weakened by years of acute asthma, Schreiner was unable subsequently to carry to full term. (Between 1896 and 1899 she endured at least six miscarriages).[12] As in her childhood, the intensity of her grief over her lost daughter was such that for ten hours she held the dead baby in her arms and refused to part from its coffin. Each time she moved to a new home, she arranged to have the coffin accompany her. In March 1907 she painted the coffin's inner shell pure white. When, later that year, she and her husband moved within South Africa from Hanover to De Aar, they added a small room with a window to their house as the coffin's sanctuary, and Schreiner designated in her will that when she died she wanted the baby buried by her side. The double loss of Ellie and her own infant found literary release in her dedication, written in 1901, revised slightly in 1911, to *From Man to Man.* It reads: "Dedicated to My Little Sister Ellie Who died, aged eighteen months, when I was nine years old. Also to My Only Daughter, Born on the 30th April, and died the 1st May. She never lived to know she was a woman."

Ellie's death aroused in Schreiner her contradictory images of nature and the cosmos. When despondent she described the cosmos as governed by capricious blind chance.[13] In better spirits she wrote of the essential order and symmetry of all being. Her efforts to surmount this conflict led her to oscillating between views of existential harmony and discord. Whereas her philosophical and religious writings articulate a harmonized cosmos, in which both the mind and the body of individuals, nature, and God are ultimately identical and in accord, her fiction and correspondence deviate from this optimism. Typical of her negative view of the universe, which did not preclude a positive, active response, is her urging of her husband, "It is so terrible to be human creatures, the universe is so awful, *we* must make it beautiful." Schreiner's reaction specifically to Ellie's death fused a repudiation of Christian doctrines of the benevolence of God with awed regard for the beauty of existence: "the whole of existence seemed to me more beautiful because it had brought forth and taken back to itself such a beautiful thing as she was to me."[14]

Schreiner's concept of the "awful universe," though sturdily rooted in

Ellie's death, had its antecedent origin and powerful subsequent reinforcement. Even before Ellie's passing, Schreiner was all too familiar with nature's malice through its slaughter of over fifty thousand Africans through famine brought on by a severe drought. She had heard, too, her parents' accounts of the helpless deaths of other siblings. Her own infancy was precarious; at nine months, she almost succumbed to lung inflammation. Four X-rays taken later revealed that in her youth she had contracted tuberculosis.[15]

Schreiner's childhood respiratory illnesses predisposed her for the asthma she developed during adolescence. In adolescence and after, too, she suffered angina spasms. Heart problems, in fact, afflicted many members of her family. Though Schreiner was to die of heart failure, asthma was her constant and most agonizing health condition. During her fierce paroxysms, she felt utterly unable to breathe, certain she would die. The severity of her attacks led her to declare: "The Kaffir woman said God couldn't be good because he made women, but I say because he made asthma."[16]

In her responses to asthma, Schreiner felt a special rapport with the life and writing of Heinrich Heine because he too attempted to deal with "the awful anguish of a *soul, striving against its own body.*"[17] Attacks of asthma sapped Schreiner's physical and mental stamina, doomed her medical ambitions, and reduced her literary output. When she resided where she could breathe without stress, her spirits were buoyant and her writing flowed. When beset with asthma, she could not muster sufficient energy to undertake large-scale projects and so turned to smaller-scale endeavors—allegories, tales, a novella, articles, brief treatises.

Revealing the limited medical knowledge of her day, Schreiner's efforts to treat her asthma did find ample evidence of environmental impact.[18] She traveled constantly in search of settings conducive to better health. At times her physical and geographical requirements clashed with those of her pocketbook or her need for compatible companionship and love, forcing her to move away from friends and endure lengthy separations from her husband. She also turned to drug therapy, a subject of dispute among Schreiner scholars.[19] Lacking a social history of female asthmatics in nineteenth-century Britain, we cannot know how unusual was Schreiner's receptivity to drug experimentation. In her struggle with the vicissitudes of nature she never became resigned or passive. Except for periods when she was simply too ill, she ignored the advice of doctors and friends to give up strenuous mental and literary labor. Though aware that disapproval from family members aggravated her asthma, she refused to let the threat of physical suffering deter her political enterprise. She suffered an acute attack of asthma, for example, upon receiving denunciatory letters from her mother and others concerning her attacks on Cecil Rhodes's racist and imperialist policies in South Africa in the 1890s, but she persisted. No extent of physical suffering in her final years deterred her from championing conscientious objectors during World War I or making plans to attend the Hague Peace Conference of international antiwar women.

Schreiner further sought to combat the "awful universe" by shaping death to human needs, evidenced not only in her attachment to her baby's coffin but in her careful planning for her own burial. During her first year of marriage, still quite hale, she and her husband climbed to the top of Buffels Hoek, the mountainous area of the extensive farm her husband managed. The summit, Buffels Kop, offered a panoramic vista so magnificent that Schreiner later wrote Cronwright, "we must be buried here, you and I," a decision he honored.[20] This moment encapsules Schreiner's belief that human beings, by such wilfulness, assert meaning in the face of senseless nature. It also resonates Schreiner's positive view of nature's holiness and harmony, a perspective that surfaces most vividly in her accounts of her mystic experiences, which I address in a later chapter.

The confidence behind Schreiner's pitting human beauty and meaning against arbitrary nature evolved slowly. Her childhood memories of being terrorized by parents and older siblings are only intermittently relieved by demonstrations of their love and caring. The most consistently gentle figure in her childhood was her father, Gottlob Schreiner, but his all-consuming work, his dreaminess, his inability to provide adequately for the material needs of his family, and his general support for his wife's child-rearing methods diluted the benefits of his tender feelings toward his offspring.[21] Although Schreiner loved her father's sensitive temperament, and although dreams served her as a source of literary inspiration and style (her volume of fictional dreams being among her finest literary achievements), she insisted that the mind be tethered to concrete reality, her ideal response to which would be an amalgam of gentleness and toughness. For this among other reasons, her mother was more decisive to her childhood sense of self. Her effort to combine intimacy and autonomy, service to others and self-realization, and to express herself frankly without hurting and alienating loved ones owed its origin in large measure to the nature of her bond with Rebecca Schreiner.

Schreiner viewed her mother's consistent and hardy realism as a valuable antidote to her father's visionary ineptitude. In *African Farm* she juxtaposed the constructive, practical, and bold realism of Lyndall (Rebecca Schreiner's maiden name) with the sweet, credulous Christianity of Old Otto (who various Schreiner family members assert was the fictional counterpart of Gottlob). Otto loses his property, dies heartbroken, and abandons his son Waldo as a result of the actions of a crafty interloper. Schreiner likened her mother's realism and self-reliance to that of men but pointedly compared Rebecca to Schreiner's idol, George Sand.[22]

Two episodes capture the polarities of young Schreiner's feelings toward her mother. When five or six years old, swinging on the door handle of their home, she exclaimed within earshot of her mother, "Ach, how nice it is outside! . . . 'Ach' was Dutch [a language forbidden within the Schreiner household] and so got my first great whipping. . . . I was taken up the little passage in the bedroom where I was born, and my clothes were raised and I was laid out on my mother's knees, and got about fifty strokes with a bunch of quince rods tied together."[23]

Schreiner's hatred of cruelty and tyranny, "the fierce rush of blood in my head when I even think of a Kaffir flogged," drew upon this episode and a similar one when she was seven. Disobeying her older sister Alice, Schreiner had loitered in her doorway when it was raining and "caught rain drops in my hand." For this her mother gave her fifty blows with a small cane.[24]

Adhering to her contemporaries' evangelical theories of child rearing, Rebecca Schreiner considered childhood submission to adults and older siblings the moral correlative to human submission to God, female to male, and blacks to whites. Schreiner observed that, though her mother permitted herself to express affection when her children were babies, she "never cared for her children" as they matured and began to test their autonomy. Moreover, she saw proper parenting as inculcating moral values that would enable a child to resist the specific temptations of a frontier region that lacked the social controls of a long-established, like-minded community. "[H]ow difficult it is," Rebecca Schreiner complained, "living as we do among gross sensual heathen, to preserve that delicacy of thought and feeling so indispensable to a right development of female character."[25] Given her fears about alien people infecting her children's morality, she was not about to share her mothering tasks with African household servants. Given, too, the geographically isolated circumstances of the family, Rebecca's power over her children was that much more concentrated. But though Rebecca might seek to extirpate Schreiner's "wildness," she could never fully tame her. Her disciplinary child raising inevitably inconsistent, she simply had too many tasks and preoccupations, and her health was too uncertain. Assisting her husband in his missionary teaching while she was also the sole teacher for all her children when they were very young (and for her daughters through their later years as well), she swung from oppressive protective ardor to exhausted indifference. Schreiner, moreover, was often not a compliant child, openly dubbing herself "koppig."[26]

Her childhood whippings aroused in Schreiner an "unutterable bitter rebellion and hatred against them all in my heart." "Them all" clearly included not only her mother and older siblings but anyone with power who abused it. "Them all" also included her father, who, despite his children's countless descriptions of him as gentle and loving, not only shared his wife's values but resorted to corporal punishment with his sons, as when he spanked Will for *his* use of Dutch.[27] "Unutterable" was a revealing word choice for Schreiner, who could not bring herself to direct overt anger toward her mother. Her religious instruction held that anger was sinful and poisoned the heart, that a good person loved and forgave even her enemies, but she could not entirely follow this dictum. As a child, when angry, she would get under her bed where no one could see her and bang her head against the wall until she was nearly senseless.

Schreiner counted as formative as these whippings her parents' exploitation of religious terror. Her mother's Victorian reliance upon religious fear was a daily motif of child rearing, memorialized in Schreiner's first two novels, *Undine* and *African Farm*.[28] Finding it impossible to accept and conform to many of her parents' precepts, Schreiner early identified with the damned. In later years she singled out as especially pernicious parental insistence upon the inevitable conflict between an individual's mind/soul and body/matter. After Ellie's death she could no longer "accept the ordinary doctrine that [one who died] was living somewhere without a body."[29] Schreiner rejected Christian and Emersonian transcendentalism along with temporal mind/body dualism. Other parental precepts likewise became suspect for their divisiveness, most specifically their Victorian views on female inferiority, separate gender spheres and traits, and the racial and ethnic superiority of white Britons to all other peoples. To the extent that these dictates rivaled young Schreiner's observations and feelings before she could adequately challenge them, she was left rebellious and confused.

In counterpoint to this physical and psychological abuse, episodes of her mother's caring touched Schreiner profoundly. One of her most cherished occasions was her mother's response to reading a story Schreiner wrote at about age twelve. Rebecca awoke her in the middle of the night, sobbing, her arms around her daughter's legs at the foot of the bed. Schreiner interpreted her mother's behavior as understanding not only the story but its relation to

Schreiner's life. In feeling understood at last, she "touched perfect bliss."[30] This episode is indicative of various other, if infrequent, occasions when Rebecca Schreiner nourished her daughter's self-respect. Prizing Schreiner's intellectual and artistic precocity, Rebecca defended her daughter against sibling mockery of her frequent spouting aloud to herself the stories she invented.[31] She also encouraged Schreiner's talents by asking her to read poetry to her while she cooked or sewed.

During her early years Schreiner fell in love with Milton and by age seven acquired a command of Coleridge and Tennyson. Simultaneously, she discovered in her mother a responsive mind, "keen as a rapier."[32] Widely read and impressively fluent in French and Italian, Rebecca was a dramatic and witty raconteur and a fluent letter writer. Possessing definite artistic tastes, Rebecca was skilled in flower painting and music. Accustomed to the comforts of a middle-class English home and wooed by two suitors prior to Gottlob, she sacrificed much in wedding this son of a German shoemaker, a youth awkward with the English language and imbued with romantic dreams of saving mankind in Africa's desolate reaches. Schreiner saw her mother as capable of being a preacher, doctor, or lawyer but resembling instead "a grand piano" functioning as a "common dining table."[33]

Rebecca's sobbing at Schreiner's bed suggests more than one striking way in which she bolstered her daughter's self-esteem. Often ill, subject to occasional fainting fits, Rebecca increasingly turned to her daughter for emotional support. Reflecting upon her mother's need for her, Schreiner later claimed, "It is *I* who have always had to think for, guide and nurse her since I was a tiny child. *She* seems to me like a favourite brilliant child of mine!" This reversal of parent–child roles both flattered and distressed Schreiner. She craved to be the recipient of such affection and resented her mother's inability to provide it sufficiently. Schreiner's yearning for maternal affection suffused a dream she recounted to her husband. In it, she had collapsed in a field from a heart attack, and "a little yellow and black cow came towards me with her head down and her long horns, and I thought she was going to poke me or trample on me. But when she came up she knelt down beside me and licked me and rubbed her face and horns against my left arm where I have great pain. . . . it seemed as if I had been in heaven!"[34]

A feature of Schreiner's narratives is her female protagonists' fluid moving back and forth between maternal and child roles. Particularly poignant evidence of this appears in *From Man to Man* when the child, Rebekah (so telling a name), engages in an extended fantasy of physical support and emotional care for her infant daughter. In turn, Rebekah both cuddles and is cuddled by her younger sister, Baby-Bertie. Later Rebekah fantasies a comparable role versatility with her husband.

Schreiner's perception of her mother's need for her clearly weakened her sense of her mother's implacable authority and afforded Schreiner the psychological space to exercise her autonomy. By adolescence she no longer felt that her family's moral approval was essential to her self-worth. No longer able to discuss politics, morality, or religion with her parents and older siblings, she continued to take pains throughout her life to avoid unnecessary conflict with them and to spare them if possible the pain and social discomfort her ideas could cause.[35]

Schreiner's release from reliance on family approval and expectations should not imply that she no longer desperately craved affection. The need for intimacy unmet in her youth haunted her for life and intensified her impulse to nurture others, often at the cost of her concentration on her writing and her overall well-being. She expressed her needs for nurturance to friends with uncommon frankness; but, somehow, she avoided the pitfall of utter selflessness so often enjoined upon Victorian women.

The roots of her independent growth are paradoxically entwined with that "awful universe" she denounced. Schreiner's contradictory outlook on nature and the cosmos drew on her reliance upon its succor in the face of human persecution. Nature's arbitrary malice faded from mind when she extolled not only the beauty of the South African karroo but its gifts of visionary insight into the symmetry of all being and the possibility of a human universe of love, peace, and equality. To the karroo she attributed her scientific curiosity and longing to become a doctor.[36] Like an elixir, the karroo's limitless horizon and distinctive flora and fauna exhilarated Schreiner as they evoked images of liberated lives and new social patterns to counter the constraints she felt as a child and a female. No matter how hungry, nomadic, and desolate Schreiner's life and the lives of her fictional characters, they could roam miles of the karroo in exalted reflection and find comfort in the radiant blue sky, the invincible rocks, the sparse but hardy vegetation, and the animal life. At times she felt that the individual plants she gazed upon spoke to her and returned her love for them. They too were isolates and lonely on a dry terrain. In effect, they replaced the careworn, chastising Rebecca. In her adulthood, Schreiner's experience of the sensual continuity between herself and natural landscape recaptured her infantile connectedness with her still doting mother and vitalized thereby that residual core of self-trust, innocent wonder, and physical delight that bore her and various of her fictional characters through the worst of times.

Not only natural surroundings but select books empowered Schreiner's struggle for autonomy. Ironically, the Bible, which her parents invoked to instill their views on human frailty and sinfulness, became the key inspiration of her early youth. Both Old and New Testaments constituted her earliest reading and her cherished companions. She committed countless passages to memory and could recall them verbatim throughout her adult life. As I will later elaborate, the Bible exerted a decisive influence upon her literary style. In self-perception, too, she not only derived comfort from the Bible's portraits of divine and human compassion but gained hope for humane power from its many narratives of heroic deeds.

In later childhood, following her rejection of Christianity, she turned for comparable inspiration to secular works.[37] However remote from cultural centers and steeped in her childhood in evangelical Christian literature, young Schreiner gained access to the works of writers who were profoundly critical of many ruling orthodoxies, exemplars and champions of independent inquiry and expression. Ralph Waldo Emerson's essays were among her treasured adolescent friends. They gave her "more strength than anything else has ever done."[38] When she was sixteen, Schreiner credited Herbert Spencer's *First Principles* with resetting her "broken leg." By her late adolescence John Stuart Mill had supplanted Jesus as her moral philosopher.[39]

A quick review of Schreiner's reading during her adolescence readily reveals her affinity with rationalist and romantic idealists who emboldened her criticism of dominant cultural institutions and values and/or reinforced her urge to ameliorate suffering. Rare on her reading lists were works by prominent conservative writers. When she did praise a conservative thinker, for example, Carlyle, what she valued were those elements of conservative criticism of societal values and structures that dovetailed with her radical objections to liberalism. By the time she completed *African Farm* she had devoured not only the writings of Mill, Spencer, and Emerson but—to list her most frequently cited authors—those of Plato, Shelley, Gibbon, Spinoza, Thoreau, Coleridge, Ruskin, Carlyle, Lecky, Goethe, and Heine. Schreiner was already familiar with the nineteenth-century school of biblical criticism as well as selected works of Darwin and T. H. Huxley.[40] Her reading of fiction, particularly by Charles Dickens, the Brontë sisters, and George Sand, as well as the poetry of Robert Browning, also molded her culture critiques and moral idealism.

The works of none of these writers mentioned here are sufficient to explain Schreiner's objections to dominant British ethnic, racial, and gender conventions. In fact, many of Schreiner's favorite authors upheld notions of white and male privilege. The spirit of their works, more than the content, mattered to her: their brave quest for truth, their love for humanity and belief in social progress, and their willingness to suffer persecution. Clearly, her early readings in biblical heroic tales and her subsequent exposure to secular heroism fostered her sense of her own epic possibilities. Indeed, the desire and self-confidence of an obscure governess from the remote rim of the British Empire to become a doctor reflected her intense heroic identification. Not surprisingly, Schreiner's fiction abounds in heroic deeds. As a governess she wove stories for her children about "hairbreadth" escapes from "wild rocky islands." As a professional writer she recounted abortive and successful feats, not only through her allegorical characters but as well in her more realistic novels, as when Rebekah in *From Man to Man* informs her children about the exceptional bravery and stamina of African women.[41]

Unfortunately, the writers she turned to did not enable the adult Schreiner to anticipate lucidly and fully the power and tenacity of opponents to her egalitarian idealism or the difficulty of realizing even her personal ideals for love and friendship. Sharing as she did the prevalent Victorian trust in individual willpower, she did not grasp firmly until years later the tidal force of elitist social structures and values. Within her adolescent years, however, the issue of political and psychological realism was secondary to her need for faith in herself as more than a weak, sinful, divided creature.

As vital and curative as natural surroundings and singular books became, they could not fully substitute for immediate human compassion. Fortunately, during her adolescence Schreiner met adults who served as alternative models to her parents and older siblings. Not all of her adolescent relationships helped to heal the emotional wounds of childhood, but had she remained beyond childhood bereft of nurturant ties it is highly unlikely, especially given her asthma, that she could have sustained as hopeful and vigorous a combative life. During her late adolescence and early adult years, she formed several intense, affectionate, and enduring friendships. These took shape during her stays as governess (1873–81)—the only respectable occupation for young, unmarried women—with various South African families. Because her intelligence and informal education far exceeded that of most white South African girls, she was easily able to secure work and win the admiration of her employers. As a governess she was proud of her economic self-reliance and competence. This buoyed her spirits despite the paltry pay characteristic of the position and despite the harangues of various domineering employers compounded by occasional physical assaults from her young charges.[42]

Schreiner's most rewarding friendship with an employer was with Erilda

Cawood, who with her husband and their six children provided a supportive, affectionate surrogate family. Beyond Schreiner's service as governess, she made clothes for the babies and conversed with Cawood at length, sitting up with her at night when her children were ill. The depth of their attachment was painfully manifest when, some time later, Cawood found herself able no longer to befriend Schreiner because of the latter's religious skepticism. Openly admitting that she cared for Schreiner "with an almost idolatrous love," Cawood decried the incompatibility of her family's love for Schreiner and for God. Apparently, however, Cawood, gripped by her own and her children's devotion to Schreiner, eventually resumed their friendship. Schreiner's letters to Cawood are filled with affection and are among her most humorous and ingenious.[43]

The Cawoods, like almost all of Schreiner's employers, were Boers, the predecessors of twentieth-century Afrikaners.[44] Sometimes for as long as eighteen months Schreiner did not set eyes on an English face. Through her friendship with these *Ach* exclaimers, she discovered the falsity and harm of British ethnocentrism. Cawood as well as other Boer women provided more appealing models for female selfhood than those Rebecca presented and prescribed. Besides admiring Boer females' physical strength, courage, and seemingly boundless self-control, Schreiner reveled in their warmth and matter-of-fact response to physical and sexual concerns. At the Cawoods she would regularly sunbathe nude on a large flat rock behind the house.[45] In later years, Schreiner exhorted Boer women not to yield their traditional ways in favor of British female material display: "the straw hat with paper flowers," "the croquet mallet," and "the mother-of-pearl card case."[46] In search of a more complete and empowering selfhood, she benefited immensely from her adolescent exposure to Boer life.

The Cawoods' regard for her talents notwithstanding, Schreiner discovered the difficulty of carving time for reading and writing. The persistent, and at times agonizing, issue in her adult life—how to integrate duty to one's self with duty to others—was just beginning to unsettle her. Although Schreiner's feminist consciousness was precociously evident in her adolescence—as passages in *African Farm* attest—it was still limited in crucial respects. She adhered to those Christian and Victorian gender ideals that elevate service to others as women's supreme duty and form of love: "[T]here is no happiness like that of giving in the world, except suffering for one you love." Determined to combine service and self-development, brimming with youthful stamina, she wrote late into the night or rose at dawn to write. Her years as governess saw her complete *Undine* and *African Farm* and begin the novel she later titled *From Man to Man*. During periods of depression in her adult years, when no longer able to combine artistic creativity with usefulness to others, she looked upon her time as governess with aching nostalgia.[47]

Besides the Cawoods, Schreiner's most meaningful and lasting friendship from her late adolescence was with John and Mary Brown. The Browns were people of personal vitality, intellectual breadth, progressive political and social views. Of no small importance to Schreiner, John Brown was the district surgeon of Fraserburg, the first doctor in South Africa to use Lister's carbolic acid method of antisepsis. He also spearheaded efforts to improve the conditions of childbirth. Mary Brown, a niece of the prominent Cape liberal politician Saul Solomon, one of the few eminent Jews in nineteenth-century Cape politics, was a writer, public speaker, reformer, social worker, and future advocate of the rights of women and Africans. Schreiner's admiration for the Browns was matched by their delight in her sharp mind and rollicking spirits. "Her laughter," Mary Brown observed, "made others laugh and was unusual in its merriment and ripple."[48]

The Browns were determined to assist Schreiner in her medical and literary aspirations. Because nurse's training was the only professional medical route available to women in South Africa (unpaid and exclusively through religious orders), Schreiner and the Browns formulated what she termed "the English plan" to enable her, once she had saved enough money from her work as governess, to travel to England and enter medical school.

In 1876, after the Browns left South Africa for Edinburgh where John obtained postgraduate qualifications in surgery and public health, Schreiner continued to correspond with them. When the Browns moved from Edinburgh to the English mill town of Burnley, Lancashire, they began to carry out "the English plan" but quickly modified it: In 1880 they sent Schreiner, at her request, the application form for nurse's training at Edinburgh's Royal Infirmary. Having funds to cover training as a nurse but not the more expensive medical school costs, Schreiner had temporarily to abandon her dreams of becoming a doctor.

The Browns also helped Schreiner secure the first publisher's reading of *African Farm*. They took the manuscript to the English publisher David Douglass (English publishing did not start in South Africa until 1893).[49] Though he turned the novel down, Douglass affirmed the author's considerable talent. With deep appreciation for the Browns' affection and assistance, and also for their model of marital devotion and comradeship, Schreiner later dedicated the published version of *African Farm* to Mary Brown.

Schreiner's friendship with the Browns was never problematic. It neither competed with the time and energy she required for her intellectual and artistic work nor compounded an already dense social calendar. Such was not true with subsequent friendships. The conflict in Schreiner between her ideals of self-development and self-expression on the one hand and intimacy and service to others on the other reached an intolerable pitch during her stay in England from 1881 to 1889 and precipitated in December 1886 her physical/nervous breakdown.[50] She referred to her dilemma repeatedly: "Life from the time one enters it, seems to be a battle between the duty one owes to one's work of life, and the duty one owes to the fellowmen one loves . . . the agony of my life. Whichever side I decide for my conscience tortures on the others. If one was a little wiser one would know how to combine all."[51] Her breakdown did have a positive outcome: its spur to her finding a more self-affirming balance among these competing claims. She came to assert with greater assurance and force the legitimacy of her own needs, a shift articulated eloquently in her fiction, most notably in several of her allegories as well as in her portrayal of the views of Rebekah in *From Man to Man*, who eventually separates from her husband and establishes a home of her own. In the wake of Schreiner's breakdown, from the solitude of the Italian residence in which she recuperated, she reflected, "The great lesson I have had to learn in the last three years is that one must be true to oneself in the first place and think of your fellow man second." She appended a smiling afterthought, "Perhaps now I shall keep the balance—at least as long as I don't see a human being."[52] Although her conflict between work and intimacy continued after her return to South Africa, it was far less intense.

What made the years in England so traumatic were the multiple opportunities for satisfying at last her emotional hunger for giving and receiving affection, and for intellectual and artistic self-realization, within a social and cultural milieu that turned seductive possibilities into confusing disappointments. Schreiner's calamity grew, too, from an ideal of intimacy (particularly when it included sexual passion) which she could not realize and which we will investigate shortly.

In many ways the 1880s were a propitious time for Schreiner to reside in England. Despite an agricultural slump and increasing European and American economic competition that would soon end Britain's industrial supremacy, English cities were flourishing, and faith in continued material progress and social improvement was at its zenith. The decade was a breeding time in the evolution of English social movements, spawning a plethora of socialist and labor associations that embodied a wide range of progressive standpoints. Concurrently, educational reforms were expanding educational options for working-class males and for women of all social classes. A decade earlier Schreiner could not have entered any British medical school. Although severe restrictions still impeded medical training for women, by 1876 legal barriers were gone.

Extending the social and political ferment of the 1880s was its cultural excitement, its aesthetic and intellectual controversies, a congenial milieu for Schreiner's feisty temperament. Intellectual clubs abounded, such as those to which she came—the Progressive Association, the woman's branch of the Democratic Federation, the Fellowship of the New Life, and especially the Men and Women's Club, in which Schreiner played a formidable role.[53] The diffusion of Darwinian ideas seeded the growth of anthropological studies, agnostic and free-thought associations, and the scientific researching of psychic experience, as well as swelling interest in Oriental philosophies. Schreiner steeped herself in the new literature that poured forth from the mounting number of publishing houses, firms in which several of her friends played leading parts.

For female intellectuals and artists, the 1880s were decidedly more hospitable than previous decades. An earlier generation of female authors had roused public respect for fictional writing by women and inspired the female authors of Schreiner's generation. Her esteem for these earlier writers was manifest in her response to a request in 1888 from the editor of the *Pall Mall Gazette* to provide a list of great women of all time. Among her twelve choices were six of the nineteenth century: George Sand, George Eliot, Emily Brontë, Charlotte Brontë, Elizabeth Browning, and Margaret Fuller.[54]

On the flip side, England's varied and swirling intellectual and social currents threatened to overwhelm the young colonial eager to seize metropolitan opportunities for self-expansion and invigorating friendships yet maintain a steady course of mental health. If isolation and loneliness were the inevitable hazards of her life as governess on the sparsely settled karroo, feverish social immersion, with its swirl of engrossing and vexing relationships, beset her life in populous England.

Had Schreiner been able to pursue her medical ambition, she might have balanced more securely her needs for self-realization and intimacy. For her, "a doctor's life is the most perfect of lives; it satisfies the craving to know, and also the craving to serve." Again and again, however, her attempts to become a nurse no less than a doctor met with defeat. When she enrolled in nurse's training at the Edinburgh Royal Infirmary, she found its regime exacting.[55] Schreiner's psychic energy was equal to the challenge but not her physical stamina. She became ill within a few days. Reverting to her goal of training as a doctor, she spent the summer of 1881 preparing for medical school entrance exams, but her unstructured education in South Africa had ill equipped her to master the requisite subject matter. Shifting career direction again, she returned to nursing as her second-best alternative. In the fall she went to the Women's Hospital in Endell Street, one of London's five lying-in hospitals, for a three-month program in midwifery. She lasted there only five days, contracting a lung inflammation. Unwilling to abandon her medical ambitions completely, she once more considered studying midwifery in 1888, but she learned that the Endell Street hospital no longer had a place for her. Despite these frustrations, she continued to read extensively in medical literature and occasionally attended medical lectures. Her desire remained fierce.

It was to a career she would always regard as inferior to medicine that she ultimately turned. Through her pen she would seek self-fulfillment and social service. Her pen became her scalpel and suturing needle. Happily, she swiftly actualized her literary aspirations. Soon after Chapman and Hall published *African Farm* in January 1883, its success was clear; a second edition followed within five months. Within a few years, it hit best-seller status, stirring worldwide interest. During Schreiner's lifetime alone, fifteen editions of the novel came into print.

Schreiner's fame, both as an author and as an exotic and vivacious woman, not only escalated her chances for valued friendships but foisted people upon her whom she did not want to see but could not turn away. As her fame swept across England she was besieged, particularly by lonely and vulnerable women eager for the understanding and support she felt compelled to offer them. In fact and fantasy, she served for many as a crucial lifeline and took pride in her ability to help: "Being a woman I can reach other women, where no man could reach them." To the economically desperate, especially prostitutes, and to aspiring career women whom she knew, she would give what limited money she had and obtain additional money from friends. At one juncture she raised a loan for a female medical student who had once nursed her, and at another she assisted her niece in her struggle for a medical career.[56]

There were limits, however, to her pleasure in being useful to women. When one female visitor told her that "if she came near me her whole life would be moulded and changed by me," Schreiner felt oppressed. Her statement "filled [Schreiner] almost with terror." She feared she would "be cruelly crushed and life's work left undone." Quite aware that her being a woman added to others' expectations of her readiness to subordinate her own needs to theirs, she crystallized Victorian gender expectations in a sardonic miniallegory:

Once God Almighty said: "I will produce a self-working . . . machine for enduring suffering, . . . capable of the largest amount of suffering in a given space," and he made woman. But he wasn't satisfied that he [had] reached the highest point of perfection; so he made a man of genius. . . . [Not] satisfied yet . . . he combined the two—and made a woman of genius—and he was satisfied![57]

Among her close friends in England, only Karl Pearson, then professor of applied mathematics in University College, London, urged her to view her desire for self-development as a moral imperative. In a vivid medical metaphor she praised his decisive contribution to her efforts to balance the claims of self and others. She felt she was bleeding to death, and he was the ice that froze her hemorrhage and saved her life. (Wryly, she described her feelings for Pearson in this context as "a curious kind of gratitude to the ice.")[58] Were it only the claims of needy friends and acquaintances and Schreiner's own long unfulfilled desires for sociability and intellectual comradeship, she might have heeded Pearson's advice and devoted adequate time to her work. The crucial debilitating elements were volatile sexual and marital issues connected with certain of her friendships. Long before Schreiner's arrival in England she had formed ideals of both heterosexuality and heterosociality which, given Victorian social realities and certain of her own needs, were exceedingly unlikely to be realized, however intrinsically worthy.

Schreiner's opposition to mind/body dualism and her emphasis upon psychological wholeness of one's self and with others led her to insist that sexual passion must form part of a larger closeness, which included spiritual, intellectual, and emotional rapport. For this reason, Lyndall in *African Farm*, despite her powerful sexual attraction to her lover, leaves him both because he calls into play only part of her nature and because he assumes toward her a position of dominance. Affirming female erotic desire and pleasure well beyond the conventional Victorian view, Schreiner claimed, nevertheless, that for a woman the experience of sexual intercourse could never be casual or severed from her emotions; "that when a man puts his penis into a woman's vagina it is as if (assuming of course that she responds) he puts his finger into her brain, stirred it round and round. Her whole nature is affected."[59]

Schreiner held as ambitious and unconventional an ideal of heterosexual friendship as she voiced for sexual passion. By the 1870s and 1880s the prevalent homosocial world of friendship, fostered by Victorian doctrines and institutions defining separate gender spheres, roles, and traits, was beginning to erode, though not nearly as rapidly as Schreiner hoped. She sought in her nonerotic male friendships the same intensity of mutual understanding and support most women believed possible only with other women. Although she spoke of her desire for "brotherly friendship" as rooted in periods of closeness with her brothers Theo, Fred, and Will, she recognized that her passion for platonic friendship was historically novel, but so, too, she argued was the electric telegraph and steamship.[60]

After many disillusioning experiences Schreiner discovered that heterosexual intimacy and friendship were not yet possible. When her efforts for an intense platonic friendship with Karl Pearson collapsed, she confided to Havelock Ellis, "I am in a state of despair. . . . My ideal has been friendship between men and women as between men and men, but it *can't* be."[61] Female and male friends kept construing her friendship with Pearson as more than platonic; landlords hounded her whenever she invited male friends to her room; and certain male friends, such as the Karl Marx family physician, H. Bryan Donkin, against Schreiner's wishes, strove to make their relationship romantic and marital.

Schreiner did form successful intense platonic bonds with two men, Havelock Ellis and Edward Carpenter, a trailblazing and influential exponent of communitarian socialism and sexual freedom. Mitigating factors permitted her to do so. Her relationship with Ellis originated as sexual as well as intellectual but became platonic when their sexual incompatibility became evident.[62] With their rapport founded upon myriad other elements of mutuality, their love for each other persisted. When Ellis did marry, his partner, Edith Lees, like Schreiner a feminist essayist and novelist, was far more attracted to women than to men and remained so. Lees revered Schreiner, and even if Schreiner was not living in South Africa by the time Ellis and Lees were married, Lees would not have viewed her as a threat to their marriage. During Schreiner's lengthy stay in England from 1914 to 1920 she and Ellis resumed their closeness in spite of the diminished accord, by then, of their political and social views. With Edward Carpenter, her physical affection and emotional intimacy were also not problematic since Carpenter was—rare for his time, of course, in the circles with which Schreiner mingled—openly homosexual.

Upon her return to South Africa, Schreiner developed many good friendships with men, but none of these approximated her youthful ideal or the depth and warmth of her interaction with Carpenter and Ellis. To a far greater degree she succeeded, though not till her late thirties, in her aspirations for sexual fulfillment. For years her ideal of a richly dimensional sexual relationship seemed doomed, and she came to fear she would never marry or marry

28

too late to become a mother. She had suffered a traumatic incident during her adolescence, and were it not for her inner resilience and her friendship with the Browns, "the two stars that shone in my sky when all else was dark,"[63] she might well have abandoned early all her personal (and professional) ambitions.

The precise nature of Schreiner's relationship in adolescence with the somewhat older Julius Gau, a representative of a Swiss insurance company, continues to elude biographers. What is certain is that Gau accompanied her, unchaperoned, on a lengthy journey to visit her parents. Shortly after her arrival she wrote to her sister Kate that she was engaged to marry Gau. Her next letter to Kate, nine days later, includes no mention of the engagement. Yet more ominous, her journal entries a month later are laced with cryptic despair. If her engagement was broken off, one theory of what transpired pivots on a momentary false assumption of pregnancy.[64] Another theory hypothesizes that, although Schreiner and Gau may not have actually engaged in intercourse, her sexual passion and emotional investment in him were so intense that she could not contain or accept without guilt the tumultuous erotic energies released. The Gau episode thus strikes scholars as the key to Schreiner's adult sexuality, leading her to create a perfectionist ideal of intimacy that warred with her true erotic desires (her apparent attraction to strong, dominant men) and was destined to failure (given Victorian male socialization).[65]

Cautious, too, about defining the extent of Schreiner and Gau's sexual activity, and sharing the view that the adolescent Schreiner was sexually troubled, I nevertheless do not concur with the analysis above. Unarguably, Schreiner's erotic impulses diverged from her ideal of love, but the divergence is complex. Although Schreiner was erotically drawn to dominant men, she was also sexually repelled by them, alienated by their denial of her passion for reciprocity and personal autonomy. Similarly, she was attracted to and disgusted by gentle, compliant males. Sexually aroused by their tenderness and nurturance, she found these traits fused with a pathetic lack of psychic and sexual vitality. Moreover, compliant men tended to invite her domination of them, a response that inflamed her negative self-image as wicked and selfish. Although in her adolescent years she longed to surrender to someone she worshiped, as she grew older she rejected such self-abasement in favor of an ideal of love between equals.[66]

Schreiner did not merely accept this sexual impasse. Within her novels written in late adolescence, she explored the self-threatening ramifications of loving both types of men. This writing clarified her sexual confusion and, at the same time, illuminated for her contemporaries recurrent heterosexual dangers. We can trace a progression in Schreiner's treatment of the issues of female attachment, intimacy, and autonomy from her first novel, *Undine*, to her final, unfinished novel, *From Man to Man*. This progression, discussed in Chapter 6, corresponded to Schreiner's personal development. From the nadir of her encounter with Gau, and a possibly parallel episode on the Isle of Wight during her first year in England, Schreiner culled the insight and realism that characterized her portrayal of Rebekah's relationships with males in *From Man to Man*. Her experiences with Gau in South Africa and with Ellis and other male friends in England also prepared her for her marriage at age thirty-nine to Cronwright. These experiences contributed to her brilliant exposition of "sexual discoordination," the gap between new sexual ideals and conventional male and female sexual socialization, in her acclaimed feminist treatise, *Woman and Labour.*

With Samuel Cron Cronwright, whom she met in December 1892 and married on February 24, 1894, Schreiner satisfied many of her marital expectations. She and Cronwright were intellectual and political comrades: freethinkers, socialists, committed to racial and sexual equality and to bringing about social change in South Africa. Cronwright was attracted to her intellectual strength, moral idealism, visionary perceptions, and creative genius. She was attracted to his mental and physical vigor. A champion athlete during his school and college years (he was eight years younger than Schreiner), he was endearingly childlike and gentle. They both desired children, yet they agreed that family life ought not restrict Schreiner's personal and professional independence.[67] Their age difference enabled her to feel a measure of maturity, even superiority, on certain moral issues, which helped to offset Cronwright's tendency to want to domineer.

Long having questioned the institution of marriage, Schreiner seemed to avow that free love was more consistent with her feminist values. When she decided on a formal marriage ceremony, she had Cronwright's support in shaping it to her beliefs. He not only adopted Schreiner's surname but agreed to a short, quiet civil ceremony, including an antenuptial contract that assured the legal autonomy of his wife's property. Schreiner wore her "everyday" blue-black serge dress and black hat, and Cronwright, too, wore his "ordinary clothes." After the ceremony, as a symbol of resolute independence, the bride drove back alone to the hotel. A more conventional "old boots and rice" send-off took place later as they boarded the train to her husband's farm.[68]

The first year of their marriage confirmed Schreiner's sense of its rightness. She was delighted with her early pregnancy and exulted to Mary Brown, "The eleven months that have passed have been a time of always coming nearer to each other and understanding each other better. Even if I were to die when the little one is born, I should never doubt that our marriage had been the right thing."[69]

No evidence suggests any sexual difficulties between them, and he openly satisfied her craving for maternal affection. She confessed to the Browns, "Cron is unspeakably tender and good to me; sometimes I feel as if I were a little baby and he was my mother."[70] A current feminist might well have trouble admitting such emotional dependence and diminution of her authority, but Schreiner felt a refreshing ease in moving in and out of child and adult identities, an ease resonant as well in her "little language" with Ellis, in Gregory Rose's treatment of Lyndall in *African Farm*, and in Rebekah's fantasies in *From Man to Man*.

Although Schreiner merged sexual intimacy with various other areas of closeness with Cronwright, she did not wholly avoid marital conflict. As their years together advanced, what began as minor problems became more serious. Cronwright's advocacy of women's rights had its limits. His acquiescence to Schreiner's desire for him to adopt her surname was not without resistance. Though he undertook household chores conventionally assigned to women, he viewed his domestic responsibilities as a concession to Schreiner's literary genius, not as an inherently proper arrangement.[71]

Schreiner's asthmatic distress forced Cronwright's most difficult concessions. Krantz Plaats, the site of his home and farm, proved inimical to Schreiner's health. Likely, the chronic source of her asthma attacks was not the climate—the karroo, on which the farm stood, usually had a salutary effect—but the animal hair and other farmyard allergens. At substantial financial and psychic cost, and risking career instability, Cronwright relinquished his farm so he and Schreiner could relocate in Kimberley, where they remained until 1898. During nearly all of this time Schreiner's health was robust.[72] However, with their savings soon exhausted, with *From Man to Man* still unfinished (the novel that Schreiner had led Cronwright to believe would bring them economic security), Cronwright had to seek other income and he embarked upon legal training.

Though he was anxious about Schreiner's physical predicament and eager to make her happy and well, Cronwright's frustrated ambitions as a farmer and his loss of economic stability gnawed at him. He became increasingly self-pitying and bitter about what he saw as the laggard pace of Schreiner's literary productivity and her continued economic reliance upon him. Though he could sacrifice for a "genius," he could not justify his deviations from conventional male roles and his loss of career for an ordinary woman.

Already guilt-stricken over Cronwright's abandonment of farming, Schreiner felt still worse about the pace of her writing. No doubt Cronwright's pressure and her own guilt impeded her work, but her literary perfectionism and early pregnancy would have delayed completion in any event. The death of her baby and subsequent miscarriages understandably impeded her writing even more radically. Indeed, doctors, in accord with general medical opinion of the time, urged her to rest and not to write if she wished to avert further miscarriage and illness. Angry and confused, longing for a woman doctor who could offer genuine consolation, Schreiner wrote a friend, "they don't see that it's the consciousness that I can't write that is killing me."[73]

The tension between Schreiner and Cronwright would have mounted still further were it not that while she slowly persevered with *From Man to Man* she also engaged in significant political writing. Her varied political output—treatises, addresses, satires, short stories, and a novella, *Trooper Peter Halket of Mashonaland*—served as balm, emphatically so in light of their joint, lonely, persecuted political stance. Because almost every South African Briton during the nineties was pro-Empire and anti-Boer (including both Schreiner's and Cronwright's families), they could turn only to each other when relatives and most friends vehemently condemned them. Similarly, their advocacy of black rights, though supported by a cluster of white and, of course, black friends, further marginalized them.[74] At stake were moral and political principles central to Schreiner's and Cronwright's integrity. Had they not shared these principles, their marriage would surely have collapsed.

Sadly, Cronwright's decision to enter a legal career complicated their residence problems and increased marital strains. Once he completed his legal training, he had to move in 1898 to Johannesburg to qualify for the bar. Inevitably, risking the recurrence of her asthma, Schreiner joined him there after a while. Her asthma did return, necessitating her departure from the city to the farm of one of her husband's cousins. When Cronwright, invited by various antiwar groups, decided to tour England to rouse British opinion against the Anglo–Boer War (which had begun in November 1899), Schreiner remained in Cape Town with her younger brother Will, now prime minister of the Cape Colony, and his family. In only a few months her asthma required that she return to the karroo, where somehow she found immediate and ironic respite on a farm at Wagenaars Kraal. After Cronwright's return from England she moved to a higher elevation in the Boer village of Hanover, famed for its excellent air and dryness. Cronwright planned to join her there, but the Anglo–Boer War intruded. On December 21, 1900, martial law brought Hanover to a standstill. Barbed-wire fences surrounded the town and the house in which Schreiner lived with her friend Aletta Vilgoen. Until Cronwright secured medical assistance to help him gain exceptional status, martial law prevented his leaving Cape Town to join her. During this time British soldiers looted their house in Johannesburg. They destroyed nearly all of her belongings, including voluminous notes for her study on women and sexuality as well as draft chapters for that book, numerous old journals, and twenty prose dreams.[75]

Schreiner and Cronwright lived together in Hanover even after the end of the Anglo–Boer War (1902). Now in a position to open his own legal business, Cronwright in June 1902 was elected a member of Parliament for Colesberg, and in the following year for Beaufort West. His political duties touring his constituencies and attending parliamentary sessions in Cape Town led to long absences, which Schreiner resented. Her anger grew when Cronwright opened what became a very successful branch of his business in De Aar. Eventually, in October 1907, Schreiner moved to De Aar, where the climate was "terrible" and the summer heat so intense that she spent that season with her family and friends in Cape Town.[76] The precise nature of Schreiner and Cronwright's marital compatibility during these years after the war is cloudy. Given their inability to have children, they shared keen pleasure in their pet animals, by 1904 possessing two dogs and six mierkats (a playful South African rodent among whom conventional gender roles are androgynous or reversed.)[77] They continued to see eye to eye on most urgent political issues in South Africa, but more than geographical distance seems to have come between them. Evidence of this mounts in a testy exchange of letters in the months prior to Schreiner's trip to England.

In 1913, Schreiner decided to sail to England after Cronwright announced that he was on the verge of a physical and nervous breakdown and needed a long vacation, without his wife, where he could escape the tiring demands of her ill health. For her part, Schreiner wanted to avail herself of new European medical discoveries to relieve her heart pains. They then planned independent trips to the Continent and would live apart, it appeared, even when they were in England together. Emerging through their discussions was Schreiner's distrust of Cronwright's friendship with an old friend of both of theirs, Isaline Philpot. Schreiner charged that Philpot had been indiscreet and critical in remarks about Schreiner that she had made to Cronwright, and he in turn accused his wife of groundless jealousy. Schreiner executed her end of the travel arrangements, but ultimately Cronwright found he could not afford to leave his business.[78]

Schreiner never imagined a lengthy absence from her husband. Whatever their marital discord, they remained devoted to each other. The onset of World War I, though, was to turn a projected brief absence into a seven-year separation. Despite the uninterrupted flow of affectionate correspondence between them during this time, Schreiner and Cronwright never recovered the full intimacy of their early marriage. When the war ended and Cronwright was at last in a position to retire and undertake his trip to England, intending ultimately to travel with or without Schreiner to America, he arrived in England to find his wife extremely ill. To spare herself another damp and chilly English winter, Schreiner sailed for South Africa just one month after her husband arrived. Sensing that death was close, she was determined to die in South Africa. After several more months in England, Cronwright abandoned his American trip, intending to rejoin his wife. Schreiner died before her husband could return to their homeland.

Despite Schreiner's commitment to realizing her ideals of heterosexual friendship and love, she never limited her concept of intimacy only to exchanges with men. She held similarly high ideals of female intimacy which, though more in accord with dominant Victorian attitudes, still challenged social realities. In fact, throughout much of her fiction and reform activity, she asserted her longing for women to form bonds that would transcend their common rivalry for male regard. Her family experience and adult observations precluded her holding sentimental notions of innate female goodness. She recognized how female subordination and powerlessness relative to men corrupted women as easily as men. She also found that her frontier manners—her ready laugh, bantering familiarity with men, mimicry and comic exaggeration, and physical expressiveness (e.g., she savagely punched her palms as she spoke)—alienated many middle-class British women. Counterbalancing this, her passion for her infant sister, her yearning for female affection and compassion, and her sympathy with women's position in society enabled her to form intimate ties with a number of such British women. In England, she became very close to Eleanor Marx, Edith Nesbit (then known as Mrs. Hubert Bland), and Havelock Ellis's sister Louie Ellis.[79] Reflective of the tenderness expressed in her friendships is Schreiner's account of how Edith Nesbit soothed her during the hectic hours prior to her departure from England to Italy in 1886 following her physical/nervous collapse. Schreiner recalled, "The last night she lay by me on the bed and drew me very close to her and pressed her face against mine, and, do you know, I have felt it ever since. I am going to get better."[80] She subsequently enjoyed a number of intimate friendships during her adult years in South Africa and especially esteemed the loving relationship between her good friends Betty Molteno and Alice Greene, who had chosen to live together. A particularly warm friendship with the prominent Dutch physician Aletta Jacobs, a leading European suffragist, pacifist, and advocate of birth control, developed following her meeting with Schreiner in South Africa.[81] Although Schreiner's relations with her older sisters were troubled, she formed strong attachments with such female relatives as her brother Will's wife (Frances Reitz) and their daughters (Lyndall Gregg and Ursula Scott). Schreiner cherished and assiduously nurtured these perhaps most unembittered emotional ties of her life.

When in the 1880s Schreiner shifted career direction to writing, she thought primarily in terms of fiction. She wanted her novels and shorter works to expose social and individual maladies and heal the socially wounded, whether lonely or poor, whether bereft of love, whether victims of religious and moral persecution. She hoped her writing would touch, too, the hearts of society's privileged members and persuade them to alter their callous and intolerant activity.[82]

Schreiner's concentration upon fiction, however, posed a serious problem when, during the 1880s, she became increasingly absorbed with England's social and political controversies. Among her major projects, she devoted much time, which would otherwise have been devoted to fiction, to collecting data on prostitution while concurrently assisting individual prostitutes to secure alternative employment. When William T. Stead (editor of the *Pall Mall Gazette*) ran a series of articles exposing the scope of greed and brutality entailed in child prostitution in England and was sentenced to three months in prison for complicity with child prostitution in his investigatory efforts to expose it, Schreiner drafted a letter (and collected signatures for it) in his support.[83] Engaged in research in anthropology, biology, and history for a wide-ranging study on women and sexuality, she also began to prepare an introductory essay for a new edition of Mary Wollstonecraft's *Vindication of the Rights of Woman*. Steeping herself in socialist writings, she yearned for direct participation in the British labor movement, but her precarious health and lack of familiarity with the movement permitted her only to take an observer's pleasure from the sidelines in the triumphs of British workers, most notably the historic dock strike in London's East End.

She still believed that fiction, not politics, was her metier, but not without reservation, as is strikingly evident in her self-critical, pendulum-swinging sequence of remarks to Havelock Ellis. First, the defense of the author over the political activist:

> When I want to go to Trafalgar Square and fight the enemies of Freedom of the hour wildly and get my head broken, *you* say I am a fool, and you are *right*. When I run about after prostitutes, ——— writes to tell me I am a *fool* and wicked for leaving my work, and he is *right*. Goethe was a far more highly moral man than Schiller. The man who sits quietly in his study, writing and writing out a great scientific truth, while his little petty state is going to pieces, is greater, more human, more moral than one who, like myself, would rush out wildly and fight.

Next, the attack: Schreiner accused Ellis, whom she identified as that admirable man of the study, as being partially dead, his retreat to the study seeming spineless detachment:

> The whole world is *crashing* about you, your dearest friends are being dragged to prison, theories you have been interested in are being practically tested, crime and wicked wrong is being done to innocent little children—and you look with astonishment and disapproval at another who is not untouched by it. . . . Give you £200 a year and you would curl yourself up in abstract study and thought for the rest of your life. In time of revolution and war you will never be in the market place.

When Schreiner returned to praise of Ellis for his social detachment and obliviousness—"Your *greatness* is your absolute absence of the enthusiasm of the market place"—her outburst rings sarcastic and hollow.[84]

Her conflict between politics and literary writing intensified when she returned to South Africa; her judgments continued to fluctuate. Not long after her arrival, she entered a brief period of reciprocated infatuation with Cecil Rhodes, the diamond and gold magnate who in 1890 became prime minister of the Cape Colony.[85] As she became acquainted with his cruelly imperialistic and racist aims and methods, the allure for her of his political passion evaporated. She became his most clear-headed and outspoken South African opponent. Yet her relationship with Rhodes, as well as her renewed ties with her brother Will (in 1890 legal advisor to Rhodes and soon to be his attorney general), had kindled her lively interest in South African affairs. Her new South African friends were not, as were her friends in England, avant-garde intellectuals but rather individuals at the center of white South African political life.[86] She plunged into histories and contemporary studies of South African life and attended parliamentary debates in Cape Town. Disqualified as a woman from pursuing a government career, she was, by the mid-1890s, through her considerable fame as a writer and her ties with Will and others, rapidly and startlingly in a position to exercise a progressive influence upon the Cape government.

Schreiner's decision to commit time and energy to South African affairs represented not only a shift in her attitudes about the superiority of the study to the marketplace but also a considerable change in her self-perception. In her youth her primary sense of connection with South Africa was, as noted earlier, with its landscape. Having given little thought to political and social reform within the colony, she at no time prior to her stay in England in the 1880s linked her identity and destiny with South Africa. No doubt her parents' references to England as their true homeland and as the pinnacle of modern civilization influenced her adolescent outlook. Even as she became increasingly critical of British cultural values and institutions, she still identified as a white Englishwoman. Because her colonial status heightened her awareness of the limitations of her education, of her general isolation and marginality, she saw settling in England as sheer self-enrichment. Yet, unlike her parents, Schreiner was deeply attached to South Africa, and this attachment became all the keener in England.[87]

During the 1880s Schreiner began to view herself as binational and transnational; that is, she felt a kinship with certain aspects of English life absent in South Africa, and vice versa. In many ways she came to admire England's intellectual and political openness and to revel in the like-mindedness and sophistication of her radical comrades. She missed this ferment and radicalism when she returned to South Africa. Conversely, while in England she craved the evocative sensual qualities of South Africa's scenery, its cultural and racial diversity, the simple and unpretentious manners of its Boer and African population.[88] Given this ambivalence about both England and South Africa, she eschewed a single national identity and preferred to designate herself a "citizen of the world."[89]

Nevertheless, in the 1890s, although still regarding herself as transnational, she emotionally and politically identified more and more with South Africa. She grew estranged from England, which had become increasingly conservative and imperialistic. The estrangement never becoming total, she retained affection for those Britons who shared her disgust with British cultural and political arrogance and who identified with those British ideals and national traits she deemed moral and progressive. When, by the second decade of the twentieth century, she had to abandon her political dreams for South Africa, her political ties to the country of her birth weakened, but her emotional attachment did not. Her final years in England only heightened her South African identity. Harassed during World War I for her German surname and pacifist views, she was understandably determined in the final months of her life to return to her native country to die.[90]

Not only did Schreiner's decision to immerse herself in South African politics manifest her expanding political identity, it also revealed her belief in her ability to convert others to her point of view. She departed from England before the disillusioning political setbacks in the 1890s for socialists and feminists, and she brought to South Africa the heady optimism of 1880s English progressives. Schreiner had clearly emerged from the rocky self-esteem and social isolation of her youth, as well as from her interpersonal upheaval in England, into a confident, resourceful woman who won respect and formed friendships with considerable ease, even in her homeland.

Prior to her marriage in 1894 to Cronwright, Schreiner saw no serious schism between her political and literary work. In her mind she was simply extending her healing urges to the body politic. She was satisfied with her literary stride: the publication of her collection of allegories, *Dreams;* the completion of a lengthy story, "The Buddhist Priest's Wife"; her current progress on her novel, *From Man to Man.*[91] She was likewise pleased with her varied political writings and began a series of essays on South African zoological, cultural, and political life that was published during the nineties in diverse English and American journals and eventually compiled and published under the title *Thoughts on South Africa* (1923). Merging fiction and document, Schreiner fired off a satire, "The Salvation of a Ministry," to excoriate Cecil Rhodes and his supporters' endorsement of the strop bill (the "Every Man Wallop His Own Nigger Bill"), which substituted lashes for fines and brief imprisonments for minor offenses.

This comfortable balance of political and literary work did not persist after her marriage. As pressures mounted upon her to finish *From Man to Man,* political turmoil in South Africa was intensifying, and she felt impelled to redirect her talents to its diagnosis and possible cure. Torn by the competing demands of her literary and political work, she composed a novella, *Trooper Peter Halket of Mashonaland,* which far more thoroughly and skillfully than her earlier satire integrated her political passions and ideals with her preference for fictional representation. In this way she virtually removed the issue of the rival claims of literary and political projects, though she recognized that her novella did not achieve its aim to convert British public opinion to opposition to its government's racial and imperial policies in South Africa. She ruefully noted, "In spite of its [the novella's] immense circulation [it had not] saved the life of one nigger, it had not the slightest effect in forcing on a parliamentary examination into the conduct of affairs in Rhodesia." Nor did the novella fully meet her artistic standards.[92] Nonetheless, she valued her accomplishment sufficiently to write Will that "if I were dead I would like them to write on my grave: 'She wrote *Peter Halket*'—nothing else."[93] At no time expressing reservations about wedding political and literary objectives in a work of fiction, she followed that path in *From Man to Man* itself, where lengthy passages treat political and social questions, and in various of her later short stories, which highlight the tragedy of the Anglo–Boer War and, later, World War I.

Fiction, however, could not suffice to carry Schreiner's political ambitions. Her major intellectual activity from the mid-1890s until her death was nonfictional political writing: *The Political Situation* (1896), a jeremiad on South Africa's calamitous state and a treatise on alternative policies; *An English South African's View of the Situation* (1899), published initially as a series of newspaper articles during June and July 1899 to expose the irrational and counterproductive warmaking policies of the British government; *Closer Union* (1909), a set of proposals for a federated, racially plural, and demo-cratic constitution for the new republic of South Africa; *Woman and Labour* (1911), a book-length analysis of the woman question and feminist apologia; and *The Dawn of Civilization*, never completed, written during World War I, published after Schreiner's death in much abbreviated form, which offers a searching examination of the causes of war and a statement of Schreiner's pacifism. Occasional periodical articles and public addresses in person and through letters to the public added to her prodigious political outpouring. Finally, her personal correspondence from 1890 to 1911 included many perceptive and prophetic letters to Will and her politically prominent friends which defined current South African political and moral issues and set forth appropriate action. Throughout all of her writing medical imagery was a recurrent motif, epitomized in a passage from her address to a woman's meeting at Cape Town in July 1900, attacking England's attempt to annex the Orange Free State and the Transvaal:

> Those who had worked in hospital, and who had some knowledge of sur-gery, knew that a very terrible thing sometimes happened. When a great surgi-cal operation was performed, and a body was cut open, it not infrequently happened that owing to the carelessness or the stupidity of the operator some small foreign object had been left within the cavity of the body. The body was sewn up; the external wound might heal; the operators might think that the

whole thing was an unqualified success. . . . But deep within the body was that foreign irritating substance, producing disease and putrefaction. It might take months, or it might take years of unutterable suffering and organic disturbance, but until, through a gangrenous wound, that foreign substance was extruded there could be no return to balanced health. The attempt to annex the Free State and the Transvaal was an attempt to introduce into the body social of South Africa such an irritating and extraneous substance.[94]

Schreiner's political activity from these last decades of her life extended beyond writing, public speeches, and personal correspondence to active participation both in South Africa and, after 1914, in England in women's suffrage and peace organizations. She personally lobbied South African parliamentary members on behalf of her proposals for a racially plural and democratic South Africa and in support of specific feminist measures, serving with her lifelong friend, Mary Brown, as vice-president of the Cape Women's Enfranchisement League until the league's refusal to extend the franchise to blacks spurred her resignation. Similarly, during her final stay in England during World War I, she joined groups lobbying the government for women's suffrage. She planned, as well, to accompany other women peace advocates in their thwarted efforts to attend the Hague Peace Conference of international antiwar women organized by Aletta Jacobs. Tellingly, though ailing throughout the last months of her life in South Africa, she collected money for the defense of Samuel Masabala of the Cape provincial branch of the African National Congress. (He was on trial for organizing a strike of black municipal workers in Port Elizabeth. The police action to end the strike caused the death of ten workers.) Her last will and testament was a political act. Deftly blending her lifelong aspirations, she provided that funds be set aside for a medical scholarship for women at the South African College at Cape Town (forerunner of the University of Cape Town) to be administered emphatically without reference to race, color, or religion, with poor women and girls accorded preference.

By her final years, Schreiner no longer expected to see her dreams for South Africa and England realized. Her last undertaking, the unfinished *Dawn of Civilization*, reflected the hard-won balance struck in her mature years between her idealism and sense of reality. Whereas in *From Man to Man* she stressed that the progressive vanguard could avoid repudiation by working in close alliance with the less advanced masses, in *Dawn* she examined why ordinary people were drawn to warmaking and would resist pacifist idealists. *Dawn* was by far her most realistic dissection of human aversion to her progressive ideals. Over the years she had acquired a complex patience with the slowness and uncertainty of social change, crystallized in her exhortation to Cronwright:

> I think this deep craving for union of thought and feeling with the mass of our fellows and this endless want when we have it not is one of the deepest elements making for growth and advance; but we must not seek for its satisfaction by trying to step back to a lower level of intellectual or emotional growth than that which we have gained, but endure the craving, til, far in the future— or never—we find our own.[95]

Schreiner's balance between idealism and realism did not achieve their successful integration. A dramatic disjunction appears in *Dawn* between her scientific and rational diagnosis of human proclivity toward war and her essentially intuitive case for pacifism. This disjuncture corresponds to her inability to resolve the contradiction in her thought between the "awful universe," which human beings alone can mitigate, and the coherence and beauty of the cosmos, which civilization corrupts. Yet, with regard to her lifelong personal issues, she had overcome much of the inner division and self-hatred of her youth. She enjoyed periods of friendship and love that approximated her ideals. She had effectively channeled her medical career yearnings into her literary and political work. In coming to terms with her illnesses, her frequent shifts in residence, and her loss during the Anglo– Boer War of her extensive notes for her study on gender, she moderated her ambitions and consoled herself with Robert Browning's "What I aspired to be, and was not, comforts me."[96]

If Schreiner on the night before she died had gazed into a mirror, as had Lyndall in *African Farm*, she would not have experienced her childhood self-disgust and alienation from herself. Those who met with her during the final weeks and days of her life found someone reconciled to herself and to impending death. She exuded cheer and humor. When Cronwright's brother, Alfred, and his two sons visited her, she was "awfully happy . . . kept us in fits of laughter." Ethel Hermann, another visitor, recalled that "when she was comfortably seated one entirely forgot that she was an old and ailing woman in the extraordinary fascination that she exercised. She talked the whole day amazingly on politics and art, literature and persons, world problems and famous people. . . . She imitated comically all manner of people. . . . We enjoyed her humour, her sprightly intellect, her broad sympathy and her attractive vivacity."[97]

Schreiner's death, when it came that December night, was eerily akin to

41

Lyndall's last moments in *African Farm*. Her death was preceded by an unusually energetic day and occurred with calm suddenness, apparently while she was reading. No sign of distress was evident. Doubtless her eyes, like Lyndall's, kept their distinctive gleam, that "wonderful yearning light." One of her final visitors, noting her "leathery and folded" skin and "rusty bellows" of a voice, could not help but comment upon how "very bright" her eyes still shone.[98]

2

"The tiny drop"

FREETHINKER AND MYSTIC

> The keynote of it [mystical consciousness] is invariably a
> reconciliation. It is as if the opposites of the world, whose
> contradictoriness and conflict make all our difficulties and
> troubles, were melted into unity.
>
> William James, *The Varieties of Religious Experience*

> I have never been able to conceive God, and man and the
> material universe as distinct from one another.
>
> Olive Schreiner to John T. Lloyd, October 29, 1892

AT A SOUTH AFRICAN and International Exhibition held in October 1892 at
Kimberley, the noted minister of the Presbyterian church there, the Reverend
John T. Lloyd, handed Olive Schreiner, then at the zenith of her popularity
and critical acclaim for her fiction, a letter in which he set forth his intellectual
difficulties with regard to his clerical work and asked for her help. Although
Schreiner was by then well known for her denunciation of Christianity and
espousal of free thought, Lloyd's regard for Schreiner as a "religious genius"
was not unique. Innumerable late Victorians, many of them figures of considerable fame, testified to the remarkable power of her religious expression.
Representative of her British enthusiasts was the famed novelist John Galsworthy who, having read *African Farm* twice, in 1891 and 1893, for its
evocation of his spiritual experience, recommended it to a friend troubled
with religious doubt.[1] In America, Pearsall Smith, a millionaire with prominent ties to social reformers, wrote to Schreiner that her treatment of religion
in *African Farm* led to his rejection of Christianity and to his social work of
thirty years. Charlotte Perkins Gilman, one of America's most original, path-
finding feminists, also prized Schreiner as a religious mentor, as did the

young Solomon Schechter of South Africa, later to become an internationally renowned Hebrew scholar.[2]

Despite such esteem for Schreiner's religious expression during her lifetime, twentieth-century scholars generally subordinate, if not sidestep, the religious dimensions of her life and writing.[3] This is particularly amiss because Schreiner's metaphysics provided the stable axis uniting her moral, social, and political views and empowered her in times of personal agony. The historic wariness of socialist and feminist theorists toward organized religion, not to mention the widespread religious skepticism of the twentieth century, has often blinded contemporary scholars to the centrality and creative force of religious reflection in the lives and social attitudes of nineteenth-century artists and reformers. Happily, the current late-twentieth-century stream of feminist thinking includes intellectual currents highly receptive to metaphysical speculation. Schreiner, it will be seen, anticipated key facets of recent feminist spirituality in addition to occupying a unique place among late-Victorian freethinkers and spiritual visionaries.

Schreiner was one of the leading Victorian exponents of the cosmic integration of material and spiritual phenomena, a position rare among Victorian religious and secular minds. Theologians of that period commonly conceived of the universe as embattled, split into opposing if not warring dualities: God versus the devil, Heaven versus Hell, soul versus body, spirit versus matter, animate nature versus inanimate, saved versus damned. For philosophers in general, the universe appeared as essentially mind (idealism) or matter (materialism and most forms of scientific naturalism). Both Victorian idealists and materialists tended to be monists; that is, they believed the universe to be one, unified according to the laws of either mind or matter. Their resolution of dualism through the subordination or dismissal of one of the two polarities necessitated conflicting, or at least differing, epistemologies.

With the exception of a cadre of Victorian scientists and philosophers, most scientific naturalists rejected nonrational sources of evidence as apt to nourish dangerous superstitions and shackle critical investigation. For them, the central task of science and philosophy involved empirical and rational delineation of the physical laws of causation, evolution, and the conservation of energy. In contrast, Victorian idealists, though many of them also promoted empirical research and rational analysis, were prone to lend credence to the insights of intuition and feelings. This tendency was especially evident among those nineteenth-century idealists profoundly influenced by, if not actual proponents of, the romantic movement. At the core of their epistemology, however, was a deep distrust of the material world and physical sensations.

Standing rational positivism on its head, they viewed the multiple external and physical manifestations of nature as fundamentally unreal. Truth resided in the inner mental or spiritual connections disguised by outward physical attributes.

Despite her inclination toward idealism, Schreiner rebelled against both materialism and idealism along with the metaphysical dualism of her Christian upbringing. She was determined to reconcile the antinomies of noumenal and phenomenal reality, to transcend oppositions of spirit and matter, oneness and plurality of being, transcendence and immanence of god. Similarly, she insisted upon the legitimacy of both objective and subjective modes of understanding, scientific and mystical inquiry, rational and subconscious avenues to truth. Though she was not always consistent in her efforts and was occasionally superficial in her vaulting of apparent philosophical contradictions, her ideas showed uncommon independence from prevailing Victorian attitudes. She carried forward the goals of a small coterie of early- and mid-Victorian thinkers who also sought to "make it whole"—from the writings of Coleridge to those of John Stuart Mill, Herbert Spencer, James Hinton, Charles Bray, George Henry Lewes, and George Eliot.[4] In their and Schreiner's integrationist ideal they hearkened back to earlier historic attempts to transmute cosmic oppositions, and they precipitated what would become a mounting twentieth-century attack on the multiple forms of nineteenth-century dualism.

Schreiner's negation of existential dualities creates linguistic problems for the scholar. When we speak of her spiritual outlook, some definition of *spiritual* is clearly necessary. Common definitions of the word assume a dualistic framework and are not adequate in conveying her outlook. First, *spiritual* in her usage was not equivalent to what is traditionally meant by the word *religious;* she used the term interchangeably with words such as *divine, transcendent, supernatural,* and *metaphysical.* Second, *spiritual* is customarily differentiated from *natural, physical,* and *material,* but again not in her usage. There simply exists no suitable term that bears her integrated meaning. Since she did not coin a new word but kept *spiritual,* I will follow her intrepid example.

Other problems pertain in delineating Schreiner's spiritual outlook. Though her critique of prevalent religious and philosophical thought is reasonably consistent and unambiguous, her substitute faith—what I designate her self-styled theism—abounded in ambiguities. She fluctuated from a modified idealism to neutral monism, from a vague interrelationship of transcendent and mundane reality to a pantheistic blending of the two. Nowhere did she systematically explain the nature of the identity of mind and body,

God and world. That these confusions should characterize her writing constitutes strength no less than weakness, testifying to her lifelong mental openness and flexibility as well as her brave defiance of many established religious and philosophical formulations. She envisioned the path that lay ahead for twentieth-century thinkers even if she could not remove its obstructive bramble.

Indeed, more a visionary than a trained, rigorous philosopher, Schreiner tended to proclaim her religious tenets rather than seek to prove them empirically or logically. Nowhere did she provide a developed religious position. Instead, though her assumptions and ideas were fundamental to her ethical and social outlook, she scattered her spiritual views within her letters and passages in her novels, allegories, and nonfiction.

The principle difference between her articulation of her religious and of her secular views was her declared reluctance to write about her spiritual beliefs. She considered spiritual convictions a purely private matter shared only in very rare and special relationships. She was all too familiar with the ease of misunderstanding and likelihood of persecution for upholding unconventional opinions, especially for women. Further, she deemed words flimsy vessels for containing her spiritual experience and views. "Religion," Schreiner has her heroine Undine assert, "flourishes best in silence, and is to be felt, not spoken of." Fortunately for us, Schreiner's resistance to verbalizing her religious views fell short of absolute. She detailed more vividly and persuasively than any of her contemporaries the loss of traditional faith, or what the historian Franklin Baumer calls "conversion in reverse."[5] At the same time, particularly through her allegorical tales, she offered alternative and inspiring visions of humanity's relationship with the universe, affirming the dignity and significance of all creation.

Of all her writings on religion, her novel *African Farm* had the widest and most profound impact. In no other work did she chronicle so carefully and graphically a Christian's loss of faith. Her account echoed the experience of innumerable Victorians, in effect validating their agonizing and guilt-ridden shift toward skepticism. Two sections of *African Farm* devoted to religious issues can best serve as prelude to a more comprehensive analysis of Schreiner's critique of conventional religion and deism.

Conversion in Reverse

Part 2 of *African Farm* begins with the chapter "Times and Seasons," which delineates the psychodynamics of human spiritual evolution. Divided into seven phases, this evolution reflects the experiences of one of the novel's major characters, Waldo, and corresponds to Schreiner's own spiritual development. "The soul's life," the narrator of the novel explains, "has seasons of its own; periods not found in any calendar."[6]

"Infancy," heralding these seven periods, is the time of diverse, disconnected, vivid sensory moments and features an experience of commanding significance: The occasion is the aftermath of a thunderstorm when "the ground, as far as the eye can reach is covered with white hail; the clouds are gone, and overhead a deep blue sky is showing; far off a great rainbow rests on the white earth. . . . We . . . feel the cool, unspeakably sweet wind blowing in on us, and a feeling of longing comes over us." The narrator, utilizing "we" as her pivotal pronoun throughout this poetic sequence, emphasizes the longing as unutterable, undefined: "we want—we do not know what"—as with an infant's dawning recognition of the ephemeral and elusive quality of natural beauty.[7]

Spanning early childhood, the second "season" is one of intensified sensory awareness accompanied by growing curiosity about nature, when "We are run through with a shudder of delight" upon beholding white wax flowers that lie between their two green leaves flat on the red sand. In awe we hesitantly pick the flowers, find their aroma intoxicating, and gently tear apart the leaves so as to gaze upon their silky threadlike composition. We sit among bushes and kiss them, believing that they reciprocate our love "as though they were alive." The alluring primary colors of nature and the intrigue of natural forms contrast sharply with drab spelling lessons taught us without care for explanation: "They tell us it is so because it *is* so." With flowers and bushes, we authorize our own experience; with spelling lessons, we invest knowledge with adult authority. The second phase terminates with our shocking discovery of selfhood, our loss of innocent oneness with nature. We ask, "This *I*, what is it?" and, powerless to answer, grow fearful, a fear heightened by our awareness of our inability to convey this realization of self to others.[8]

During the third season of spiritual growth, loosely ranging from ages seven to ten, we discover that the Bible is more than a grim storehouse of prohibitions. One day, we read the fifth chapter of Matthew, and it stirs us with its message of love. Adults, however, do not share in our enthusiasm.[9] Still, we are passionately committed to Christ's exhortations to self-denial and charity: "Our little wagon that we have made, we give to the little Kaffers. . . . We conscientiously put the cracked teacup for ourselves at breakfast and take the burnt roaster-cake. . . . We are exotically virtuous." We begin to reflect upon the doctrines of Heaven and Hell. When occasional doubts surface, we find grownups' answers satisfying only "more or less."[10] Our mature moral and intellectual rejection of these doctrines develops later. Initially, we absorb unquestioningly the many hymns, sermons, didactic tales, and parental remarks warning us of damnation.[11]

In late childhood, circa ages ten to twelve, the fourth phase of our spiritual drama, we undergo, as did Schreiner, traumatic sufferings.[12] Our pivotal issue is God's alleged goodness and justice, what Piaget might refer to as the child's sense of fair play. We find incomprehensible the affirmation of our Christian God's perfect benevolence when it includes divine readiness to consign us to eternal damnation. No less a challenge to our sense of justice is the doctrine of atonement. We ask, "Is it good of God to make Hell? Was it kind of Him to let no one be forgiven unless Jesus Christ died?" Our feelings swing from rapturous delight in the heavenly sounds of harpists serenading God on his throne to terror at the horrible groans from the damned below. The fires of Hell and Christ's torment seem more potent than the joyful sensations of childhood. Flowers once so glorious metamorphose into "fuel waiting for the great burning."[13]

The primary image to evoke the terror of God's judgment for Schreiner is the watch or clock. Whereas for many the timepiece might signify the mechanical regularity and order of a rational universe, for an evangelical youth such as Waldo the clock was a fearsome symbol of time passing, of the final heartbeat, of death and eternal damnation.[14] In an early section of the novel, Waldo broods upon the great silver hunting watch of his father: "'Tick-tick-tick-tick! . . . it went on inexorably; and every time it ticked *a man died!* . . . 'Dying, dying, dying!,' said the watch; 'dying, dying, dying!' . . . where were they going to, all those people?" Waldo saw before him "a long stream of people, a great dark multitude, that moved in one direction; then they came to the dark edge of the world and went over. . . . 'Stop them! Stop them!' cried the child. All the while the watch kept ticking on; . . . 'Oh, God, God! save them!' he cried in agony."[15]

Ultimately, we come to wonder whether God cares about our souls. One very hot day Waldo tests the biblical promise that "Ye shall receive." Clearing a small space in the bushes, he creates an altar from twelve small, identical stones. From the bag that holds his dinner he takes out a mutton chop and sets it on the stone altar. He next prays to God to send fire down from Heaven to burn it. Then he kneels down with his face upon the ground, certain that when he looks up he will see God. He is half-suffocated with fear, but when he looks up God has not responded. After repeating his prayer three times, he receives as answer only a mass of devouring ants. After waiting the entire afternoon without further response, Waldo concludes that God hates him, that he is lost.[16] The disappointment and hate he is not permitted to feel toward God, Waldo turns upon himself.

Compounding Waldo's desolation is his persistent feeling of being alone. Waldo comes to learn "that the cup of affliction is made with such a narrow mouth that only one lip can drink at a time, and that each man's cup is made to match his lip." Indeed, "the barb in the arrow of childhood's suffering," observes the narrator in *African Farm*, is "its intense loneliness, its intense agony."[17]

Relief does come, though. The fourth season contains an interlude, a rest from the state of fear and trembling, as "the spring long bent recoils." This interval of calm, characterized by the evaporation of doubt and the filling of the soul with "soft waves of bliss . . . 'the peace with God,' " is suffused with feelings of having been forgiven.[18] Key to this transformation is a shift in psychic concentration from the powerful, prohibitive God to the victimized Jesus; the sufferer exclaims, "We feel him! Oh, Jesus Christ, through you, through you this joy!" Upon the fading of this transient, blissful state, doubt returns and with it torment. Three courses lie open to us: "to go mad, to die, to sleep."[19]

The last of these options, mental sleep, dominates the fifth season of the soul's development, which corresponds to early adolescence in Schreiner's characters' fictional lives and in her own. While the questioning intellect slumbers, we adopt a dreamlike, sentimental religion, one that simply suppresses evidence of evil and cruelty in the universe. In place of the ticking clock, our new world view posits "a Mighty Heart, which, having begotten all things, loves them; and . . . beats with great throbs of love toward them."[20]

Ultimately, our sentimental Christian beliefs bring us neither peace of mind nor community approval (at least not in evangelical circles). Where Christian communities and their ministers insist upon a God of judgment we now consider that doctrine an abominable lie, one that condemns those who claim Jesus loves and saves even the atheist and heathen. The church appears riddled with hypocrisy, a breeding ground for ministerial egoism, a place for parishioners to flaunt their new clothes, engage in heterosexual flirtation, and practice mundane forms of respectability.[21]

With the sixth season, roughly the time of midadolescence, we awaken to life's brutalities and the inadequacy of sentimental Christianity. Our God of love retreats before the harsh facts of life, of "eyes that we love with worms eating them."[22] Waldo watches his aging father, Otto, who epitomizes the sentimental Christian, succumb to the rhetoric of Bonaparte Blenkins as the latter exploits Otto's credulity and love for all Jesus' brothers in order to evict him from his homestead and usurp his property and position. These actions precipitate Otto's heart attack and death as Blenkins conducts Sunday services for the members of the homestead. Waldo, who has shared Otto's religiosity, finds himself whipped by Blenkins, his prized sheep-shearing invention crushed, and his few precious books burned. Later he watches a savage wagon driver whip oxen to their death and learns of the death of his beloved Lyndall. Throughout the novel, he absorbs as well the effects of nonhuman suffering—droughts killing cattle, larger animals preying upon the smaller. Yet, despite a period of atheism ahead, Waldo can never wholly relinquish his dreamlike beliefs. They will remain his only consolation.[23]

The impact of reality upon the sixth phase of a soul's growth is devastating. In the seventh season doubt has triumphed. Cynicism and atheism replace earlier convictions. Injustice appears rampant: "The black man is shot like a dog, and it goes well with the shooter. The innocent are accused, and the accuser triumphs." The cosmos appears without order or meaning, not only irrational but also hostile. The sky becomes a "blue rag stretched overhead," existence a great pot stirred by Old Fate who cares nothing "what rises to the top and what goes down, and laughs when the bubbles burst." The seventh stage, however, does not conclude with pessimism and atheism. Gradually an alternative world view emerges. Resigned to the death of religious truths, we redirect our energy into the acquisition of secular knowledge—arithmetic, Latin, grammar, "poring over them as over our Bible of old." With these sobered eyes, we discern remarkable patterns in nature, not as a young child filled with the simple joy of our planet's sensory appeal or as the troubled believer but as a naturalist, a budding scientist. We experiment with plant and animal dissection and seek to understand the structural correspondences in nature, from the delicate network of blood vessels in a dissected gander to the shape and outline of "our thorn-tree seen against the sky in mid winter." This awareness rescues us from despair over a chance and chaotic universe. From a shabby blue rag, the sky becomes "an immeasureable blue arch over our heads" and nature "a living thing, a *One.*" The rebirth recounted here is truly a nineteenth-century secular counterpart to the evangelical conversion experience.[24]

Schreiner develops the final segment of the seventh phase as a haunting allegory, later excerpted for separate publication as "The Hunter." Told to Waldo by a visiting stranger, the allegory embodies nineteenth-century belief in scientific rationalism. The Hunter's goal is not salvation but Truth, an elusive and captivating white bird with outstretched silver wings. The Hunter, having seen her reflection in a lake, is so determined to capture her that he abandons his shooting to find her. As the narrative proceeds, the Hunter learns that the quest for Truth requires acute suffering. He must abandon comforting beliefs (e.g., immortality, an afterlife) as irrational superstitions, and he finds himself spurned by everyone as insane in his denunciation of human credulity. Wisdom tells him he must wander alone into the Land of Absolute Negation and Denial, make that his temporary home, resist further lures of superstition and despair, and finally leave that land by climbing the mountains of Stern Reality. Even after he ascends these mountains beyond where Wisdom can continue as his guide, he will not be able to grasp the white bird of Truth. At most he can hope to pick up one feather dropped from her wing.

The Hunter accepts the challenge. Though the mountain grows steeper, less marked, and though the mountain peaks loom higher, the air gets harder to breathe, and blood oozes from his fingertips, he perseveres. Finally, old, weak, and exhausted, no longer able to climb, he loses hope of ever grasping Truth. He comforts himself, nevertheless, that his work has not been in vain, for the footholds he has secured will enable others to climb more easily, and they will advance closer yet to Truth. The allegory concludes on a delicate uplifting note, so resonant that the influential nineteenth-century philosopher, Herbert Spencer, requested this allegory be read to him on his deathbed. As the Hunter dies, a white feather flutters toward him from the sky.[25]

Not even this seventh and climactic phase, the scientific rationalist solution, constituted the full scope of Schreiner's philosophical and religious outlook. At most, it represented one significant dimension of her thinking, the one most closely in accord with dominant patterns of Victorian free thought, which she would spend her whole life both affirming and questioning.

The Creed of a Freethinker

When Schreiner identified her religious position she opted for the Victorian term *freethinker*,[26] broad enough to accommodate a widely diverse range of beliefs. Though *freethinker* can fall under the general category of religious skepticism, it is not equivalent to agnosticism or atheism or scientific naturalism. Adherents to these cousin varieties of skepticism considered the quest for metaphysical truths futile and/or wrongheaded. Freethinkers, on the other hand, embraced those willing to include metaphysical questions within the valid sphere of human study. Karl Pearson, whose writing on free thought echoed and reinforced facets of Schreiner's complex stance on religion, drew the careful distinction: "The Freethinker's position differs to some extent from that of the Agnostic. While the latter asserts that some questions lie beyond man's power of solution, the former contents himself with the statement that on these points he does not know at present, but that, looking to the past, he can set no limit to the knowledge of the future."[27]

Having suffered intellectual deprivation as a result of orthodox religious training, Schreiner was hardly prepared to have her appetite for knowledge in any field thwarted. Rebekah in *From Man to Man* voices Schreiner's commitment when she describes her "hunger for an exact knowledge of things as they are, of naked truth about all things small or great, material and also psychic."[28] In this respect, the Hunter allegory personifies the freethinker's refusal to abandon hope for even a glimpse of ultimate Truth.

Although Schreiner's critique of Christianity was singular in certain respects, it also shared Victorian freethinkers' dominant arguments.[29] The essence of their attack on religion was (1) its inculcation of credulity through its stifling of human curiosity and subordination of reason to the dictates of religious authority; (2) its tendency to divert human attention from pressing social problems; and (3) its license to bigotry and tyranny in the name of true belief. Freethinkers also drew upon history, anthropology, and, of course, evidence from the physical and biological sciences, most notably Darwinian, to argue for the relativity of systems of belief and against traditional notions of providential will and design. All of these criticisms are present in Schreiner's writing. In early adolescence, in her struggle against parental religious teachings, she turned to John Stuart Mill's *Logic* and Herbert Spencer's *First Principles*. Her reading of Darwin enhanced her scientific passion for facts and for a sound grasp of the physical world. Throughout her adult life she found ammunition against religion in the works of Higher Criticism and in Gibbon's compelling account of the historic reasons for Christianity's triumph in the ancient world. Gibbon inspired her as well with his skeptical detachment from the doctrinal squabbles that gripped early Christianity.[30]

No less salient for Schreiner were moral criticisms of religion. Some scholars allege that these moral considerations were more decisive than the rationalist arguments for most freethinkers, scientific logic serving as a rationalization of prior moral rejection of religion. The cardinal tenets of Christian orthodoxy—damnation, vicarious atonement, original sin, and, among certain Calvinist strains of Christianity, predestination and election—were, for freethinkers, fundamentally immoral.[31] Even for those Victorians who eventually developed a liberal version of Christianity, the cruel and savage God of orthodox tenets was incompatible with the moral demands they imposed on themselves and others in their daily lives.

Historically, Christian thinkers have resolved two seemingly incongruous personae, a god of love versus a god of judgment, either by surrendering to faith what seemed inexplicable or by opting for one of the two personae as the Deity's primary characteristic. The Victorian Christian, however, faced this dilemma with new urgency. The widespread nineteenth-century belief in social progress and individual self-help was predicated not only on the utility of educating human reasoning powers but even more on the merits and possibility of training moral sensibility and willpower. An expanding of social conscience and human sympathy, if not love, seemed a precondition for social improvement. How, then, could a god, who turned his back on the predestined fate of sinners and consigned them to Hell, be worshiped by anyone instructed in compassionate behavior?[32] Among political liberals and radicals, Victorian ethics of social amelioration also involved an assault upon exclusivity, whether of the right to vote or of educational opportunities. Their stance against social privilege, which became increasingly egalitarian as the century advanced, was hardly consonant with an aristocratic god of arbitrary and selective grace.

Both Victorian confidence in social progress and the liberal and radical attack on social privilege flowed from a sense of the possible mastering of agonizing vicissitudes of fate. Belief in an arbitrary and omnipotent deity had served to reconcile people to staggering mortality statistics, recurrent plagues, drought, and famines, and other "acts of God." Fatalism, however, began to erode during the eighteenth and nineteenth centuries with England's rapid technological and industrial advance. As human capacity for control of life enlarged, people became less willing to invest divine providence with powers for self and social well-being. Such deference to fate came to seem destructive of the very character strengths—acquisition of initiative, responsibility, industry, ambition—that Victorians valued as essential to each individual's moral growth.

Schreiner's critique of religion incorporated the full range of moral objections. There can be no question that for Schreiner—as for her fictional characters—the doctrines of Hell, vicarious atonement, predestination, and election turned hollow adult professions of God's infinite love and goodness. Her stories often pivot on the evils of selective love in the human world, highlighting the hypocritical morality of those who preach love but abuse "fallen" women and "illegitimate" children while restricting love to those of the same religion, race, and way of life. Schreiner once wrote to Havelock Ellis that one of her brothers claimed his insensitive responses were a consequence of his belief in Hell and damnation, which made impossible his preserving tender feelings and still remaining sane. Appropriately, inside the front cover of her Journal for the years 1881–86 Schreiner wrote, "If God should dare to let one living soul into Hell he would defeat himself for he would not be there."[33]

Though Victorian moral and rationalist objections to Christianity figured prominently in Schreiner's thought, additional sources of her alienation from conventional religion marked her originality. Voicing feminist criticisms of religious institutions and values, she explored in *Undine*, for instance, how women and men conflate obedience to God and obedience to men. Mrs. Barnacles and Miss Mell, two pillars of the community, gossip about Undine's "idiotic ideas" on religious matters, which, they warn, will discourage all potential suitors, since "for clever learned men it's all very well" to be a skeptic, but for a woman it is immoral and self-defeating. "True" women were naturally spiritual, the moral redeemers and models for Christian behavior, saviors of men from the clutches of skepticism, materialism, and hedonism. This bears on Undine in painful fashion when Albert Blair, whom she adores, insists upon female religious piety and social submission.[34] Schreiner's fictional children discover from their earliest years that men are the arbiters of religious belief and social mores (the former sanctioning the latter). In Schreiner's own life, of course, males conducted family prayers and monopolized preaching whether in a chapel in England or on an isolated homestead in South Africa. Family prayers were among those many occasions when a Victorian father could incontrovertibly assert his dominance over his wife, children, and servants.[35]

Since religious skepticism posed so great a risk to a woman's psychic cohesion and personal reputation, no wonder so few women figure among prominent Victorian freethinkers.[36] The literary scholar Valentine Cunningham points out how emancipation from religious structures necessitated rebellion against patriarchal authority and vice versa. He cites such female literary rebels as George Eliot, Geraldine Jewsbury, and Schreiner, contrasting them with other Victorian writers, for example, Charlotte Yonge and Elizabeth Sewell, who knuckled under to male authority and permitted male family members and clergy to alter the content of their writing.[37] Schreiner's defiance was all the more remarkable in that she was not only a woman but a comparatively young one and from a cultural context far more homogeneous and rigid in its religious attitudes than Victorian England. As a result, her isolation as a freethinking adolescent was far more complete than that of English male and female skeptics.

Although in her fiction Schreiner uncovered some of the ways in which patriarchy and Christianity reinforced each other, she did not offer a comprehensive feminist critique of Christianity. She neither analyzed church organization nor advocated female ministry. At no time did she apply her feminism to a critique of the Old and New Testaments such as her American contemporary Elizabeth Cady Stanton dared to undertake in her infamous *Woman's Bible.*

Schreiner's feminist critique of Christianity extended, nevertheless, beyond sheer uncovering of the ways religion held women in their place and stifled personal development. Penetrating to the heart of Western religious conceptions, she denied the maleness of God. Not until the current wave of feminist religious and philosophical writing do we encounter comparably determined efforts to dethrone God-the-Father (and efforts to resist replacing that god with a god of any gender stereotype). In Schreiner's allegory "The Sunlight Lay across My Bed" God escorts the narrator through Hell and then into a multitiered Heaven. Describing these heavenly levels, God declares, "In the least Heaven sex reigns supreme; in the higher it is not noticed; but in the highest it does not exist." Schreiner's allegory "In a Ruined Chapel" posited a deity without gender. Such a view clearly departed from the androgynous view of God promulgated by gnosticism and certain forms of medieval mysticism, as well as from that of the American feminist Elizabeth Cady Stanton and from Mary Baker Eddy's definition of God as Father-Mother.[38] Had Schreiner explicitly distinguished her views from those who favored an androgynous deity, she would have decried the perpetuation of stereotypical feminine and masculine role and trait assignments still embodied in androgynous conceptions.[39] Though she never stated directly that the concept of God-the-Father is the bedrock of the insidious alliance between organized Christianity and male social privilege, it is evident from her intense dwelling upon a genderless god that she intuited this connection. Of course, a genderless god equally deprived women of a female-identified object of worship. Its toll is evident in Schreiner's continued use of male pronouns for God when not employing "it."

An array of current scholars allege that the rigid demarcations of God and man, transcendent realm and mundane, human being and animal, soul and body, stem from an original assumption of reality as radically bifurcated into male and female principles, with the male principle superior.[40] In advance of these scholars, Schreiner targeted this historic framework for overhaul. In her unpublished, never completed introduction to an edition of Mary Wollstonecraft's *Vindication of the Rights of Woman,* she maintained two protean principles, male and female, governing biological and human evolution but insisted they were not inherently in opposition or in hierarchical sequence but, rather, interacting, often united in the same organisms, fundamentally identical.[41]

No less distinctive than the feminist dimensions of Schreiner's religious outlook was her paramount objection to Christianity as incompatible with overwhelming mystical experiences of her childhood. Her five-year-old vision of "the unity of all things, and that they were alive, and that I was part of them," had a factual certainty that she was "never able to doubt."[42] Her experience of pervasive cosmic integration was starkly at odds with her family's insistence upon the doctrines of God's transcendence, selective grace, dualism of soul and body, and the depravity of man versus God's perfection. I. M. Lewis, in his provocative examination of comparative ecstatic religions, documents the predominance of women and oppressed males in noninstitutional forms of religious and, particularly, ecstatic experience. Through such spiritual episodes, women, long denied access to the texts and techniques of religious power, have cross-culturally tapped vital alternative power sources in their struggle against male authority and have validated their freedom from institutional dependence. For some nineteenth-century women this led to various forms of formal spiritualism and Christian Science. Schreiner, however, disdained both as escapist, simplistic responses to existential enigmas. Her intuitive religious experiences functioned as a weapon against credulity, not as a back door to another form of dogma and superstition. She was especially irritated by Mrs. Eddy, whom she regarded as "the greatest humbug who ever lived," and found her books "revolting."[43]

Schreiner's reliance upon religious visions represented an ironic turning of evangelical methods of belief upon themselves. In John Wesley's mid-eighteenth-century opposition to the religion of his day, he summoned individuals to spurn theological and intellectual understanding and conformity and, instead, engage in "heart-work," the stirring of their deepest emotions in soul searching and love of God as they quested for salvation and underwent eventual conversion. Waldo's agonies in *African Farm* were no more romantic in their ardor than that of innumerable other evangelicals, who recorded their experiences of conversion as rhapsodic, mystical, and trancelike: The sinner was now possessed and illuminated by God's grace. By the mid-nineteenth-century, however, with the spread of evangelical respectability and popularity, and especially with the maturation of organized Methodism, the ecstatic force of the original rebellion against conventional, lukewarm belief dissipated. Historically, as religions become entrenched, the more hostile they became toward haphazard, wildcat forms of inspiration. The religious enthusiast with direct claim to divine truth constituted a threat to the newly established order. And, yet, evangelical parents still demanded of their children a fundamentally emotional and intuitive relation to God while simultaneously insisting upon self-restraint and conformity in all matters of doctrine and social mores. Whereas most freethinkers jettisoned both the tenets and the techniques of conventional religious belief, usually subscribing to a rationalist and naturalist explanation of religious inspiration, Schreiner cherished the evangelical sanction of passionate religious expression, whether in describing states of being bereft from God or states of blessedness. In her metaphysics and, as we shall see, in her aesthetics, she believed in personal "illumination" and divine "flashes."

Schreiner's stress upon intuitive spiritual experience was allied to her romantic conviction that book learning was not indispensable to authentic spiritual understanding. For her, nature alone could suffice. In *Thoughts on South Africa*, she adduced various illustrations of the simple, nondogmatic faith of unlettered Boers. There is the silent, introspective, brawny cart driver who, with disarming naiveté asks, after driving about two hours, "When you are alone in the veld like this, and the sun shines so on the bushes, does it ever seem to you that something speaks? It is not anything you hear with the ear, but it is as though you grew so small, so *small*, and the other so great. . . . Do you hear it, too—you who are so learned?"[44]

There was also the African woman who, educated by the veld, with its blue mountains meeting the sky, was "animated by a great, direct perception of certain facts in life," those which Schreiner noted the Essenes sought in their rocky caves. She discerned a natural tolerance among these uneducated people, recalling a Boer woman who inquired why she never went to church. After a brief discussion, the Boer woman dropped the matter, but two years later the woman referred to it again:

> You told me once that your religion differed from mine; but the more I know you the more I begin to think we must have the same religion. When I sit alone with my sewing I think very far away sometimes; and sometimes it occurs to me like this: If I had many children, and each one spoke a different language, I would try to talk to each child in the language it understood; it

would be always me speaking, but in a different language to each child. So, sometimes I think, it is the same God speaking, only He speaks to you and to me in different languages.[45]

In claiming that education was not crucial to religious knowledge, Schreiner underscored not only the elitism of established religions but also the elitism of the leading freethinkers of her day, for whom the study of science, philosophy, and history was essential. In effect, her evangelical validation of emotional and intuitive understanding when divorced from doctrinal and institutional strictures served as a valuable resource in her challenge of both established religion and even male authority.[46]

Religious Commitment: Schreiner's Self-styled Theism

When we move from Schreiner's critique of established religion to her own brand of freethinking theism, we discover again an amalgam of philosophical concepts held in common with other freethinkers alongside views decidedly her own, some of which harbinger twentieth-century philosophical and religious approaches. In her self-styled theism the dichotomous universe of her Christian upbringing and "the awful universe" of her adolescent and adult skepticism yield to a vision of an integrated and neutral, if still not benevolent, cosmos.

Schreiner was indebted to John Stuart Mill and Herbert Spencer for more than their verification of her skepticism toward prevailing religious belief and more than their support for open and critical investigation. They also guided her toward an understanding of universal order and coherence. In *From Man to Man*, Schreiner has Rebekah compare the cosmos of modern science to that of the Christian conception of the universe, the latter "a thing of shreds and patches and unconnected parts." By contrast, the majesty of the scientific view of the cosmos was its rational presentation of a regulated, unified whole, knowable to the human mind. Science had replaced the universe of capricious design, of arbitrary miracles and interventions, with one bound together by "internetting lines of action and reaction." Like most Victorian freethinkers, Schreiner assumed that these laws of interconnection and causality were not merely constructions of the human mind, the fabrication of genius, but directly corresponded to objective reality. The wise stranger in *African Farm* asserts, "All true facts of nature and the mind are related."[47]

Correspondences were a central motif in Schreiner's conception of reality. She took particular pleasure in discovering nature's analogous and symmetrical patterns. Faith was not necessary to perceive these patterns; they were accessible to anyone with a sharp eye or, better yet, a microscope. For young Rebekah in *From Man to Man* the microscope is the premier scientific instrument. She fantasies herself entering a house equipped with a microscope just for her. In later years, owning a microscope, she uses it to examine lichen and roses. At one point, she reflects upon how the "physiologist, when he seeks to study an organism, puts beneath his microscope an almost invisible spot of blood or shred of animal tissue . . . because he knows that once rightly understood it may explain to him the nature of the entire organism of which it is a part . . . may unlock for us the meaning of part of that great universe of which it is an integral fragment."[48]

Schreiner's affirmation of correspondences was a corollary of her monist view of the universe: "The Universe is One, and, It lives."[49] Within this unity, every natural phenomenon, be it human, a leaf, whatever, bore at some level a common imprint. In much of Schreiner's writing she described the underlying unity as mental, suggesting thereby her adherence to an idealist form of monism, the form most typical among Victorian freethinkers. In her allegories she insisted upon the common identity of the mind of God and human beings. And like most idealist monists, she appeared at times to uphold a dualist conception of the relationship between mind and matter: The unity of mind is cloaked by the diversity of matter. Strip away this mantle of individuation and separation, and the essential unity of the spiritual and mental becomes disclosed. Consider Schreiner's allegory "In a Ruined Chapel": The narrator in this story has a dream in which a man approaches God in despair over his inability to forgive one who injured him. God's angel, after futile efforts to induce forgiveness in him, receives divine assistance. God endows the angel with the power to unclothe a human soul. The angel proceeds to strip away "all those outward attributes of form, and colour, and age, and sex." The man beholds the exposed soul as identical to his own. The angel then bares the soul further, taking from it "all those outward attributes of time and place and circumstance whereby the individual life is marked off from the life of the whole." The man now discovers "in its tiny drop" the whole universe, the inner nature of stars, lichen, crystals, outstretched fingers of infants. Gazing upon the fully naked soul, he bows his head, shudders, and whispers, "It is God." The angel then discloses that this is the soul of the one who offended him. The man declares it beautiful.[50]

Given the distinctively transcendentalist nature of this moral/metaphysical tale, Schreiner might well have dedicated it to Ralph Waldo Emerson. She acknowledged frequently her keen admiration for Emerson, after whom she named Waldo in *African Farm*.[51] The transcendental features of her philosophy are transparent in her view of the "tiny drop" as a microcosm of all material appearances. She attributed to Emerson not the creation of her views but the confirmation of her basic convictions. Even had she never read Emerson, she would have encountered, as an avid reader of the German romantics and of Plato, confirmation for and articulation of the idealist world view she intuited as a child during her mystic trances.

With her inimitable independence, Schreiner also rejected certain tenets of monist idealism and transcendentalism. She was unwilling to subordinate matter to spirit and could not "understand the scorn of men towards matter." She repudiated Christian and Emersonian concepts of immortality, as much for their derision of matter as for their lack of scientific credibility. When Lyndall dies in *African Farm*, Waldo reviews the various religious and philosophical justifications for an afterlife. Moaning as he dismisses traditional and Victorian Christian doctrines of immortality, he "heard the Transcendentalist's high answer. 'What have you to do with flesh, the gross and miserable garment in which spirit hides itself? You shall see her again. But the hand, the foot, the forehead you loved, you shall see no more.'" Waldo recognizes these as lofty words, but he longs not for pure spiritual essence but "for a little woman full of sin" in her flesh as he remembered her. He ultimately exclaims, "Your immortality is annihilation, your Hereafter is a lie." Here he echoes Schreiner's response to the death of her little sister. Sitting by her sister's grave she found it impossible, then and thereafter, "to accept the ordinary doctrine that [her sister] was living somewhere without a body." For Schreiner, the material universe was an indispensable and inherently real dimension of all being.[52]

Schreiner's sense of the integration of material and spiritual reality led to her struggle to resolve the dualism inherent in both an idealist and a materialist monism. At times she suggested an animating spirit, which, at once material and spiritual, constituted all reality. In *From Man to Man*, she speculated that, rather than mind, perhaps it was a great heart that pulsated throughout nature. Unable to articulate in discursive language a position that seemed akin to what twentieth-century philosophers label "neutral monism," Schreiner explained, "except in my own language of parables I cannot express myself. If I say that in a stone, in the wood, in the thoughts of my brain, in the corpuscles of a drop of blood under my microscope, in a railway engine rushing past me in the veld, I see God, shall I not be darkening counsel with words?"[53]

The issue remains puzzling to this day, as philosophers continue to wrestle with the relationship between mind and matter. In Schreiner's generation most writers were content to remain within a dualist framework. The most notable exceptions were Samuel Butler, James Ward, George John Romanes, Alfred Russell Wallace, and Frederic W. H. Myers, who developed ingenious schemes for the coexistence and inseparability of mind and matter in the same substance.[54]

As a freethinker, Schreiner evoked criticism from those, generally her socialist friends, who objected to her continued use of the word *God*. For a time she refrained, agreeing with her critics that the word carried connotations she had long discarded. To Ellis she wrote:

> I must have a long talk with you some day (perhaps in a letter) on your use of the word "God" and the old symbols generally. The use of them by people like you and me is never quite true. . . . We *cannot* always stop to *define* what *we* mean by "God," etc., so the best way is not to use the terms at all. I have taken care that the word "God" does not occur in this last book of mine, hateful damned name that it is. A word may become so defiled by bad use that it will take a century before it can be purified.[55]

Within a few years her resolution faltered. By 1888 she was admitting to feeling self-conscious and defensive about "God" appearing in all her dreams and allegories. Usually, as she explained to Edward Carpenter, there simply was no surrogate term possible, but she challenged others, "If any one can give me another name for it, I'll use it."[56] Still, we may wonder why Schreiner did not resort to Spencer's "The Unknowable" or Emerson's "Oversoul." I am convinced an answer lies in her experience of a profound personal relationship with divine reality. Spencer's and Emerson's abstractions were too sterile for her rich and immediate perception of God's presence. Rather than invent or adopt names for divinity, she vascillated between using familiar vocabulary and remaining silent.

Despite all said so far, Schreiner's theism would remain compatible with liberal forms of Christianity (e.g., Unitarianism and Broad Church Anglicanism) were it not that her views on Jesus completely precluded her belonging to any Christian denomination. She found the doctrine of his special divinity odious. In a letter to Mrs. Francis Smith, she exclaimed, "Christianity, with its horrible doctrine of man as God!!" Not only did she deny Jesus divinity, she refused to regard him as the greatest of religious teachers, declaring that except for the fifth and sixth chapters of Matthew, "I owe nothing to the teaching of Jesus." She faulted his limiting love to the human world, judging his wisdom as inferior to that of Buddha, whose compassion encompassed all created beings. In a letter to Ellis she projected a conception of love she considered more advanced than Jesus': "Neither Christ nor Tolstoy nor any one of us living has yet seen and preached that doctrine of love and forgiveness as it will be preached in ages to come."[57]

By no means absolute on this issue, Schreiner still regarded Jesus as a "great rare soul." She regretted how spare were the records of Jesus' life, longing to know more about him between the ages of twenty and thirty, "those years, the most important and intense, in which amid agony and temptation his view of life was forming."[58] She especially admired "his intense emotional nature, whether in anger or tenderness." She visualized him as a "dark little Jew, with flashing eyes and a hooked nose," who with a scourge of cords drove the merchants from their tradings in the temple; and who, turning affectionate, saw himself taking Jerusalem under his arms as a hen gathers her chickens under her wings. In addition, Schreiner valued Jesus' egalitarianism, writing with a twinkle, "To *me* Jesus was a poor working-man Socialist of genius, a sort of Keir Hardie."[59] In her novella *Trooper Peter Halket of Mashonaland,* Jesus appears as the champion of the common man of all races. He exposes the immorality of British racism and imperialism and ultimately converts Peter Halket, the callous racist, into a Christian idealist willing to sacrifice his life to liberate persecuted African blacks. What we witness here is revolutionary Christianity, the kind of religious idealism that has historically spurred radical social and political transformations. Recognizing the nominal affiliation, at least, of most Britons, Schreiner was perfectly willing to deploy Jesus when necessary for propaganda purposes.[60]

Though incompatible with even liberal Christianity, Schreiner's theism had a certain affinity with both Judaism and Buddhism. Her attraction to Judaism was intellectual and psychological. Persecuted for her beliefs and way of life, she identified with the historic outcast plight of the Jews and even fancied that one of her distant forebears was Jewish.[61] One of her most eloquent public addresses was a letter written in defense of Jews, which was read at a large public meeting in Cape Town in July 1906. In the letter she denounced the Russian pogroms as well as anti-Semitism in South Africa and elsewhere. She also set forth the intellectual contribution of the Jewish people to human civilization, crediting them with humanity's preeminent religious and ethical genius, a contribution she thought surpassed that of all other peoples. Similar praise reappeared in *Woman and Labour* and *Thoughts on South Africa* as well as in her correspondence.[62] Admittedly anti-Semitic stereotypes are present in *From Man to Man,* and in *Thoughts on South Africa* she referred to the *smous,* an unflattering term for a Jewish hawker of old clothes. As I discuss in Chapter 3, Schreiner was prone at times to simplistic national and ethnic characterization, though her remarks included rare praise and sympathy for groups commonly scorned.

Among the dimensions of Jewish thought that Schreiner singled out for acclaim, foremost was its simple, lofty monotheism. None of the terrifying doctrines of original sin, damnation, predestination, and vicarious atonement contaminated Jewish theology and ethics. Furthermore, the dualism of mind and body so vehemently instilled through Christian doctrine was far more muted in Judaism. It is not surprising, then, that she often cited in her writing the Jewish philosophers Spinoza and Maimonides.[63] Schreiner's respect for Spinoza and Maimonides may well have been part of a small but vigorous current of mid-to-late-Victorian intellectual life. Karl Pearson devoted an entire chapter of his *Ethics of Freethought* to both of these philosophers and seized opportunities elsewhere in this work to extol their thinking and deplore the anti-Semitism of Luther and his followers. Likewise, Havelock Ellis touted Spinoza's genius.[64] For Ellis and Pearson as for Schreiner, Spinoza and Maimonides represented compelling alternative viewpoints to the prevailing Victorian derision of physical appetites and material reality.

For obvious reasons, Schreiner could never adopt Judaism as her religion: Its claim, at least in mainstream Jewish thought, of a transcendent, patriarchal deity, separate from and above human beings and animals, conflicted with her insistence upon the identity of all being and the pervasive immanence of God in the natural world. She regarded the Old Testament presentation of ideal love in the same light that she judged the New Testament's, as far too limited for her all-embracing compassion. In this light, Schreiner found Buddhism (though she never adopted it either) the most satisfying of existing religious systems.[65]

The story of the inception of Buddhist thought into English life and letters has yet to be written. It is clear that some mid and late Victorians, disenchanted with Christianity though still seeking religious guidance, turned eastward for spiritual sustenance. They were precursors of surging numbers of twentieth-century writers who undertook an intellectual if not actual journey east.[66] It was during the nineteenth century that most of the principal texts of Oriental philosophy were translated into English. Among these major projects, a group of Victorian scholars were translating from Pali the earliest records of Buddhism. These records, preserved on the palm leaves of Ceylon, Burma, and Siam, preceded the Vedantic Sanskrit writing, which, already available in English translation, had infused the thinking of American transcendentalists such as Emerson. Among the leading Pali scholars, Professor and Mrs. T. W. Rhys Davids were special friends of Schreiner, her letters amply testifying to her admiration for their lives and work.[67]

In 1881 Rhys Davids founded the Pali Text Society and, in the same year, offered at Oxford University a series of seminal talks, the Hibbert Lectures, subsequently published as *Lectures on the Origin and Growth of Religion as illustrated by some points in the History of Buddhism.* It was apparently at this time that Schreiner's friends Ellis and Pearson became acquainted with Buddhist thinking, Pearson specifically acknowledging his debt to Rhys Davids.[68]

From that point on a steady stream of books and articles on Buddhism greeted the British public. By the mid to late 1880s many avant-garde intellectuals, including, crucially, Edward Carpenter, were studying Oriental philosophy and religion. Carpenter found the Bhagavad-Gita physically and sensually liberating. He likewise hailed the Upanishads' affirmation of erotic experience, in particular its merging of erotic and spiritual reality.[69]

It is unclear whether Schreiner was acquainted with Buddhist ideas prior to her arrival in England. Obviously she had imbibed many of the cardinal concepts of Vedantic and Buddhist thought through her reading of Emerson. (In *African Farm* she refers to a Hindu philosopher alone under his banyan tree meditating on God.)[70] Certainly by the time she had formed close bonds with Ellis, Pearson, and Carpenter she shared their enthusiasm for Buddhism and favored it over Christianity. The precise date when she became friends with Mr. and Mrs. Rhys Davids remains unknown. No doubt her respect for Gandhi's nonviolent campaign for Indian rights in South Africa reinforced her attraction to Buddhism as well.

In Buddhism, Schreiner found responsive chords to both the rational and intuitive sides of her religious thinking. Buddhism's emphasis upon critical inquiry was, of course, its major appeal to most British freethinkers. Gotama Buddha's lack of dogma, his dismissal of definitive supernatural knowledge, his distrust of received authority, rendered Buddhism, as Pearson declared, "perhaps the most valuable study among concrete religious systems for the modern freethinker."[71] Along with Gotama's distrust of dogma, what appealed to Schreiner was the Buddhist refusal to settle for atheism or agnosticism and its affirmation of the individual's independent spiritual searchings.

Above all, it was the universal breadth of Buddhism that Schreiner prized. She held that "Buddhism is so much more wide and satisfying than Christianity can ever be because it takes in the animal world, and *sees* that all life is one."[72] Buddhism corresponded to Schreiner's perception of the interpenetration of transcendental and mundane phenomena and the absolute identity of God's mind with the mind of human beings. The allegory "In a

Ruined Chapel," examined earlier as Emersonian, serves equally well to convey essential Buddhist insights into the relationships among God, nature, and humanity.

A dimension of Buddhist philosophy Schreiner does not refer to but which is in distinct accord with her own is its validation of intuitive spiritual understanding. Any account of Schreiner's theism that fails to explore the scope and significance of her mystical experiences is at best partial. It is this dimension of her theism that, as indicated earlier, distinguished her critique of Christianity from that of most freethinkers, even those who admit of an Unknowable or Ultimate Reality. If we attend only to the Hunter allegory, as most Schreiner scholars do, a distortingly incomplete view of Schreiner's religious life results: She comes across as just another Victorian rationalist. In focusing upon her mystical life, we not only grapple with some of Schreiner's finest writing and most provocative insights but understand far better her struggle to surmount conventional Victorian dichotomies.

Furthermore, in Schreiner's lifelong perception of the sacredness of the universe and her intrinsic place in it, she clearly stood apart from the spiritual homelessness of most freethinkers. Her sense of cosmic belonging separated her from another remarkable late-Victorian writer and freethinker, George Eliot, whose "homeless" feeling was far more characteristic of religious skeptics. The mystic connection to life that Schreiner felt also enabled her to preserve a biblical style even when jettisoning the Bible's doctrinal content.[73]

In asserting how crucially Schreiner's mystical experiences shaped her religious outlook, I am using the customary definition of mysticism, ably expressed in Elizabeth Petroff's recent study of thirteenth-century female saints, "the personal experience of the divine—ultimate, immediate, beyond ordinary sense perception, and beyond discursive reason."[74] Schreiner's personal experience of the divine differed from traditional Western mysticism, however, since it lacked a sense of communion with a personified god. In this respect her experience was closer to that of Eastern mystics or twentieth-century secular accounts of a rush of seemingly transcendent energy and light.[75] Had she chosen not to speak of God in describing her experiences, I would have preferred to use either the psychologist Abraham Maslow's term, "peak experiences," or the term most common among anthropologists, "ecstatic experiences,"[76] but since, throughout her writing, she alluded to these experiences as revelations of God, *mystical* seems more appropriate.

Schreiner, significantly, never applied the term *mystical* or any other label, except *vision*, to designate these moments. They were simply another, more emotionally intense variety of religious understanding. There is both humility and wisdom in her linguistic restraint. She viewed her transports, though intermittent in anyone's lifetime, as common to sensitive and intuitive children and adults.[77] Moreover, these experiences were part of a unity of knowledge which, she may have feared, would be subverted by a linguistic differentiation that suggested their unusual quality.

Schreiner was as stymied as other mystics in attempting to articulate precisely what she experienced. She wrote of her sense of the dissolving of fragmentations and polarities within living experience; for her, subject and object, figure and ground, time and space blurred.[78] She found only poetic language capable of bearing the full weight of these occurrences. "We human beings have not framed speech for the purpose of expressing such thoughts," she wrote John Lloyd, and added, later in this same letter: "This is a poor answer to send you to your beautiful letter. But except in my own language of parables I cannot express myself. . . . Words are very poor things."[79]

Among Schreiner's friends, only Havelock Ellis seems to have shared with her similar experiences of rhapsodic unity with nature; no doubt this rapport served as a powerful bond between them, as powerful a source for their intimacy as any adduced so far by Schreiner scholars. Schreiner's husband was not such a spirit. His comments on her mystical transports mingled detachment and awe: "This intense phase of feeling, as though an illumination, was part of her strange organization throughout; when it was on her she seemed something holy. You were hushed."[80]

The triggers for Schreiner's ecstatic moments, at least as recorded in her letters and fiction, were highly diverse, ranging from terrible events, such as her younger sister's death, to features of natural scenery, such as certain moments when she beheld the vast, silent stretches of the karroo or the play of sunshine on vegetation or the dew on the English grass or an isolated ice plant on the sod wall of a pigsty. Characteristically, the youthful experience of gazing at one large white cloud excited her to the point of "quivering. . . . I almost fell on the ground with feeling."[81] Since, for her, "all life was a miracle," any event was potentially mystic.

Schreiner shared the recognition of most mystics that certain settings and states of mind were preconditions for mystic awareness. Solitude was essential. It involved both geographical and psychological detachment from ordinary distractions.[82] The desert was her literal and metaphorical inspiration. In *Thoughts on South Africa* she wrote:

That which the Buddha left his kingly palace and sat beneath his Bo-Tree to seek; that which Zoroaster found in his solitary sojourn on the mountain top, and Mohammed in his secret cave, . . . this reality is not easily perceived as present and always over-arching when the individual is swathed in by conditions of life . . . when the tumultuous sounds and minute details forced on it at every moment almost blind and deafen the individual to the consciousness of anything beyond the fragmentary and present.[83]

Not merely free from mundane preoccupations, however, the seeker must be in a receptive and alert state, able to concentrate intensely but passive as well. These conditions served as a prelude to one of Schreiner's most formative visions, occurring when she was nine years old, one that would provide the intuitive fount of her later pacifist and egalitarian convictions:

and then as I sat looking at the little damp dark island, the sun began to rise. It shot its light across the long, grassy slopes of the mountains and struck the little mound of earth in the water. All the leaves and flowers and grasses on it turned bright gold, and the dewdrops hanging from them were like diamonds; and the water in the stream glinted as it ran. And, as I looked at that almost intolerable beauty, a curious feeling came over me. . . . I seemed to *see* a world in which creatures no more hated and crushed [one another].[84]

Unlike her spurning of gender associations with God in her philosophical and allegorical writing, female imagery abounded in Schreiner's articulation of her visions. For example, in *African Farm*, the narrator notes that nature comforts the distressed individual by showing "herself to you. So near she draws you, that the blood seems to flow from her to you, through a still uncut cord: you feel the throb of her life." Elsewhere, nature is manifest as large white snowflakes softly fluttering down, soothing the agonized soul "as though our mother smoothed our hair, and we are comforted." Schreiner was fond of quoting a passage from Emerson, which began, "Embosomed in wonder and beauty as we are . . ." Not only nature but God is feminized when Schreiner depicts God as a long-robed, gently protective being covering her, as a mother covers a child when putting her to sleep.[85] Schreiner's female imagery was akin to the religious imagery of medieval female mystics who envisioned the cosmic order as "the law of the mother." For them, Jesus became this mother: "He behaved like a mother with her favourite child," declares Saint Catherine, and she proceeds in her vision to suck his wound as though she were sucking milk.[86]

The umbilical relationship of the individual with God is one of intimate, nonjudgmental nourishment, a fluid bonding of two beings. This represents a thoroughly contrasting image to that espoused in conventional religions, wherein the separation between God and the individual is emphatic and permanent. Moreover, the sensuality of the umbilical image contrasts with the rational, ideational relationship with the divine that male freethinkers espoused. Schreiner, in endowing the divine with strongly maternal imagery, was expressing her various yearnings to mother and be mothered: her deprivation of consistent maternal affection, her youthful pleasure in mothering her younger sister, and her lifelong desire to bear and raise a child.[87]

A foremost characteristic of Schreiner's visionary experience was its individualistic mode. The ecstatic experiences of collective ritual, integral to many religious and spiritual communities, were alien to Schreiner, who experienced the cosmos as responding to and affirming her individual selfhood simultaneously with her integration into divine reality. Elizabeth Petroff argues that this heightened sense of self is particularly prominent among female visionaries. Women tend to form a relationship of mutuality with God, Petroff claims, wherein divine absorption does not jeopardize autonomy of self. Male visionaries, she contends, on the other hand, tend either to incorporate the divine or to be incorporated by the divine, blurring or erasing the self in the process. In the reciprocity of relationship with the divine that is common to female mystics, reverence for both God and one's self is preserved.[88] Mary Daly, in her feminist analysis of female ecstasy, notes the infrequency among feminist visionaries of words like *awe* and *dread.* Rather, they experience, like Schreiner, a sharpened sense of their integrated personality, self-centering not self-loss.[89]

Only such an individualistic approach to visions was possible for Schreiner. After all, she had defied the communion of Christian believers, and she could support no extant alternative religious congregation: Feminist religious communities did not exist in her day. What recourse in practical terms did she have? Just as her freethinking was of necessity lonely and individualized, so too her theism.

And yet, for all her spiritual individualism, the function of her visions was as much communal as personal. Not only were these experiences of incalculable worth in rescuing her from despair and fueling her to grapple with her personal dilemmas, they also undergirded her social and political activism. They did not, however, resolve the basic moral contradiction between her "awful universe" and her benevolent cosmos that inspired visions of peace, love, and equality.

Schreiner's spiritual outlook eschewed the question of the origin and nature of evil. She offered no persuasive theodicy, no effort to explain how the one, wondrous majesty of creation, at once transcendent and immanent, can simultaneously include the cruelty of human beings and nature—not that, in her extensive probing of the relationship between religion and morality, she denied evil's presence or somehow rationalized that nature was overarchingly beneficent.

Victorian freethinkers were sensitive to the frequent charge that moral behavior without a metaphysical sanction was ungrounded and would therefore collapse. They met this accusation with the claim that a thoroughly natural and rational basis for morality was not only possible but far preferable to a religious base. So concerned were they, nevertheless, with countering moral suspicion that, scholars allege, they shared to some extent popular anxieties about the social consequences of their skepticism. Consequently, their freethinking moral creeds were in most respects conservative and conventional.[90]

Schreiner recognized her peers' uneasiness. The Stranger in *African Farm* concedes: "To all who have been born in the old faith there comes a time of danger, when the old slips from us, and we have not yet planted our feet on the new. . . . We have proved the religion our mothers fed us on to be a delusion; in our bewilderment we see no rule by which to guide our steps day by day; and yet every day we must step somewhere."[91]

Schreiner recalled her own moral confusion when she first abandoned Christian belief, "that condition in which I was from about 14 to 15 or 16, when there seemed nothing but a blind chance ruling life and no right and no wrong and no ideal ruling life." She referred to a similar period from 1883 to 1885, but she insisted that such moral confusion was preferable to the insidious relationship between traditional religion and morality. Criticizing freethinkers who raised their children in religion so as to assure their moral behavior, she believed such a policy boomeranged. To the contrary, she agreed with Ellis, "the more one teaches children morality and right doing and love for all animals and people in the world, *without* fastening it on to any system of theology . . . *the safer will its roots be.*" Given the likelihood of young people shedding their religious convictions in the late-Victorian era, it was crucial that from the outset religion and morality not be thought of as wedded. The Stranger in *African Farm* likens the parasitism of religion toward morality to rotten weeds and creepers clinging to a wall which, however solid, appears to be disintegrating when the rot of the sucking vines is exposed.[92]

In common with eighteenth- and nineteenth-century advocates of a natural morality, Schreiner insisted that morality's essence resided in rational and responsible choice. In *African Farm* Lyndall is upset that religious people assume no responsibility for their behavior, attributing their evil acts to the devil's influence and virtuous deeds to God's will. This, she feels, does not constitute a morality befitting dignified human beings. Schreiner maintained that traditional condemnation of such acts as murder, adultery, violent revenge, or self-aggrandizement could survive without recourse to religious fear and authority. "Experience *will* teach us this, and reason will show us why it *must* be so," instructs the Stranger.[93] Still, Schreiner was vague in *African Farm* as to how experience and reason would guide people. She advocated neither a utilitarian nor any other secular moral system. Though she cited John Stuart Mill as her most important moral mentor, she never articulated his modified utilitarian logic in her own writings. The levers of pleasure and pain, the principle of the greatest happiness of the greatest number, were phrases that never entered her vocabulary. What she absorbed from Mill appeared mostly to be his moral commitment to empirical and logical reasoning.

Although Schreiner's moral philosophy is somewhat clearer in *From Man to Man*, it still remained haphazard. In this novel Rebekah posits as her overriding moral axiom fidelity to truth or reality:

> the greatest wrong a man can commit towards his fellow is the willful misleading of him as to any reality; and the sin against the Holy Ghost—the sin which hath no forgiveness—is the conscious, willful blinding of our own eyes to any form of reality. . . . the soul which lies in itself to itself, acting always a part before itself, becomes a poison, a deadly fungus that scatters its poisonous seeds unconsciously whenever it is touched.

Rebekah pursues the moral ramifications of this axiom in child rearing, in the practice of art and literature, in political action, in marriage, and in all personal communication:

> That which makes us shift restlessly from side to side, as if we were trying to shake off something, is often not the remembrance of what men and women of the past would have regarded as our greatest crime; it may be no infringement of any decalogue that ever yet was written; it may be just some written or spoken word or some act, perhaps seeming to us, even at the moment it was written or spoken or done, to be right and even magnanimous, but which falsified our relation with another or that other's relation to someone else.[94]

Exactly how such a sensitive conscience matures, as well as the ultimate justification for such honesty, remains unexplained. Underlying Schreiner's ethics was an adherence to the moral idealism of the German romantic tradition, which she absorbed through her reading of Goethe, Schiller, Kant, and Heine and indirectly through Emerson. In the final analysis, to sanction her morality she must summon intuition and a reconceived yet familiar metaphysics:

> As vast and incomprehensible in its ultimate nature as light or time, or space, or matter generally, is that other vast reality, which we know and feel more intimately than anything else in the universe, the will within us that is not time nor space, that is not light nor heat; incomprehensible in its ultimate essence . . . yet never for a moment to be ignored if we do not wish to wreck our lives and make a fool's play of our existence.[95]

In short, Schreiner retained the concept of a truth, if not a god, beyond human fathoming. She assumed an indissoluble conscience, emerging from neither the blind piety of the ages nor the socially formed superego of twentieth-century psychology but from a deeply rooted human sensitivity and will that are somehow intrinsic to the personal/divine self.

Next to unswerving loyalty to truth seeking and truth telling, the obligation to love all living creatures and ameliorate their physical and spiritual suffering constituted the second principal pillar of Schreiner's moral creed. On her deathbed, Lyndall, rather than recant her freethinking, issues such a moral call: "I see the vision of a poor, weak soul striving after good. It was not cut short, and in the end it learned, through tears and much pain, that holiness is an infinite compassion for others; that greatness is to take the common things of life and walk truly among them."[96]

Schreiner's emphasis upon compassion was completely within the mainstream of Enlightenment and Victorian moral thought. Traditional religious and freethinking moralists alike adhered to the Victorian positivists' Religion of Humanity, though Schreiner never went so far toward such "humanism" as to deify the human being as the ultimate and only truth, a view she dismissed as ignorant and superstitious.[97] She felt no need to deify humanity in order to commit herself to the amelioration of human misery.

An important nonrational source did contribute to Schreiner's healing passions: A faith in human progress, which functioned in certain senses as a religious creed, sanctioned her commitment to a morality of love and compassion. She shared this faith with Victorian secular thinkers generally, for whom the doctrine of human progress replaced Heaven and Hell as the incentive to search for truth and social betterment. Though Schreiner, as will become clear, held a far less sanguine and more complete view of human progress than most of her contemporaries, her morality, like that of her mentors—Mill, Spencer, Emerson—rested upon faith, faith in the possibility, if not the reality, of individual and collective human improvement.

In advancing free thought, these Victorian skeptics, including Schreiner, did at the very least reduce the misery of religious persecution and terror. By the end of the nineteenth century, philosophical and religious toleration was broader than at any prior time. The grip of the doctrines of Hell and damnation upon the minds of children and adults had loosened if not utterly disappeared. Schreiner's niece, Joan Hodgson, contrasted the bitterness of her aunt's freethinking with that of Hodgson's generation, among whom freethinkers had become familiar and respectable. Hodgson asserted, "we found our feet more easily because of the pioneering that had been done." Yet, with a note of nostalgia, she qualified her freedom from her aunt's bitterness with envious reflection; "there was no mistaking the fierce joy of the pioneer."[98]

3

"An ass masquerading in . . . lion's skin"

FROM THE FOLLY OF SOCIAL DARWINISM
TO AN ALTERNATIVE THEORY OF THE
NATURE OF RACE, GENDER, AND CLASS

> the continued development of the human race on earth (a
> development, which, as the old myths and dreams of a
> narrow personal heaven fade from our view, becomes
> increasingly for many of us the spiritual hope by light of
> which we continue to live) . . . shall make the humanity of
> a distant future as much higher in intellectual power and
> wider in social sympathy than the highest human units of
> our day, as [the best of humankind today] is higher than
> the first primeval ancestor.
>
> Olive Schreiner, *Woman and Labour*

TO US IN THE SECOND half of the twentieth century, survivors of two global wars and potential perpetrators/victims of nuclear holocaust and ecological disaster, belief in progress appears no less a superstition than belief in afterlife. Collective human extinction, not to speak of a moral and material backslide, threatens us as never before. Because for most Victorian freethinkers the religious tenet most difficult to relinquish was that of immortality, eighteenth- and nineteenth-century deists generally clung to some concept of an individual or collective afterlife, and, of course, such a notion was integral to both Western and Eastern religions. Those Victorian thinkers who, like Schreiner, spurned doctrines of an afterlife as superstition appear to have preserved it in another guise, specifically within the creed of human progress. Even traditional religious believers found in the idea of human progress further validation for their faith in a meaningful universe, and they too promoted the idea. For many reasons, throughout nineteenth-century Europe and America the belief in progress enjoyed an unprecedented popularity.[1]

Despite the many ways she deviated from established views of progress, Schreiner spoke in a language familiar to her contemporaries. She could inspire their social idealism because she, like them, believed that their reform efforts were not in vain. Some future generation would benefit. Indeed, as she tells later generations of readers of *Woman and Labour,* "it was in the thought of your larger realization and fuller life that we found consolation for the futilities of our own."[2]

By the time Schreiner reached adulthood an array of compelling ideologies of progress influenced popular thought: Enlightenment rationalism, French positivism, German idealism (Hegelian in particular), Marxism and the evolutionary theories of Chevalier de Lamarck, Herbert Spencer, and Charles Darwin. For Schreiner's generation, it was, above all, these evolutionary theories that stirred the intellect. Application of various aspects of these theories to human social relations resulted in what became known as Social Darwinism, a misleading label since the ideology owed its origins as much to the writings of Thomas Malthus and Herbert Spencer.[3]

Whereas most Victorian intellectuals found the reigning evolutionary ideas and Social Darwinist applications compatible with their own attitudes, Schreiner saw much that disturbed her, kindled some of her most fiery critical writing, and spurred her to develop an alternative concept of progress, a unique blend of prevalent theories with her original research and interpretation. Basically, the prevalent theories of species development tended to strengthen the widespread hierarchical and conflict model of social life inimical to Schreiner.[4] These theories served to rationalize Britain's imperial aggrandizement and militarism, its racism, its socioeconomic class stratification, and its patriarchal patterns—all targets of Schreiner's attack. Her measure of progress was the degree to which patterns of domination had diminished. Phrased in broad, sometimes platitudinous terms, her concept of progress was of global unity, "not in the extermination of earth's varied races, or in the dominance of anyone over all, . . . but in a free and equal federation of all." In Schreiner's view, the great moral and intellectual expansion humanity must undergo involved the submerging of superficial differences of sex and class "in the greater personality of the human creature" and the extending of the social instincts of each individual beyond family, nation, and race to all of humanity. She envisioned a world in which "intellectual power and strength of will combined with an infinite tenderness and wide human sympathy" would characterize the personality of both men and women.[5]

Schreiner witnessed the upstaging of religion by science as the final authority for social doctrines. Scientific racism, sexism, and social class elitism dominated the reasoning of social theorists. Marvin Harris's definition of nineteenth-century scientific racism can extend to other varieties of scientifically endorsed social prejudice. Scientific racism assumed that "the significant socio-cultural differences and similarities among human populations are the dependent variables of group-restricted hereditary drives and attitudes." Nineteenth-century writers on "race" displayed little concern for precision or consistency: "Race" could designate cultural, religious, national, linguistic, ethnic, or geographical groupings, and yet these racial categories passed as objective facts of nature.[6] Assumptions of inevitable and salutary struggle and division among classes, races, and nations compounded this fiction. Although integrationist concepts occasionally entered into Victorian portraits of progress—for example, social scientists' favoring of a socially cohesive England, free from class conflict, so as to compete more effectively in the struggle among nations and races—a hierarchical ordering of nations and races was still clearly assumed and predicated upon a biological paradigm of ascending complexity and dominance among nature's creatures (as a result of natural selection of the fit competing for limited resources).[7]

For Schreiner to establish the validity of her egalitarian and integrationist social and political proposals, she had to demolish this biological paradigm and substitute an alternative theory of human evolution that would be equally scientific and logical. She was fully aware of this requirement, which accounted for the many years she devoted to her "sex book." As originally designed, the book demanded extensive reading and data collection. With the destruction of her copious notes as well as of the book's initial chapter as a result of the raid on her Johannesburg home during the Anglo–Boer War, what remains of her formidable enterprise, in addition to the truncated *Woman and Labour,* is the considerable number of deeply reflective passages in her fictional and nonfictional writing that confront evolutionary thought and Social Darwinism. Given the dispersed nature of her writing on evolution during different points in her lifetime, inconsistencies in her reasoning inevitably appear. My construction, therefore, of her evolutionary outlook is necessarily cobbled together, suggesting greater coherence than is perhaps warranted. Fortunately, her writing on human evolution was far more abundant than on religion; it encompassed the fields of animal and human biology, comparative physical and cultural anthropology, history and sociology.

In all her prodigious reading in the new biological and social sciences,[8] Schreiner was cautious and independent, sifting out those arguments compatible with her own and rejecting others. The most recurrent statement of hers with regard to scientific doctrines of species evolution was that they were unproven.[9] She worried about the susceptibility of scientific explanations of sex and race differences to crass exploitation by the powerful. At one point, Schreiner has Rebekah warn in *From Man to Man*, "Let him not imagine when he prates the survival of the fittest that he is enshrouding himself and his desires in impenetrable armour; he is only an ass masquerading in the scientific lion's skin put on hind-side before!"[10]

As significant to her evolutionary theories as the books she read were Schreiner's lifelong interest in and distinctive observations of South African plant and animal life. Like many other amateur Victorian naturalists, her approach to her native country's natural phenomena was decidedly romantic. She delighted in the "colossal plentitude" and heterogeneity of South African natural forms as well as in the odd efflorescences so akin to her sense of her own individuality. In "Our Waste Land in Mashonaland" (1891), she called for a halt to the wanton destruction of South Africa's flora and fauna. She proposed that a vast tract of Mashonaland be set aside as the "World's Zoological Garden" where scientists could study animals in their natural habitat and where tourists could marvel at nature's prodigiousness.[11]

Schreiner's avid naturalist concerns found frequent expression through Rebekah's activities in *From Man to Man*. At age five, Rebekah has a small collection of stones, a very large bright crystal, fossils, and brightly colored dead beetles and grasshoppers. By her adolescence, Rebekah owns a microscope and a glass cabinet for her specimens, as well as numerous scientific texts. She aids her father in cultivating new varieties of wheat and advises him about "grafts and flutes" and new remedies for cattle disease. At one point, she cuts a large, many-horned gall growth from one of the branches of the mimosa tree in order to compare galls on different species of mimosa. As a wife and mother of four children, she studies in her spare moments little cups of moss under her microscope. The entire novel teems with names of familiar and exotic plants and animals and with analogies among plant, animal, and human life.[12]

Schreiner was determined to penetrate her joyous concrete examples of nature to their patterns, correspondences, and unifying features. Her attention oscillated between noting diversity and noting uniformity. In her approach to human as well as plant and animal variety, she struggled for that blend of artistic and scientific apprehension of reality she admired in the life and writing of Goethe. Underscoring the importance of critical detachment so as not to be overwhelmed by the specificity and diversity of humanity, and so as to comprehend larger social and historical patterns, she considered her stay in England indispensable to the objectivity and rationality she could apply to her accounts of racial variation in South Africa. Yet, she also found scientific detachment insufficient. "Subjective emotional sympathy" was vital if one was not only to identify surface patterns but to grasp "the nature and origin of the passions" shaping those patterns. The empathetic imagination of the artist was essential to delineate the connections between the inner reality of individuals and groups and their external social behavior. Schreiner's emphasis upon the integration of these two modes of understanding sharply distinguished her from her contemporaries, who tended in this matter, as in many others, to opt for one or the other approach.[13]

In her effort to provide a scientific base for her egalitarian and integrationist social and political outlook, it would have been easy for Schreiner to jettison Social Darwinist theories in favor of earlier, more optimistic views of nature and human progress. To some extent, in clinging to Lamarckian environmentalism and John Stuart Mill's insistence upon a universal human identity, Schreiner did just that. But she was too honest to ignore the obvious brutal patterns of competitive struggle, domination, and submission evident in the natural world. Indeed, such Darwinian observations had contributed to her repudiation of Christianity and the sentimental romanticism of so many Victorian writers. As a result, she faced a quandary, one with which a minority of other late-Victorian thinkers wrestled: Was there a way to reconcile one's egalitarian and pacifist social beliefs with the seemingly antithetical biological insights and deductions of Darwinian research? Schreiner in Britain, like Lester Frank Ward in America and Peter Kropotkin in Russia, represented the first generation of revisionist (or reform) Darwinists, individuals at odds with the ascendant Social Darwinist ideology yet still devoted to much of Darwin's work.[14]

Among this small band of revisionists, Schreiner was unique in the comprehensiveness of her critique of Social Darwinism. She alone faulted Social Darwinism for its rationale in defending race, gender, and class inequality, and she alone realized in its logic the interconnectedness of all three modes of domination. Less successful in creating an alternative scientific interpretation of evolutionary dynamics, she had glimmers of what would constitute that alternative, but she never worked it out. Her failure to do so was primarily responsible for occasional moments of murky thinking in her egalitarianism. It also contributed to tangled skeins in her view of historical processes. Of course, no one, during or since her time, has offered a trenchant synthesis of biological and social evolution compatible with radical egalitarianism and

77

pacifist ethics. For all their deficiencies, Schreiner's evolutionary ideas, particularly as they shaped her overall analysis of race, gender, and class differences, revealed a patient, daring, and original mind.

Critique of Social Darwinism Close Up

Neither Schreiner's romantic nor her rationalist approach to nature led her to the Social Darwinist belief that the laws governing nonhuman evolution were automatically applicable to human evolution. Instead, she posited a selective, critical stance toward nature, namely, viewing the diverse repertoire of nonhuman forms and behavior as composed of both models and antimodels for human society. Implicit, of course, in her judgments as to what in nature was and was not exemplary for humans was her egalitarian criterion of human progress.

Not only did Schreiner question the uncritical application of nonhuman models to human organization, but she was not convinced that the dynamics of evolution were primarily violent and competitive. She discerned in nature's processes not one but two laws of species survival and proliferation. Whereas Social Darwinists postulated competitive and brutal struggle within and among species for dominance, Schreiner concluded that species evolution was contingent no less upon cooperative and mutually protective behavior.

Schreiner did readily recognize the empirical basis for Social Darwinist belief in struggle for dominance as the engine of evolution. "Almost everywhere," Schreiner through Rebekah observed in *From Man to Man*, "are the traces of rapine and slaughter and the suppression or destruction of the weak form by the strong." In *African Farm* Schreiner portrayed species domination through Waldo's dog, Doss, as he tortures a beetle: "The beetle was hard at work trying to roll home a great ball of dung . . . but Doss broke the ball and ate the beetle's hind legs, and then bit off its head." Rebekah laments in *From Man to Man* the tragic losses that result from the domination by the more powerful, the extinction of wonderful forms of life such as beautiful winged reptiles (a fossil of which she owned and treasured) falling victims to "the strong jaw and the long claw and the poison bag!"[15]

Schreiner's perception of a hidden oneness and harmony in the cosmos would not let her rest, however, with a view of nature purely as a jungle in which destructive competition was key. She considered such an emphasis "a strange inversion," for an opposing natural law equally shaped species evolution. This law of "love and expansion of ego to others" assumed various modes, the foremost being parental love and protection of the young by both males and females of diverse species. Further, Schreiner noted among certain species a nurturing of the weak that extended beyond their immediate kin; for example, the survival of the small and defenseless mierkat required collective action: "not for their own young only, but for each other, and, for the younger and more helpless, all labor and sacrifice themselves."[16]

The roots of this loving behavior Schreiner located in the sexual instinct. She suggested that, "to kill, man might have been silent; but to communicate with and bind himself to his fellow . . . man was obliged to blossom into speech." Rebekah likens the impact of species struggle on evolution to pruning, modifying through hatchet blows forms of life already present but in no way creating the essential vitality of a tree or a flower bud. She conjectures that the pruning process was so haphazard that "forms of life, perhaps higher than any we know or even shall know . . . in their first incipience were cut away."[17] Clearly, through Rebekah, Schreiner challenged the sanguine Social Darwinist assumption that the outcome of the struggle for survival was inevitably progressive and, however bloody, justified.

Much theoretical similarity emerges between Schreiner's views and those of other critics of late-nineteenth-century Social Darwinism—Peter Kropotkin, Lester Frank Ward, Samuel Butler, F. W. H. Myers, the French vitalists. But though Schreiner met the Kropotkins in England, she nowhere mentioned reading *Mutual Aid* or, for that matter, the writing of these other evolutionists. No evidence yet exists to determine whether she was familiar with the work of Henry Drummond, a Scottish preacher who set forth in *Natural Law and the Spiritual World* (1883) and *The Ascent of Man* (1894) how the law of the struggle for the life of others coexisted with the struggles for one's own life. This altruistic principle emerged for Drummond as for Schreiner from family sexual, reproductive, and food-sharing activities; but Drummond injected into his account providential design, whereas Schreiner's perspective was wholly naturalistic.[18] Whether or not she ever read these writers, they could at most only reinforce the direction in her thinking, since her ideas on evolution were formulated well before any of the writings referred to here were published in England.

Despite Schreiner's wary attitude toward "tooth and claw" processes, the fact that she did accord them considerable influence in species development posed a problem for her integrationist concept of the cosmos. The antagonism between the often arbitrary and reckless pruner and the flourishing tree suggested a dialectic incompatible with Schreiner's nondualistic approach. A comparable problem emerged in her account of human nature and evolution, which, according to her, encompassed both the aggressive blood and power lust of animal ancestors and their sexually rooted caring and cooperative drives. The interplay of these destructive and creative impulses operated on an unconscious level, she felt, spurring humankind into ghastly wars and, at the same time, magnificent acts of love and art.[19] She shared with Social Darwinists the view that the more brutal drives prevailed because the individuals in whom such drives were less pronounced were "killed off by the individuals most incarnate of the lower nature and not allowed to perpetuate themselves freely either physically or spiritually."[20] She saw the caring sexual instincts corrupted by the tenacity of destructive impulses and called that corruption "lust." Applying Darwin's theory of sexual selection, she declared that women chose as their mates the more skillful hunters and warriors, thereby rewarding the more aggressive, bloodthirsty males. Despite their penchant for nurturance, women to the present day were complicit in "lust": They enjoyed violence vicariously, basked in the protective strength of their men, and emboldened males to acts of military heroism.[21]

If Schreiner granted that humanity was at least as much given to violence as altruism, how, then, could she maintain that the cosmos was essentially harmonious? She partially attempted to resolve this logical impasse by redefining human nature yet more inclusively. Beside the creative and destructive drives that humans shared with animals was a third, peculiarly human instinct. Schreiner alleged that "the deepest necessity of our being" was our ability to create and communicate ideals, "that strange and lovely power" that enabled us to transcend animal instincts and "to picture that which we have not in all parts ever fully seen." Our complex brain and nerve structure, which made visionary impulse possible, also endowed us with powers of reasoning and of devising ways to implement our ideals. Tellingly, Schreiner suggested the often nonconscious character of this strictly human implementation through analogies she drew from animal behavior—the sea insects who raise a sandy bank through infinite accretion of specks or the locusts whose dead bodies mount as a bridge for living locusts to pass over.[22]

Although Schreiner acknowledged that human nature's "triune instincts"—hunger, thirst, sex—were the raw animal tools of survival, subject to countless creative and destructive forms of expression, she described the ideal-making instinct in exclusively creative terms.[23] Her optimism here corresponded to her artistic confidence in intuition and subconscious "flashes" (see Chapter 8). Since humankind's visionary and reasoning potential allowed it to promote self and social improvement, however slowly, it had no need to abide by the crushing rule of "tooth and claw."[24] Schreiner could therefore adjudge the Social Darwinist sanctification of competitive struggle as unscientific, reductive, imprudent, and regressive.

Schreiner never made clear how much of this visionary impulse was naturally determined and irresistible and how much was subject to free will and moral choice. Much like the "new psychologists" at the turn of the century—William James, G. Stanley Hall, and William McDougall—she did not define the regions of instinct, habit, and free will. She was closest to James in allowing for any degree of free will. McDougall simply reduced social exchange to the interplay between pugnacious and parental instincts, whereas Hall insisted that human conduct is fundamentally biopsychological and innate.[25]

In positing uniquely human attributes, Schreiner also implied a separation of some sort between the inborn and the learned, that is, between nature and culture, even if the visionary impulses through which idealistic human learning could proceed were natural and physical in their origin. In this respect, she joined that small minority of evolutionary thinkers, most notably A. R. Wallace, T. H. Huxley, and Lester Frank Ward, who insisted that ethical and cultural purposes were formative in human evolution. Schreiner's analytic stance was particularly akin to that of Ward, who shared her view that nature often presented a negative model for human development. Rather than accept and imitate nature's wasteful and destructive methods, she argued, human beings should and could actively transform their environments to assure a progress nature would deny.[26]

Schreiner was convinced that in the course of history the need for physical prowess and combat for survival had not only diminished but had become increasingly antiprogressive. In *Woman and Labour* she recorded this shift: "The day of the primary import to humanity of the strength in man's extensor and flexor muscles, whether in the labors of war or of peace, is gone forever; and the day of the all-importance of the culture and activity of man's brain and nerve has already come." Accordingly, she sketched a new hero: "In the new world which is arising about us, . . . the type of human most useful to society and best fitted for its future conditions . . . will be, not the muscularly powerful and bulky, but the highly versatile, active, vital, adaptive, sensitive, physically fine-drawn type."[27]

Schreiner stressed the role of changing environments in defining "fit" and adaptive traits, a process of change much accelerated by centuries of major inventions. The greater the human control of the dynamics of natural selection, the more outmoded historic definitions of fitness became. She devoted significant passages of *From Man to Man* to describing how the absence of social habitats that foster caring and cooperative behavior had suppressed brilliant human forms as surely as, in earlier times, inimical environments had crushed the beautiful winged reptiles. Her evidence: the fates of Socrates, Jesus, and talented women throughout history. Though Schreiner could not anticipate how swiftly twentieth-century military technology would gain the capacity for annihilating the human species, she perceived how increasingly self-defeating to species evolution such technology had already shown itself. Fearing human control of nature as it contaminated and depleted natural resources, she was motivated in her concern for conserving the plant and animal life of South Africa by scientific and romantic values, not by a sense of how precarious human survival can become in a disturbed ecology. But she insisted the time had arrived when humanity, past the need of and benefits from brute physical prowess, could alter social systems and, hence, social training.[28]

In her complex moral deliberations, Schreiner conceded that certain inhumane practices might at one time have been a condition of survival, but with changing technology and modes of subsistence these practices became dysfunctional and either modified or died. She cited as an extreme example the destruction of "superflous" infants and old people in times of food scarcity. So, too, polygamy, though it wrought great suffering to women, might have been a necessary survival method when men, outnumbered by women, were centrally employed in warfare and hunting.[29]

Schreiner's critique of Social Darwinism was unqualifiedly corrosive when she treated common assumptions of racial and sexual inferiority, questioning both their scientific and their moral validity. Scientifically, she claimed, no proof existed for the biological inferiority of women and darker peoples or of Jews, Boers, and other of the allegedly less than "fittest." The privileged position certain groups of people commanded during any given period of human evolution was the consequence of shifting environmental influences and not, as Social Darwinists contended, a sign of innate superiority. The extent of human plasticity was such that Europeans living among "primitive" races, who could neither emulate the strengths of these races nor preserve the strengths of their own culture, have in their cultureless state "gone back in the scale of being."

> the mere climatic and physical differences would, at the end of forty years,
> have rendered them highly dissimilar in physical constitutions and in many in-
> tellectual and material wants, while their descendants at the end of six genera-

tions would certainly represent distinct human varieties, for which distinct laws and institutions would be requisite.[30]

For Schreiner, moral differences too, no less than physical and cultural differences, were circumstantially formed. In *African Farm* Waldo propounds this view when he asserts his sense of kinship with convicts and alcoholics: "A convict, or a man who drinks, seems something so far off and horrible when we see him. . . . We wonder what kind of creature he is; but he is just we, ourselves. We are only the wood, the knife that carves on us is the circumstance."[31]

Waldo's statement is consistent with Schreiner's many remarks on fundamental human identity and malleability. The strength of her environmentalism was particularly significant in light of her close friendship with Ellis and Pearson, both of whom advocated eugenics to promote human progress by ridding the world of the biologically unfit.[32] As a Lamarckian who believed in the transmission not of genetic but of acquired traits, Schreiner allowed for biological and cultural progress and regression within one generation. Arguing, for example, that lazy, self-indulgent parents, no matter how mentally and physically vigorous they potentially may be, breed less hardy youngsters,[33] she went a crucial step further: Though the parental upbringing of the child is the most formative influence, the child even in the womb can be aided or damaged by the parents' behavior. Both female parasitism and male overwork, in her example, can impair the vitality of offspring. As her positive model, she linked the Boers' developed farming skills and their academic excellence and stamina to their parents' simple, hardworking agrarian life, which did not overtax their nervous system. She assumed that such strenuous but not excessively laborious lives would best improve the biological quality of the human race by generally assuring both reproductive and "germinal" vigor as well as salutory infant and childhood surroundings.[34]

On Racial Differences

Unlike her anthropologist contemporaries who plotted a linear, progressive line of evolution from early history to the nineteenth century, stationing different races at points on that line, Schreiner rejected such a linear scale of progress and any attempt to evaluate races accordingly.[35] Given her definition of human progress as essentially moral progress—the steady expansion of sensitivity to and empathy with other human beings, the growth of personal freedom and collective self-determination in tandem with increasing cooperation and reciprocity among social groups—the very judging of certain persons or races as inherently inferior and justifiably subservient would constitute an act of sheer retrogressive insensitivity and prejudice.[36] As she saw it, Englishmen and Jews were alike in exhibiting both exceptional moral idealism and crass materialism; the African Boer could be unusually self-disciplined, courageous, free from greed, and also close-minded, stubborn, and bigoted; the African "Bantus," though illiterate, possessed a sophisticated communal organization in light of which Britain's flaunted economic and social system appeared backward.[37] In Rebekah's words:

> Is there really any superiority at all implied in degrees of pigmentation, and are the European races, except in their egoistic distortion of imagination, more desirable or highly developed than the Asiatic? . . . We scorn the Chinaman because his women compress their feet, not perceiving how infinitely more deadly and grotesque is the compression of our bodies; . . . We accuse of immorality the Asiatics who consume the opium we forced upon them at the point of the sword; but we fair Northerns . . . our chief pleasures . . . drinking and gambling; our race courses and card tables are as essential to our happiness as the dice and knuckle bones to our forebears.[38]

In reply to conventional Europeans who regard Africans and Asians as uglier than themselves and condemn their nudity, Rebekah asks: "Which is lovelier here, now, or in any place or time—the troop of men and women on a South Sea Island, naked and gladly disporting themselves in the water . . . sharing their love in the open light of day, or the scene that night by night our great cities witness?"[39]

Schreiner was not championing the "noble savage" here; rather, she was insisting that nobility and vice are prevalent in roughly comparable degrees in all creatures. In sum, all races constituted mixtures of vices and virtues, with no particular race monopolizing positive attributes or the reverse.

Not only each race but each individual, in Schreiner's view, displayed a range of strength and weaknesses. A poetic genius could be physically weak; a remarkable athlete might well possess criminal inclinations; an illiterate person could display rare courage and devotion to others. Through Rebekah, Schreiner attacked the eugenicists who would judge the criminal and social deviant as unfit but would acquit the exploitative factory owner or the myopic magistrate who imprisoned prostitutes without penalizing the men who used their services.[40]

Despite Schreiner's Lamarckian view of the transmission of acquired traits, there were areas where she substantially qualified her environmentalism with regard to both racial and sexual variation. The inconsistencies reveal the loose ends of her evolutionary outlook, the fact that some fraction of her thinking was still swathed in Victorian biases. In exploring racial differences, like many of her contemporaries, she applied the term *race* loosely; for example, she referred to Boers, Jews, the French, and Britons as "races" even as she also employed the more generic, human "race."[41] As was literary custom, she labeled characters in her fiction according to race and ethnicity: for example, "The Dutchman chuckled," "The Hottentot boy," "The Jew gazed at her."[42] Sometimes she spoke of specific "races" as human "varieties," "peoples," and "groups," an idle categorizing that fused with another Victorian assumption: that racial distinctions had objective scientific reality. Although she did not believe racial attributes were fixed from the inception of the human species, or even soon thereafter, and although she insisted at length upon individual variation within racial categories, she still held, as was evident in her very highlighting of the positive and negative attributes of certain cultures, that a cluster of shared physical and psychological traits dominated the majority of any designated "race."[43] Environmentally induced, these racial differences represented adaptation to specific natural ecology and social habitats. To illustrate, she traced the nineteenth-century Boer's fierce rebellion against imposed alien authority to the circumstances of a small band of seventeenth-century Dutch sailors and soldiers, "children of fortune," who originally settled in South Africa and whose "blood . . . modified truly and powerfully by other elements" flowed actively in the latter-day Boer, especially since these early Dutch adventurers had intermarried with French Huguenots who had boldly resisted Catholic efforts to dragoon them into the Catholic Church. The geographic isolation of the Boers, their adoption of South Africa as their homeland, their linguistic isolation (the Taal separating the Boers from modern European cultural influences), and their close inter-breeding assured a constellation of Boer physical and cultural attributes. Schreiner cast the Boer's situation in romantic Darwinian terms: "[O]n certain isolated mountain peaks, or on solitary islands, surrounded by deep oceans there are sometimes found certain unique forms of plant and animal life. . . . Such unique human species is the true South African Boer."[44]

Offering similar cultural explanations for the distinctive traits of other races, Schreiner's primary motive appeared to be that of subverting belief in the ineradicable and biological character of negative racial characteristics, but her effect was mixed. She agreed, for example, that South African "half-castes,"[45] as she unfortunately called them, were generally antisocial, that is, prone to crime, prostitution, and psychological disorders, even as she argued that these racial traits were not inherent but socially conditioned. Her attempt to redirect the impact of a stereotype she would not deny went as follows: With significant exceptions, parents of South African "half-castes" represented the least responsible and cultured members of their respective races. Damned as young "half-castes" were by both black and white communities, their poverty and social isolation heightened the peril of their inadequate parental influence. Lacking a family or community that respected them, "half-castes" despised themselves, most pointedly their blackness. Given such inner and external alienation, the "typical" antisocial behavior of the outcast became socially explicable and subject to change.[46] In *From Man to Man* it is a "half-caste," the offspring of a union between Rebekah's husband and a black African servant, whom Rebekah proceeds to raise with the same love and respect she gives her blood children. As portrayed in the novel, the "half-caste" daughter, Sartje, is expected to be, and is, as socially mature and responsible as any white child.

Schreiner often focused on the environmental and cultural origins of positive traits. Noting that the "English are the least musical of all European nations," in marked contrast with the Germans' extraordinary musicianship, she claimed that "a family of English children reared in Germany exhibit often the same serious passion for music, the same knowledge of it, and even the same power of producing it."[47] Likewise, "a French boy reared from birth in English surroundings would love rough outdoor games," and, feeding on beef, pudding, and ale, he would come to resemble the stereotypical John Bull. To those who alleged that Jews possess an instinctive greed, Schreiner replied that circumstances afforded Jews limited occupational choice. If the Jews were released from these constraints, "though his descendants would undoubtedly inherit his nose they would probably show no inherent tendency to lend money at sixty percent."[48] It is obvious that though she intended by this remark to counter anti-Semitic prejudice, she subtly reinforced common hostility to Jews all the same.

Schreiner's combined stereotyping and environmentalism permeated her discussion of South African blacks. On the one hand, distinguishing among ethnic groups, she did not succumb to the usual European monolithic view of black people. On the other hand, she rooted these ethnic divisions in mistaken Victorian anthropology. Like all nineteenth-century British historians and anthropologists, she called the Khoikhoi "Hottentots" and the San "Bushmen," much as she thoughtlessly kept the "half-caste" designation. She spoke of "Bantus" interchangeably with "Kaffirs" and "natives." In order to capture the timebound features of Schreiner's thought I am employing her language, placing quotation marks to signal their dated reality.[49]

In defining differences among blacks, Schreiner found "Hottentots," "Bushmen," and "Bantus" highly different from one another, but when she spelled out those differences she abundantly generalized in directions of cultural if not biological inequality. She praised the "Hottentots'" artistic imagination, acute perceptions, and complex language, yet she found them generally lacking in intellectual stamina. She accepted the "Hottentot" and "Bantu" judgment of the "Bushmen" as childlike, less culturally sophisticated than themselves, and cited their rudimentary social organization, weak interpersonal ties, and simple language. She went so far as to suggest that on the scale of evolution the "Bushmen" were intermediary between human beings and nonhuman primates. The "Bantus," on the other hand, were free from negative racial attributes. She lauded their physical, moral, and intellectual prowess, their proud reserve and independence. Chuana women (Chuanas—or Bechuanas—were a "Bantu" branch; other branches included the Kuz and Basutos) delighted Schreiner with their brilliant performance on matriculation exams at Cape University where they acquitted themselves as capably as European males. The "Kaffirs," among the most populous of South African blacks, exhibited unusual resourcefulness, personal honor, and self-reliance, according to Schreiner, who felt them capable of genius. She noted that some black tribes were more submissive to slavery than others. Those from the East and West Coasts of Central Africa were easier to enslave, though "sometimes the human in them woke" and they became as fiercely opposed to slavery as South African blacks.[50]

Many of these mistaken racial generalizations, particularly her assumptions that enslaved Africans who did not revolt were less human and were in a position to resist, were commonplace among Victorians;[51] yet, in comparison with her contemporaries, Schreiner credited diverse African black groups with many more positive moral and intellectual strengths. She insisted that even if a people were at a lower stage in cultural evolution they possessed the same potential as any other people for pain and love. Cultural inequality was a fluid and complex reality and could in no way justify practices of domination and racial insensitivity.[52]

Though Schreiner stretched her racial egalitarianism further than her contemporaries, she obviously did not completely relinquish elements of racial condescension. Her emphasis upon the impact of environment and culture on human personality was fraught with inconsistencies. At times she would have it appear that a people's physical and cultural traits persisted regardless of environmental forces, as when she noted how European Jews for centuries were victims of "more muscular, physically powerful and pugilistic peoples." Somehow, she did not see such circumstances as modifying the traits of surviving Jews toward greater muscular development and pugnaciousness. Instead, she proposed that cultural flux had turned desirable those Jewish traits so long associated with their victimization:

> The Egyptian taskmaster and warrior have passed; . . . after long ages of disgrace and pariahism . . . those qualities which the Jew possesses and which subtilely distinguish him from others, are in demand. . . . Exactly that domination of the reflective faculties over the combative which once made him slave . . . are the very qualities the modern world . . . crowns.[53]

Given the ignorance of nineteenth-century scientists about genetic transmission and the paucity of statistical data on racial patterns, Schreiner was no better able than Darwin or Spencer to explain the relationship between nature and nurture or to reach reliable conclusions about typical and exceptional racial behavior.

Schreiner's struggle to resist biased thinking about racial matters was most evident in her oscillating views on interracial breeding, her inconsistencies revealing both her time-bound shortsightedness and her more progressive inclinations. Interracial breeding was a matter of paramount interest to her, situated as she was in South Africa, where "half-castes" were increasing in numbers each year and where taboos against racially mixed unions correspondingly intensified. These taboos pertained, of course, preeminently to black and white unions. Strictures against Boer and British mating were rapidly eroding. The shared white supremacist outlook of Briton and Boer led numerous whites to appropriate scientific propositions concerning the biologically unsound consequences of interracial mating. And though it was quite obvious that "half-castes" were not, as many leading scientists alleged, infertile or of impaired fertility, no evidence appeared to counter the belief in Darwin's notion of biological reversion: that when species are crossed, the offspring tends to manifest long-lost, more "primitive" characteristics possessed by neither parent nor immediate progenitor.[54]

Whereas Schreiner refuted general opinion that "half-castes" were innately antisocial, she balked at discounting altogether the theory of reversion. She pointed out that the mating of two distinct breeds of pigeons (she presumed blacks and whites were equally distinct breeds!) results in progeny unlike their parents, resembling instead the original parent stock from which both varieties descended. While admitting that the reason for this atavism was unknown, she felt its occurrence raised serious questions about human heredity. Were a Zulu and an Englishman to mate, she suggested, the offspring might resemble neither of these brave, socially sophisticated races but rather an earlier breed from which both races descended, a breed weaker perhaps in both courage and social feeling.[55]

By the same token, Schreiner viewed the crossing of so-called allied races as beneficial. She drew upon Ellis's scientific studies of the nature and causes of genius and seemed convinced of his contention that a significant percentage of European men of genius were offspring of mixed "race" (by which term she meant, this time, nationalities). If reversion did take place, the ancestor of an Italian and a Briton would be a figure only a few thousand years earlier, a "known racial type" familiar to readers of history, in contrast to the unknown remote progenitor common to the Zulu and Briton. When thinking in this vein, Schreiner worried that insufficient knowledge made the risks of interracial breeding all too high, possibly costing humanity "the results of hundreds of years of slow evolution."[56] Though she held that all human breeds were branches of an original human type, she clearly assumed that the original human ancestors were biologically as well as culturally inferior to later generations; otherwise, the "law of regression" would pose no problem.

On occasion, Schreiner came closer to surmounting her racist fears. She reasoned that the same law of reversion "might, under certain conditions, produce development and not regression." She speculated as to a cross between English and Japanese individuals, both races having attained, she believed, "the same high point of intellectual and social development, the Japanese being probably more artistic and refined, the Englishman possibly more dominant." She surmised that the outcome of their mating might be "a creature higher in the scale of life and more desireable than either parent species."[57] Eager to suspend judgment on this issue, Schreiner observed that her only encounter with an offspring of an Englishman and a "Kaffir" woman challenged the reversion theory completely: the offspring presented a simple blend of both parents.

Although most anthropologists were exclusively concerned with the biological consequences of interracial mating, Schreiner dwelt upon its psychological feasibility. By and large, she considered cross-racial unions psychologically viable only among races that were comparably culturally advanced. She assumed, exhibiting further her residual racism and unwillingness to confront the issue of prevalent interracial liaisons directly, that highly disparate individuals tended not to be drawn to each other. She asserted that if a George

Sand or even "the average cultured females of a highly evolved race" were marooned on an island where the only males were "savages of the Fuegan type, who should meet them on the shores with matted hair and prognathous jaws and with wild shouts, brandishing their instruments of death," no possible sexual attraction could occur and the females' "race" would become extinct. The same would be true for a man like Darwin, Shelley, or Keats if he were cast into a circle of "Bushmen" females "with greased bodies and twinkling eyes, devouring the raw entrails of slaughtered beasts."[58] Though Schreiner acknowledged these were extreme cases and allowed for sexual compatibility between, for example, an educated "Bantu" woman and an educated British man, her virtual cartoonlike illustrations of gross sexual revulsion between intellectually developed white races and "primitive" black tainted her egalitarian cultural pluralism.

Schreiner's fluctuations as to the wisdom of interracial breeding carried trouble in her vision of the ideal society. As a romantic and cultural pluralist she gloried in the preservation of racial variety, opposing the dilution of human variety into a bland uniform mass. But she also proposed that the "ideal human creature, for whom the centuries wait . . . [may be] half China-man, half Aryan, or African-Aryan and Mongolian blend."[59] Of course, neither position is inherently racist, and in Schreiner's time the idea of interracial blending was by far the more radically antiracist. Ultimately, she resolved her ambivalence over interracial mating by leaving the matter to spontaneous impulse: "where nature herself obliterates the distinction of race, and allows a mighty and permanent affection between man and woman to cross its limits of race, then I should be inclined to say nature herself gives sanction . . . and consecrates the union of distinct breeds."[60] In effect, Schreiner granted sexual desire, if uncontaminated by coercion, the freedom to dictate social ethics, a most unusual position for a Victorian, particularly for one who, according to many scholars, presumably held repressive attitudes about sexuality. In this matter she was as much a sociobiologist as any nineteenth-century Social Darwinist. Her position, I suspect, would totally reverse itself were the natural erotic drive to lunge toward conflict and subjection of the weak; then, of course, nature's sanction would count with her for little.

On Sexual Differences

Schreiner's critique of Social Darwinism went even deeper when she dealt with questions of sexuality and gender. Like her contemporaries, she could not account scientifically for sexual dimorphism, but unlike them, her igno-rance did not impede her from challenging prevalent assumptions about the origin and nature of sex and gender differences.[61] When even feminists of her time were touting separate male and female traits and roles, which they believed reflected biological differences, she suspected that both their biology and their sociology were corrupted by the scientific biases then current.[62] In her analysis of sex and gender differences, she anticipated later twentieth-century directions of feminist thinking.

Schreiner allowed for limited biological differences between the sexes only in the matter of reproduction and overall muscular mass. Apart from that, she felt that the two human sexes possessed essentially identical characteristics. She drew supporting evidence from her study of animals, observing that although some animals do appear to conform to Victorian assumptions con-cerning sex traits (e.g., gallinaceous birds) countless others manifest a com-pletely opposing pattern. For instance, "with the great majority of species on earth, the female form exceeds the male in size and strength, often in predatory instinct." Among insects, fish, birds of prey, and certain mammals, Schreiner noted, the female is more pugnacious, physically active, and domi-nant. Her skepticism toward the notion of innate and universal sex roles was aroused early on when, as a young child, she gazed at various African birds—cock-o-veets, the Cape Kapok, doves—"building their nests together, and caring for and watching over, not only their young, but each other."[63] She watched the male ostrich daily relieve the hen at a fixed hour to sit on her eggs; and she watched, too, his tender care for the hatched young. Later she learned that among certain toads the female deposits her eggs in cavities on the back of the male, where the eggs are preserved and hatched.[64] Among South African mierkats, "it is the males who from the moment of birth watch over the young with the most passionate and tender solicitude, . . . exhibiting exactly those psychic qualities which are generally regarded as peculiarly feminine."[65] The Social Darwinist contention that nature ordained the Vic-torian sex/gender system was patently unempirical and not a whit more substantiated than the prejudices of "the pure-blind inhabitant of a modern social state [who] seeing no further than the shapes which happen for the moment immediately before him, sees in sex manifestation something un-alterably fixed and unchanging, a mathematical axiom."[66]

Given the diversity of gender traits and behavior among most animal species, Schreiner declared that scientific evidence was lacking, too, to prove innate human gender-role differences. She held that environmental determi-nants fully accounted for gender traits and roles. Teasing conventional readers' sex biases, she mused, "It may possibly be that, when the historian of the future looks back over the history of the intellectually freed and active sexes for many generations, a decided preference of the female intellect for mathematics, engineering, or statecraft may be made clear."[67] So various have been human gender roles throughout history—Schreiner supplied plentiful evidence from an array of cultures and eras—that she deduced both males and females showed essentially similar potential for any given behavior beyond reproductive functions. She stressed that "The eye, ear, the sense of touch, the general organs of nutrition, respiration and volition are in the main identical, and often differ far more in persons of the same sex than in those of opposite sexes; even on the dissecting-table the tissue of the male and female are often wholly indistinguishable."[68] With this statement, Schreiner parted ways with the late-Victorian obsession over craniometrical analysis of brain tissue differences and late-Victorian notions that men inherently possessed greater psychic and mental variability.

Though Schreiner acknowledged that men's bones and muscular structure were somewhat larger than women's, she found little anthropological or historical evidence to justify viewing women as physically weak and dependent. To the contrary, the strenuous activity of the nineteenth-century Boer and "Kaffir" women was more the historical rule than the relative passivity and flaccid muscles of comfortable "modern" European women. Unlike Spencer, Geddes, Thomson, and their cohorts, who viewed the muscular disparity between Victorian men and women as a positive sign of cultural progress, Schreiner judged it as a symptom of diseased social values and institutions.

Her insistence upon the superficiality and cultural relativity of gender differences included her assessment of erotic appetites and parental impulses. Both of these categories of instincts were almost universally regarded among nineteenth-century scientists, and by the public at large, as sharply sex-differentiated. Many feminists couched their arguments for women's right to a political voice in terms of their belief in women's biologically rooted maternal protectiveness toward the weak and in women's superior moral purity. Schreiner strongly disagreed. Men and women, she declared, were "alike even in the possession of that initial instinct which draws sex to sex, and which differing slightly in its forms and manifestations, is of equal intensity in both."[69] Similarly, whereas men's parental impulses were embryonic, little encouraged by society, their potential nurturant impulses were no less intense than women's. The parental instinct of women, she noted, was itself far from universal. She asked, "Who farm little babies and starve them to death? Women in most cases, not men. Who keep brothels and betray young children and girls into a life which means disease and generally early death? . . . Women! . . . I don't for one moment believe in the moral superiority of women."[70] She then proceeded to name male friends who equaled the finest females in tender, unselfish, nurturant behavior.

For a time Schreiner subscribed to the popular opinion that the biological and social experience of pregnancy and child raising did arouse keener feelings of human sympathy and a more ardent love of peace among women than among men.[71] She eventually rejected this flattering notion. Her experiences with feminist and nonfeminist attitudes and behavior during World War I undermined her earlier assumption of biologically rooted female pacifism. (See the discussion of pacifism in Chapter 7.)

Schreiner disputed the argument, widely advanced by scientists, doctors, and educators, that women's reproductive activity, including menstruation, diminished their mental stamina and could be jeopardized by excessive physical or mental labor. From her own experience, her studies, and her discussions with female friends, she determined that a woman's menstrual period in no way impaired her intellectual functioning. In fact, she discerned an increase in mental energy during the last two days of her period: "My acquisitive power, my power of learning is not *at all* weak just at the time." Given her perception of the reciprocity between emotions and thought, she concluded that the greater "hyper-sensitivity" of many women during their menses enriched their imaginative fertility, citing as evidence that during one of her menses "the solution to all difficulties with *From Man to Man* flashed into me."[72]

In present-day analyses of sex and gender differences, much is made of physiological distinctions between men and women in erotic response, with comparable intensity of appetite and pleasure generally acknowledged. Schreiner may have addressed these distinctions in the original destroyed manuscript of *Woman and Labour*, but in her published writings she rarely alluded to them. Perhaps here more than in any other area she revealed the limits of her crusade against Mrs. Grundy. Although able to assess erotic matters openly in private discussions, she held back in public. Her published essay on Boer courtship patterns, for example, omitted details of specific erotic styles. But she had no trouble treating sexual questions frankly in her correspondence and even in discussions at the Men and Women's Club. She reported solid evidence to refute the dominant medical opinion that women and men disliked and avoided intercourse during a woman's pregnancy and lactation time, and she admitted to gender difference with regard to the physioemotional effects of coitus.[73]

As with her treatment of ethnic and racial differences, Schreiner's desire to champion an oppressed group—women, in this instance—occasionally led her to contradictory statements. In controverting the Victorian consensus that males of a species were primarily responsible for the mental and physical strength of offspring, she was adamant that both parents were equally responsible but then stressed the mother's decisive role. At times, like other nineteenth-century feminists, she regarded women alone as the standard bearers of their race, arguing there was a direct link between the fearless and hefty Boer mother and her hardy children, just as there was between the affluent, idle, narrow-waisted and delicate British woman and her effete youngsters.[74] Schreiner asserted that as the mother's—and only the mother's—muscle softens, so does the child's; "as she decays, decays the people." Drawing an analogy from ant life to human life, she noted that the parasitic behavior of female ants inhibited the evolution of ants as a species; after reaching a point of remarkable mental development, ants "become curiously and immovably arrested."[75] But Schreiner also rallied numerous examples of how the most worthy qualities of certain illustrious men came from their mothers: for one, Alexander the Great's indebtedness to the "fierce, vital and indomitable Olympia." She saw Olympia as the source of Alexander's courage, intellectual activity, and ambition. For Schreiner, the female was "the final standard of the race," because, as she explained, "with each generation the entire race passes through the body of its womanhood as through a mold."[76] At other times, however, she underscored the simultaneous role of both sexes in transmitting traits. Holding that particularly progressive periods in human evolution were marked by coordinated development among both genders, she suggested that, as the convolutions of the brain of one sex occurred, so too that of the other sex: "now this sex and then that, so to speak, catching the ball of life and throwing it back to the other, slightly if imperceptibly enlarging and beautifying it." At such times she argued that future progress required that "male and female must march side by side."[77]

Schreiner also qualified her position on essential sexual identity with regard to women's muscular abilities. At various points, she credited women with small-motor coordination, physical agility, and stamina superior to men. This superiority compensated women for their smaller bones and muscles: their fine, agile, small-motor coordination was particularly advantageous in an era of modern technology, whereas men's broader physical prowess, such as their ability to wield a battle-ax, had become less socially useful.[78] Clearly, when it served Schreiner's purposes to assert sex differences, particularly when doing so boosted female status, her constant emphasis on sexual similarity gave way. Compared, however, with her contemporaries, feminists and nonfeminists alike, she was remarkably consistent in her claim of inherent similarity and equality between the sexes and their shared ability to embrace the full range of gender roles and traits.

Given this intrinsic gender similarity, environment and culture were for Schreiner the chief sources of gender behavior in any place and time. I will explore the manner in which Victorian culture shaped gender identity and roles when I analyze her feminism; what is pertinent here is her opposition to Victorian biological and anthropological accounts of gender distinctions. Marshaling copious examples from early cultures, she conceded that in early society male muscular prowess and female reproductive activity held greater sway than in later centuries and may have accounted for the division of sex roles between hunting males and suckling females. But even in early society, she argued, this pattern was not universal, as witness women warriors and chieftains and men supplanting women as weavers and planters. Stressing the role versatility of women in early cultures, Schreiner maintained that women were responsible for the discovery of the uses of fire and the creation of language, art, pottery, and medicine. Women, she asserted, were humanity's first doctors, priests, artists, theoretical and applied scientists.[79]

Although at times Schreiner seemed to describe early society as essentially matriarchal (eliding distinctions among matriarchal, matrifocal, and matrilineal, as was the wont of her contemporaries), that was decidedly not her intent. In presuming the prevalence of patriarchal domination in early cultures, she differed from Victorian writers such as Bachofen, Bebel, Engels, Ellis, and Pearson. In her allegory "Three Dreams in a Desert" she labeled this early period the "Age of-dominion-of-muscular-force." She argued that long before the advent of private property and the institution of slavery, male authority was the ultimate coercive power in society, a power rooted in men's comparatively greater muscular strength.[80] She cited the persistence of these early patterns into nineteenth-century "Kaffir" society. The male "Kaffir," she contended, "may kill, flog or subject her [his "Kaffir" wife] to any use," abusing her verbally and physically throughout their marriage.[81] Subject to such an imbalanced organization of sexual politics, early women, Schreiner observed, for all their impressive array of economic and social roles and contributions, were "often more or less enslaved."[82]

Despite her awareness of the predominance of female subjection in early cultures, Schreiner emphasized that no one sex/gender system prevailed everywhere: "Here we find the female form free and unenslaved, bearing its young and transmitting its rights to them; there we find it in absolute subjection to the male form; here polygamy, there monogamy; there group marriage."[83] In sum, anthropological evidence could not be fairly invoked to buttress the Victorian distribution of gender roles. Though Schreiner's thinking was limited by the availability of nineteenth-century anthropological records, the main lines of her argument are upheld by many late-twentieth-century social scientists, apart from her emphasis upon the decisive role of large-scale hunting. Further impressively, her skepticism about early matriarchy and her stress on female role diversity and versatility are in accord with current feminist anthropological findings.[84]

On Social Class Differences

Schreiner's study of human evolution shaped her biological and cultural analysis of not only racial and gender development but also social class differences. Her critique of Social Darwinist analysis of class differences relied primarily on historical reflections rather than on the evidence of biology and ethology. She discarded Social Darwinist assertions of the biological inferiority of the poor and lower classes, her aim not to account for the origin of class hierarchies but to refute the accepted bias that class differences benefited social progress. As Schreiner studied historical accounts of the rise and fall of various civilizations, she deduced that any enduring social strength required the organic, simultaneous, and reciprocal development of all participant groups. She attributed the decay of Rome, Greece, Egypt, Assyria, Persia, and India to the failure of these civilizations to heed this principle. Through Rebekah, she asked rhetorically, "What had they [the ancient civilizations] been but the blossoming of a minute, abnormally situated, abnormally nourished class, unsupported by any vital connection with the classes beneath them or the nations around?" She then proceeded to debunk Victorian reverence for Ancient Athens by pointing out that its culture was bound to decay since Athenian cultural and political leadership was "a delicate irridescent film overlying the seething mass of servile agricultural and domestic slaves and women."[85]

For her, the danger of social class divisions transcended national boundaries. Human progress was impaired if one culture enjoyed privilege at the expense of another. Schreiner has Rebekah ruminate, "Is it not a paradox covering a mighty truth that not one slave toils under the lash on an Indian plantation but the freedom of every other man on earth is limited by it?"[86] For this very reason she titled her novel *From Man to Man*. For this reason, too, she could not tolerate the position of various social reformers and socialists who would advocate legislation to help the poor in England only to unify the nation and better enable it to advance its imperial domination of other territories.

Given her view that not only race and gender hierarchies but also severe class differences were antievolutionary (Schreiner nowhere posits the total absence of class differences), she rejected nineteenth-century historians' elevation of their century as the pinnacle of human progress. Rather, she lamented that nineteenth-century European society was in precipitous decline, as diseased as cultures of antiquity, corrupted by its materialism and stark social inequality.[87] In an eloquent appeal to the rural South African Boer attracted to European material and cultural accomplishments, she warned:

> Be not too ready to give up the past, we pray you. All that is new is not true, and that which comes later is not always an improvement on that which went before. . . . There are times when, looking carefully at this nineteenth-century civilization of ours, it appears to us much like the concretion which certain deep-sea creatures build up about themselves out of the sand and rubbish on the deep-sea floor, which after a time becomes hard and solid, and forms their grave.[88]

Yet for all her antagonism toward Victorian civilization Schreiner would not return humanity to the relatively stationary condition of up-country Boer communities. In alerting Boers to the deceptive appeal of modern civilization, she was urging not rejection of all that is new but a careful sifting of the new for what is genuinely conducive to human progress. She recognized that such a sifting process was neither easy nor always highly conscious.

Her view of historical progress combined ideas of material necessity with those of human choice, the former exerting greater influence. Consider her treatment of youthful marriage among up-country Boers. Though she personally opposed such marriage as oppressive for most women, she recognized specific conditions in Boer culture that accounted for durability. Vital economic reasons were foremost: The Boer male depended upon a wife as domestic laborer and nurse if he was to leave his father's homestead, begin his own household, and assume mature independence. Reversing the British pattern, the Boer did not seek to make money in order to marry but rather married in order to secure economic needs. No less decisive were social considerations based upon the Boer male's geographical and intellectual isolation.[89]

In a similar fashion, Schreiner explained why abused "Kaffir" women did not revolt against their subjected state. She reasoned that however bitter the "Kaffir" woman was over her plight, she recognized her social role as indispensable: "Her labour," she wrote, "formed the solid superstructure on which her society rested; her submission to her condition was the condition of social health and even national and tribal survival."[90] That "Kaffir" women recognized both social necessity and their unjust circumstances was evident in Schreiner's conversation with a "Kaffir" woman, "a woman of genius" who in "language more eloquent and intense than I have ever heard from the lips of any other woman" detailed the anguish of the conditions of her life. And yet, this woman's fierce bitterness did not ignite her desire to rebel. Indeed, she exhibited a "stern and almost majestic attitude of acceptance of the inevitable." Schreiner concluded that no race, sex, or class will ever collectively revolt unless social conditions change to the extent that submission to existing patterns of authority is no longer essential to collective survival and growth.[91]

The complexity of historical resistance movements is such, Schreiner proposed, that not even the most perceptive and articulate leaders of those movements fully understand the historical dynamic involved. They and their followers are "driven to action as the result of the immediate pressure of the conditions of life." Schreiner likened the development of a social movement to the slow, unconscious growth of a child within a womb, to the piece-by-piece creation of the great Gothic cathedrals, and to the process whereby a starfish eventually climbs a sloping rock, each of its million fine tentacles engaging in separate labor. Forced or artificially hastened social transformation will be unstable because, like a structure built on a shaky foundation, it will lack that broad base of support which is essential to durable change.[92]

Even when historical conditions create ample momentum for progressive change, Schreiner recognized that historical change introduces social stress regardless. Social institutions may change while individual psyches lag behind. Further, the rapidity and unevenness of structural changes in modern society generated "a large amount of disco-ordination, and, consequently, . . . suffering." Schreiner knew full well from her own tribulations that "agonizing moments must arise, when the individual, seeing the necessity for adopting new courses of action, or for accepting new truths, or conforming to new conditions, will yet be tortured by the hold of traditional convictions."[93] She was certainly neither naive nor sentimental in her optimism about the potential for progressive historical change, but her belief in the innate human longing to create positive ideals, coupled with her confidence in the power of the individual to follow a new course of action, however painful, sustained her faith in the possibility of human progress. As subsequent chapters will elucidate, Schreiner's perception of the complexity of social change occasionally grew blurred when she was in the midst of a campaign for social justice. At such times, she held a faith in the power of political and cultural leaders that overrode her own more reasonably skeptical insights into the complex dynamics of human progress.

4

Axing "the upas-tree"

ANTIDOTES FOR RACIST
AND IMPERIALIST POISON

If the South Africa of the future is to remain eaten
internally by race hatreds, . . . our doom is sealed;
our place will be wanting among the great, free
nations of earth.

The ultimate chant of the human race on earth is not to
be conceived of as a monotone chanted on one note by
one form of humanity alone, but rather a choral
symphony chanted by all races and all nations in diverse
tones on different notes in one grand complex harmony.

Olive Schreiner, *Thoughts on South Africa*

SCHREINER'S EVOLUTIONARY THEORY, particularly her critique of scientific and Social Darwinist rationale for white race supremacy, molded her views on Empire and the political welfare of South Africa. Between 1890 and 1914 she emerged as both the foremost South African critic of British imperialism and the leading exponent of an independent, federalist, and democratic union of South Africa. She set as her major project to diagnose and cure the diseases infecting South African politics. The forms of her political activism proved various: works of fiction, such as the novella *Trooper Peter Halket of Mashonaland,* the allegory "Eighteen-Ninety-Nine," and long, ruminative passages and parables in *From Man to Man;* nonfiction articles and books, most notably, *Thoughts on South Africa, An English South African's View of the Situation* (published also as *The South African Question*), *Closer Union,* and addresses to meetings held in opposition to the Anglo–Boer War. Besides her public campaigns, she exerted considerable personal influence before and after the Anglo–Boer War through her private letters and conversations with prominent South African and English government leaders, including her brother Will. Friends and foes alike among her contemporaries testified to the effectiveness of Schreiner's political activity. The biographer of onetime South African prime minister J. C. Smuts accused her of inciting Smuts "almost always, towards extremist action."[1] And Sir James Rose-Innes, chief justice of South Africa in 1914, ranked Olive and Will Schreiner among that indispensable band of idealists "who had consistently maintained that racial problems can never be satisfactorily solved on the lines of oppression."[2]

Schreiner's admirers frequently extolled her political foresight, citing her tragically ignored prophecies of implacable Boer resistance and devastating British and Boer losses should war break out between Boer and Briton, as well as her unheeded predictions of the disastrous outcome of a unified South Africa that deprived African blacks of civil rights. The editor of the *Nation*, H. W. Massingham, typified British liberal esteem for Schreiner's prescience, designating her as the "true spiritual founder of the South African Union, the scourge of its base betrayal and the intrepid preacher of a gospel of rights and duties for all its peoples, black and white." Mohandas Gandhi similarly applauded Schreiner's espousal of the rights of Indians in South Africa.[3]

Although many of Schreiner's English and South African contemporaries appreciated her remarkable role in South African affairs, later writers and scholars, with some stellar exceptions, have ignored her.[4] Even the spate of recent books on the Anglo–Boer War and on British pro-Boers have overlooked her.[5] General histories of South Africa and biographies of eminent South African political figures usually treat her briefly. Invariably, the results are superficial. Scarcely more satisfying is current discussion of Schreiner's views on race and Empire among South African and English scholars and literary critics. Slighting her radical critique of Empire and her daring, egalitarian federalist proposals, with a very few exceptions they focus instead on the extent to which her residual racist views cast her as a typical white liberal.[6] To be fair, these time-bound features of her antiracism and antiimperialism must be juxtaposed with those of her South African and English liberal, socialist, and feminist contemporaries. From this perspective, her opinions and proposals, though evincing inescapable tensions between political idealism and realism and between radicalism and liberalism on the race issue, sparkle with humanity, freshness, and audacity.[7]

British critics of Empire in the nineteenth century were predominantly racist and ethnocentric. Rarely did concern for Africans assume any importance in their thinking, and very few were pro-Boer.[8] Anti-Semitism was rampant in antiimperial agitation. Jewish financiers in Johannesburg and London were assailed as insidious abettors of British imperial policies in South Africa. Caricatures and stereotypes abounded in virulent antiimperial descriptions of Africans, Jews, Boers, and Asians. Whether antiimperialists were liberals, radicals, or socialists made little difference in the character of their ethnic bias. Even Edward Carpenter, an ardent champion of women and the working class and a rare nineteenth-century defender of homosexuals, fueled his antiimperial rhetoric with blatant ethnic prejudice. To justify Transvaal's President Paul Kruger's desire to restrict immigration into Transvaal and circumscribe franchise rights, Carpenter used an openly racist analogy: "[What if] Liverpool were to be overrun by 100,000 Chinese, smothering our civilization and introducing their hated customs?" No less ethnocentric was Carpenter's belief that Britain's world mission was to love, educate, and heal "lesser races."[9]

Even when Victorian antiimperialists did not assert the inherent inferiority of other nations, they claimed that, whereas other races were potentially on a par with England, they depended upon British tutelage to achieve cultural equality. Until the 1890s, Schreiner, though she objected to the notion of "lesser races," held the idea, common among Victorian radicals and liberals, that among nations Britain was uniquely committed to the preservation and diffusion of human freedom. She envisioned England as the protector and strengthener of weaker and smaller states and also viewed it as a neutral arbiter, a power fulcrum, and primary global peacemaker. With specific regard to South Africa she "dreamed that when, in forty or sixty years' time," the states of South Africa had grown "internally enough, healthily and without sacrificing their different systems of internal self-government to federate," the new confederacy would take its place beside the other great nations of the world.[10] Nurtured by British liberalism and idealism as well as by its own experience of cultural diversity, South Africa might even surpass its tutor as political and moral leader for the world. Throughout the period of South Africa's maturation, the relationship between England and its colony, as Schreiner conceived it, would conform to the most enlightened and generous notions of colonial stewardship. She relied upon two vivid images to convey her sense of this nurturant colonial relationship. One was the "tree of life . . . the great banyan tree . . . among whose sheltering roots and under whose protecting shadow, endless forms of life may spring up and flourish that might otherwise be destroyed."[11] Her second image was of the brave, kindly, and devoted stepmother, opposite to the evil stepmother of folklore and fantasy, who protects and raises her stepdaughter as lovingly as if the child were her own. When the child attains full adulthood, stepmother and stepdaughter enter into a new relationship of peers, tied together by "a peculiarly close and tender bond."[12] English history, sadly, proved otherwise.

By the mid-1890s Schreiner had lost faith in England's special tutelage because of its persistent and stark betrayal of its own principles of human freedom and national self-determination.[13] Concomitant with her disillusionment was Schreiner's critique of the self-serving and spurious biological and social-scientific rationale that the English adopted to further British racial hegemony. In view of Britain's policies in Ireland, India, and South Africa, the Empire now struck Schreiner as a monstrous stepmother; the banyan tree now appeared as "a colossal upas-tree" whose leaves distilled poison. "Under its branches, plants, flowers and animals suffocated." The Empire, as the tree, became sole monarch "over a bared earth."[14]

With unsparing scorn, Schreiner denounced the British Empire as "sulphurous lava," "a deadly disease," "a drunken orgie," "a death shroud of nations," "a vast mass of adipose tissue," and as "John Bull, seated astride the earth, his huge belly distended by the people he has devoured." In a particularly powerful medical metaphor, Schreiner observed that "for ages England has tried to fasten Ireland artificially on to herself, and after four hundred years it still hangs at her side a dislocated arm, almost as ready to drop off as when four hundred years ago Oliver Cromwell tried to plaster it on with blood and sword."[15]

Of course, Schreiner's critique of Empire was not without precedent. Apart from her quite original attack on Social Darwinism and her espousal of cultural pluralism and interracial international relations, her antiimperial ideas drew from traditional Victorian thinking. Initially expounded by Adam Smith, then carried further by Richard Cobden and John Bright, and epitomized by the speeches and writing of Gladstone and Morley, this antiimperialist viewpoint was commonly referred to as the "Little England" position, and it dominated liberal and radical politics until the 1870s. Schreiner was emphatically a Little Englander. As she surveyed the history of Western civilization, she concluded that intellectual, social, and political changes were likely to be most organic and progressive where the political unit was small. She contrasted the immense creativity of the city-states of Athens and republican Rome, of the small Jewish tribes of antiquity, of Renaissance Holland, and of Elizabethan England with the comparatively enervated condition of the "bulky, unwieldy and unnatural" historic empires.[16]

Like most nineteenth-century radicals and liberals, Schreiner believed that extended territorial control favored the growth of centralized, authoritarian rule. Even within nations, it was often the small town rather than the large city that spearheaded national progress. She claimed that "the small town of Concord, in America, has been immeasurably greater than, up to the present, have been the cities of New York, Chicago, and San Francisco combined; they might pass away as a puff of smoke to-morrow and be forgotten, but the little town is immortal in the heart of humanity for the great deeds that have been done there and the wise men who have walked in her quiet streets."[17]

Schreiner's Little England position reflected a blend of Enlightenment and romantic social theories—for example, when she echoed the sentiments of both Montesquieu and Herder in stressing that the imposition of an artificial government, no matter how enlightened, on a people was an act of "national slavery . . . disease-producing and freedom-limiting." So, too, when she argued for varieties of social freedom and well-being: "Freedom and health for a folk desiring a tribal head is the right to possess him and to live and die for him; for a people with republican instincts is the right to republican institutions, for a folk with an inclination towards monarchy, a monarchical rule." She likened the conditions for the health of nations to that of other natural forms. For example, she noted that a shellfish cannot live in a shell other than the unique one it secretes. Even the hermit crab, who inhabits shells that it has not secreted, must still choose his own shell. He would die if compelled to adopt a shell not his own, no matter how beautiful or capacious it was. Spurning abstract philosophical discussions of political theory, Schreiner held that "human institutions or governments are good or bad exactly as shells are . . . as they harmonize with the wants of the living creatures they are bound to."[18]

Schreiner was not only sensitive to the need for organic political forms; she also viewed cultural forms as equally vulnerable to toxic imperial shells. Intertwining cultural and political modes of imperial domination, she voiced her ideas through Rebekah's dream in *From Man to Man*. The dream concerns alien invaders from space who impose their ways on earthlings; resistance to their superior military techniques is futile. More technologically advanced, these invaders assume that they are morally, culturally, and politically superior to earthlings, whose ways they scorn. That scorn then becomes internalized: "Because they despised *us*, we began to despise *ourselves!*" Rebekah underscores the colonial displacement of self-respect: "[W]hen they took from us all our old laws and our old customs, when they told us all we thought right was wrong and all we had known foolishness. . . . we despised ourselves; . . . we faded and faded, as the leaves fade on an uprooted tree."[19]

Schreiner's unswerving emphasis upon cultural self-determination was uncommon among Little Englanders. In addition to her affirmation of culturally diverse customs, her focus on language preservation revealed a perceptive understanding of self and cultural identity. Since she likened a people's language to the spine of their collective awareness, she strenuously opposed British efforts to ban the Taal, the Boer tongue.[20]

She did not view a people's customs as static, however. Given her faith in the superiority of democratic forms of government, she believed that worldwide social ferment would eventually stir democratic desires. But she cautioned that democratic nations must not rush this process of social and political change; coercion in the name of democracy was still imperialism.

To be sure, her apparent resolution of the disparity between the political ideal of global freedom and equality and her advocacy of national self-determination was fraught with unexamined problems that continue to perplex us today. For example, if a people appear to want monarchical rule, how can this be determined without democratic suffrage? And is monarchical rule, even freely chosen, inimical to self-determination? Moreover, what ought to be the role of a democratic nation when faced with the denial of human rights in another nation? In short, are there no limits to achieving political and cultural self-determination? And how fundamentally is self-determination defined?

Although Schreiner ducked direct treatment of these troubling questions, she contended that dual sensitivity to cultural diversity and democratic progress was not an impossible ideal. The methods and accomplishments of a few enlightened nineteenth-century British administrators convinced her of this. Her political writing abounds in praise of the performance of three in particular: Sir George Grey, Sir William Porter, and Saul Solomon. Occasionally, Schreiner added Livingstone to her list of exemplary Englishmen in South Africa.[21] She also credited Prime Minister Gladstone with moral and political wisdom when, in 1881, he restored to Transvaal the independence England had earlier appropriated.

The model actions of these British leaders set the measure for the many others who woefully fell short. Though Schreiner singled out those who were especially intolerant, for example Lord Somerset, she condemned their faults as extensions of the ordinary Briton's limited empathy.[22] In general, she claimed, the British lacked the tact that arises from perception into another's distinct problems and needs. "We are not a sympathetic or a quickly compre-hending people; . . . we are slow and we are proud; we are shut in by a certain shell of reserve." In an English setting, this disposition was an "innoxious, venial defect," Schreiner deemed, but in South Africa it became a "deadly deficiency."[23] As a result, British officials sent to the Cape, though brave and earnest, made major mistakes, the most constant and noticeable of which were their callousness and air of superiority. The Boers resented "the cold indifference with which they were treated by their rulers, and the conscious-ness that they were regarded as a subject and inferior race."[24] According to Schreiner, if the British public and its leaders had possessed the broad understanding of the Greys, Porters, Solomons, and Livingstones, they would have recognized the fatal folly of late-Victorian British imperial policies. They would, for example, have realized how thoroughly they misunderstood the franchise issue in the Boer states, which became a major cause of the Anglo–Boer War.[25]

The Little England outlook altered during the final decades of the nine-teenth century. Those who remained wedded to the idea (most liberals had abandoned it in favor of imperial arguments) punctuated their arguments with anticapitalist overtones, but these attacks, whether they were advanced by Schreiner or by other "new radicals" and socialists, did not constitute a coherent socialist analysis of imperialism. No such analysis emerged in nineteenth-century England, a factor contributing to the division among British socialists over the wisdom of Britain's imperial and military policies.[26] The closest to a Marxist economic analysis in print was that by J. A. Hobson in *The War in South Africa* (1900). By then, Schreiner had already articulated her own economic analysis of British policies in South Africa, prefiguring Hob-son's views. Indeed, in his treatment of the South African situation, Hobson paid homage to her influence.[27]

Schreiner was anxious to dispel various misunderstandings that accom-panied the conventional use of the terms *capitalist* and *monopolist* in the discussion of South African affairs. She pointed out that the issues facing South Africa were more complex than the international problem of gross disparities in the control and distribution of wealth. Rather, this general disparity was compounded by the failure of South African monopolists, speculators, and millionaires to identify with their developing nation's future by investing in South Africa. Since the nation had an essentially agrarian economy hindered by a largely stony and barren terrain, it was, apart from its recently discovered mineral resources, poor. Consequently, its fate, its cul-tural institutions as well as its material welfare, depended almost wholly on careful development of its vast stores of mineral wealth. But before South Africans of all races could act to protect their country's natural resources, foreign speculators had seized control. Schreiner pointed out, "That they were not South African–born would in itself matter less than nothing, had they thrown in their lot with us, if in sympathies, hopes, and fears they were one with us. They are not." Not only did these speculators rape South Africa of its wealth and future security, they used this wealth to corrupt South African political life in order to augment their wealth still further.[28]

Conscious of how deeply vested British capitalist interests were in South Africa in the 1890s, Schreiner indicted the British government for conspiring with South African commercial interests. Her views, regarded in her day as overly cynical, proved sound. Though scholars debate the relative roles of the Colonial Office, the British Treasury, financial interest groups that sought new fields for investment, and "humanitarian" lobbies that promoted impe-rial policies, they now concur that an informal alliance existed among the governor of the Cape Colony, the high commissioner in South Africa, Sir Alfred Milner (1897–1905), and the firm of Wernhes-Beit (the dominant Rand mining house). As prime minister of the Cape Colony, Cecil Rhodes shaped this alliance.[29] The economic and political greed of the Uitlanders, that is, the European newcomers to the Boer republics, abetted by Rhodes and Beit's millions, became an irresistible invitation over time for the British government to take over the Boer territories. The British bribed poor Boers to attack the Uitlanders, hoping the ensuing violence would serve as a pretext for British military involvement. Schreiner was horrified by these machina-tions as well as by British inflexibility in the face of the Boer republics' President Kruger's willingness to make concessions on the franchise ques-tion.[30]

Schreiner's emphasis upon the role of international mine owners and speculators in fomenting war was a common socialist position.[31] Less com-mon was her awareness of how racism and racial inequality exacerbated general socioeconomic inequality. She saw the "labour question" of Europe simultaneously as a race question in South Africa, noting that "the natives form almost the entire body of the true wage-earning labouring class in South Africa. The European, working in mines or elsewhere, becomes almost at once in the majority of cases simply the overseer or guider of the native labourer." The large syndicates, companies, and chartered bodies that orga-nized the mineral industries in South Africa treated the skilled and unskilled natives as "machines . . . to extract the wealth of the South African conti-nent." It was in their interests to exploit their African workers, for "the more the machinery costs to keep at work, the smaller the percentage of South African wealth which reaches the hands of the speculator."[32]

Schreiner stressed that if South African laborers organized to agitate for improved working conditions they would face two formidable obstacles. Unlike their European and American counterparts, South African laborers toiled for company executives and shareholders who, as nonresidents, felt no stake either in South Africa's general economic development or in expanding mass purchasing power there. Solely interested in lowering the black workers' wages, the leading speculators and manufacturing executives wanted to create a united and uniform labor system, enacting laws that would dispossess the African of his tribal land and, in effect, force him "into a purely proletariat condition . . . always glad to sell his toil for the lowest sum that will maintain life."[33] Of even greater significance, racial politics complicated class conflict between employer and employee. Given the Social Darwinist racism of most Europeans, injustices against black workers were rationalized by both employer and employee as inevitable and right. As Schreiner explained, "even those white men, whose economic interests are identical with those of the black labourer, may be driven by race antagonism to act with the exactors." [34] In effect, working-class solidarity, indispensible to successful labor organization and strike action, was vitiated by racist sentiment among white laborers who, along with the mining executives, feared an eruption of racial warfare if the great masses of Africans mobilized for economic justice. As a result, no viable working-class resistance was possible.

Until the 1890s Schreiner had assumed that England's imperial control of South Africa would curb capitalist exploitation of Africans. Indeed, that assumption was the chief reason why many British and American liberals and clergy as well as American black groups supported England during the Anglo–Boer War. But well before the outbreak of war, Schreiner realized that England could not be counted upon anymore than the Boers to protect South African blacks.[35]

Schreiner's concern for black laborers enabled her to see through the complacent ethnocentrism that led so many liberals to assume that England protected African interests. In her attack on British imperialism, she not only drew upon traditional liberal and radical reasoning but incorporated as well a frank critique of self and national racial sentiment. She admitted from the outset that no white person was free of racial bias. At most, a "very few, most fully evolved and exceptionally endowed humans have been in the past or are even at the present day capable of carrying the sense of solidarity and social obligation across the limit of race." She acknowledged that even such rare individuals, while sympathizing with black people, still felt culturally superior, "the mists of racial prejudice occasionally blinding them too."[36] She herself could not wrest free from her own feelings of cultural superiority, as revealed in her candid reply to the question of whether she was a "negrophile." With mingled compassion and condescension toward blacks she responded:

> No—we are trying to be [a negrophile] but we are not yet. . . . It would be a lie to say that we love the black man, if by that is meant that we love him as we love the white. But we are resolved to deal with justice and mercy towards him. *We will treat him as if we loved him*: and in time the love may come. . . . we shall perhaps be able to look deep into each other's eyes and smile: as parent and child.[37]

For most people, she observed, so rudimentary was the human social instinct that a sense of collective solidarity rarely extended beyond family and class. Even a sense of identity with those of one's own nation and race was often too dim to assure "truly socialized action." An "abysmal hiatus" in morality characterized interracial relations, whether between Boer and black or Briton and black. A sensitive, generous, and caring white husband and father in one context could justify participating directly or indirectly in the mutilation and dismemberment of a black neighbor in another context.[38]

Lest Englishmen believe themselves less racist than Boers, Schreiner flaunted the record of past and current British racism. As one example, she cited the hideous cruelty that England inflicted upon the natives of India. She marshaled such evidence as that of the British compelling Indians to lick up the blood of those of their people blown from a British cannon. Further, where the Boers rather than the English formed the majority of the population, as in the Cape Colony, the legal and political position of the African and Asiatic person was far better than where the English dominated, as in Natal. Where the British were totally in power, as in Matabeleland and Mashonaland, the condition of the African was worst: "Large numbers of black Africans have been exterminated and, in recent years, a determined and practical attempt has been made to introduce a modified form of slavery under the name of compulsory labour."[39] So much for British moral superiority.

Schreiner has been accused of being harsher on British than on Boer racism.[40] Although she could be quite scathing in her criticism of Boer bigotry, she did castigate England far more severely. Aware of this charge, she justified her stance through the words of a minister in her novella *Trooper Peter Halket of Mashonaland*. The minister explains that the reason he soft-pedals the iniquity of non-Britons and focuses instead upon British racism is because he and his congregation are British: "It is my own nation, mine, which I love as a man loves his own soul, whose acts touch me." Since he yearns for England to be a truly Christian nation, its sins cut him more deeply.[41]

As Schreiner weighed the various forms of white racial bigotry, she concluded that the most cruel manifestation came from newly arrived European—including British—immigrants. In their attitude she saw complete callousness and cold contempt, rare among those who grew up among African blacks. Newcomers would often treat black men as sheer sport, delighting in "the pleasures of Bantu-hunting." By contrast, the racism of longtime residents of South Africa tended to include elements of fear of and respect for blacks.[42]

Schreiner found particularly offensive the widespread moral cant of British racial attitudes, that "greasy whine of affected sanctity and humanity." Given Britons' need to view themselves as righteous, they adopted bizarre and sordid self-defenses. When, Schreiner noted, an Englishman "desires an adjoining Native territory, he sighs, and folds his hands; he says: 'It's a very sad thing the way these Natives go on! They believe in witches and kill them. I really can't let this go on! It's my duty to interfere.'" He then proceeds to kill several thousand blacks in the name of saving witches, and he takes over their land with its rich mineral reserves, while "the dishomed and beaten Natives" become his laborers. Whereas the Boers, like most peoples, are forthright about their aggressive intent, the British, with a "hideous deformity, peculiar to ourselves," try to "gloss over our acts of greed, injustice and self-seeking."[43]

Schreiner might have concluded, of course, as the British Marxist H. M. Hyndman did, that the exploitative patterns of both Boer and Briton justified complete neutrality with regard to their conflict, that the only worthy cause was that of the African.[44] Such a perspective was far easier for Hyndman to take, removed as he was from the daily reminders of British abuse of both Boers and blacks in South Africa. Schreiner ultimately reached a similar conclusion, but only after heartbreaking evidence of the extent of Boer racism after the Anglo–Boer War.

Until the outbreak of the Anglo–Boer War Schreiner hoped it was possible to pierce British cant through an appeal to the British conscience. She sought to demonstrate how the notion of imperial "duty" generated political behavior at odds with traditional Christian and secular principles of human dignity, freedom, and fair play. The Jameson Raid and consequent British conquest of Matabeleland and Mashonaland stirred her to write a novella of rage and hope for moral change in British policies. The incident most immediately inciting her book was the hanging of black political prisoners in Bulawayo, a photograph of which, serving as a frontispiece to her novella, depicts the casual demeanor of the nine British men involved. They loll with calm pride around the swinging bodies, one man smoking a cigar.[45] In this novella, *Trooper Peter Halket of Mashonaland* (1897), Schreiner highlighted the nature and consequences of British moral hypocrisy, particularly with regard to racial violence. Since most English men and women professed Christian values, Schreiner, despite her antipathy to Christianity, deliberately cast her moral issues in Christian terms.

The heart of her story is an allegoric dialogue between a stranger, representing Jesus in contemporary guise, and a young British soldier employed by Rhodes's Chartered Company. Schreiner took pains not to frame through the words of her Jesus values that she did not uphold as well. Though most of her nonfiction writings on South African affairs (excluding public addresses) were directed to policy makers and to the politically educated and sophisticated public, her novella was aimed at the broad reading public, especially in England. Their conversion to antiimperialism was her goal, and she hoped to reach them through their ability to identify with Peter Halket's evolving moral maturity. Although scholars and literary critics disagree over both the political and the literary value of this work, it offers us valuable insight into the intensity of Schreiner's antiimperial and antiracial approach.[46] It also reflects her faith in the power of words to change minds.

Trooper Simon Peter Halket, the eponymous protagonist, is a quintessential late-Victorian young British male. He aspires to emulate Cecil Rhodes, make a fortune in South Africa, and return to England as director of a mining company. For him, wealth is a means to political power, for he hopes in time to become a member of Parliament and then, "when he had millions, Sir Peter Halket, Privy Councillor!" He views his acquisition of wealth and power as a way to disguise his humble origins, longing to rescue his beloved mother from the drudgery of washing clothes "for those stuck-up nincompoops of fine ladies!" Given his Christian training, he has qualms about his ambitions, but during the daytime he ignores these qualms and participates in routine forms of racial violence. As narrator of the book, he makes clear to the reader that he stops short of floggings and hangings, though he proudly affirms that with his rifle he has "potted as many niggers as any man in our troop, I bet." With comparable delight, he describes his callous treatment of "nigger girls" but claims pridefully that he is not a sadist. Admiring men who treat blacks as mere property, he warmly approves Rhodes's plan for forcing blacks to till

British land. He prizes Rhodes as "death on niggers" when Rhodes refuses to punish a white man for thrashing a black man to death.[47]

In time, however, Peter Halket's Christian upbringing makes him susceptible to occasional nightly flickers of conscience. One night, alone on an isolated kopje, he dreams of a stranger, a Jew from Palestine, paying him a visit. The Jew stokes the flames of Peter's conscience and gradually converts him to a humanism that embraces all people. During this conversion, the stranger exposes the hypocritical Christianity practiced by the Chartered Company and, through vivid imagery, depicts the dignity, sensitivity, and heroism of individuals of all races and classes.

Peter's conversion forms the first part of the novella. The second part treats the behavioral implications of his moral metamorphosis. The stranger invites Peter to become a messenger to the English people, to summon them to end their support of imperialism. Peter resists; he thinks he lacks credibility with the English because of his working-class background. Nor would his credibility in South Africa be greater, he argues, because the Dutch would refuse to listen to an Englishman and the South African Englishmen would regard him as too new to the country and, again, too poor. The stranger urges Peter to take his message to one man, clearly Cecil Rhodes, though his name is never stated. The lengthy, probing questions the stranger wants Peter to ask of this man disclose Schreiner's sense of Rhodes's decisive role in sustaining imperial violence in South Africa. Transmuting her fury at Rhodes into metaphor, she has the stranger instruct Peter to hold before the man the image of his soul as a healthy streamlet that, instead of flowing to a great sea to nourish new areas of beauty and fertility, cascades into a chasm where it forms a stagnant and poisonous marsh. Though the stranger offers other rhetorical strategies if Peter's initial forays fail, Peter, again, pleads his humble origins and incapacities. The stranger assures Peter that it is not the messenger but the message that matters and argues further that if Peter confesses to his own sins his credibility will be enhanced. Ultimately, realism wins out: The stranger recognizes that he is asking too much of Peter. He retreats, urging Peter simply to enact the gospel of love in his own life. This, gratefully, Peter does.

The conversion of Peter Halket from "nigger-hunter" to Christian protagonist is complete when, in the final part of the novella, Peter opposes the British policies that foment large-scale slaughter of African blacks. After a comic episode in which Peter's comrades mock his awkward efforts to convey his newly acquired Christian idealism, Peter releases a black captive whom he has been charged with guarding and shooting or hanging the next day. In the fracas following the captive's release, Peter is killed. The other troopers view him not as the tragic martyr into whom Schreiner has transformed him but merely as one who had lost his mind.

Unfortunately, few real-life readers identifed with Peter's moral transformation.[48] Even more troublesome, Schreiner encountered humanitarian Britons who defended Rhodes and British policy to crush the Boers as a means to promote black interests. Schreiner rejoined, "*Now* no person feels more strongly our duty to the native than I do. But we cannot do wrong today that good may come tomorrow." She added that one must treat both Boer and black as "a man and a brother," according to the Golden Rule.[49] Unable to convert public opinion through her novella, Schreiner turned to direct political polemic in which she combined appeals to both conscience and self-interest. This last attempt, completed four months before the Anglo–Boer War broke out, was *An English South African's View of the Situation*, also published as *The South African Question*. In this treatise, she still felt somewhat optimistic that an appeal to traditions of daring and enlightened British statesmanship would evoke the desired response.[50] Though moral and humanitarian arguments continued to shape her rhetoric, she focused more directly than ever before on how British ambitions to conquer the two Boer republics so as to establish a unified South Africa patently did not serve English self-interest. Such enterprise, she reasoned, would lead to needless cost in British lives and resources. She pointed out that the British assimilation of the Dutch population was advancing rapidly without coercion. The Boers were steadily adopting English manners and language. Swelling numbers of young Boer males matriculated at British universities and entered occupations with British colleagues. Even more significant, intermarriage between Briton and Boer, rare a generation ago, was becoming commonplace: "As a result . . . in another generation the fusion will be complete."[51] If an impatient England forced that union prematurely, Schreiner argued, the unifying process would be imperiled. Casting England as both a fool and a vulgar rapist, she assailed it for having "torn and forced . . . the rose of South African national existence before its time . . . A flower pushed artificially open by coarse fingers . . . premature and violent."[52]

Further appealing to British self-interest, Schreiner predicted that the cost of military conquest and unification would be enormous. In the final section of *The South African Question*, she repeatedly asked "WHO GAINS BY WAR?" Reviewing the consequences of war for everyone involved—England, its soldiers and queen; British, Dutch, and black South Africans; and even the financiers and speculators whom many regarded as the most likely beneficiaries of English conquest of the two Boer republics—she could in every instance discern only tragic loss. Whereas military and political experts held that 20,000 soldiers could crush the republics in a few months, Schreiner foresaw that such "victory" would take at least 150,000 soldiers and several years. Although her fears about the war were ignored as unduly pessimistic, the toll of the war exceeded her grimmest forecasts.[53] British predictions that the war would be over by Christmas 1899 and cost the British taxpayer little in lives and money were, as Schreiner prophesied, miserably short of the truth.

Amply familiar with the history and psychology of the Boers, Schreiner warned that their democratic political and military structures assured their zealous mass struggle to preserve their national autonomy. She foresaw that their staunch loyalty and fierce courage in resistance guaranteed that, "though every city be taken and every village and farmhouse burnt, the people is yet to crush."[54]

Central to Schreiner's espousal of the Boer cause and to her certainty of dauntless Boer resistance was her special reverence for Boer women. Even as late as 1910 when she was thoroughly disgusted with Boer politics, she reflected upon the female Boer spirit: "When you saw that room full of strong, determined, iron-willed women, you understood all of the South African war afresh, the glory of that struggle of a handful of folk against a mighty folk, and also the narrowness and hardness of South African life."[55] A victorious England would need to leave an army of occupation to try to sustain its supremacy. But though a temporary silence might follow the end of war, there would be no peace, since Boer women would "breed up again a race like to the first." On various occasions, in describing the Boers' invincibility, Schreiner evoked the image of the South African red mierkat. Overcome by a mastiff and almost dead, the little mierkat would creep back into its hole in the red African earth, "torn and bleeding" as though in total defeat "but alive—" and, crucially, prepared to resume a normal independent life at a later time.[56] England's triumph, in short, would be Pyrrhic.

Schreiner's appeal to British self-interest was no more persuasive than her exhortations to the British moral conscience. As war grew imminent, her hopes of converting the British public faded. She realized that she had overestimated the integrity of the British conscience. She had "never believed possible" that the nation she had long admired could "set her knee on the necks of two small, brave peoples, striving to force life from them while with eager hands she grasped their gold and lands." England, she declared, "is dead to me."[57]

With the eruption of war, Schreiner released her anger and sadness through bitter prophecies. The dominant motif of her wartime writing was the self-defeating stupidity of the British decision to pursue war: "[E]very farmhouse which the British soldiers were burning down to-day was a torch lighting the British Empire in South Africa to its doom; every trench which the brave English soldiers dug was a part of the tomb of England." Although England appeared to be committing murder in South Africa, in reality, Schreiner claimed, it was really committing imperial suicide.[58]

This prophecy informs her short story "Eighteen-Ninety-Nine." The quotation beneath the title of the story is "Thou fool, that which thou sowest is not quickened unless it die."[59] Briefly, the story surrounds two independent, sturdy, and brave Boer widows, one whose husband and three sons were lost in various early- and mid-nineteenth-century conflicts, and the other, her daughter-in-law, whose husband likewise dies in battle. Surmounting their tragedies, the two widows live intimately together, capably managing their farm while raising the daughter-in-law's son. This remarkably gifted boy becomes the center of their lives and of their hopes for the future. The son adores both women, especially the grandmother, whose inspiring accounts of Boer history spark his imagination and heroic resolve. His adolescence coincides with escalating tensions in the 1890s between England and the Boer republics. When he is eighteen and packing for college, the Anglo–Boer War breaks out. No less fervent in his love for his country than other Boers, he abandons his college plans, despite his mother's bitter tears, and joins the army with his grandmother's silent blessing. Predictably, the boy dies in battle, but he is so adroit in warfare that his death requires three bullet wounds and four bayonet stabs, arousing awe as well as grief over his death. Undaunted, his grandmother sets out to sow seeds on their property to sustain her people in battle and affirm her faith in the future. Though by 1901 both women have died, their farmhouse burned down, their belongings the subject of amused curiosity to English soldiers, and their land the property of speculators, all is not lost. The dead still possess their own country and, "from among the long waving grasses, keep watch over the land."[60]

Schreiner's forecast of the resurrection of Boer culture and South Africa's political autonomy is yet more explicit in her allegory "Seeds a-Growing," composed during her internment in Hanover. In this first-person narrative, The Spirit of Freedom visits Schreiner while she meditates on the side of a kopje. The Spirit assures her that in spite of the devastation that envelops her, indeed because of it, freedom grows: "At the foot of every scaffold which rises in town or village, on every spot in the barren veld where men with hands tied and eyes blindfolded are led out to meet death, as ropes are drawn and the foreign bullets fly, I count the blood drops a-falling; and I know that my seed is sown. . . . The day will come when I will return and gather my harvest."[61]

After the signing of the Peace of Vereeniging in May 1902 and the establishment of self-government in the two Boer republics in 1907, South Africans pondered the nature of an independent union. The same arguments that Schreiner enlisted before and during the Anglo–Boer War to oppose imperialism in general and British policies in South Africa in particular form the core of her postwar thoughts on the development of South Africa. She called the various schemes for a new South African union, popular among South African politicians, "absolutely monstrous" and threatening the rights and self-determination of all people, especially blacks.[62]

Schreiner articulated her constitutional ideas in *Closer Union* (1909), a work that initially appeared in the December 22, 1908, issue of the *Transvaal Leader* as an extended reply to twelve questions the journal's editor had submitted to her. She responded with statements of political principles as well as specific policy recommendations. She was deeply committed to a federal plan for union. Among the various constitutional proposals that the South African National Convention considered during winter and spring 1908–9 was a federal arrangement, a proposal advanced by the delegates from Natal, granting considerable autonomy to the participating states. The proposal's chief advocates outside of the convention were Olive and Will Schreiner and J. H. Hofmeyr. As an exponent of the federal union, she was clearly this time not alone. In fact, in the years immediately after the Anglo–Boer War, most political leaders assumed that the only way political unification of South Africa could come about, if at all, would be by a federal plan. Nevertheless, by 1908, with the resurgence of Afrikaner power in the Cape and self-government in the Boer republics, Afrikaner leaders concluded that, since they were no longer subject to the dominance of British South Africans, a unitary rather than a federal form of government would be more suitable. The supporters of federalism dwindled when key federalists such as Smuts, John Merriman, and Sir Henry De Villiers, the chief justice of the Cape who presided over the National Convention, shifted their support to a unitary constitution. For Schreiner, however, the case for federalism remained incontrovertible.

Schreiner's loyalty to federalism was founded upon her belief in both cultural pluralism and small units of government, an outlook rare among South African politicians. She argued that federalism was preeminently appropriate for South Africa because of the nation's vast territory and diverse populations. A centralized government, she feared, would favor authoritarian control whereas "a number of strongly organized and individualized though confederate states, will present a far greater obstacle to the undue dominance of any interest, class or individual."[63]

Guided by her vision of decentralized federation and racial equality as the foundation for a new constitution, Schreiner addressed a variety of questions specific to the constitution's design. In regard to the distribution of power between a central parliament and local parliaments, she favored local control of all matters except transportation, communications (posts, telegraphs), external coast defense, interstate and external commerce, and, once South Africa gained autonomy, foreign affairs. Like the American Congress, the central parliament would be composed of two houses: a lower house elected on the basis of population and an upper house composed of an equal number of representatives from each state (as a means of protecting the smaller states). Schreiner had long admired the American federal system with its bicameral legislature.[64]

Among various other advantages of decentralization, Schreiner noted, was that of permitting distinct states to pilot experiments in government, education, and the arts and thereby stimulate one another's political and cultural growth. Such flexibility would be more likely to spur progress than if South Africa were to attempt a wholesale transformation of political and cultural life with its accompanying infringement on traditional tribal or regional rights, possessions, and privileges. In any event, a federal plan would leave open the possibility for greater unification in the future, whereas to shift from centralization to a federal plan would entail severe dislocation.[65]

To those who feared that political decentralization would foment war, Schreiner reminded her readers that brutal wars often occurred among peoples who were united and where one party felt the union "to be unequal and not for their advantage." Even practical economic factors mitigated against centralization. Schreiner refuted the argument that unification would alleviate the ongoing economic depression, promote rapid economic growth, and reduce taxation. She feared that the advocates of unification were kindling illusions of a "new Father Christmas who will drop a pound into every empty pocket." She explained that wide-scale depression was an inevitable aftermath of war and "the reckless indulgence in building and other speculations" that had ensued. Since landowning people had invested their money in restoring their farms and property, capital was lacking for other enterprises. What South Africa needed, she suggested, was not unification but "three successive good agricultural years," which would supply the surplus capital for industrial and commercial investments. Though free trade within a unified South Africa would be beneficial, the taxes on intercolonial trade were not the problem. The taxes on overseas imports were what was choking the nation's economy.[66]

Schreiner was convinced that the seeds of unity in South Africa were present and simply needed time to mature and flourish. She was relieved that the political boundaries of existing states did not generally correspond to racial divisions. Races were woven everywhere "like the tints in a well-shot Turkish carpet. They cannot be separated." Races had mingled, in fact, for decades. Schreiner alluded to the common South African household composed of an English father, a Boer mother, children of both nationalities, a German governess, a "half-caste" cook (part Boer, part black), "half-caste" housemaid (part English, part "Hottentot"), pure "Hottentot" nurse girl, Basuto groom, and "Kaffir" bootboy.[67] Not only did races cut through political boundaries but so too did commercial interests. Consequently, though the historic political divisions were important, they lacked the deep organic cohesiveness that bred inflexibility. For Schreiner, the essential unifying reality of South Africa was indeed its racial/cultural diversity. Its very multiplicity of cultures, as of its plant and animal life, created a unique national bond.[68] Unless the new constitution permitted a racially pluralistic and egalitarian society to emerge, South Africa and, along with it, Schreiner's vision of a racial "choral symphony" would be doomed.[69]

Hoping that races would continue their public and private intermixing, Schreiner thought that the most supportive method to encourage this was through the strengthening of individual political states. Her concern for local freedom made her cautious about efforts to include in the new union Rhodesia, Basutoland, Swaziland, the Bechuanaland Protectorate, and Nyasaland. Eventually, hoping these territories would become part of the union but "with due regard to the rights of all concerned," she advocated deferring this question to a later time. She argued that if the small native states were left alone for fifty or sixty years to follow their own course of evolution, blacks would be far more culturally vigorous and progressive than "if they are all forced into the vortex of our so-called modern civilization."[70] She therefore regretted the annexation of Bechuanaland and the Cape Colony and opposed the annexing of Mashonaland and Matebeleland with any other African state. So too she opposed the merging of Natal with the Cape Colony.

Schreiner stressed both the number and significance of blacks to South Africa's well-being. She reminded her readers that of the roughly nine million inhabitants of South Africa, approximately eight million were Africans, primarily Bantus, with a much smaller number of "yellow varieties of African races," "half-castes," and Asiatics. She noted that the black population was steadily on the increase and that South Africa relied on blacks as producers and consumers: "We want more and always more of him [African]—to labour in our mines, to build our railways, to work in our fields, to perform our domestic labour, and to buy our goods."[71] She did not approve of delegating manual labor to blacks, but her eagerness to persuade white readers to adopt more progressive views on black rights led her to appeal to white self-interest in this fashion.

In *Closer Union* Schreiner defended the extension of the same political and economic opportunities to blacks as were available to whites. Unless such treatment prevailed, a host of horrors would befall the country. The suppressed talents of blacks would become "subterraneous and disruptive forces." Though in the short run white supremacist policies would "pay us admirably both as to labour and lands," benefits would be short-lived. A modern-day Jeremiah, Schreiner enumerated the various racist policies she feared being adopted and etched their pernicious consequences.[72] As her final appeal to white self-interest, she held that whites themselves could not progress amid millions of subjected peoples. The white disdain for physical and manual labor and the continued assignment of that labor to unfree peoples would "ultimately take from us our strength and our freedom. . . . If we raise the dark man we shall rise with him; if we kick him under our feet, he will hold us fast by them."[73]

There were a few South Africans who sympathized with Schreiner's position on the "native question," but even they thought unification would hasten an egalitarian society. Schreiner foresaw that British guilt over the Anglo–Boer War would prompt England to be swayed by Dutch antagonism to any black political rights, even to the point of eradicating the limited black franchise in the Cape Colony.[74] She understood that the drive for unity was a drive for white unity only, as revealed in the Englishman's frequent comment "that it was only by Unification that we could 'wash out' the native."[75]

Schreiner strongly advocated that the federal franchise be absolutely democratic, with no distinction as to race, color, or sex. Some residency requirement would be reasonable. On the other hand, with regard to local and state parliaments, she proposed a strategic rather than principled policy. Knowing the Dutch-dominated states would probably not accede to black voting rights in the near future but wanting at least to protect the Cape's limited franchise to blacks, she preferred to let each state decide its own criteria. She deviated from her commitment to racial democracy even further in her espousal of a rigorous educational test, because "it may serve as a stimulus in the direction of education to both poor whites and natives." She admitted that such a test, whose "passage" level she never clarified, would exclude many blacks from voting, particularly those living under tribal systems. She, therefore, proposed that "some arrangement should be made for their electing a certain if small number of direct representatives."[76] Clearly uneasy that such temporizing measures might halt the realization of full racial democracy, she advocated linking the voters' roll of each state to the number of representatives each would send to the central parliament, thereby encouraging states to widen the basis of their franchise.

Schreiner more unambiguously revealed her commitment to expunge the divisive prejudices of the past in her solution to the location and design of the new capital. She envisioned it "built in a small, neutral territory and entirely anew." Most of South Africa's lovely old towns were saturated with local British and Dutch traditions and chauvinism, which alienated outsiders. Moreover, all existing state capitals were closely connected to commercial or financial centers, arousing anxiety that business influences would exert undue power in the new government. Consequently, the capital would best be situated in its own territory, under its own laws, "a city in which every South African was equally a citizen and at home, . . . there should be nothing in the new capital to recall the divisions of the past."[77]

Schreiner's enthusiasm for the new government, and her belief in a federation that respected differences and healed ethnic divisions, shaped her vision of the capital's architecture and layout. The buildings would blend simple Dutch design ("the old farm-house ideal") with African and Moorish patterns. In homage to South Africa's distinctive topography, the buildings, no more than two stories high with "simple, square, solid, white pillars forming colonnades around our squares," would be laid out in wide squares, evocative of the country's spacious landscape and wide skies. The adjoining Moorish and African courtyards and cloisters would enhance the flow of air, yet exclude excessive heat and wind. Schreiner expected that the capital would also serve as a center of culture, with libraries, museums, art galleries, sporting events, and scientific conventions.[78]

Concluding *Closer Union*, Schreiner described the political leadership South Africa would need in the years ahead: racially pluralist and democratic. The country's governing figures must understand and sympathize with all of South Africa's people, prize the unique virtues of each of its people's culture, and work to reconcile the races. Schreiner allowed that these leaders need not be saints or heroes but simply men (in this treatise she did not raise the matter of female political equality and leadership) "with a clear head and large heart, organically incapable of self-seeking or racial prejudice."[79] Aware that she seemed naive in expecting to find such humane navigators of state, she claimed to have known men of this kind in private life and cited exceptional leaders in the history of all races. Without such guidance, the South African union would "be a poor peddling thing when we [finally] have it—perhaps bloody."[80]

Not content simply to call for such leadership, Schreiner lobbied among various South African political figures who seemed equal to the challenge. She devoted most of her energy to her brother Will and, to some extent, to Cronwright. Even after the Anglo–Boer War, Will exercised formidable influence in South African affairs. Schreiner was cognizant of how unpopular were Cronwright and Will's views on native rights and federation, but she urged them to exert their utmost to attract converts. She acknowledged that neither of them commanded the true politician's psychological gifts of "simply a perception of what *is*, and what is not possible."[81] It troubled her that they did not plan strategy in concert. She chided Will for losing allies by failing to inform them in advance of his actions, for being too disputatious, arrogant, and tactless, and for alienating potential followers through his unconcealed lack of sympathy with them.[82] Still, she conceded that those who did have remarkable political instincts rarely possessed the moral clarity and courage for which a country had much more need.[83] It was patently difficult for South African political leaders to combine shrewd political pragmatism and moral tenacity with democratic principles in a time of such political ferment. Not surprisingly, Schreiner verified her naiveté; she did not find the quality of leadership for which she longed.

Schreiner's constitutional proposals, moreover, received scant support. The South African Parliament adopted a white supremacist unification scheme, the Act of Union (1909), which easily secured British parliamentary approval (1910).[84] Schreiner was not surprised by the outcome. The cozy complicity of former British and Boer foes—"buttering down of each," as she described it—emerged from their shared interest in white domination of South Africa as well as British guilt over the treatment of Boers during the war.[85] Indeed, in negotiating the Peace of Vereeniging, the British acceded to white demands that the franchise of blacks not be considered until after the introduction of self-government, and then only upon the consent of the white electorate.[86] Despite Schreiner's years of support and harassment in defense of the Boers, she, too, became a target of Boer abuse, ostracized for her unconventional ways. She finally saw that the same narrow morality and intolerance that led Boers to scorn her for taking a walk with a male friend infected their treatment of blacks.[87] Together, Briton and Boer colluded to snuff out black hopes for a racially egalitarian society.

This joint Boer and British racism took many forms. In 1906, Schreiner noted that Natal and Johannesburg Boers and Britons were planning a mighty native war as a pretext for the complete subjugation of blacks. By 1909, Schreiner viewed blacks as pawns in the clutches of Rand capitalists and retrograde Boers: If the black workers strike, they "will be shot down like dogs." She noted that Indians were being "hunted like wild beasts."[88] These policies prior to the Act of Union were intensified by subsequent legislation. In 1911, Schreiner wrote Carpenter of her fury over white working men's agitation to enact a law excluding blacks from skilled-labor jobs.[89] It was passed shortly thereafter as part of the Mines and Works Act (1911). Worse was to follow. The Defence Act of 1912 established a white active citizen force, and, a year later, the Parliament passed the Native Land Act, which laid down the principle of territorial segregation, restricting black ownership of land. The Native Land Act confined land occupancy rights of four million Africans to less than 8 percent of the country's land area, whereas one and a half million whites had unlimited access to the remaining 92 percent. Prohibited from buying or leasing land in their own country, except in infertile sections, blacks were doomed, Schreiner proclaimed, to slavery within their own infant nation.[90]

Schreiner wrestled with the question of how best to support black rights without arousing even stronger white racism or abetting black revolutionary violence. She was so fearful of black uprisings and interracial warfare that, until she wrote *Closer Union*, she deliberately refrained from speaking publicly about Briton and Boer plans to eliminate black rights. Confiding her fears to Will, she wondered: "[O]ne dare not speak the full fact about the future for fear of rousing the native to despair . . . and yet how is one to act and write with force unless one does speak of the 'great open secret.' "[91] Until 1910 she worried that an appeal by black Africans to the English government might aggravate racial tensions still further. With extraordinary prescience, she warned that white anxiety over possible black political power in the Cape Colony would spark whites to stir up a war scare to deprive blacks of such power.

Schreiner's inability to stem the surging of white racism sorely challenged her political and moral idealism. Occasionally she lapsed into cynicism. The nadir of her political engagement came in 1905 when she lamented: "[P]olitics interest me very little at present one way or another. The apostolic days are passed and the day of politics pure and simple has arrived, and party politics . . . are most highly distasteful to me."[92] Usually, however, she refused despair. She took refuge in the words of one of her favorite poets, Robert Burns, which she paraphrased to Will: "I dont [sic] know whether the highest moments in life are not those when we fight on in blank dispair [sic], with no hope, fighting just because we must." She also took comfort in acknowledging that human intentions are often betrayed in their implementation.[93] She voiced this compassion for human limits in a key passage in *From Man to Man* when Rebekah hears her son burst out angrily about his mixed-race half-sister, Sartje, "She is a nigger! . . . and I'll never walk with her again." Rebekah responds, "I hope, I believe, I know the day will come when you will regret utterly every slighting, every unkind word or act, that you have given place towards Sartje."[94]

It is difficult to discern what Schreiner's views on black insurrection were following the passage of white supremacist legislation after the Act of Union. When she spoke earlier of racial violence, her phrases were saturated with the same vague, terrified images of anarchy and revenge that filled the imaginations of white racists. She never delineated the constructive dimensions of black militance as she did for suffragette militance or for other European and American revolutionary movements. Perhaps in this respect more than any other, Schreiner exposed the white liberal prejudices that some scholars and writers have accused her of harboring.

Yet, compared with the women's suffrage movement in the early twentieth century, the state of African black political organization and collective resistance was at best embryonic. Two rival black associations dominated the period between 1902 and 1914, representing a small segment of the black population. Neither group was able to mount concerted resistance to the Act of Union. Because of historic religious and tribal differences among Africans, black leaders faced considerable difficulty in uniting their disenfranchised constituency for political resistance. Consequently, black rebels, Schreiner rightly predicted, would be "shot down like dogs."[95] Given the slim chance that their revolts would produce positive results, Schreiner's failure to explore the viable alternatives within black militancy possibly reflected both her pacifist disposition and her political realism.

At heart, any appraisal of Schreiner's amalgam of liberal and radical approaches to South African politics pivots on the question of whether a peaceful transition to a multiracial democratic government and society was possible, whether the acute fragmentation and divisions could be healed. If we conclude from hindsight that racial and economic forces precluded this prospect and that a black revolutionary struggle was inevitable, then Schreiner's tireless campaigning among South African white leaders exposes her blindness to the depths of white liberal racism. Yet, if we attempt to assess the situation from her perspective within the still politically fluid times in which she wrote, we may legitimately claim that it was too early for her to reach such a pessimistic conclusion.

Like so many other facets of her thought and behavior, Schreiner's politics defies easy categorizing. Were she a man, able to enter directly into political processes, we could more clearly assess the precise character of her blend of realism and idealism, or liberalism and radicalism, in her treatment of South African political questions. Lacking that kind of evidence, we can at best explore the variety of her political voices, from her thundering jeremiads and evocative, original visions of a transformed South Africa to her cogent political arguments for a decentralized and culturally pluralistic constitution; from her penetrating criticisms of all forms of imperial domination to her shrewd appraisals of South African leaders and political processes. The sweep and grandeur of Schreiner's political outlook admittedly involve much that is superficial. At times she was certainly naive. (Did she ever truly believe white South Africans would vote for a racially plural, democratic constitution or that a charismatic leader would appear to garner support for such a constitution?) At other times she surpassed her most brilliant political contemporaries in South Africa in her understanding of the nature and course of South African affairs.

Postcard photograph of the mission station at Wittebergen, captioned by Olive
Schreiner: "The window of the room I was born in is hidden by the tree. The
building on the left is the church." (Photo: NELM Grahamstown, South Africa)

Ruins of Fouché's house, Klein Ganna Hoek, Cradock, where Schreiner was
governess in 1875 and 1876 and began *The Story of an African Farm*. (Photo:
NELM Grahamstown, South Africa)

Olive Schreiner, early 1870s. (INIL 1138. South African Library, Cape Town, South Africa)

Eastbourne, England, 1881. Olive Schreiner with her brothers Fred (far left) and Will (far right), Fred's wife, Emma, and Fred's son, Wilfred. (The Library, University of the Witwatersrand, Johannesburg, South Africa)

Frontispiece for original edition of *Trooper Peter Halket of Mashonaland.* (J1337:
Cape Archives Depot, Cape Town, South Africa)

S. C. Cronwright-Schreiner and Olive Schreiner, The Homestead, Kimberley,
1895–1898. (Photo: NELM Grahamstown, South Africa)

1899

Olive Schreiner, 1-7-1899, Rembrandt Studio, Johannesburg. (INIL 3183.
South African Library, Cape Town, South Africa)

Olive Schreiner, 1908, E. Peters, photographer. (INIL 3186. South African Library, Cape Town, South Africa)

August 13, 1921: The tomb where Olive Schreiner is buried at the summit of Buffelskop. (Photo: NELM Grahamstown, South Africa)

5

"The highest heaven"

THE ANDROGYNOUS VISION

Throw the puppy into the water: if it swims, well;
if it sinks, well; but do not tie a rope round its
throat and weight it with a brick, and then assert its
incapacity to keep afloat.

Olive Schreiner, *Woman and Labour*

AMONG SCHREINER'S VARIOUS social causes, feminism was preeminent. Its favored place did not stem from a belief that women's plight was more desperately in need of redress than racial or social class oppression but stemmed, rather, from her daily experience of the injury to women and society resulting from the Victorian construction of gender identity and relationships. Unlike her campaigns for other public causes, which commanded her attention intermittently, feminism was a lifelong absorption, evident in her fiction and nonfiction from adolescence to her death. If she could identify and help remove the "rope" and "brick" submerging women's lives, she would have realized her premier curative goal.

Given how steadfast Schreiner's feminist advocacy remained, it should not surprise anyone that her feminist writing is most responsible for her worldwide reputation as a pioneering thinker. Schreiner's most focused treatment of the women's question, *Woman and Labour,* became widely regarded as the "Bible of the Woman's Movement." Constance Lytton spoke for countless feminists when she hailed Schreiner as the author, "more than any other . . . [who] has rightly interpreted the woman's movement and symbolized and immortalised it by her writing."[1] Far fewer people were familiar with her writing on race, South African politics, religion, pacifism, and socialism.

The urgency of Schreiner's feminism has, of course, specific biographical roots: the earlier discussed trauma of her sister Ellie's death, Schreiner's longing to mother and be mothered, her search for a more viable model of female authority and power than that represented by her mother and by British women in general, and her anger over constraints on her opportunities for education, employment, and heterosexual friendships and love. As we have seen, she discerned an insidious, symbiotic alliance between patriarchal norms and Christianity, which judged her adoption of free thought unfeminine as well as sinful. The need to redefine her female identity was imperative if she were to move from her persecuted, marginal status to a more central, agential place in her culture.

Although the personal wellspring for Schreiner's feminism is obvious, no less formative was her deeply felt compassion for the distress of other women. Crucially, she recognized that her circumstances were not idiosyncratic and unrelated to other women's concerns. Yet she was also sensitive to gender sources of female misery quite different from her own, and her empathy for these women extended to her feminist consciousness. When, for example, she detailed the psychologically bruised lives of married women in conventional middle-class settings and of women of mixed race, she drew upon personal observation as opposed to direct personal experience. Her compassion for these women fired her criticism of dominant Victorian gender assumptions and arrangements as surely as her own suffering.

Schreiner's feminism involved a tripartite transformative process: the overcoming of female self-hatred and dependency through equal opportunity with men for meaningful, productive, wage-earning labor; the reformulation of individual identity freed from the socially constructed bifurcation of feminine and masculine personality; the resolution of sex antagonism through the comradeship of "new women" and "new men" in work, friendship, and love. To be sure, Schreiner never set forth her commitment to this triple goal systematically. Despite her unremitting engagement with women's issues and her international fame as a cogent feminist writer, she offered no comprehensive and coherent feminist philosophy. I doubt that even her extensive, interdisciplinary study on women, destroyed during the Anglo–Boer War, would have met her ambitions to provide just that. Nevertheless, the entire fabric of her feminist thought becomes evident in her lifework looked at whole.

Particularly with regard to gender identity formation, Schreiner relied upon her fiction to communicate the subjective reality of gender. Frequently, too, it is her correspondence that glistens with nonsystematic insights into women's lives. In her letters she permitted herself tentative, unresolved broodings on gender and sexuality, which she would not bare in public.[2] As a result, though *Woman and Labour* set forth Schreiner's feminist views more completely and convincingly than any of her other published works, it must be seen as the "fragment" she termed it.[3] She recognized that its fragmentary nature could easily lead to a distorted conception of what her feminism encompassed.

Much of *Woman and Labour* deals with middle-class female parasitism, conveying the impression that Schreiner's basic concern was with middle-class women. Subsequent scholars, relying heavily upon this work, naturally conclude that she was oblivious to the straits of working-class women. Failing to study her other writings, they are unaware, for example, of her staunch support for female trade unions.

In Schreiner's original version of *Woman and Labour*, middle-class parasitism constituted only one chapter. As initially drafted, the volume included a number of chapters on working-class women's labor and over 100 pages addressing male parental and sexual roles, matters scarcely touched upon in the published version.[4] The destruction of pertinent notes in the military looting of her home in Johannesburg precluded her piecing back together that original draft. A study, then, of her other writings on gender issues, including correspondence, is indispensable to putting the scope of her feminism in proper perspective.

In calling Schreiner a feminist, I apply a term foreign to her vocabulary. The word rarely appeared in turn-of-the-century English.[5] In her time she would be designated a "new woman," a champion of the women's movement or "the cause," and a theorist on "the woman question." As with feminist ideology in our own time, these Victorian and turn-of-the-century concepts cover widely divergent attitudes. The common denominator was a shared sense of gender inequity and constraint in some or many facets of living. Most feminists deplored the sexual objectification and abuse of women and sought greater female autonomy in redefining gender relationships. Feminists then as now, however, held markedly divergent views on family, marriage, sexuality, female nature and destiny, strategies for social change and for relationships among women of different social, ethnic, and racial groups. Schreiner's place in this panorama of beliefs was a complex one and, as will become clear, often at odds with mainstream feminist opinion in Western culture.

Until World War I the organized women's movement in England and South Africa was primarily concerned with the interests of white middle-class women. It focused upon such liberal issues as voting rights (at least for propertied women), legal equity with men of their class on matters of property holding, divorce, and educational opportunities. Though the struggle for sexual autonomy permeated their campaigns for legal and political rights, a preponderance of feminists adhered to most Victorian strictures on proper female behavior and appearance.[6] Though they would dispute scientific allegations of female intellectual inferiority relative to men, most feminists assumed women were fundamentally different from men: less aggressive, violent, and egoistic; more nurturant, self-sacrificing, peace-loving, intuitive, and adroit in interpersonal relations. Very few Western feminists believed women to have sexual appetites as strong as men or to be as sexually assertive and expressive as men. Indeed, proponents of women's suffrage argued that women's greater purity and sensitivity to others' needs would, if empowered by the vote, rein men's lust and contribute to a more moral, cooperative, and compassionate society.[7]

Schreiner's feminism involved a blend of dominant feminist opinions as well as thoughts sharply opposed to these. The intellectual lineage of her ideas was that of Mary Wollstonecraft and John Stuart Mill. Unfortunately, Schreiner never recorded when she first read their feminist texts. Indeed, she nowhere declared her debt to any feminist writer. She differed most sharply from Wollstonecraft and Mill in her close examination of women's work, in her discussions of working-class women and women of color, in her treatment of sexual desire, and in her vision of the comradeship between the "new woman" and "new man."[8] Invariably, those of her views that deviated from mainstream British feminism prefigure positions adopted by feminists of the 1970s and eighties. In Chapter 3 we saw that Schreiner denounced prevalent scientific views on sex and gender differences held by feminists and nonfeminists alike. She repudiated both flattering and demeaning "scientific" implications with regard to exclusively female potential. Summoning her own social and biological evidence, she upheld the similarities between the sexes, as well as the circumstantial, heterogeneous, and versatile nature of gender traits and roles. Writing, however, prior to the diffusion of Freudian and other twentieth-century interpretations of female personality, she ignored the intricacies of infantile attachments, separation issues, and the ways cultural taboos and norms are encoded in the unconscious. Nonetheless, her careful probing and eloquence not only stirred many of the finest minds of her day but strike current feminists, too, as exceptionally discerning. An examination of her analysis of the nature and consequences of gender socialization can serve as a fruitful starting point. It leads organically into her articulation of new modes of gender identity and relationships and new forms of collective as well as individual political struggle.

On The Victorian Construction of Gender

In chapter 4 of *African Farm*, the female protagonist, Lyndall, explains to her friend Waldo how gender differences emerge:

> They begin to shape us to our cursed end . . . when we are tiny things in shoes and socks. We sit with our little feet drawn up under us in the window and look out at the boys in their happy play. We want to go. Then a loving hand is laid on us: "Little one, you cannot go," they say; "your little face will burn, and your nice white dress be spoiled." We feel it must be for our good, it is so lovingly said; but we cannot understand; and we kneel still with one little cheek wistfully pressed against the pane. Afterward we go and thread blue beads, and make a string for our necks; and we go and stand before the glass. We see the complexion we were not to spoil, and the white frock, and we look into our own great eyes. Then the curse begins to act on us. It finishes its work when we are grown women, who no more look out wistfully at a more healthy life; we are contented. We fit our sphere as a Chinese woman's foot fits her shoe, exactly, as though God made both—and yet knows nothing of either.[9]

The female characters in Schreiner's other novels, *Undine* and *From Man to Man*, are similarly "branded" and "cursed." Parents, older siblings, relatives, and ministers apply the branding iron. Should the young woman attend a boarding school, she would receive further indoctrination. Lyndall describes to Waldo how the name *finishing schools* indicates precisely what they are: "They finish everything but imbecility and weakness, and that they cultivate. They are nicely adapted machines for experimenting on the question, 'Into how little space a human soul can be crushed?' "[10]

Unlike Lyndall, adolescent Undine does not attend school. Rather, it is the men she meets who reinforce her early gender training. Albert Blair, her first love, seeks to erase what remains of her deviant traits. She already deems herself unworthy of this man, whom she adores as "a piece-of-perfection" and whose approval she craves. She struggles to conform to Blair's instructions about true femininity:

> A woman to be womanly should have nothing striking or peculiar about her; she should shun all extremes in manners and modes of expression; she should have no strong views on any question, especially when they differ from those of her surroundings; she should not be too reserved in her manners, and still less too affable and undignified. There is between all extremes a happy medi-

ate, and there a woman should always be found. Men may turn to one side or the other; women never must.[11]

In line with these instructions, Blair demands that Undine abandon books and take up music and dancing. In tones Henrik Ibsen was soon to have theater audiences hear from the lips of his patronizing husband, Torvald Helmer, in *A Doll's House* (1879), Blair counsels ample rest, for "my wife must be always bright and beautiful."[12] He presumes to adjust her gloves and presses her to avoid crude gestures such as punching her palm when she grows agitated. The climactic humiliation is his insistence that though she be a religious skeptic she attend church with him. No authority figures in the novel dictate to Blair how a man ought to behave. In general, gender prescriptions pertain to women alone, not only in Schreiner's writing but in much of Victorian literature.

Occasionally, Schreiner touched upon male socialization. Discussing gender behavioral differences as artificial, she observed that infant males were forcibly prevented from amusing themselves with needles and thread and dolls, just as infant females were denied climbing and shouting.[13] Though Schreiner's close male friends, Havelock Ellis and Edward Carpenter, addressed male acculturation more fully than Schreiner, both of them believed in certain "natural" gender distinctions that Schreiner disavowed; for example, criticizing men's childish dependence on women's maternal and domestic skills, they argued that women were inherently passive and men the born initiators. In accord with dominant Victorian gender notions, Carpenter insisted that women were "the more primitive, the more intuitive, the more emotional . . . nearer the child than men."[14] He meant this, of course, as praise.

Unfortunately, Schreiner's superficial understanding of male socialization compromised her fictional portrayals of men. Whereas her female characters are usually richly dimensioned personalities, her males, with the possible exception of Mr. Drummond in *From Man to Man*, fall into two classes: insensitive, domineering, possessive authorities (some attractive, others repulsive); sentimental, introspective, ineffectual dreamers (aggravating, yet lovable). Curiously, in her nonfiction and correspondence, she highlighted male exceptions to these two classes through her prototypes of the "new men" who were to be comrades for the "new women" reshaping the world. Perhaps the absence of such men in her fiction stemmed from her overriding abreactive concerns: to evoke compassion for victimized women, to lend support to feminist efforts to curtail male power, to release anger at male abuse of women, and to vent her frustration with apolitical men like her father whose sentimental idealism stymied social change.

In her exploration of how female gender traits are acquired, Schreiner underscored the way in which the general organization of society into separate gender spheres bolstered rigid gender patterns and deterred women from bucking the gender prescriptions that perpetuated those patterns. To wit, Lyndall's contrasting of the divergent fate of a poor female and male:

> We stand here at this gate this morning, both poor, both young, both friendless; there is not much to choose between us. Let us turn away just as we are, to make our way in life. This evening you will come to a farmer's house. The farmer, albeit you come on foot, will give you a pipe of tobacco and a cup of coffee and a bed. If he has no dam to build and no child to teach, to-morrow you can go on your way with a friendly greeting of the hand. I, if I come to the same place to-night, will have strange questions asked me, strange glances cast on me. The Boer-wife will shake her head and give me food to eat with the Kaffers, and a right to sleep with the dogs. That would be the first step in our progress—a very little one, but every step to the end would repeat it. We were equals once when we lay new-born babes on our nurses' knees. We will be equals again when they tie up our jaws for the last sleep![15]

Lyndall's monologue points to the devastating effect of the double standard of sexual morality. Not only did the general public commonly assume the socially independent woman to be sexually independent, but the ease with which innuendos about a woman's sexual nonconformity would soil her reputation forcibly kept women from striking out on their own. Any suspicion of premarital sexual activity would preclude a woman's making a proper marriage or even finding respectable employment. In all of Schreiner's major novels a "fallen woman" suffers social ostracism and a wretched destiny: prostitution, insanity, starvation, or suicide. The only practical route toward lifelong security for women was a stainless reputation leading to legitimate marriage. With an image of a cat set afloat in a tub in a pond, Lyndall dismisses the argument that women are free not to choose marriage. Theoretically the cat is free to sit in the tub until it dies; it is not forced to touch the water. Such "freedom" is patently sham.[16]

Faced with a societally defined destiny of women as wives and mothers, women early learn strategies to secure their future. Denied a variety of socially useful outlets for their energies, they exploit the most powerful instrument at their disposal, their sexual powers, to guarantee their survival and self-respect. The consequence can be ironic and sinister, as Lyndall elaborates:

> Power! . . . Yes, we have power; and since we are not to expend it in tunneling mountains, nor healing diseases, nor making laws, nor money, nor on any extraneous object, we expend it on you. You are our goods, our merchandize, our material for operating on; . . . we make fools of you, . . . we keep six of you crawling to our little feet, and praying only for a touch of our little hand; . . . We are not to study law, nor science, nor art, so we study you.[17]

In this light, Schreiner's fiction demonstrated that women whose sexual attractiveness cannot assure male affection experience a powerlessness in romantic rejection that is foreign to men, who can look to drown their emotional disappointments in other sexual affairs or in the absorbing careers denied to respectable women. Once romance turns hopeless, women's lives seem bereft of purpose or gratification. In a characteristic situation, Undine, after Blair jilts her, collapses into self-pity, despair, and ultimately emotional numbness.[18] Though she recovers her grip on life, she remains deeply scarred. A similar fate befalls Baby-Bertie in *From Man to Man*. After being seduced and abandoned by her male tutor, she is rejected by her subsequent suitor, who had harbored sentimental views of her delicate purity. Twice spurned, she enters into morose withdrawal, a prelude to a life of fear and (eventually) prostitution.

The fragility of the female ego in the face of male rejection led Schreiner to dwell on the need for a rudder to a woman's life other than love attachments. She exhorted her friend Alys Pearsall Smith to adopt some definite life plan. "Men," she wrote, "have always some object for which they live, if it be nothing higher than business or horse-racing. Therefore their lives are more complete and great." She urged Smith to surmount her diffidence and cultivate her considerable talents through continued studies. Too many women, Schreiner lamented, drift with life's tides, instead of swimming in a chosen direction.[19]

As long as marriage served as women's only safe and respectable profession, female gender training was bound to stress the life-fulfilling character of love, wedding vows, and motherhood. Tant' Sannie, the robust and earthy Boer woman of *African Farm*, voices traditional religious arguments for women's marital destiny. Tant' Sannie asks Em, Lyndall's younger cousin, "If the beloved Redeemer didn't mean men to have wives what did He make women for?" In Schreiner's analysis of Boer life in *Thoughts on South Africa*, she showed how practical needs as well as Christian injunctions sustained conventional gender values. Free of the romantic gloss and self-deceit with which English men and women approached marriage, Boer women and men were primarily concerned with a spouse's more mundane attributes. In one Boer mother's view: "If a man is healthy and does not drink, . . . and is a good Christian, what great difference can it make to a woman which man she takes?"[20] And, behold, when a Boer spouse died, the widow or widower soon remarried. The homogeneity among Boers with regard to cultural values, educational background, and way of life, Schreiner conjectured, guaranteed a remarkable extent of marital compatibility.

Schreiner found such compatibility absent in nineteenth-century British society where social class, educational privileges, and value structures were far more diverse. A young woman's expectation of marital happiness, even with her assiduous training in "femininity," was naive. Young women, such as Rebekah in *From Man to Man,* were not warned of the likely emotional frictions resulting when the persons wed held discordant values and came from dissimilar backgrounds. Under these circumstances, separate male and female gender training aggravated marital discord since the common ground of shared concerns and communicative styles was so limited. Schreiner anguished over "that painful hiatus which arises so continually in modern conjugal life, dividing the man and woman as soon as the first sheen of physical attraction . . . begins to fade."[21]

Of Schreiner's novels, *From Man to Man* most forcefully exposed that "painful hiatus." Rebekah struggles against the widening incompatibility between herself and her husband, Frank. Though given to "mannish" interests, specifically her botanical and anthropological research and her pleasure in intellectual meditation, she centers her life on her husband and children. She never questions that it is her role to raise their children and carry out household tasks. At no time does she criticize Frank for his inattention to child rearing, for his long absences on business trips, and for his preference for billiard games with male friends over leisure time with her. Though she is conscious of being exhausted by the travails of her frequent pregnancies, her children's illnesses, and mounting household chores, she never contemplates resorting to birth control or forsaking her fated maternal role.

Still, Rebekah longs for emotional intimacy, for genuine marital friendship, for open and honest communication. At one juncture she blurts out, "Oh, can't we speak the truth to one another just like two men?" At no time does she see the link between separation of gender spheres and her sense of inadequate marital contact. It is not until she discovers Frank's dishonesty toward her that she is driven not only to measures to preserve her integrity and sanity but to an analysis of the relationship between gender identity formation and marital discord. Though the immediate catalyst is Frank's various sexual infidelities, what most upsets her is Frank's lack of frankness in owning up to them. She finds abhorrent, as well, his infidelity with a woman he did not love. Trained to view sexual intimacy as contingent upon deep love, Rebekah comes to regard her husband's casual attitude toward sex as distinctly "male."[22]

As Rebekah expands upon the significance of socialized gender differences, she notes how Frank takes relish in stalking and killing wild animals. By contrast, she rescues wild animals in order to nurse and love them.[23] As opposed to Frank, who enjoys animals as prizewinning possessions, the dog Rebekah loves is a mongrel who sleeps at night on her bed with its two paws resting on her chest. Angrily, she parallels Frank's view of animals as prey to his delighted conquests of women, though he regards women after his triumphs, in Rebekah's sexually reeking image, as dead fish "through whose gills you have put your fingers." Ultimately, Rebekah wonders whether love, marriage, and human relationships have the same meaning for Frank as for her. She concludes that, in her impasse with Frank, there may not be anything unusual:

> that perhaps in all these houses with their tender gardens and their little front gates, and between all these men and women whom one sees walking smoothly to church together and going out to dinner and sitting on the stoep, there lies the same ghastly reality that the strange joy which fills the heart of the man and the woman . . . in the end comes to this . . . an hour's light, and then a long darkness; the higher the flame has leaped, the colder and deader the ashes.[24]

With many of its sections drafted during the 1870s and 1880s, *From Man to Man* foreshadowed numerous fictional critiques of turn-of-the-century marriages. By the second decade of the twentieth century, the controversy over Victorian/Edwardian marriage as a most pernicious human arrangement was well established in British feminist and nonfeminist fiction. Though anticipating many later debates, her analysis differed in its claim that the roots of marital incompatibility lay not in the "nature" of the sexes, or the inherent instability of monogamy, but rather in social discrimination against women and systematic socialization of women into dependence upon men.

Not all facets of female gender socialization flatly diminished women's lives, Schreiner conceded. The effects of societal emphasis upon female nurturant behavior could indeed instill a more compassionate and committed form of love less common among males who were rewarded for self-regarding and domineering traits. Although some women, in the style of Veronica in *From Man to Man*, fit the jealous, predatory, romantic stereotype, most women, as Schreiner viewed them, shared Rebekah's gentler and enriching modes of caring. Evincing this perspective with a bit of tongue-in-cheek, Lyndall likens her cousin Em, whom she terms a thoroughly "feminine" woman, to an accompaniment to a song "but a great deal better than the song."[25]

Female gentleness, Schreiner happily asserted, carried into relationships between women and mitigated the rivalry often present among women to win male suitors. In letters and fiction, Schreiner conveyed the special warmth and understanding of female intimacy. She fondly recalled caring, tender moments with Louie Ellis (Havelock Ellis's sister) and the novelist Edith Nesbit. In Schreiner's short story "On The Banks of a Full River," the sixteen-year-old narrator falls asleep with her head on the shoulder of a comforting older woman, and in the morning she awakens to find that the woman allowed her head to remain there. One of Schreiner's most moving and sensuously rich passages in *From Man to Man* depicts the affection binding Rebekah and her younger sister, Baby-Bertie:

> Almost every night when, as a very small child, she had been moved into that room, Rebekah had lain by her to sing her to sleep; and when she grew older Rebekah had still crept in to lie beside her to talk and caress her before she slept. Tonight Rebekah put the light down on the floor and knelt beside the bed. She put her head down upon Bertie's breast, under Bertie's arm, and pressed it there. It was as though, to-night, it was she who wanted to be caressed.[26]

Unfortunately, the tenderness between the two sisters, though it persisted following Bertie's seduction, did not enable Bertie to confide in Rebekah the truth of her "fallen" state. If she had been honest, *From Man to Man*'s story would have unraveled quite differently, and perhaps Schreiner could have finished the novel. Key to the climactic narrative is Bertie's decision, after overhearing women gossip about her adolescent liaison, to flee from Rebekah's home to an aunt's up-country residence. Were Rebekah privy to Bertie's loss of virginity Bertie would not have been motivated to leave. Schreiner's loosened plot coherence and inability to complete this novel hinge on this matter. If Rebekah and Bertie had not been intimate sisters, sleeping together, warmly affectionate and communicative, Bertie's secrecy and Rebekah's reticence to inquire would make sense. But these two sisters were wonderfully attached to each other. Moreover, Rebekah's values, as Bertie certainly must have known, were for her time liberal, if not radical, on sexual and moral matters. In Rebekah's philosophical ruminations and extended letter to her unfaithful husband, she amply reveals her compassionate, forgiving, and open nature. Rebekah would have prized Bertie's disclosure, finding in such a confession, had it occurred, splendid evidence of their special rapport and bonding.

Schreiner projected two possible endings to the novel, but despite Rebekah's acceptance in both of Bertie's "fallen" condition, neither of the two would have resolved the novel's unspoken contradiction between, on the one hand, the sisters' loving openness and Rebekah's commitment to honesty and compassion and, on the other hand, a plot development premised upon melodramatic concealment and distance between the sisters.[27] Perhaps, if Schreiner could have given Bertie reflective passages in which she explains her reluctance to inform Rebekah, or if Rebekah had tried, even in vain, to encourage Bertie's frankness, one of the potential major themes of the novel—sisterly love—could have a clearer, more complex and effective role in unifying the novel's disparate forces.

Since male gender training undermines the fullness of expression of tender feelings that such women as Rebekah and Bertie could exchange, Schreiner perceived, men sometimes find that they can assume female caring roles only by posing as women. In *African Farm*, Schreiner offers a startling illustration: In order for Gregory Rose to care for the dying Lyndall, he shaves off his beard, dons women's clothes, and offers himself to her as a nurse. When Lyndall asks him to rub her swollen and unsightly feet, "He knelt down at the foot of the bed and took the tiny foot in his hand . . . bent down and covered it with kisses." Rose's action is a telling counterpart to women who disguised themselves as men so as to join the army to follow a loved one or simply to enter a profession barred to women. Their transvestism was no result of sexual fetish or hormonal dysphoria but the rationally calculated behavior of individuals determined to transcend their culture's gender limits.[28]

Schreiner's account of gender socialization extended beyond its impact on women's and men's lives to its larger toll on society. Her fiction and nonfiction abounded with passages exposing the social dangers of polarized gender traits and roles. Whereas her fiction emphasized the social victimization of women wrought by Victorian gender values, her nonfiction accented the ways conventionally acculturated women do social harm.

The pressure upon women of all social classes to find life's meaning in marriage and motherhood, Schreiner contended, led to excessive child breeding. With declining infant and maternal mortality, frequent procreation meant a dangerous population explosion. An avid supporter of the birth control movement, she cited the growing problem of unemployment and, most crucially, the need for women's energies and talents in professions and trades rather than in continued enslavement to childbearing. Margaret Sanger expressed her gratitude for Schreiner's help during a critical point in Sanger's birth control campaign.[29]

Despite soaring population statistics, Schreiner claimed that more and more women were limiting the number of their offspring or were bearing no children at all. Although such family planning, where demonstrable, would have obvious social benefits, this strategy posed evident problems in light of persistent female socialization. As child rearing became "an episodal occupation," a woman was left without absorbing labor for much of her life, an irony escalated by most women's lengthening life-span. Along with the social waste of women's unrealized talents came their restless self-dissatisfaction and parasitic frittering with vanities. Schreiner likened many modern women to their predecessors in the late Roman Empire who madly pursued pleasure and sensuality "to fill the void left by the lack of honorable activity; accepting lust in the place of love, ease in the place of exertion, and an unlimited consumption in the place of production."[30] Schreiner coined the term *sex-parasitism* to indicate the moral danger such behavior posed to women and to society at large.

Schreiner's choice of term rings jarringly to the contemporary historian of women's lives. Even if the group of women she indicted were affluent, with few or no children and ample domestic servants, their "leisure" veils the multiplicity of their domestic responsibilities and chores, for example, managing household staff, acting as sophisticated hostesses and consumers, caring for older parents, maintaining kin ties, mediating kin conflict, and offering moral and psychological guidance to the few children they bore. Many privileged women were also busily involved in church and charity activities.

"Sex-parasitism" may be a misleading coinage, for the essence of Schreiner's critique was not the issue of wealthy women's idleness but the questionable value of much of their work, the relative waste of female talent, the consequences of both their reliance upon men and their social reliance upon others' labor for many of their comforts. In her portrait of Rebekah's comfortable, middle-class marriage, sex-parasitism as such is hardly evident. Like Schreiner's most kindred American analyst of women and work, Charlotte Perkins Gilman, she pinpointed as the crux of their parasitic dependence their reliance upon their sexual services as their payment for men's labor and protection. Articulating a view common among Victorian feminists, she declared that a married woman was no less a prostitute than those women who had no alternative to professional prostitution for adequate means of self-support: "[W]hether as kept wife, kept mistress, or prostitute, she contributed nothing to the active and sustaining labors of her society."[31] Schreiner calculated that "probably three-fourths of the sexual unions in our modern European societies, whether in the illegal or recognized legal forms, are dominated by or largely influenced by the sex purchasing of the male." Consequently, in modern society, not the man of the strong arm but "the man of the long purse" took primary advantage of the woman's economic dependence on her sexual functions.[32]

Schreiner was appalled by a proposal by "an eminent friend" (most likely Karl Pearson), which recommended that the state provide pensions for all middle- and upper-class women without regard to any productive or reproductive activity they might perform. This proposal, in her view, injected into society a most virulent strain of the sex-parasitic disease. Sex-parasitism, she charged further, contributed to the two widespread social evils: middle-class male "overwork" and the enslavement or exploitation of working-class and racial-minority male and female labor. With regard to the former, she wrote:

> That almost entirely modern, morbid condition, affecting brain and nervous
> system, and shortening the lives of thousands in modern civilized societies,
> which is vulgarly known as "overwork" or "nervous breakdown," is but one
> evidence of the excessive share of mental labor evolving upon the modern
> male of the cultured classes, who, in addition to maintaining himself, has fre-
> quently dependent upon him a larger or smaller number of entirely parasitic
> females.[33]

With regard to the latter, Schreiner declared, "It has invariably been by feeding on this wealth, the result of forced or ill-paid labor, that the female of the dominant race or class has in the past lost her activity and has come to exist purely through the passive performance of her sexual functions."[34] This theme reared its provocative head in her fiction, most directly in two allegories: "I Thought I Stood," in which a woman is denied entrance to Heaven because she is unaware of her guilty abuse of working-class women; and "The Sunlight Lay across My Bed," in which feasting men and women in a banquet house, intoxicated by their pleasures, are oblivious to the hardships endured by the common toilers who slaved to construct the building in which the privileged carouse.

In the original draft of her study on women, Schreiner apparently pursued a thorough examination of domestic labor. Since so many nineteenth-century wage-earning women were domestic servants, and since for many years single middle-class women could make a living only as governesses, a study of household organization of labor would additionally expose how the relative idleness of some women relied upon unrecognized exploitation and drudgery of many other women. *Woman and Labour* touches upon this oppression when Schreiner itemizes various forms of female labor—"from tea pickers and cocoa tenders in India and the islands, to the washerwomen, cooks, and drudging laboring men's wives, who, in addition to the sternest and most unending toil, throw in their child-bearing as a little addition."[35] She adds to this list the cleaning and ironing women, the seamstresses in sweatshops, and the floor scrubbers. But of all the modes of oppressed working-class female labor, prostitution struck her as the most hideous. For her, it combined the effect of social class inequality, sex-role stereotyping, male economic privilege, and female dependency. When in the mid-1880s she read the government Blue Books on prostitution they made her "blood boil." She was most infuriated by the government rationale of sanctioning "healthy and regulated" prostitution as inevitable and necessary. Bent upon eradicating the causes of female exploitation, she was prepared "to pull down the whole structure of society to get out that stone [prostitution] that lies at the foundation of it." She deplored the fact that, until white men introduced venereal disease in Africa through their prostituting of native women, venereal disease was unknown to blacks.[36] The insensitivity of middle-class women to the very causes of prostitution they knew firsthand particularly aroused Schreiner's ire. Complacent about their own restricted work opportunities and often glorying in socially sanctioned domesticity, they helped to maintain the taboos against female employment that forced so many women into the crassest form of sexual dependence.[37]

Given Schreiner's evident concern for the economic exploitation of working-class women, the military destruction of her expanded analysis of their labor was especially unfortunate. This volume would have broadened our understanding not only of her feminism but also of her protest against modern capitalism. We glean only hints of her sense of the integrated character of capitalism and patriarchal patterns in the published *Woman and Labour.*

As oppressive as was much of working-class women's labor, Schreiner claimed that at least it prevented their physical and moral flaccidity. She feared that in the future more and more working-class women would also become parasitical, displaced by modern technology and emulating affluent women's life-styles as soon as they had the financial opportunity to do so. She noted that the labor movement endorsed Victorian notions of femininity, upholding the concept of the male breadwinner, thereby also threatening working-class women's physical and emotional vitality. Her alternative obviously did not lie simply in assuring that all women labor, for as long as any society typed labor by gender it deprived itself of the maximal use and benefits of human talent. Persistent sexual division of labor that excluded women from statecraft and law, she reasoned, deprived an entire citizenry of women's distinct angle of vision, particularly on such issues as prostitution, divorce, child custody, and warfare.[38]

But her critique of gender socialization encompassed more than a probing of the toll on women's well-being and on society as a whole. It cleared the way for an alternative vision of female identity and social relations. What Schreiner had in mind was a far more radical social transformation than the sheer enactment of legal and economic reforms. Though specific reforms could remove barriers to female opportunities, these reforms could not assure the removal of tacit antifemale public and domestic sanctions or uproot internalized modes of female self-limitation. She was adamant that women and men must come to view themselves and their relationship with one another in a new way. Her refashioned society required "new men" and "new women" who privately as well as publicly defied sex-role stereotyping and pursued love and comradeship as equal partners.

"New Woman" and "New Man"

Schreiner's call for a "new woman" was not an oddity. Progressive-minded and unconventional women from the 1890s and after were often labeled new women by both their critics and their supporters. Schreiner herself was hailed by avant-garde writers as a forerunner of the new woman. To the conventional the term conjured images of irresponsible, selfish, self-indulgent, and promiscuous women. Many literary critics linked the new woman with the fashionable "decadent" of the 1890s and early twentieth century, describing both phenomena as socially subversive and anarchic, "harbingers of the apocalypse." Though from our present perspective these critics exaggerated the impact of the turn-of-the-century "new" figures, there were certain grounds for their unease. Despite the fact that most new women were ardently heterosexual and eager to become mothers, their insistence upon a "masculine" freedom in dress and behavior and their criticism of Victorian marriage, sexual prudery, and hypocrisy, compounded by their freethinking on religious matters, were genuine threats to the survival of conservative Victorians' family and world order.[39]

In reality, of course, many new women were not nearly as socially deviant as the general public and critics supposed. Along with the boldly defiant was the less radical, "purity school" contingent. These women shared most of the conventional views on sexual display and female behavior while preferring to see women's "natural" compassion and altruism function more widely in the public arena. The feminists among them were critical of gender discrimination, outraged by the sexual double standard and government-sanctioned prostitution; nonetheless, their social attitudes and behavior were decidedly "feminine" and respectable.[40] Even the radical new women often believed in innate sex differences and confined their revolt to demands for greater sexual openness and candor. In short, the new woman could range from prototypes of the superficial "flapper" of the 1920s to serious, searching individuals.

Schreiner's conception of the new woman differed pointedly from prevalent public and literary images. Though she applauded women wresting control over their lives, women's independence from social norms was not her central concern. Despite her plea for greater erotic expression and bodily affirmation, sexual freedom was not her pivotal concern either. In fact, she feared the public equation of the new woman with sexual promiscuity.[41] At the core of Schreiner's model of the new woman was her belief that only an androgynous woman could fully realize her abilities and enter as an equal with men in all fields of labor. Her concept of androgyny and of the "new man" are complex and are crucial to her stature as a unique and farseeing thinker of her time.

Schreiner, admittedly, did not use the term *androgyny*, but that was precisely what her description of the new woman and new man connoted. For her "the highest ideal . . . of human nature" was of "intellectual power and strength of will . . . combined with an infinite tenderness and wide human sympathy." She indicated that such a person was her friend Lady Constance Lytton, to whom Schreiner dedicated *Woman and Labour*. She claimed to have known "one or two other men and women" who embodied her ideal. As she elaborated her vision of the blending of conventionally masculine and feminine traits, she spoke of the new woman and new man as "laboring and virile . . . free, strong, fearless and tender."[42] She did not specify through concrete circumstances, though, the implications of these general traits so as to deal with complication: Patently, in daily living a "fearless" act may conflict with "tender" behavior, as when a woman decides whether to sue for a divorce. Moreover, such traits are historically situational; the word *virile*, for example, would vary in meaning in the ear of a sixteenth-century Asian peasant woman or an Edwardian middle-class suffragist. (Curiously, Schreiner's use of *virile* merits the same criticism that Havelock Ellis rendered when he chided Schreiner for her overuse of the word *manly* in her praise of certain women: He argued that a nonsexual word would be preferable since *manly* implied that men possess some special secret that it is women's supreme ambition to attain.)[43] Although Schreiner's descriptions of the androgynous personality could be this vague and inconsistent—sometimes embodying gender-specified traits, sometimes omitting gender labels altogether—her desire to undercut women and men's fear of displaying attributes of the opposite sex led her to riveting proposals.

To induce readers to consider her radical ideas regarding female personality, Schreiner insisted that the new woman was neither new nor rare. In *Woman and Labour* she alleged that the new woman was simply the nonparasitic woman of the remote past in contemporary dress. She cited the bold Teutonic woman who wore no veil, had no bound feet, received for her wedding gift not a "contemptible trinket" but a shield, spear, sword, and yoke of oxen, and then marched, fought, and labored with her spouse. With the exception of their military ardor, the physical prowess and economic self-sufficiency of these forerunners of the new woman underscored the "masculine" traits Schreiner idealized for women.[44] Comparably, she often invoked hardy, rural, nineteenth-century Boer women as closer to her ideal than women of nineteenth-century England. She applauded the Boer women's "keen, resolute, reflective, and determined" personalities, and she attributed these traits to a life of economic and physical parity with Boer men and to the legal dignity that women's equal inheritance of property accorded them.[45] Still closer to Schreiner's androgynous values were her allusions to such women as George Sand, Sophia Kovalevsky, George Eliot, Elizabeth Barrett Browning and such men as John Stuart Mill, Shelley, Keats, and Goethe, who blended intellectual range and discipline with breadth of human feeling.[46] To be sure, she overlooked the fact that neither Browning nor Shelley was a model of physical prowess and economic self-sufficiency. Though all of her historical examples falter in some respect from the ideal she elevated as a standard, they deviated all the same from conventional gender prescriptions and inspired a more flexible view of gender traits and roles.

Neglected by scholars, Schreiner's vision of the new man was one of the most original and subversive features of her social thought. She herself was aware that, whereas the new woman could find historical antecedents in the bold, industrious, self-reliant women of less technologically advanced societies, the new man was a type "more diverse from his immediate progenitors." She pointed out that, given male social and cultural privilege, men were understandably reluctant to support or adopt for themselves gender ideals that would threaten their public advantages and position. As a result, men who renounced their gender dominance and aggressiveness were far less common than new women. Schreiner underscored how the blinding effects of power, habit, and custom led men to oppose equal pay for women engaged in work equal to that of men, an opposition she deemed "the nearest approach to wilful and unqualified 'wrong' in the whole relation of woman to society today." She further speculated as to a male's fear of losing sexual attractiveness should he conform to her view of the new man. She surmised that men were worried that, without the economic and social power they enjoyed because of their muscular strength and economic privilege, women would no longer depend upon them for their protection and might therefore no longer find them appealing.[47] Despite these compelling reasons for male resistance, Schreiner was emphatically optimistic about change. She held that the impact of new social and material conditions for individual and collective human welfare, combined with the emergence of new women, would foster the emergence of more and more new men.

With Schreiner's passion for transforming gender identity, she might have used her novels as a vehicle for exploring gender alternatives. She did so only partially. Situated in nineteenth-century England or Africa, all her novels present essentially realistic figures, some of whom are struggling to surmount conventional gender expectations, next to none of whom are living the victory. To an extent they succeed and evince the qualities of her ideal personalities, but in many respects they remain constrained in imagination and behavior by the assumptions and restrictions of their time and place. An evolution does occur in her novels, from her early fiction where androgynous men are depicted in crucial respects as frail to the emergence in her last novel of an exemplary new man.

In *African Farm* the male characters who, to any extent, defy customary role scripts tend to display some fundamental weakness. Gregory Rose, who dons female attire to pose as a nurse and care for the dying Lyndall, is otherwise a rather insipid, sentimental, and fickle person. Waldo, a thwarted artist and scientist hobbled by poverty, religious doubt, existential ennui, and eventually Lyndall's death, evokes our sympathy for his gentle, freedom-loving ways and his reflectiveness and imagination but not our admiration. His enfeebled spirit lacks the tough, rebellious mettle we find in Lyndall. By contrast, among Schreiner's male characters in her later writing, we encounter Mr. Drummond, who enters *From Man to Man* near the story's end and who most closely approximates Schreiner's vision of the new man. An urbane, world-traveling scientist, he is the first man Rebekah has ever met who takes her intellectual pursuits seriously. Drummond differs as well from Rebekah's stereotypical husband in his devotion to the arts and in his exceptionally gentle and caring manner with children and animals. This tenderness is epitomized in a statue that Drummond gives to his wife of Hercules holding a little child. Rebekah purchases the statue from Drummond's wife, so deeply does she treasure this androgynous mix of male strength and gentleness. Drummond's deviance is also manifest in his urging of Rebekah to smoke a pipe, just as he does, to ease her intense life.[48]

Schreiner's realism, however, prevents her from projecting Drummond as thoroughly free from male gender socialization. He tends to view life more simplistically than Rebekah. When she confides in him that she is torn between duty to her own talents and a sense of obligation to aid social victims, and adds that as she grows older the right course to follow appears less and less clear-cut, his reply is cavalier: "Life doesn't become more complex to me. . . . it lies right ahead." By responding in this way, he evades what Rebekah identifies as the "agony of life," which "is not the choice between good and evil but between two evils or two goods." Drummond's moral simplicity is matched by no less oblivious an optimism. When Rebekah expresses her despair about ever finding her sister, Baby-Bertie, after years of frustrated searching, Drummond confidently assures her that "When we fix all our desires in one direction, I think one is almost bound to find what one hungers for at last." His jaunty temperament, though a tonic for troubled Rebekah and arguably a human rather than a peculiarly male trait, is set in the context of his disregard for the multiple tugs and constraints Rebekah as a woman must face. His lack of understanding about women's circumscribed lives, compounded by his carefree marital situation (he and his wife are virtually separated, and he has no children), is crystallized when, delighting in Rebekah's garden, he reflects that life might "be lived more satisfactorily a little hedged about with narrow conditions which compelled one to expand oneself in that circle—there's such a thing as being dissipated with too large an horizon and too much liberty to expand in it." Of course, as a man he has had the privilege of the wider horizon and cannot see the meaning of his words for a woman. Rebekah wisely rebuts, "If the hedges are too close round, they may kill the plants." To Drummond's credit, he readily agrees.[49]

If, despite Drummond's lacunae, he remains Schreiner's single progressive fictional male, Lyndall and Rebekah are her only fictional representations of conscious female mavericks. (Although Undine deviates in many ways from conventional gender expectations, she appears to do so more from temperamental disposition than from principled choice.) In certain respects, Lyndall is more a feminist rebel against gender norms than Rebekah, who in her unhappy marriage is an uncertain model for the new woman. Lyndall scorns marriage as slavery, as in effect placing her neck beneath a man's foot.[50] Consequently, she insists that her domineering lover submit to a "free love" union. Though pregnant, she separates from him when he fails to satisfy her craving for autonomy and a many-sided intimacy. She insists throughout *African Farm* on her right to self-determination, and her critique of current gender mores is fierce, filled with bitter sarcasm and steely logic.

Indeed, Lyndall possesses what Schreiner called a virile mind. Lyndall is resolute in her search for truth, in her refusal to succumb to Christian or romantic softening of harsh reality. She does not want to be sheltered by the many conventions designed to protect feminine innocence and sensibilities from raw experience. Though Waldo's eyes weep, hers do not. She holds that crying does no good and bites her lip instead. Whereas Waldo's, Em's, and Old Otto's good hearts and Christian precepts make them gullible to the moral manipulation and cruel tyranny of Bonaparte Blenkins, Lyndall alone among the members of her African homestead is clear-eyed about the danger Blenkins presents. Without words and with her piercing eyes, she alone can intimidate him. Her gaze can both discern Waldo's pain and stem the rage of a Blenkins or of Tant' Sannie.[51]

Seeking both autonomy and truth, Lyndall is constantly yearning for psychic and physical room: The farm and finishing schools compress souls within crabbed spaces. When Gregory Rose offers to seal the space of a broken window, Lyndall refuses: "No; we want air." Unlike Em, who adheres to domestic and familial expectations and remains on the farm, Lyndall strikes out into the world. Her incentive to leave home is heightened by the economic fact that, unlike Em, she cannot inherit the farm. Having nothing at stake, she can escape from external and internal dependency only through venturing forth to cultivate her mind and find employment. She even fantasizes becoming rich one day. She writes her lover, "I am not afraid of the world—I will fight the world."[52]

All the same, Lyndall is afflicted at times, much like Waldo, with a strange passivity and lack of focus. When weary from her futile struggles to win understanding for her values and hemmed in by restrictions on her personal development, she exudes self-pity and despair. At these vulnerable times she longs for someone to save her, surrendering to that fantasy all her usual effort to exercise initiative and command her own life: "I will do nothing good for myself, nothing for the world, till someone wakes me. I am asleep, swathed, shut up in self; till I have been delivered I will deliver no one."[53] The roots of Lyndall's gloom lay in her lack of both meaningful work and fulfilling love, which for Schreiner were indispensable to the new woman. Lyndall's adventures away from the farm, though they instruct her in the limited and faulty nature of female education and restrictions on female work options, do not inspire her resolve to pioneer new arenas for the work women can perform. Unlike Schreiner, Lyndall seeks neither to enter medicine nor to become a major novelist; nor does she strive to alter women's lives through political actions. Her assertion of autonomy is strictly limited to the realms of intellectual freedom and romantic love. Lyndall's rebellion is fundamentally individualistic and isolated, mirroring her restricted circumstances as a young woman in South Africa.

Yet, even in less restricted settings, many young women interpreted their liberation in wholly personal terms. Many of the new women of the 1890s rarely acted on a responsibility to alter the collective plight of women or to reconceive the role of work in women's lives. They rarely assumed the risks of social activists who were struggling to dismantle the edifice of institutional patriarchal control. These new women no more lived up to Schreiner's new women than did Lyndall.

On occasion, however, Lyndall did perceive that women needed more than love relationships to strengthen them. In a passage from a letter to her lover, whom she is rejecting for his traditional male traits, a passage interpreted usually as showing her desire for a strong man she can worship, Lyndall suggests instead, in my opinion, her need for a cause of some kind to mobilize her idealism and energy: "One day—perhaps it may be far off—I shall find what I have wanted all my life; something nobler, stronger than I, before which I can kneel down. . . . One day I shall find something to worship." At no point in this letter does she state her ideal "someone"; repeatedly, her word choice is a deliberate "something." This understanding of her letter is not incompatible with her earlier emphasis upon needing "someone" to deliver her; in both instances, she is looking for the catalyst that will unleash her own passions and ability to commit herself to something larger. Lyndall grasps the need for independent growth, but not firmly enough. She chides Waldo for lacking a life focus: "If you go into the world aimless, without a definite object, dreaming—dreaming, you will be definitely defeated, bamboozled, knocked this way and that. In the end you will stand with your beautiful life all spent, and nothing to show. . . . We have only one life. The secret of success is concentration."[54] Unfortunately, neither she nor Waldo follows this advice.

In different respects, Rebekah comes closer to Schreiner's standards for the new woman. Though conforming outwardly to conventional domestic patterns—she is married, bears children, enjoys needlework, gardening, kneading bread, mixing salads, and ventures little into the world—she is intellectually and emotionally as autonomous as Lyndall, if not more so. Her social criticism extends beyond sex roles and religious structures to include attacks on Social Darwinist rationale for the many forms of social inequality and domination. Except for the one time she verges on suicide when shaken by her husband's infidelity and her own impotence in overcoming her continued love for him, she never plunges to the depths of moral lassitude that on occasion beset Lyndall. In fact, she turns Lyndall's longing for a deliverer on its head and insists that women must initiate and direct their own delivery. In a fantasy dialogue she engages in with the Spirit of Humanity, the Spirit whispers to a morose Rebekah, "Despairing one, no deliverer will ever come. You, you, yourself must save yourself."[55]

Although Rebekah does not pursue a career or even engage in wage labor, she does have work she finds meaningful. Unlike Lyndall, she interlaces manual and domestic tasks with her mental activity. When uncomfortable with the weight of the fetus within her she finds comfort in mulling over domestic details: "She thought of little household things; she saw pictures of them, saw the kitchen shelf with the row of tins on it and the dust she must dust off to-morrow, saw the large bag of wash-clothes she must count; then she saw the little cups of moss she had been looking at under her microscope that day, so delicate and so minute the naked eye could not see them."[56]

A parallel is clearly intimated between the invisibility of housework, a woman's psyche, and microscopic reality. Rebekah's mind is focused and systematic: Her cabinet of scientific collections, her many books, her intermittent but serious journal keeping, all testify to an intellectual dedication beyond Lyndall's scope. It is fitting that Rebekah can separate from her husband and attempt to secure a level of economic independence, and that when she does so the source of her psychic and material well-being is horticulture. Earlier in her marriage Rebekah purchased a small fruit and vine farm with money her father had given her upon marriage. When her marriage capsizes she can turn to that farm to stay afloat.

Unlike Lyndall, Rebekah recognizes the need for collective organization to bring about social change. Though she too neither launches nor joins any reform groups, her rebellion is not wholly personal. Her philosophical reflections give weight to the necessity for mass participation in social reform, and she constantly instructs and molds her children in her democratic values. Whereas we may fear that when Lyndall dies her values die with her, with Rebekah we know they will live on.

Rebekah's identity as a woman includes certain androgynous features not present in Lyndall. Rebekah merrily sees herself as "mannish" in her enjoyment of carpentry and house painting and in her refusal to wear stays.[57] As a young child she envisioned one day being a mother raising an androgynous female. In the first chapter of *From Man to Man*, "A Child's Day," a five-year-old Rebekah, angered by the many restrictions on her life, fantasies herself living on a distant island replete with dazzling flora and graceful swans. Her paradisiacal house is filled with books and a microscope of her own. As she wanders about her island garden, she discovers an infant girl asleep in a strange, silver-frosted pod, as of a mimosa tree. Rebekah adopts the infant, feeding her milk from a tiny bottle, though wishing she could breast-feed her. When the child grows older, Rebekah promises herself, she will let her climb trees, even if they tear her clothes; indeed, she will sew her a pair of thick trousers so she can climb more easily, and she will spare her the terror of "horrid" Bible stories and religious hymns. If the child wants to invent stories, "I shall never let anyone laugh at *you*, when you walk up and down and talk to yourself." She also cautions her baby about male cruelty, young boys stealing bird eggs and holding cats by their tails and later, as adults, abusing their wives.[58] Rebekah's fantasy includes not only telling the infant stories but setting an unconventional example herself: She builds a playroom for the baby, digging the room's foundation, mixing mud (even dancing in it), and skillfully mortaring bricks with a trowel.

Although Rebekah can never act on her childhood utopian fantasy of motherhood, she does deviate somewhat from conventional parental practices when she actually becomes a mother. She uses stories to instill countercultural values in her children. In these stories to her four sons and Sartje (her husband's daughter by their black servant, whom Rebekah raises as her own child), she portrays make-believe and historical women as heroic figures.[59] She also explicitly encourages her sons to strive toward a nobler conception of manhood than her husband and most males display. The true man, she instructs them, would not be drawn to domination and destruction but would engage in a life of compassionate service to others.[60]

Rebekah's edge over Lyndall as authentic new woman stops short of

Lyndall's willingness to foresake conventional femininity. Compared with Lyndall's feistiness, Rebekah's compassion and gentleness make her a much less militant feminist. Lyndall would never stoop to Rebekah's obsequious behavior with her husband, nor would she tolerate the sacrifices Rebekah makes to sustain her marriage. The stormy indignation and pluck that enable Lyndall to leave her family farm, stride out into the world, and repudiate marriage are lacking in Rebekah, whose caution and patience resemble Em's benign temperament. In a lengthy and at times mawkish letter, Rebekah explains to Frank why she hesitates to leave him despite another of his adulteries. Her most painful tug is of maternal attachment to him: "[S]omething cries out in me, 'If he should need me!—If he should want me!—.' . . . When I have thought of leaving you against your will, it has been as if I left my little child while it cried for me; something begins to bleed inside of me."[61]

Rebekah's feelings are a far cry from the words of the wise man in Schreiner's "Three Dreams in a Desert" who exhorts women to turn away from their male loved ones, who metaphorically suck on their breasts, even if in consequence their breasts should bleed. Tellingly, when Rebekah imagines a better world for herself, she imagines herself not as a new woman but as a man, strong in body and protective urges. She dreams that she is a man sleeping with a woman he loves, whom he treats with astounding tenderness and care.[62]

If we bear in mind Schreiner's image of the new woman as a social activist, confidently entering new fields of labor and political movements, neither Lyndall nor Rebekah is an ultimately satisfying example.[63] Yet, for all their shortcomings, they clearly stand in the vanguard in their social milieu. Both are passionate in their search for truth; both disdain social disguises and evasions. Their quest for personal integrity and their "mannish" ways make them undeniable, if incomplete, new woman prototypes.

The New Comradeship and Love

For her model new woman and new man Schreiner envisioned not only individuals who transcended and in some fashion reassembled prevalent gender-distinct traits and roles but also a new world of relationships formed among them. Throughout her life she clung to her ideal of heterosexual friendship and love no matter how warped the test of that ideal in reality. Repeatedly she encountered the charge that the women's movement intensified sexual antagonism. She allowed that if the relationship at issue was between a new woman and a conventional male, the claim was valid. But if the tie was between a new woman and a new man, the result would be vastly superior.[64]

At the very least, Schreiner anticipated that the social and economic independence of women would evoke more respect from men, "new" and conventional men alike. The sheer fact that economic considerations need not enter into marital decisions would enable men and women to love whom they wished without the taint of disguised prostitution. For the first time, economic and social freedom would "fully enfranchise" love. Her experience with certain progressive men led her to believe that the new man, no less than the new woman, longed for love relationships of partnership and interdependence.[65]

Schreiner expected that marriages between new men and new women would possess a far more stable center: "A certain mental comraderie and community of impersonal interests," she argued, "is imperative in conjugal life in addition to the purely sexual relation, if the union is to remain a living and growing reality."[66] This was Lyndall's conviction when she refused to marry her lover.

Given a fully enfranchised love, Schreiner's views with regard to sexual passion fluctuated. Her most consistent position was that, since sexual intercourse both augmented and conveyed the rapport that the new man and the new woman experienced in other dimensions of their relationship, their erotic union would release a "life-dispensing" energy that heightened not only love but artistic expression. By contrast, sexual pleasure divorced from emotional and intellectual reciprocity or fettered by sex-role stereotyping and female dependence was an angel with "feather-shafts broken," "white wings drabbled in the mires of lust and greed."[67]

The extent of Schreiner's denunciation of the impurity of mere sexual satisfaction varied. When angered by the Victorian feminist and nonfeminist equation of sexual appetites with crude animal needs, she became an ardent champion of erotic pleasure, affirming the equally intense erotic desires of both sexes and hailing these desires as emphatically human proclivities.[68] Accordingly, she urged women to combat Mrs. Grundy in all her guises and, as a member of the Men and Women's Club and in her correspondence with Ellis and Pearson, engaged in open discussion among both sexes of all facets of sexual behavior and feeling.[69]

Specifically refuting religious prescriptions, Schreiner insisted that sexual activity had other worthy ends besides procreation, including sheer pleasure and emotional bonding. In supporting birth control, she argued that its purpose was not only family planning and limiting population but also helping women to achieve greater ease in sexual expression. Her emphasis upon the importance of sexual expression is further evident in her linking it to artistic pleasure. She defined both aesthetic and sexual pleasure as joy, a valid joy, in the act itself.[70] She admitted certain dangers to viewing sex as aesthetic, one its debasement into mere hedonism, the other an overintellectualizing of it; but these dangers could be avoided by preserving its emotional, sensual, and intellectual unity.

To those antifeminists who charged that the new woman scorned sexual desires and could well become sexually repulsive to men, Schreiner rejoined that sexual appetites in both sexes were fortunately too vigorous, too elemental an imperative, to be crushed by such changes. In fact, she conjectured, sexual gains would ensue from women's emancipation: Women with money (now that they had careers) would be even more sexually appealing. "The female doctor or lawyer earning a thousand a year will always . . . find more suitors than had she remained a governess or cook, laboring as hard, earning thirty pounds." Schreiner argued as "axiomatic" that "the value of the female to the male varies as her freedom. . . . The study of all races in all ages proves that the greater the freedom of women, the higher the sexual value put upon her by the males of that society." Historically, by no means have intellectual women been unattractive to men, namely, such figures as George Sand, George Eliot, Elizabeth Barrett Browning.[71] In short, for admirable and crass reasons, humanity had no need to fear that the sexual attraction between the sexes would wane with women's greater autonomy.

Schreiner's defense of sexual expression also appeared in her discussion of monogamy. Her positions on this issue wavered. In her more radical moments she prophesied that in a highly developed culture a desirable multiplicity of forms of sexual relation would arise. She wrote Ellis of agreeing with a mutual friend that what would emerge would be an erotic arrangement higher than monogamy.[72] In fact, she maintained, conscious experimentation in sexual arrangements was a precondition for cultural evolution.[73]

Her position on homosexual unions, however, was more qualified. She condemned homosexuality in ancient Greece as a reflection of female subordination and social decadence but felt comfortable with Carpenter and his homosexuality and, in a letter to Mrs. Francis Smith, praised the decision of two of her female friends to live together intimately: "[They are] so closely united that I can never think of them apart, but as parts of one whole. They are both so noble and beautiful, each in her own way."[74] It is unclear whether Schreiner assumed an erotic union between the two women. Though what she pays tribute to is a "Boston marriage," even that degree of her affirmation of alternatives to conventional marriage represents an uncommon Victorian mental freedom. Further, to the extent that she regarded male homosexuality as a function of the social inequality of women and not the willful perversion of immoral individuals, she expressed a measure of understanding and sympathy for social deviance surpassed by few of her contemporaries.[75]

Schreiner's more conservative reactions surfaced when she no longer felt the need to defend sexual pleasure against Victorian feminist and nonfeminist prudery and when, instead, she feared that the women's movement was being misconstrued as a movement primarily for erotic freedom. For strategic purposes, she stressed, "The direction in which the endeavor of woman to readjust herself to the new conditions of life is leading today is not towards a greater sexual laxity or promiscuity or an increased self-indulgence, but toward a higher appreciation of the sacredness of all sex relations."[76]

At these times she wrote of the new woman's conception of love between the sexes as more "than crudely and purely physical." She insisted that, although for most people marriage was essentially a physical union, for natures "more highly developed" a true marriage was one of both mind and body, and a purely physical bond would be a travesty of this ideal. This same attitude spurred her to write Ellis that her feeling for him was purer and closer to perfect for being free of erotic passion.[77] As indicated earlier, in *From Man to Man* Rebekah's unrequited passion is less erotic than a longing for psychic communication and emotional reciprocity. When erotic passions were evident in Schreiner's novels, they were often destructive to her characters: They undermined Undine's integrity and Lyndall's struggle for autonomy and self-realization. Though affirming various examples of "free love" relations—for example, George Henry Lewes and George Eliot—Schreiner could also be a scathing critic, as when she denounced the pernicious "free love" bond between Eleanor Marx and Edward Aveling.[78] In this instance, Aveling, who engaged in multiple sexual liaisons, benefited from his freedom at Marx's expense. At no time did Schreiner propose that marriages between new men and new women be free-love arrangements.

Schreiner's caution about sexual freedom was evident in related issues. Although bold in her advocacy of birth control, she was reticent to detail specific techniques of birth control and the psychological ramifications of these methods. She accepted masturbation as a valid sexual outlet, but she never publicly stated her support, and her approval was limited to masturbation's physical and emotional benefits.[79] Moreover, she nowhere discussed the physiological dimensions of erotic pleasure, as, for example, Ellis did in his frank, albeit highly male-biased, accounts of foreplay in *Studies in the Psychology of Sex*. Much like Edward Carpenter, Schreiner retained a romantic, if not Victorian, reluctance to delve into the practical and realistic requirements for sexual reciprocity and ecstasy. Her prose, also like Carpenter's, would suddenly waft into rhapsodic nebulosity when she described the transformation of sex from sheer physical reproductive ends to a source of heightened personal intimacy: "As the first wild rose which hung from its stem with its center stamens and pistils and its single whorl of pale petals had only begun its course, and was destined, as the ages passed, to develop more and more, stamen upon stamen to develop into petal upon petal, and to assume a hundred forms of joy and beauty."[80]

Her fiction likewise avoided any frank discussion of details of erotic arousal and expression. Indeed, despite her frequent claim that women's sexual appetites were as voracious as men's, her female fictional characters were sexually passive; unlike her male characters, they responded rather than pursued. When they did initiate affectionate physical activity it had emotional rather than sexual intent. Typical of this is Rebekah's yearning to be close to her husband in bed, "to slip her arm under his and wind it softly round his waist—just to feel him and hear him breathe . . . without waking him." Though her thoughts dwelt on "his soft light hair pressed to the pillow and his strong shoulder showing above the cover" and though a wave of feeling "rose and surged through her," this feeling was one of "great tenderness . . . as when one thinks of one's little child, as if all the heart were being drawn out of her to him."[81] Sexual magnetism and emotional needs are sublimated into the grand passion of mother toward sleeping child.

In her avoidance of physiological realism—to the degree, too, of having no character menstruate or masturbate—Schreiner compromised her feminist attack on sex-role stereotyping.[82] If wholeness of self and intimacy required economic and social autonomy as well as versatile androgynous traits, it no less required transformed sexual interplay. In unchanged traditional erotic behavior, conventional female acceptance of a male-dominated sexual script would clearly lock women into a contradictory bind as they simultaneously struggled to enter fields of male labor as equals in the public sphere.

Of course, none of her contemporaries, even Ellis with all his delineation of sexual physiology, critically examined the impact of gender assumptions upon sexual play and gratification. Only recently have studies interconnected gender socialization and erotic experience as researchers explore the discontinuities between common erotic scripts and advocacy of female liberation. Nor can we fault Schreiner for not matching Ellis in his sexual explicitness. It was brave enough for a male doctor such as Ellis to publish shocking studies on sexuality; but it was altogether another matter for a woman, with no medical or scientific credentials, to detail sexual physiology. The audacity of Schreiner's public writing and, even more, her private inquiries and commentary on sexual topics should not be overshadowed by an undue emphasis on her ambivalence and points of omission.

Schreiner's impediments in fully articulating her sexual attitudes stem, too, from the absence of appropriate vocabulary to convey her view of the blend of physical and spiritual sensations in love. Just as she found Victorian vocabulary distorting her religious experience, traditional as well as new scientific language for erotic feelings and love eviscerated her amorous experience and understanding. She anticipated the dilemma of early-twentieth-century feminists who, having spurned the erotic language of their mothers as inadequate, rejected the language of medicine and psychoanalysis as equally insufficient.[83] It should be noted, however, that Schreiner never explicitly stated that she encountered a linguistic problem with sexual expression comparable to that bearing upon her religious thought.

Schreiner's discussion of the comradeship of the new woman and new man neglected a further key ingredient to its success. In her extant writings, she rarely considered domestic social relations. Unlike either early-nineteenth-century socialist-feminists, such as Anna Wheeler, Frances Wright, and Emma Martin, who enunciated a radical material feminism of communal domestic arrangements, or late-nineteenth-century feminists, such as Charlotte Perkins Gilman, who envisioned new neighborhoods and collectives that relied upon professional services for many household and child-care chores, Schreiner left vague how domestic life should be organized to maximize heterosexual partnership.[84] Rare among feminists of her time, she did call for the equal sharing of the "physical and moral" tasks of child rearing, but she never spelled out what this entailed.[85] This oversight, due most likely to her lack of child-care responsibilities, minimal household chores, and deep longing to be a mother, also qualified, as the next chapter will underscore, her socialist outlook.

Feminist Praxis

The new comradeship that replaced sexual conflict could not come about through individual actions alone. Unlike the feminism of her fictional heroines, Lyndall and Rebekah, Schreiner's feminism involved collective political action. Her view of historical progress, as we have seen, required "bringing up the rears," a collective organic social transformation built upon popular participation and responsive, visionary leadership. She expounded her feminism publicly, through published writings and through addresses to women's suffrage and trade union groups. In 1907 she helped form the Women's Enfranchisement League in South Africa. During World War I in England, she joined in various forms of suffrage agitation, including marches and demonstrations.[86]

Compared, however, with the activity of an Emmeline Pankhurst or a Mary MacArthur, Schreiner's political activism was limited and erratic. During her adolescence, no women's movement existed in South Africa, and during her stay in England in the 1880s, her chronic asthma attacks, her frequent changes of residence, and her travel abroad made sustained organizational work an impractical goal. Worse, during Schreiner's years in South Africa from 1890 to 1914, the racist ideology of organized feminism, once the suffrage movement arose in 1907, disgusted her.

Although she abhorred efforts to prioritize certain feminist objectives over others, Schreiner had difficulty with a narrow, white liberal feminist construction of the women's movement. The typical liberal placed inordinate importance upon winning the franchise and tended to overlook other essential preconditions for collective female equality. Whereas in South Africa the liberal oversight ignored sisterhood with black women, in England what divided suffrage advocates tended to be class and age differences. When a woman's franchise bill finally became law in England (1918), it granted women the vote only if they were thirty years of age or older. Schreiner was among a small minority protesting.[87]

Though she did not go so far as to disparage the vote, because she linked progress to more radical social and economic changes, Schreiner differed from feminists who regarded the vote as a panacea for women's subordination. She did not share the majority feminist belief that the vote was a means of redefining sexual culture and wresting autonomy. To Mrs. Francis Smith she remarked: "Long ages must pass before we really stand free and look out on a world that is ours as well as man's. The poor little political franchise is just a tiny, little, wee step towards it."[88]

Consonant with her aversion to rigid ideological boundaries, Schreiner adopted a pluralistic, pragmatic, tolerant approach to feminist political objectives: "I feel that the woman's movement is so vast that we all have quite distinct work to do in it." She added that "If I, personally, had to devote myself to working for women's emancipation in some special branch, I would devote myself to aiding women to enter professions and business, and to reform in dress." But she cautioned, "that is not to say that the vote and dozens of other things are not as important and more so."[89]

Schreiner's emphasis upon "aiding women to enter professions and business" was, of course, a central theme of *Woman and Labour*. With regard to training women for conventionally male vocations, she assumed that equal access to higher education would assure such entrance. In this light she was moved to tears by the sight of women graduates at the University of Cape Town.[90] Unlike Virginia Woolf, she did not question the effect of school and professional competition and hierarchy upon those truth-seeking, self-determining, and compassionate traits she considered paramount to personal integrity. She further neglected the vital need for women in professions to create informal networks of support to protect themselves from prostituting their values in order to preserve their jobs and advance within their occupational hierarchy. The very real threat of sexual harassment in all spheres of employment never entered her discussion.[91] Finally, she did not set forth what political and economic changes were necessary to enable working-class and black women to pursue middle-class education and careers, an oversight particularly striking in light of her socialism and antiracism.

The strength of Schreiner's examination of political strategies centered on her awareness of the psychological implications of specific tactics. With regard to the agitation for suffrage, she exclaimed that the value of militance lay in cultivating courage and self-esteem among women:

> it's not the vote they are fighting for. . . . It's *freedom* for women! It's the fact, that, in some cause they believe to be of benefit to woman and promoting human freedom, there *are* found women ready to fight, to face ridicule, abuse, suffering and even death if necessary, that is so grand! If I didn't believe in the vote being of use, the fight would be equally glorious to me![92]

Although as a pacifist she opposed some of the militant tactics of the suffrage movements, such as the destruction of property, she nonetheless felt, "If it put the vote off in England for twenty years, the freedom of action they have given an example of to all women, makes their fight of infinite value." Despite her ambivalent feelings about violent tactics, she recognized in the militant suffrage movement the same positive character training that revolutionary movements often afford.[93]

Schreiner's psychological perspicacity is further evident in her comments on men's participation in the women's movement. Though she strongly adhered to her vision of cooperation and intimacy between the new man and new woman, she thought women must not turn to or rely upon men's assistance in their struggle for autonomy and justice lest they perpetuate their inclinations toward dependency and passivity and uphold male political domination. Fearful of such deference to men, Schreiner had the Woman in "Three Dreams in a Desert" recount, "And I said, 'Surely he who stands beside her will help her?' And he beside me answered, 'He cannot help her: *she must help herself.* Let her struggle till she is strong.' "[94]

To enable this struggle to succeed, Schreiner called for female self-pride, mutual female respect and solidarity.[95] How these aims were to be effected other than through sheer verbal persuasion, she never described. (It may be perhaps the most important achievement of the current women's movement that vehicles for such change were created: for example, consciousness raising and support groups.) But, akin to current feminists, Schreiner understood that the personal arena of change (interpersonal and intrapsychic dynamics) was inseparable from public transformative processes, an understanding few of her contemporaries shared.

Schreiner was optimistic about the eventual triumph of the women's movement. She deemed the women's movement as the most recent manifestation of those "vast controlling movements which have in the course of ages reorganized human life." Though she was uncertain of the impact of movement leaders on the course of historical events—sometimes regarding them as critical, highly conscious trailblazers, other times as semipuppets, half-aware of the conditions propelling them—she had no doubt that they were "the foremost crest of a great wave of human necessity."[96] Her faith in the gradual appearance of new men and new women inspired one of the most stirring passages in her writing, a passage that has buoyed feminists of our own time as well as hers. When the Woman in "Three Dreams in a Desert" cries out in loneliness after abandoning her man-child and all other human comfort in order to swim across to the land of freedom, the old seer consoles her:

"Have you seen the locusts how they cross a stream? First one comes down to the water-edge, and it is swept away, and then another comes and then another, and then another, and at last with their bodies piled up a bridge is built and the rest pass over."

She said, "And of those that come first, some are swept away, and are heard of no more; their bodies do not even build the bridge?"

"And are swept away, and are heard of no more—and what of that?" he said.

"And what of that—" she said.

"They make a track to the water's edge."[97]

This vision of incremental, if erratic, progress enabled Schreiner in her allegory "Life's Gifts" to exhort women, when offered a choice between the gift of love and the gift of freedom, to opt for freedom, since the end result of this choice will be the possession of both gifts, if not by that particular woman then by a future generation of women.[98] Christian traditions of heroic self-sacrifice for the sake of others merge with utilitarian ethics based on the greatest happiness for the greatest number in Schreiner's hopeful image of women with oars, rowing hard against the stream, the horizon they aim to reach veiled in mists, but convinced that what they see dimly ahead is not a delusion and that, even if they fail, subsequent female rowers will ultimately guide themselves and other women to a new Garden of Eden.[99]

6

"Interknitted sympathy"

ETHICAL SOCIALISM

The man who dreams to-day that the seeking of material
good for himself alone is an evil, who persistently shares
all he has with his fellows, is not necessarily a fool
dreaming of that which never has been or will be; he is
simply dreaming of that which will be perfectly attainable
when the dream dominates his fellows and all give and
share. Working it alone, it fails, because the individual
is part of an organism which cannot reach its full
unfolding quite alone.

Olive Schreiner, *From Man to Man*

If I thought Socialism would bring the subjection of the
individual to the whole I would fight to the death. . . .
Better to die of cold or hunger or thirst than to be robbed
of your freedom of action, of your feeling that you are an
absolutely free and independent unit.

Olive Schreiner to Havelock Ellis, March 29, 1885

THE TUG SCHREINER felt between service to others and her own self-
development as a writer had as its political counterpart the question of how to
combine collectivism and individualism, an issue that perplexed her much of
her adult life. Liberal and socialist writers commonly voiced this dilemma,
which prompted some of the most penetrating political writing of the turn of
the century. Leonard Woolf described his political stance in 1912 as "a liberal,
but not a Liberal, and half way to Socialism."[1] Schreiner hovered in a similar
limbo in the early 1880s; by the mid eighties she had joined the socialist
movement, assisting seven other women to launch the woman's branch of the
Democratic Federation, though still insisting that "Socialism is only one-half

159

loaf of truth; individualism is the other half."[2] Her earliest declaration of socialist leanings was in a letter to Havelock Ellis dated April 8, 1884, in which she stated, "I am glad you feel sympathy with socialism."[3] In formally becoming a socialist, she appropriated those modes of socialism compatible with her commitment not only to individualism but also to internationalism, antiracism, feminism, and pacifism.

Compared with her writing on behalf of other social causes, Schreiner's socialist output is frustratingly sketchy. The original manuscript for *Woman and Labour*, with its projected consideration of working-class women's lives and household labor, might have provided a much-needed limning of Schreiner's socialism. Apart from her allegory "The Sunlight Lay across My Bed," which she referred to as her "long dream on socialism," she never composed a socialist treatise per se.[4] Her brief address in 1905 in support of striking female shop assistants in Johannesburg constitutes her most focused socialist statement. By and large, her socialist ideas are framed in passages scattered throughout her fiction and nonfiction. As we cull these together, the broad contours of her socialism grow visible. What emerges is an outlook, comparable to her approach to race and sex antagonisms, that seeks to heal the injuries of class inequality by eradicating the injustices of social organization and reformulating socioeconomic relationships. Her vision of classes combining "in interknitted sympathy" presents yet another manifestation of her nonviolent, integrationist social theory. Despite her close friendship with Eleanor Marx and her regard for the writings of Engels and Bebel, she rejected the premise of militant class conflict embedded in Marxism. Her socialism was closest to that of late-Victorian "ethical socialists." She differed from them in her effort to balance individual and community interests and to include feminism, antiracism, and internationalism in her socialist program. Again, as elsewhere in her social theory, she was not always successful in cohering within her socialism her multiple commitments, but her struggle to do so marks her originality and farsightedness as a socialist thinker.

Like many socialists, Schreiner considered the upper classes leeches on the less privileged and was far more detailed in her attack on capitalists and capitalism than in her defense of the working class and socialism: "[T]he man who lives and grows wealthy on underpaid human labor is as essentially a parasite, feeding on human brain and nerve and muscle, as the insect which fastens itself on another organism and saps its life."[5] Her critique of capitalism was sparked more by moral outrage than by "scientific" economic analysis, although her desire was for a scientific critique.[6] Her excoriation of the rich and of class inequality belongs more properly among traditional religious and literary diatribes against greed than with Marxist and Fabian studies of the marketplace and class relationships. Nonetheless, her eagerness to delineate historical and material foundations for social theories and policies led her to unravel threads linking class, gender, and race absent in the writing of her more sophisticated and "scientific" socialist contemporaries.

We have already seen that a premise of Schreiner's approach to history was the inevitable collapse of a culture in which an affluent or educated elite ignores the conditions of the majority of the population. In her critique of Social Darwinism, she refuted the various arguments marshaled in defense of the rich as the more "fit," deserving their privileges by virtue of competitive success. Rarely in Schreiner's writing do we meet admirable wealthy people, despite the fact that she counted a number of such among her cherished friends. The most she would concede was that vast wealth might "upon certain rare and noble natures exert hardly any enervating or deleterious influence."[7] Ordinarily, she viewed wealth as won at the expense of suffering masses. The advantages of status and power that accompanied wealth struck her as a social affliction. She defined that disease as insatiable greed, "the horse-leech of our material civilization." In her view, the wealthy, intoxicated with their possessions, thirsted to possess still more, a thirst that ultimately bred internal moral decadence, national self-destruction, and war.[8]

Schreiner clarified that it was not material wealth in itself that produced social decay. Rather, wealth infected "at that point exactly (and never before) at which the supply of material necessaries and comforts, and of esthetic enjoyments, clogs the individuality, causing it to rest satisfied in the mere passive possession of the results of the *labor of others*."[9]

She argued that if men and women have no incentive to exert themselves their intellectual, physical, and moral fiber rots. Such a point in a nation's history comes when substantial wealth accumulates and is unevenly distributed among its population so that the affluent become relatively idle and dependent upon the labor of others. She stressed that such exploitative imbalance was not limited to a single nation's population, because the rich of any one country required the exploited labor of people all over the world: The wealthy who stand at Monte Carlo and "throw down coin as though it were not the life-blood of the peoples" are utterly oblivious to the drudgery of "the Hindoo with a cotton cloth about his loins toiling at his loom for twopence a day . . . [and] a needle girl between snatches of weak tea and bread and butter and fits of coughing."[10] More subtly and immediately for Schreiner, the comforts of the British working class were at the expense of exploited African and Asian laborers.

Applying metaphors of disease to her socialist critiques carried eugenic implications for Schreiner. Invoking the historical experience of ancient civilizations, she claimed that those societies and individuals who became muscularly and mentally flaccid weakened their offspring. She predicted that the relatively affluent Western European peoples would inevitably succumb to more energetic, hardworking communities, probably Africans and Asians, upon whom the menial work of Victorian industrial capitalism was increasingly being foisted.[11] In short, social inequality was a curb, not spur, to the "human progress" for which the Europeans strove.

In her dissection of capitalist's exploitation of the working class, Schreiner focused upon consumption as well as working conditions. A capitalist's search for profits led to trading in deceptive wares, from specific material items to an entire life-style. Exhorting South African Boers to select carefully what of modern industrial society they wished to adopt, Schreiner summoned an image familiar to the Boer, that of Jewish smouses (itinerant vendors). In a deplorably anti-Semitic characterization, she equated the economically marginal smous who sells a glittering but defective clock with modern capitalists writ large who not only deal in deceptive clocks but "will traffic with you for your land, your freedom, your independence, your very souls."[12]

In Schreiner's fictional writing as well, wealth is invariably the product of deceit and cruel exploitation of the poor and ignorant. In *Undine*, George Blair and his eldest son, Albert, are almost one-dimensional caricatures of malignant wealth: brutal, domineering, possessive, and intolerant. George Blair has a "flesh-incrusted soul," and Albert's eyes gleam as a "moonbeam falling on a glacier." Undine captures the indifference of the rich to others' well-being in an image of a rich man's carriage rolling through city streets: "[T]he mud from its wheels sprang up into the faces of the two who were poor and hungry and stood at the corner of the street talking."[13] As an ironer and seamstress in the South African diamond fields, Undine receives scant renumeration and often finds her work wholly rejected.

As insensitive to the less privileged as the Blairs are, the character of Bonaparte Blenkins in *African Farm* surpasses them. Blenkins personifies the man-on-the-make, who acts fully upon acquisitive and mercenary impulses. No moral scruples interfere with his readiness to crush those who would thwart his desire for Old Otto's homestead. Class differences became heightened when Waldo, with whom Schreiner hoped poor working-class men could identify, leaves his homestead for a South African town and experiences brutal economic exploitation and class snobbery. Waldo's shamed consciousness of his class inferiority initially strikes him when he meets some elegantly dressed ladies: "I never knew before what a low, horrible thing I was, dressed in tancord." The shopkeeper who hires Waldo as a salesman forces him to sign a six-month contract, pays him only half the wages that he pays others, and expects him to behave with customers in an obsequious, fawning way.[14] After his six-month term in the shop, Waldo hires himself out to drive one of a transport rider's wagons. He ends up driving three wagons, subjected to his drunken employer's verbal abuse and with no time or energy to read or even think. The situation grows worse than intolerable when, in order to drive starving oxen pulling a stuck wagon up a hill, his employer flogs, stones, and knife-slashes the poor animals. Enraged, Waldo attacks his employer until other assistants drag Waldo away. Miserable from his experience of town life, Waldo returns to his homestead.

Although no character in *African Farm* is truly affluent and class differences pivot on limited contrasts of property and status, in *From Man to Man* representatives of wealth and social class are prominent. With Rebekah's husband, Frank, and with Baby-Bertie's unnamed Jewish protector, we encounter more fully developed bourgeois male personalities. Frank, a reasonably successful businessman, is not as ruthless and ostentatious as the Blairs, but he is no less acquisitive, competitive, materialistic, and insensitive to women and blacks. He often treats Rebekah as a prized possession, expecting her to behave in a way appropriate to their station in life. In Frank and Rebekah's attractive suburban Cape Town home, Frank passes his leisure hours playing in his billiard room with friends, smoking cigars on the veranda, and scheming sexual conquests.

A gentler person than Frank, the Jewish moneylender and diamond speculator whom Bertie accompanies to London also treats women as a possession, regarding Bertie as a rare jewel. He is somewhat more sympathetically portrayed than Frank in that Schreiner provides the reader with reasons for the man's economic and personal insecurity: Religious persecution and economic deprivation are presented as the goads to his quest for material ease and social power.[15] Moreover, he genuinely cares for Bertie. Never placing sexual demands upon her, he is eager to make her happy through whatever means are at his disposal. On the other hand, his essential insecurity leads to overprotective, jealous behavior, the price Bertie must pay for his rescue of her and his lavish material attentions. Within a brief time, trapped and suffocated in her opulent surroundings, Bertie becomes idle and obese, increasingly hysterical and depressed. The circumstances of London's poor, coupled with the emptiness of her own life, heighten her self-image as a useless parasite.[16]

As she depicts the destructive behavior of materialistic men, Schreiner employs Rebekah as her *raisonneur.* More fearsome and criminal than the desperate soul who turns to gambling, prostitution, robbery, and even murder, Rebekah claims, is the man of property who makes his wealth from "the ill-paid labour of those in mines and factories working at the cost of life" and who uses the law to his own advantage.[17] Although Frank and Bertie's protector do not neatly fit that category, both of their incomes can be traced in part to South Africa's flourishing exploitative diamond industry.

In keeping with Schreiner's love of argumentative ironies, Rebekah herself is an indirect beneficiary of Frank's exploitation of others. Despite her opposition to class inequality, she, too, enjoys the services of a servant. Her household servant poses a particularly interesting challenge to Rebekah's views, especially since most servants are not white and British. With colonial privileges enabling even poor white families to hire black servants, Rebekah's childhood home itself is served by "a score of Hottentot and Kaffir servants."[18] Among these, Old Ayah, a "Hottentot," and Griet, a "Bushman" girl, come forth with shrewd observations on the ways of white people.

Of course, the English-speaking South Africans, such as Rebekah, were not the only employers of black servants. The Boer Tant' Sannie in *African Farm* also employs African black maids and field servants. Although Schreiner gives black servants a measure of respect in her novels, she neglects to depict adequately, whether through the words of characters or through other authorial devices, their constrained, vulnerable, and ill-rewarded working and living situations. A focus on the arduous labors of Rebekah and her parents may account somewhat for her failure to examine employer–servant relations, but given Schreiner's antagonism toward class and race privilege, the shadowy treatment of household help is disappointing, reflecting the vestiges of classism and racism infecting her imagination.

Schreiner's most evocative and angry presentation of the sufferings of the poor appears in her allegory "The Sunlight Lay across My Bed." Here, God takes the narrator's soul on a journey through Hell and Heaven, with Hell epitomizing the dynamics of modern industrial society. Initially attractive, verdant, and fruitful, Hell gradually emerges as toxic and revolting: "I stood a way off watching in the sunshine and I shivered," the narrator asserts, observing beautifully clad women delicately kiss, bite, and poison pears still luscious on their branches. He then sees men dig holes among bushes that they camouflage so that "their fellows may sink." When he asks God why men do this, God responds, "Because each thinks that when his brother falls, he will rise."[19] The narrator proceeds to view the pleasures of the rich, symbolized by an immense banquet house, where numbers of men, women, and children are greedily quaffing great bowls of wine, not to quench thirst but for the sheer pleasure of intoxication. He sees children floating rose leaves as boats in the bowls and blowing wine bubbles while their inebriated parents revel in song and dance, thanking God for their material prosperity and praying for its continuance. To the narrator's horror he learns that these festivities rest on the exploitation of wine pressers hidden behind a thick curtain. Anyone who seeks to end this exploitation faces slaughter. God assures the narrator that this society is doomed, for the earth will become sodden with spilled wine and the oppressed will successfully revolt.

The abominations of the rich in Hell appear all the more horrible next to the behavior of the inhabitants of Heaven. In Heaven a cooperative rather than competitive spirit reigns, with property shared by all and everyone, including the crippled and the blind, contributing to the welfare of all. So powerful is mutual caring in Heaven that the literal light it emits nourishes plant and human development.

In "The Sunlight Lay across My Bed," as in all Schreiner's fiction and nonfiction, the specific circumstances of the urban poor are vague. Although she aims her barrage of criticism at factory and mine owners, financiers and speculators, she scarcely paints the lives of the laborers on whom these men rely. Her intensive research in the 1880s into urban prostitution enters her writing only in the most general way. When she reflects upon the unpropertied, the urban poor are not her immediate association. Because her childhood and adolescence were spent in South African farming and small-town settings, for her the materially deprived and vulnerable are the Undines, Lyndalls, and Waldos of the world, toilers of the mind as well as the hand: missionaries, governesses, laundresses, dispossessed white and black farmers, unrecognized artists and writers.

Although Schreiner encountered industrial and corporate capitalism in the gold and diamond fields, these were not the typical settings that gave rise to late-Victorian literature of class distinction. Curiously, she seemed little interested in visiting English factories. She learned about factory conditions through reading and conversation with socialist friends and mill workers during her brief stay with the Browns in Burnley, Lancashire. Aware of her firsthand ignorance of urban poverty, she intended to enter midwifery so as "to learn to know our poor," but, as noted earlier, these plans failed.[20]

The only characteristically Victorian form of urban exploitation with which Schreiner had direct knowledge was prostitution. During the 1880s she came to know prostitutes of varied classes, from the desperately poor to wealthy consorts of rich men. Although this knowledge intensified her rejection of liberal approaches to social reform—she wrote Will that liberal measures were useless in eradicating prostitution; its demise required the radical transformation of social relations—it provided her with only a partial understanding of urban, industrial conditions of labor.[21] When in the 1880s Schreiner grappled with socialist theory, she could never feel that it adequately accounted for social injustice as she knew it. Understandably, too, given her agrarian and small-town background, she fantasized about traveling to Russia and joining nihilists in their struggle for a new Russia, rather than lending her shoulder to industrial labor struggles in England.[22] In sum, although she traced the greed and idleness of the rich directly to capitalism, her attack was primarily a moral one, and her language was metaphorical rather than empirical.

A similar philosophical, moral, and literary bent guided Schreiner's concept of socialism. At its base was her belief that human beings instinctively seek unity with others.[23] Likewise, she posited a natural human yearning for communal well-being and cooperation, which, she felt, a progressive social order must permit and encourage. Her earlier-described socialist Heaven offered such an ideal vision. Through passages in *From Man to Man* and *Thoughts on South Africa*, she articulated, too, her utopia founded on social class equality and reciprocity among diverse individuals and groups.[24]

To the extent that Schreiner validated socialism empirically, she turned to history and anthropological observation, citing, for example, the highly developed social empathy of the "Bantus" as indebted to the absence of private property. For the "Bantus," the idea that land could become someone's private possession was "morally repugnant."[25] Indeed, one of the sad results of European imperialism was its forced conversion of the "Bantus" to a system of private property holdings.

Although the "Bantu example" is a commendable effort at empirical justification, it is hardly a substitute for a comprehensive, comparative, socioeconomic analysis of capitalism and socialism.[26] Most of Schreiner's socialist friends were equally devoid of scientific rigor. They, like Schreiner, made their most significant contribution to the evolution of socialism through the depth of their moral outlook. As numerous scholars have elucidated, the socialist revival in England in the 1880s, even among "scientific" Marxists, was primarily grounded in a moral vision of a transformed community and remained so into the early 1890s.[27] An allegory such as "The Sunlight Lay across My Bed" conveys the quintessential spiritual and ethical fervor of socialism within this roughly fifteen-year period. Many socialist recruits shared Schreiner's evangelical background. No longer adherents of conventional Christianity, they found in socialism, particularly when articulated in moral and religious language, a substitute religious belief.[28]

The most exemplary writing of the "ethical socialism" of this period was Edward Carpenter's *Toward Democracy* (Stanley Pierson, who designates this prevalent late-Victorian outlook "ethical socialism," refers to Carpenter's work as the Bible for ethical socialists).[29] When Schreiner became close friends with Carpenter in the mid eighties, visiting him at length at his Millthorpe home, she was already impressed by his book, though Carpenter's influence upon Schreiner and many other socialists emanated as much from his charismatic personality as from his writing.[30] In later years, prominent members of the Independent Labour party and Labour party testified to Carpenter's formative role in their conversion to socialism. They recounted how his Millthorpe home became a supportive center for trade unionists and socialists to meet, explore ideas, and plan actions. Schreiner found her ideas, harbored in isolation, affirmed, clarified, and expanded in these conversations.[31]

Carpenter's magnetism closely drew upon his lyrical expression of his social views. He also declaimed that the English live "frozen up, starched, starved, coffined, each in their own little cells of propriety, respectability, dirty property and dismal poverty." In the next breath, however, he could summon young English men and women to rescue their country from such evil and create a millennium of love for every human being on earth.[32] In his writing and speaking, Carpenter carried into late-Victorian England the romantic anticapitalism of Ruskin and Carlyle, the thundering moral diatribes of evangelical ministers, and the visionary socialism of Owen and Fourier, all modes of expression with which Schreiner had strong affinity.

Schreiner further shared Carpenter's and Ruskin's distress with the ways industrial capitalism and social inequality demeaned manual labor. She supported their emphasis upon the need to integrate manual and mental labor.[33] But in contrast with Ruskin and Carlyle, and in common with Carpenter, Schreiner's antiurban bias did not kindle in her romantic feelings for pre-capitalist modes of work or earlier political modes of authority and hierarchy. She shared with Carpenter the conviction that the new world would be a comprehensive rural and urban democracy, utilizing modern technology in the service of human needs. In her appeal to old-fashioned Boers in *Thoughts on South Africa* to avoid the corruptions of modern society, she urges them to sift through the wares of Victorian culture for what may be valuable. Applying the image of a box of clothes from a dead elder sister, Schreiner imagines a twentieth-century critic declaring, "This bit of real lace is still good, and that silk scarf; but the rest is all brummagem."[34]

In accord with other ethical socialists, Schreiner believed that the process of socialist transformation involved simultaneous societal and personal change. Societal structural changes mandated the abolition of private property, economic and political decentralization, and equal rights for all men and women. Personal change required heightened social compassion and conscience, egalitarian feelings, and openness to new ideas and social arrangements. This tandem process of societal and personal change would rely upon the participation of working-class as well as middle-class citizens, as Schreiner, like ethical socialists generally, sought to avert the possibility that working-class men and women would adopt middle-class corruptions and insensitivity as they gained property and privileges.

Despite their shared emphasis upon a new set of values and interpersonal relations, ethical socialists held diverse views about specific changes. Few among them would share the extent of Schreiner's antiracism, feminism, internationalism, and pacifism or Carpenter's plural forms of eroticism. Ethical socialists avoided facing how potentially conflicted and sometimes inherently contradictory were their perceptions of the ideal community. A telling example, which bears on Schreiner's personal and political development, was their demand for altruism and self-sacrifice. Sidney Webb spoke positively of "self-deadness," that is, egolessness, in order to serve the collectivist social whole.[35] John Stuart Mill, for all his emphasis upon individualism, designated self-sacrifice for the public good as the highest virtue.[36] William Morris's call for altruistic struggle sparked the seemingly indefatigable crusading of leading socialist missionaries such as Tom Maguire and Carolyn Martyn.[37] Undoubtedly, such an ethic of self-denial intensified Schreiner's own inner battle in the mid eighties between serving others and seeking self-realization. Rare was the socialist akin to Karl Pearson who urged Schreiner to reject the many requests for her help and instead concentrate on her research and writing. And yet, ethical socialist definitions of the welfare of the whole frequently stressed as essential components individual freedom and self-expression. Fundamentally, the issue revolved around what Schreiner initially set forth as central to her uneasiness with socialism—the collision course between individualism and collectivism. She hoped, in the words of John Stuart Mill, to integrate "moral community and personal freedom, so as to be both genuinely 'social' and genuinely libertarian."[38]

Antagonistic to pressures for group conformity, Schreiner feared that the "self-deadness" Webb championed would promote a collective lacking in diversity. While extolling, on the one hand, a cooperative, integrated, organic community, she equally insisted upon heterogeneity of life-styles. She feared that a collectivist ideal rooted in altruism and self-denial would subvert female efforts to struggle free from dependent, submissive modes of behavior. In fact, many prominent female socialists, such as Eleanor Marx and Katherine St. John Conway Glasier, constantly subordinated their own needs and rights as women to serve working-class and socialist ends. Marx, Glasier, and other female socialist colleagues also charged the women's movement with self-interest, a charge Schreiner took pains to repudiate, arguing that female liberation advanced male and female welfare alike.[39]

Schreiner's acceptance of Karl Pearson's affirmation of self-service was one of the principal ways her thinking differed from that of most ethical socialists. Though she could rarely escape vague and sentimental expressions of socialist belief, she opposed most socialists' romantic orientation, particularly Carpenter's prizing of feelings over intellect. She longed for a rational theory of socialism that she could more happily adopt. To no surprise, she was drawn to Fabian socialism, though she never explicitly declared her allegiance to it. (Schreiner had good friendships with various leading Fabians, such as Beatrice Webb, Edith Nesbit, and Nesbit's husband, Hubert Bland.) She shared the Fabian admiration for the ethical, political, and economic thinking of John Stuart Mill and Herbert Spencer.[40]

It was Karl Pearson's complex socialism, as he elucidated it in the 1880s, that most thoroughly won Schreiner's support. However, Pearson's contention that he was indebted to Schreiner's ideas (along with those of Carpenter, Ruskin, and Morris) no doubt contributed to her ready accord.[41] His was a mingling of utilitarian ethics with political and economic analysis. His specific proposals included complete democratic suffrage, the formation of a Labour party, strong trade union organization, and parliamentary legislation that would nationalize land and large concentrations of capital. Schreiner emphatically supported all these programs.[42]

Yet, in two vital areas Schreiner differed from Pearson. First, she questioned his view—Engels's and Bebel's as well—that prior to the advent of private property a classless society existed where men and women were roughly equal comrades in work and power. As alluring as such a notion of an early Golden Age could be to socialists seeking historical antecedents for a new society, it was alien to Schreiner's reading and experience in South Africa.[43] Her anthropology, as we have seen, drew heavily on African history and posited the presence in primitive societies of multiple patterns of sexual politics, with male dominance the most prevalent. Additionally, the Golden

Age theory placed primary causation for class and gender inequality on the institution of private property, whereas Schreiner knew that those African communities where property was communal were no less patriarchal or devoid of class differences.

Second, Schreiner differed with Pearson over his advocacy of state support for the childbearing woman. Although she did not explain her opposition, we can infer from her other writings that she feared such support would lock women into child-rearing roles and promote an excess population.[44] Possibly she discerned the buds of his later eugenic zeal to promote the breeding of white Anglo-Saxons. She may also have feared the power of a highly centralized state administering such a policy. Her writings on South African constitutional matters made her antipathy to concentrated state authority unmistakable.

Despite Schreiner's immense admiration for Karl Marx and later Lenin, Marxist analysis did not appeal to her.[45] Her socialism was decidedly anti-Marxist in its approach to the question of who initiated social change. Like other ethical socialists she denied the inevitability of violent class conflict and upheld the educability of members of all social classes.[46] Though she believed that the pathfinder of the new social order could emerge from any class, she tended to designate the more highly educated to facilitate the growth of those less culturally advanced. Her clarion call was "Bring up your rears!"[47] In later years, reflecting back on the 1880s, she asserted, "The solid, stolid (call it sordid if you will) but *real* advance of the condition of the working classes in England is the result of that movement, begun and carried on almost entirely by a small handful of men and women mostly of the 'upper' classes and all of ability."[48] However, Schreiner qualified her view of elite leadership through her stress on collective solidarity. With characteristic botanical metaphor, she argued that for individuals and nations as for plants the more advanced shoot was generally doomed unless it could secure broad support.[49] Maintaining that no ideal transformation of interpersonal and group life could be instituted by coup d'état and endure, she asserted that social progress was possible only through fostering "interknitted sympathy" among all classes.[50]

Schreiner differed further from most Marxists in her sober view of the working class. Both her feminism and antiracism distanced her from any romanticization of the white working-class male as societal savior. She pointed out that despite socialist and labor union statements in support of comprehensive social and political democracy, the vast majority of working-class leadership and rank-and-file members balked at the prospect of female equality and shared the racist and imperialist impulses of their upper-class countrymen:

> Our hope that the English working man and the woman when freed will impart their gain to all the world . . . is belied at least by two symptoms—that the man who is trying to free himself from the tyranny of class still does in certain instances strive fiercely to maintain that of sex, and that, as he gains or thinks he is gaining his own freedom, he strives jealously to exclude men who are not of his blood from sharing it.[51]

The blatant exclusionary policies of white male workers toward African and Asian workers deeply disturbed Schreiner as trade unions restricted access for Asians and Africans and readily supported the official policy of color discrimination.[52] Schreiner reviled the injustice and self-defeating nature of such policies; they deprived South Africa of valuable human skills and not only bred destructive hostility and violence among excluded workers but also thwarted the class solidarity essential for an effective labor counterweight to capitalist power.[53]

Schreiner's awareness of the preconditions for effective working-class solidarity and triumph spurred her to oppose a working-class organization that was merely national. She called for unity with workers of other nations, regardless of their race and ethnicity. A morally consistent and politically sound working-class movement would espouse the rights of workers of all colors and nations. Schreiner warned the Johannesburg Shop Assistants' Union that "as long as there is an Italian girl willing to take the work for five shillings which a French girl did for ten, or a Chinaman who will take the miner's work for half that the Englishman or Kaffir demanded, there is always a hole in the bottom of the boat through which the water will ultimately creep in."[54]

Deeply bitter about English working-class support for imperial undertakings, Schreiner cast Peter Halket in the earlier-discussed novella *Peter Halket* as representative of working-class moral myopia and self-interest. Seething with a sense of class injustice, Halket, rather than direct it toward constructive social change, releases it on vulnerable Africans and in fantasies of revenge against the upper classes. When, for example, he broods about his mother's drudgery as a washerwoman, he vows, "Wait till I've got money! It'll be somebody else then who . . ."[55] Accordingly, in a letter to Ellis, Schreiner asked, "What will it benefit us to seize away the money from the rich? At the same moment that the greedy hands are seizing it there will pass over it the disease of which the rich are dying, the selfishness, the hardness of heart, the greed for material good."[56]

To be sure, Schreiner was sympathetic to working-class impatience for material goods. In her opening remarks to the Johannesburg Shop Assistants' Union, she emphasized that "Among all the reforms necessary to improve the life of modern civilized nations the first in importance in its bearing on human good is that a just return of the worth of his labour should be made to the worker."[57] When English workers struck for improved wages and working conditions, she heartily approved and was pleased at their collective assertion of their just due. She recognized that, unless a certain level of material security was attained, self-respect, independence, and self-expression were problematic. What she could not countenance, and what ethical socialists generally could not countenance, were class revenge, hatred, and greed as wellsprings of social change.

Schreiner's objections focused not only on the absence of a constructive social vision but also on the probable arousal of hatred and violence in return. Her lifelong aversion to and guilt over expressions of anger played into the psychology and ethic of socialist and pacifist transformation, wherein love and forgiveness produced the ideal community. Resentment, as graphically depicted in her allegory "The Sunlight Lay across My Bed," was toxic: When the narrator in the allegory feels angry over how his fellows have misunderstood and mistreated him, he emits a breath that withers the plants in Heaven.[58]

The competitiveness and misdirected revenge white workers displayed toward workers of different races, nations, and ethnic groups were also targeted at women workers. Schreiner's inability to commit herself wholly to working-class and socialist agitation stemmed as much from white workers' sexist attitudes and behavior as from their racist and narrow class interests. She bristled at trade union resistance to female labor; this resistance was reflected in policies that denied women access not merely to new fields of labor but even to their traditional work in textile manufacturing and handicrafts.[59] She inveighed against the principle of "the family wage" with its consequent exclusionary labor policies and differential pay scales, underscoring its shortsighted understanding of the marketplace. Without equal wages for equal work, she pointed out, women inevitably deflate wages, especially in skilled fields of labor.[60] Exclusionary policies and unequal pay, she believed, arose from erroneous notions about the nature of unemployment, not merely from historic patterns of male domination. Such erroneous notions, she felt, also diminished the efficacy of those socialists who likewise subordinated the women's movement to the working-class cause instead of realizing that these two movements were equally legitimate, independent, and complementary processes.[61]

The problem of unemployment was not the same for both sexes, Schreiner emphasized. Although both sexes suffered from technological displacement and the dehumanization of industrial capitalism, men had no choice but to keep their labor for hire or perish. Women, however, could succumb to various forms of economic dependency upon men, whether as prostitutes or as wives, avoiding the labor market altogether. Women's labor struggle, therefore, was not only against the same economic forces males encountered but also against social institutions and practices that rewarded women for relying wholly on their sexuality for subsistence. Although the ultimate goals of the female and male labor movements were similar—that is, saving human beings from want, dependency, and degradation—their intermediate objectives differed. The male labor movement was primarily concerned with material ends—seeking jobs, improving wages and working conditions, and securing a more equitable distribution of property—whereas the female labor movement, in the short run, sacrificed material gains for meaningful work. Schreiner reasoned that affluent women—the leading figures of the female movement—were faced with the prospect of severe material and social loss in their struggle to gain access to job opportunities, at least for future female generations. Their renunciation of the comforts of comparative idleness linked the female labor agitation not to "the large mass of economic movements" but to the vast religious developments aimed at elevating humanity.[62]

Given these differences, Schreiner warned against politically conflating them, for even if the males reached their various economic and social goals, women's lives would not necessarily improve. In fact, if greater social equality among men prevailed, it might possibly encourage even greater female sex-parasitism. Millions of working-class women who had led vigorous lives might well degenerate, like their parasitic wealthier sisters, into economic dependency and nonproductive activity. Schreiner concluded that the male and female labor movements must fight separately.[63] She longed for close cooperation between the two movements; such coordination would hasten and ease the pains of social transformation while, for the time being, the two movements would ideally remain distinct.

However clear Schreiner's imperative for two distinct labor movements, she failed to address the practical political issues that agonized most socialist feminists of her time. At the Second International's conference at Stuttgart in

1907, the members called upon European and American women socialists to pursue feminist objectives within the socialist movement, scoring middle-class feminist organizations as too limited and self-serving in their aims. At the same time, socialist women were reminded that feminist objectives, valid though they may be, were secondary to the effort to eradicate capitalism, an effort to be achieved through groups of socialist women and men working together. In both England and the United States, with historic traditions of effective separate women's political organizations and cross-class female alliances, the decisions of the Second International stirred socialist feminists to heated controversy.

Even before the Second International's position was formulated, socialist and working-class women were divided over the relationship between the women's movement and the labor movement. Most working-class trade union and socialist women favored separate female organization, viewing the majority of male socialists and trade union members as insufficiently sensitive to working-class women's needs and unwilling to accord more than lip service to equal female economic, political, and legal rights.[64] Male unions did consistently display either hostility or indifference to feminist demands. From the outset, the Social Democratic Federation leadership was antagonistic to the women's movement, although rank-and-file members were occasionally more receptive.[65] The leading British socialist labor organization, the Independent Labour party (ILP), was divided on the issues of women's rights, with Keir Hardie one of the few staunch advocates for women. Women active in local branches of the ILP "had to assert themselves if they wanted to do more than make tea and run fund-raising bazaars," but few women had the time, energy, and combative spirit to assert themselves against male prejudices.[66] Not surprisingly very few women enjoyed key posts in the ILP. By contrast, the Women's Cooperative Guild, composed of working-class wives with a sprinkling of middle-class women, concerned themselves with a broad range of female and class issues. The guild provided ample opportunity for women to gain leadership and organizational skills and to form supportive political and social networks with other female labor groups.

Despite female preference for separate organization, many working-class women shared the male view that the women's movement nationally was dominated by middle-class women who were not concerned with the destiny of working-class men and women. The particular nature of the women's suffrage bills under parliamentary deliberation kept this belief alive. While supporting complete adult suffrage, the leading women's suffrage groups were willing, for pragmatic reasons, to support a suffrage bill for women on the same property basis as then existed for men. The effect of this position would be to enfranchise roughly 80 percent of working-class women, leaving a substantial number still disenfranchised.[67] Schreiner's position on female separate organization varied according to circumstance. Given her belief in both separate and mixed-sex organizations, she threw her support to one or the other depending on her sense of shifting consequence. For example, in her support of the Johannesburg Shop Assistants' Union demonstration in 1905, she praised the union for being sexually mixed, "because men and women are the right and left sides of humanity, capable of moving anywhere together and nowhere alone."[68] Though she realized that in South Africa, which lacked England's history of female trade unions and cooperatives, the only viable approach may well have been sexually mixed, she approved of separate female political groups in England.[69] In general, she avoided entering into quarrels over separate and mixed associations.

Concern for the needs and rights of racial minorities and women distinguished Schreiner from most socialists and working-class advocates of her time. Her sense of the breadth of the future cooperative commonwealth awaited a later generation of socialist feminists to elaborate. Yet, her far-reaching vision of ethical socialism had its limits, such as her scant attention to the nuclear family as a prop of capitalism. Although in the 1880s she was skeptical about monogamy and sympathetic to free love as elemental to a nonpossessive community, by the time she wrote *Woman and Labour* she no longer questioned monogamy and the nuclear family, so long as the marriage bond was based upon sexual equality, shared parenthood, female independence, and mutual respect and love. Unlike socialist feminists who advocated collective organization of child care and household tasks, her inattention to marital and family work arrangements precluded her ability to grasp capitalism's interconnections of domestic and public modes of work and love, the symbiosis between the unpaid domestic labor of the housewife and both capital accumulation and cross-class male privilege.

Schreiner's views on the organization of the work sphere were no less cloudy. She nowhere indicated whether her opposition to hierarchical structures implied a complete industrial democracy. Would she preserve any status and income distinctions within the professions? Had she remained in England in the 1890s, she might have wrestled with these matters and, possibly, joined the Fabians. On the other hand, since she was engaged in such an array of social causes, her practical socialist thinking might well have remained thin. She certainly would have experienced the same disillusionment so many ethical socialists endured in the 1890s as racism and imperialism swept through the labor movement and as pragmatic economic issues upstaged the moral questions and vision that dominated eighties socialism. However, unlike numerous socialists who yielded to the prevalent narrow trade unionist pragmatism, Schreiner held fast to ethical socialism. In 1908, she recalled for her brother Will

> that glorious time in the '80s when socialism was in its dawning, and we were all fighting in the conviction that full day lay just over the next hill. . . . It does lie over the hill; but the day is hot, and it takes the race a long time climbing. I never have any doubt that the end of the twentieth century will have witnessed as wonderful a moral and emotional evolution in mankind as the nineteenth century witnessed one in material matters.[70]

7

*"Love begets love and war begets hate and war"**

FLYING THE OLIVE BRANCH

The supreme moment to me is not when I kill or conquer
a living thing, but that moment its eye and mine meet
and a line of connection is formed between me and
the life that is in it.

Olive Schreiner, *From Man to Man*

SCHREINER'S LONGING FOR connecting rather than separating living forms aroused in her a passionate hatred of militarism and war. She viewed violence as the chronic, looming threat to her mediating and reconstituting social and cultural oppositions. Her longing to heal conflicts within and between individual souls and national states, as we have seen, had multiple intellectual and experiential sources. If she had harbored any illusions as to the justice and efficacy of warfare, the Anglo–Boer War had disabused her of them. The death of so many and the extensive loss of property had not saved South Africa from racial tyranny or paved the way for more democratic policies. When World War I broke out, Schreiner was utterly detached from the naive optimism and war fever of most Britons. The widespread conviction that World War I would make "the world safe for democracy," that it was "a war to end all wars," struck her as an all too familiar and dangerous illusion.[1]

The minority of war critics during World War I derived inspiration from Schreiner's pacifist advocacy. When Emmeline Pethick-Lawrence, early in her campaign to stir American women to organize for peace, spoke to a large audience in New York's Carnegie Hall (October 30, 1914), she invoked Schreiner's words and reputation in two striking ways. Behind Pethick-Lawrence on the platform hung a placard that bore a peace message from Schreiner. She gave prominence as well to another statement from Schreiner, this time read aloud, exhorting women to "overstep the miserable bounds of

*Olive Schreiner to Edward Carpenter, January 1915.

177

nationality and race" that engender war. Pethick-Lawrence announced Schreiner's pledge to assist an international organization for peace in Europe and South Africa that would be open to all women of all races.[2]

As is quickly evident, Schreiner's peace advocacy went beyond traditional liberal approaches. She was an avowed pacifist.[3] The nineteenth-century peace movement had early (1838) split into two groups, with some overlapping membership. One was composed mainly of liberal humanitarians who sanctioned defensive wars in just causes. They worked to develop legal instruments for peace as well as modes of international cooperation and arbitration. Allied at times with these peace proponents, though radically different in political and social ethics, was the second group, a small minority of pacifists who abjured all wars. Usually they belonged to one of the historic peace churches, either Mennonites, Hutterites, Plymouth Brethren, or, dominant in England, Quakers. Less numerous yet (neither large nor unified enough to be called a third splinter group) were socialist objectors to wars conducted by a capitalist nation. Finally, there were those such as Schreiner who were utterly isolated, part of no religious or socialist pacifist group, and opposed to all wars, be they capitalist or socialist. Until World War I, no organizational setting existed at all for such peace crusaders.

As both a freethinker and a pacifist, Schreiner was a forerunner of the substantial minority of nondenominational members of the 1930s English pacifist movement. Though her philosophic impact on later pacifists was negligible, her antiwar stance during World War I was widely known, her addresses, public letters, and political actions adding prestigious weight to antiwar campaigns.[4] The nature of her pacifism, though little known to the public of her time, has historic significance in its distinctive realism and original amalgam of secular and spiritual elements.

No less distinctive was the way in which feminism intersected with her pacifism. True, the vast majority of pre–World War I feminists in Europe and America were peace proponents, some also pacifists; most of them were active in same-sex and/or mixed-sex national and international peace groups.[5] Nevertheless, in their rhetoric, they upheld the gender stereotypes of the era, that women are predisposed toward peacemaking whereas men incline toward confrontation and fighting. The feminist dimension of their peace advocacy was their belief that only if women were equal participants in public affairs could wars be prevented. Until the outbreak of World War I, Schreiner shared this outlook, although she disagreed with their broader notions of gender differences and belief in female moral superiority. Chapter 4 of *Woman and Labour*, "Woman and War," represents the most eloquent statement of such prewar feminist pacifist optimism. However, with the onset of World War I she altered her views and argued that women were as prone to warmongering as men. Though she distinguished herself from most feminist pacifists in this crucial regard, her feminism did not abate, nor did her cooperation with feminist peace advocates. The fact, however, that the majority of prewar feminist peace advocates shed their pacifism and supported England's entrance into the war did challenge Schreiner to reconsider her earlier assumptions about women's peace propensity.[6] She developed a psychology and sociology of war passions that was rare in her time and remarkable in its perceptions.

These qualities were most fully evident in her unpublished manuscript, *The Dawn of Civilization.* An examination of this manuscript, supplemented by Schreiner's briefer writings on peace and war, will clarify the typical and atypical features of her pacifist outlook.[7] As prelude to this discussion, a brief overview of Schreiner's prewar feminist pacifist theory can help to clarify the dramatic evolution in her thinking.

Although in *Woman and Labour* Schreiner eschewed any social theory of gender that postulated biological sex differences, she deviated from her position with regard to human response to violence. She held that women were biologically disposed to nonviolence. She countered those who claimed women's antiwar outlook arose from cowardice, military incapacity, or inherent moral superiority. Rather, it sprang from her distinctive knowledge of "the history of human flesh; she knows its cost; he does not."[8] Schreiner argued that women who experienced or anticipated the physical and emotional trials and risks of pregnancy as well as the formidable demands of child rearing felt more keenly than most men the preciousness of human life:

> There is, perhaps, no woman . . . who could look down upon a battlefield covered with slain, but the thought would arise in her, "So many mothers' sons! So many young bodies brought into the world to lie there! . . . So many baby mouths drawing life at women's breasts;—all this, that men might lie with glazed eyeballs." . . . No woman who is a woman says of a human body, "It is nothing!"[9]

Schreiner qualifies her maternalist thesis by conceding that certain men, steeped in pacifist religious and philosophical doctrines, also recoil from war. Their aversion, however, remains for her more abstract than women's. She concludes that, given women's profoundly sensual knowledge of the costs of war, "on that day when the woman takes her place beside the man in the governance . . . will also be that day that heralds the death of war."[10]

World War I shattered Schreiner's faith in pacifist womanhood. Despite the ravages of aging she reformulated her pacifism. The outcome, *Dawn*, her only extensive inquiry into the causes of war, began with a general attack on the usual prescriptions for preventing war. She contended that though some of the proffered superficial remedies for war might be useful, "the root of the evil is not even touched." Turning to medical metaphors, as was her wont, she first likened these remedies to "the efforts of a good nurse attending a patient with a deep-seated virulent internal disease; . . . if the disease should show itself in an external ulcer or sore, [the nurse] applies salves and lotions to it . . . but the disease is still there; the patient . . . may yet die of it."[11]

Adding that such well-intended palliatives were dangerous if they aroused complacent resistance to a quest for more radical and real remedy, she warned that "by [the nurse's] artificially healing the external symptoms, the disease may be driven inwards, to break out later in a yet more intensified form."[12]

Tackling one misguided pacifist fantasy after another, Schreiner discredited the suggestion that altering a nation's form of government would abolish war. She pointed out that wars have been endemic to humanity since earliest societies and have coexisted with all known forms of social and political organization. Equally untrue, she maintained, was the belief that individual political leaders could by themselves generate war. The overwhelming recurrent fact, borne out historically, she stressed, was that warfare is popular.[13]

Schreiner considered the sources of warfare's popularity, first taking up the argument based on human greed. Admitting that even so-called religious wars and wars for human rights have often veiled underlying economic motives, she conceded that argument had some validity. There was, for her, an important irony here: War would ultimately frustrate greed, an insight she derived from Norman Angell's then well-regarded economic treatise, *The Great Illusion*, a work often cited by peace advocates and pacifists between the two world wars. Angell's proof of the economic irrationality of war, particularly among modern nations with their complex intertwining of international economic interests and activities, reinforced Schreiner's historical account of war's damaging economic consequences. There was no question in her mind that, overall, the material cost of both offensive and defensive wars outweighed the gains; but whereas Angell was hopeful that closer economic ties among countries and fuller public awareness of war's economic costs would prevent future war, Schreiner found no such comfort and hope. She pointed out that Angell's logic, with its characteristic liberal optimism, assumed greed to be the decisive human passion and assumed greed, too, to be subject to people's enlightened understanding of their country's economic self-interest. She disputed both premises.[14]

Schreiner argued that as long as some individuals and classes in a society materially gained from war, even if the gain was ephemeral, they would disregard the economic interests of the nation as a whole: "It is a commonplace of history that continually . . . a race dominating over races which it has subjected, or a class dominating over the masses of society, has believed that its highest material good and the maintenance of its hold on wealth and lands was often only to be maintained by war."[15]

Further, a dominant race or class often promoted war among the subjected races or classes as a means to divert potential civil rebellion against itself. Schreiner acknowledged that those in power might dimly realize that their economic interests depended on the economic well-being of the country as a whole, yet would still pursue their class or race domination, disregarding their economic interests in the satisfaction of deeper-seated urges.[16]

More powerful than greed, though at times closely interknitted with it, Schreiner declared, was the human desire for dominance, "top-dogism," "the thirst in some form or other to have the better of our fellows." This thirst, she perceived, often lurked under the seemingly noble guises of "love of glory, love of power, ambition, love of competition." Even the overtly ignoble quest for wealth often served a deeper yearning for mastery. The ironies of greed were manifest, she observed, in the ascetic behavior of the brutal exploiters of human labor, the sharp speculators, the multimillionaires who spend very little of the money they amass. She argued that "three quarters of that struggle for excessive wealth which tortures our modern societies" was motivated primarily by "top-dogism."[17]

The lure of competitive status had such potence that subordinate individuals and groups, Schreiner noted, often sought to identify vicariously with the dominant group rather than further their own best interests. As one example, she invoked the poor black caddies in South Africa who refused to carry the golf clubs of losers though it cost them their supper.[18] The longing to identify with the triumphant party, she argued, lurked behind popular enthusiasm for war. Foreshadowing Virginia Woolf's classic essay on the causes of war, *Three Guineas* (1937), Schreiner held that educators abetted the lust for dominance through awarding prizes for competitive achievement and, by so doing, dismissed the pursuit of knowledge and truth for their own sake just as warmakers inflamed direct and vicarious top-dog impulses through propaganda speeches, flag waving, and drum beating intended to stir war fever that drowned out objective thinking. With the mass war frenzy in the early stages of World War I obviously in mind, Schreiner lamented that once people adopted a cause as their own and were convinced that "its victory is theirs, its loss their disgrace . . . millions will rush forward to die and to slaughter, which neither directly nor indirectly can bring them any material gain, and of which they may intellectually understand nothing."[19]

Commingled with greed and top-dogism, another all too pervasive human instinct, perhaps yet more deeply irrational and certainly more disturbing, incited war: "the sheer, inborn, animal delight in shedding blood, in destruction, in causing death."[20] Schreiner traced this instinct, as with the former two, to survival conditions in early societies. Like Thorstein Veblen, whose writing she appeared not to have known, she viewed a range of modern sports and games as atavistic expressions of primitive blood lust. The thrill that spectators in the Roman amphitheater experienced as they watched the quivering anguish and saw the blood gush forth when animals mauled animals and men killed men has its modern counterpart in the audience whooping it up at boxing matches. Schreiner described at length the parallel rites of combat in early and modern societies, the various methods of arousing blood lust and the animated faces of participants.[21] If human evolution was, as she claimed, shaped by both altruism and brute conflict, with altruistic impulses preeminent, then the historic frequency of warfare reversed that evolution. Without elaborating upon the erotic features of blood lust, she intimated its sadistic allure when she quoted a military correspondent's response to wielding a bayonet, "the almost indescribable sensation of pleasure . . . 'when you feel it [the bayonet] pass through the soft non-resisting human body.' "[22] She seemed to forget her claim of the power of nurturant and ideal-making human drives when she asserted that civilization had placed only a fragile, deceptive veneer over destructive pleasures.

Schreiner addressed two other irrational components of fighting—hatred and fear. She deemed those equally embedded in the human psyche, rooted as they are in early conditions of survival. So intense was the drive among some individuals to satiate their hatred, she noted, that they readily forsook material well-being and even their lives. Among her illustrations of those prepared to sacrifice their economic interests to hatred was the planter who flogged his black slave to death, though his loss of the slave ran counter to his economic welfare. Unless hatred was kindled, Schreiner argued, the masses of people would not go to war. Knowing this, warmakers vilified the enemy, projecting onto foes every loathesome attribute.[23] Those who upheld the humanity of the enemy and opposed the tendency to cast the conflict as a moral struggle between righteous and evil were condemned and persecuted.

However, beyond hatred, Schreiner proposed, possibly the most universal and elemental animal and human instinct was fear, a response manifest in the tiniest amoeba. Fear, she observed, was unusually infectious and recalcitrant in the face of reason. It was fear, as much among the empowered as the oppressed, that aroused people to the most merciless forms of cruelty. Schreiner speculated that the thrill of blood lust was often, at base, a phobic response to fear of attack and fear of one's own cowardice.[24] Like other spurs to fighting, fear was highly susceptible to political manipulation. In democratic nations especially, national leaders relied on awakening fear and panic to rally popular war enthusiasm.

In examining the prevalence of these warmaking urges Schreiner was careful to include women as no less subject to their goading power. As noted, this inclusion constituted a shift in her thinking, since in her prewar writing she placed hope for peace in women's distinctive efforts. Although she continued to grant some degree of truth to the belief that women have more at stake emotionally in preserving life than do men, she, characteristically, found proof in history and anthropology that women derive various psychic satisfactions from warfare. Not only did women in some early societies become military chiefs and form warrior bands, when deprived of such direct martial activity they eagerly assisted male combatants.[25] In her own lifetime Schreiner witnessed Boer women aiding their men during the Anglo–Boer War and, in World War I, British women handing out white feather insults to suspected draft dodgers and readily serving as recruits in munitions firms.[26] In Schreiner's allegory "Who Knocks at the Door?" women cheered men on to slaughter each other and supplied men with fighting tools.[27]

Schreiner discerned among both sexes a fusing of combative sexual feelings. Just as men often indulge in sexual excesses after a bloody fight, so, too, Schreiner recalled having "seen fifty women rush to kiss one fighting male." She conjectured that such behavior was a holdover from early societies when wars were fought for the possession of women, and the custom of female capture by brute force tended to merge sexual sensations, war, and masculine dominance. She further observed that males and females alike were sexually aroused by war dances.[28] Schreiner presumed here some sort of collective unconscious, early patterns of response persisting centuries later, though considerably modified by changing circumstances. She seemed unaware that her psychology of warmaking was at odds with the plasticity of human nature that she maintained in her other writings.

Schreiner took pains to probe women's attraction to military clothes and ornaments, whether worn by soldiers of their own or their enemy's country.

Though she did not judge female response to military garb sadomasochistic, she asserted, "there is something destructively sexual in this passion . . . shown by the readiness with which from the Duchess to the servant-girl, women tend whether in legal marriage or illicit relations to throw themselves into the arms of men who suggest war."[29]

Schreiner remarked that the coal miner's job was as risky and as vital to the country's well-being as the soldier's work, but news of a terrible accident to thirty miners did not comparably impel anonymous women to rush out and console friends of the victims. Likewise, the heroic act of a man rescuing hundreds of lives in a train crash scarcely evoked much public female attention.[30]

With respect to female behavior in her own time, Schreiner speculated that the interlacing of sexuality and violence in women's psyche was most evident among "celibate women between twenty nine and forty five" and less developed among mothers.[31] She did not indicate the basis of her generalization, and, clearly, she overlooked mothers of the order of Emmeline Pankhurst, a woman touted as the "queen of the Hun-haters." Perhaps Schreiner arrived at her hypothesis from watching the countless single women in 1914 and 1915 who plunged ferociously into war work and taunted peace advocates. Unfortunately, she offered no insight into the baffling processes of sexual sublimation.

Schreiner's focus upon female warmaking propensities set her apart from both feminist and nonfeminist writers on war and peace in her time. Their views, not Schreiner's, however, prevailed during the interwar years and formed an integral plank of the "new feminism," which dominated the women's movement.[32] In more recent years, "new feminist" assumptions undergirded the opinion of Erik Erikson that women's political participation was indispensable to preserving humanity from a nuclear holocaust.[33] Moreover, a version of the interwar new feminism has supported current peace advocates who place great faith in the alleged maternal impulses and/or experiences of women.[34] The premise of women as peacemakers did not always serve women's best interests, as Schreiner well knew.[35] Victorian male writers warned that women's compassion, if empowered through suffrage, could jeopardize the security of the nation and Empire, a view Lionel Tiger recently upheld when he asserted that women's weaker aggressive and bonding instincts could threaten national security.[36]

Not only did Schreiner's inquiry into the causes of war puncture conventional, sentimental linking of women with peace, but, through her survey of irrational martial drives, she challenged the premises of typical liberal and

Marxist antiwar thinking. Unlike most peace advocates of her time, she harbored no illusions as to the goodness and rationality of human nature, averring, "I have tried to look nakedly in the face those facts which make moot against hope."[37] Neither the arguments of liberals, such as Angell, that the public could be persuaded of war's damage to economic and political interests nor the Marxist assumptions that working-class consciousness and solidarity would avert war adequately grappled with the powers of unreason. The enthusiasm in 1914 of throngs of working-class men and women, as well as of most socialist and labor organizations, to rally behind their nation's flag stunned Marxist theorists. Those Christian pacifists who expected that their churches would transcend national boundaries and work for peace were also sorely disappointed. Even the Quakers divided over whether, and in what manner, to support England's war effort.

The one other notable British peace proponent to stress the irrational roots of warfare was Bertrand Russell, whose tract *Why Men Fight* (1916) bore the influence of his wartime friendship with D. H. Lawrence. Though Schreiner admired Russell's writings for the *Labour Leader*, the one antiwar Labour periodical, she probably did not read Russell's tract. As with *Dawn*, Russell's *Why Men Fight* was intended to make sense of the war delirium that seized England in 1914. With regard to the causes of war, the chief differences between his tract and Schreiner's were his more sophisticated use of psychological vocabulary and the absence—as his title suggests—of any consideration of gender issues in relation to fighting.[38]

In *Dawn*, Schreiner's analysis of the general causes of war strikingly neglected institutional considerations. By contrast, her explanation of specific wars consistently identified particular historical forces—social and economic systems, demographic factors, cultural patterns—as causative. In her analysis of the causes of the Anglo–Boer War and World War I, Schreiner never attributed primary responsibility to sheer human nature. Instead, she blamed narrow national and racial loyalties, artificial national boundaries, imperial ambitions, and competition for national supremacy and wealth.[39] In accord with the reasoning of the *Labour Leader*, she exposed England's World War I economic ambitions. She argued that England backed Russia because millions of British pounds were invested there "and millions more in France, whose money system will break if the Russian autocracy falls." In this light, England fought Germany both to protect these interests and to crush Germany as a trade rival. All the crusading rhetoric to free Germans from military rule was mere government propaganda.[40]

Schreiner weighed the long- as well as short-range causes for World War I.

She reminded Havelock Ellis that the behavior of Germany must be understood in light of the Napoleonic occupation, when Germany "was trampled under the feet of France, torn and desolated." The hypocrisy and duplicity of England's war policies became glaring when placed in historical context. Schreiner juxtaposed "the villainy of our proposal to dismember Turkey" with England's having "bathed the world in blood" to keep Russia out of Constantinople so as to maintain English hold on the Balkan peoples. She moralized, "A nation, no more than an individual, can wash its hands of the past."[41]

In contrast, the stress on human nature that informed Schreiner's analysis in *Dawn* can best serve as an explanation not so much for the origins of a specific war but for its overall irrational expression—muddled diplomacy, popular war frenzy, the government's need to distort and suppress information, the credulity of the educated. This last trait, manifest among her closest friends, was particularly disturbing to her. When Ellis expressed outrage at German treatment of the Belgians, Schreiner chided him about his hypocritical double standard. He had conveniently forgotten British executions of innocent individuals in India, Ceylon, and Burma and the British depopulation of entire districts in these regions. Schreiner exclaimed, "I don't believe one Englishman in 10,000 can see straight."[42] How absurd the English pretense to crusade for peace and justice when, even in the midst of the peace conference, "We are a race of devils—shooting the Indians, starving the Russians and Germans, trying to crush the Irish, and so pleased with ourselves!"[43]

A component of wartime credulity that particularly disturbed Schreiner was casual optimism about the effects of the war on English society and on future international relations. When England's leaders and Schreiner's friends predicted a short war, she must have heard the echoes of 1899 and optimistic forecasts about the Anglo–Boer War. She countered, accurately, that the war would be long and devastating, affecting the lives and property of innocent noncombatants. As the war intensified, Schreiner foresaw that trench combat between England and Germany could continue indefinitely.[44] Were it not for America's intervention on England's side in 1918, the conflict might well have lasted much longer; its toll in British lives, as it was, surpassed that of World War II. When Schreiner's friends claimed that the war would improve women's lives by providing more work opportunities and greater material self-reliance, she contended that for most women these opportunities comprised sheer drudgery: "[W]omen were drafted into men's places with hours as long, but pay far smaller." Further, heavy male casualties on the battlefield, Schreiner knew, would place intense pressures upon women to replenish lives lost, in effect reducing women again to breeding machines. Their desire for alternative work would be scorned and restricted, halting the feminist momentum of the prewar years.[45]

In response to those who believed the war would elevate the moral tone of the nation, Schreiner predicted the reverse. Her friend Adela Smith recalled that early in the war Schreiner prophesied that "an orgy of self-indulgence . . . and going in for every kind of extravagance and dissipation" would accompany the war and its aftermath. It was inconceivable to her that a country that sanctioned the perversion of truth and rampant hatred of Germans could in the thick of such activity undergo moral improvement.[46] When her friends insisted that the war would inaugurate a long period of peace, she refuted that it would, instead, mark "the beginning of a half a century of the most awful wars the world has seen." Wars with Russia, China, India, Japan, and the black peoples of Africa, she warned, lay ahead and would lead to fifty years of bloodshed worse than any time since the Roman Empire.[47] She regarded J. M. Keynes's *Economic Consequences of the Peace* as a work "worthy of J. S. Mill in its large truth-loving spirit."[48] Keynes's cogent delineation of the legacy of economic instability and national antagonism bequeathed by the war and the Peace of Versailles was in full accord with her perspective.

Though the war delirium, credulity, and naive optimism of the well educated could be explained as products of years of acculturation, Schreiner alluded to this cultural accrual only passingly, as when she lambasted competitive and patriotic patterns of school instruction. She did acknowledge the immense power of the media in sustaining war morale when in her allegory "Who Knocks at the Door?" she equated a reader seeking truth about the war in newspapers to "a small animal under a pile of decaying mould seeking to find the way to one ray of light."[49]

Given the depth and range of irrational instincts toward battle even among the educated, Schreiner found the usual pacifist appeal to reason and conscience, however crucial, inadequate. Akin to the approach of Bertrand Russell and Jane Addams and as earlier voiced by William James, she urged peacemakers to galvanize counterpassions no less elemental and powerful than those that fueled war.[50] Unfortunately, Schreiner's original unfinished manuscript did not develop this strategy systematically, nor did she explore it elsewhere in her writing. She never extended her anti–Social Darwinist thesis of innate, unconscious altruism and ideal-making instincts to questions of war and peace. Whereas in regard to other issues she maintained that social policies and institutions could reinforce human constructive impulses and discourage less civilized ones, she neglected this fruitful avenue of thought when she enunciated her pacifist philosophy.

After extensively diagnosing the causes of war and determinedly basing a peace movement upon the irrational forces of human nature as well as rational cognition, Schreiner emphasized her faith in ultimate human unity. Perhaps, had she time and energy, she would have provided a bridge between her grim account of human pugnacity and her confidence in an eventual peaceful world. She might have bridged, as well, her rational and irrational foci. Though she believed that "cool reason can find grounds to justify" her hope for a peaceful world community, she never explained why. At most she voiced the utilitarian thesis, brilliantly elaborated by Russell, that "no immediate gain conferred by war, however great, can compensate for the evils it ultimately entails on the human race."[51]

Although the rational features of Schreiner's pacifism sprang from this pragmatic judgment, she rooted her hope for human unity and peace in her admittedly nonrational, childhood spiritual visions of human identity, equality, and cooperation. So charged and ever-present was her vision of human possibility that she declared a "psychic compulsion" had forced her to be a pacifist and made her no more able to hold another position on peace and war than to ignore the beating of her heart.[52] In *Woman and Labour* she declared that men and women who perceived the fundamental unity of all sentient life regarded warfare as an early stage of human evolution and were "compelled" to struggle for higher levels of human harmony. Their ideal, like hers, could be viewed as "metaphorically prefigured by the ancient Hebrew, when he cried, 'the wolf shall dwell with the lamb; and the leopard shall lie down with the kid; and the calf and the young lion and the fatling together.'"[53]

Though it would be tempting to suggest that Schreiner, despite her militant freethinking, revealed in her pacifism the vestiges of her Christian training, such an interpretation would be erroneous. Since her devout Christian siblings, Theo and Ettie, never had moral qualms about warfare, she could not help viewing Christian piety as breeding war. Non-Christian sources, particularly Buddhism, inspired her pacifism.[54] As discussed in Chapter 2, her references to the superiority of Buddhism over all other religions focused on its emphasis on the unity of all sentient life. No doubt her personal acquaintance with Gandhi during his rigorous nonviolent campaigns in South Africa heightened her respect as well for the pacifist content of Indian philosophy.

Since Schreiner was too realistic to believe pacifist behavior would be grasped and practiced by more than a small minority in her time, she did not condemn those who fought for what they believed to be a just cause.[55] Her pacifist ethics even accorded a degree of heroism to the noble warrior, be he an American soldier in 1776, a Boer in 1899, or a Briton in 1914. Similarly, she hailed the militant suffragette, though she herself could neither counsel nor resort to violence. Like Gandhi and Quaker pacifist theorist Robert Barclay (*An Apology*, 1802), she contrasted a personal witness on behalf of pacifism (to which the majority population could not at the time adhere) to a second-best alternative she counted still honorable. In her 1916 address to conscientious objectors, she urged them not to judge British soldiers harshly: "Let us allow no bitterness to enter our hearts and no misunderstanding of these our fellows, who, not having seen that which it is our joy to have seen, cannot, therefore, of necessity, see their path of duty stretching where we see ours."[56]

The difficulty with such a position was its ambiguous implications for pacifist politics. Schreiner fluctuated between espousing a lonely pacifist witness and advocating active political struggle against war. She adhered to a strictly personal stance when she felt most overwhelmed by the futility of persuading others. At such times she likened her pacifist statements to two small leaves in a forest clapping together unheard beneath the din of human rampage.[57] She recognized that "You cannot by willing it alter the vast world outside of you; you cannot, perhaps, cut the lash from one whip; you cannot stop the march of even one armed man going out to kill . . . but this one thing only you can do—in that one, small, minute, almost infinitesimal spot in the Universe . . . *strive* to make that you hunger for real!"[58] That "infinitesimal spot," which she left undefined, seemed to mean only her inner consciousness, the space for one tiny body, and her immediate personal relations, but, to judge from Schreiner's varied antiwar activity, that spot could also loom rather large. Her devotion to small personal effort became unsteadier yet when juxtaposed with her comment to Emily Hobhouse that "anything one individual ever does to diminish this hideous nation-hatred does do good."[59]

The ambiguity in Schreiner's complex pacifist ethics was mirrored in her character Rebekah's reflections on conscientious objection in *From Man to Man*. Insisting at length that the vanguard individual has a responsibility to "bring up the rears" and secure solid support if s/he is to be historically effectual, Rebekah asserts that the pacifist is ineffectual and effectual at once. She concedes that unilateral disarmament invites predators to annihilate the pacifists and less advanced folk to scorn them but then claims, "Those men, who rise as high above the laws and conventions of their social world as the mass who violate them fall below, are . . . the new pathfinders of the race . . . the saviors and leaders of men on the path to higher forms of life."[60]

Schreiner's fluctuations between a view of social change that obliged the idealistic to seek a popular base of support or face failure and a view that credited the "failed" idealist with significant long-term influence corresponded to a historic division within British pacifism (and, no doubt, within most radical political movements). In the England of the 1930s when pacifist societies abounded and recruited their largest numbers of adherents, the leading pacifist organization, the Peace Pledge Union, was severely split over this very question of the nature of pacifist social change. There were those who believed it possible to garner enough popular support to pressure the government to refrain from military activity and to adopt constructive peacemaking policies. The more radical among these "political" pacifists planned strike actions in the event of war. Opposed to these pacifists were those, partly in the tradition of the spiritual witness, who doubted the efficacy of these policies and focused upon training small cadres of deeply dedicated pacifists, who would be able, even in the face of war and the extreme unpopularity of their position, to remain staunch and serve as nuclei for the rebirth of civilized values. Both camps addressed the issue of efficacy, though with regard to very different ends. Had Schreiner lived in the 1930s and belonged to the Peace Pledge Union, she would have felt drawn to both sides, but to judge by her actions, rather than by *Dawn*, she would have leaned toward political efforts no matter how useless.

One political "peace-minded" undertaking Schreiner refused to endorse was the League of Nations movement. She realistically predicted that the League would easily become an instrument of coercion by the more powerful nations against the less. As such, it would "lead to the most cataclysmic wars which the earth has ever known."[61] Though she fervently advocated international cooperation and transnational identification (while preserving cultural plurality), she never outlined the form of international government she would support.

Despite her objections to a League of Nations, Schreiner joined the Union of Democratic Control (UDC) early in its formation. The espousal of an international league was only one of the organization's many peace proposals. Composed primarily of nonpacifist Liberals and Labourites, Schreiner belonged to the pacifist minority. Nonetheless, she shared the group's commitment to do more than verbally oppose the war. In her published letter in support of the peace efforts of the UDC (March 1916), she urged her readers to consider the nature of the peace settlement they would favor. Her experience with the peace treaty that ended the Anglo–Boer War convinced her that insufficient care as to peace terms sowed the seeds of conflict for many years after. She called for a peace founded upon compassion and justice, not revenge. Without this, the result would be "a luxuriant growth of those national resentments, consciousnesses of injustice and hatreds, which are bound to create wars—wars which may be immeasurably more destructive and widespread."[62]

Schreiner applauded the two major objectives of the UDC: the organizing of individuals eager for a durable peace and the education of "ourselves and others" so that "when the time comes, we may be able effectively to act."[63] But she did not spell out what she meant by effective action. She evidently had collective strategies of some sort in mind when she wrote that, rather than "feebly gushing" over the evil of the war, it would be an "immense good . . . to combine as the Labour Party under Keir Hardie and some Social Democrats in Germany, to protest against the action of *their own government.*" She added her admittedly futile wish that women would combine to defeat prowar politicians in their own countries and also prevent their husbands and sons from enlisting in the army.[64]

Generally, however, Schreiner avoided discussion of political protest tactics and focused on public education. She urged people to study closely the long- and short-range origins of war, the history of international relations, and political psychology. She hoped the outcome of such study would be a firm grasp of "general principles on which we are determined to act, and hold by them as a guide through all the labyrinth of complex details." Ultimately, she expected this study to kindle a transnational consciousness that would lift people from "our wretched little trenches of national hatred and antagonism, dug for us by ignorance and the desire for vulgar dominance and empire." True to her socialist leanings, she also called for modification in the unequal distribution of wealth and power among nations.[65] Clearly, despite her emphasis upon the tenacious irrational roots of warfare, her faith in the efficacy of such knowledge indicated some measure of confidence in enlightened human reason as an antiwar force.

Schreiner's wartime peace activism also included her effort to accompany a contingent of roughly 180 British women to the International Congress of Women at The Hague, set for April 28–May 1, 1915.[66] The writer of the call to the Hague conference and its guiding spirit was her dear friend, Dr. Aletta Jacobs. This conference spawned an array of women's international peace efforts and ultimately gave birth to the Women's International League for Peace and Freedom, the principal women's peace organization of the twentieth century. Unfortunately, the British government and dock workers aborted the plans of the British delegation, including Schreiner, to travel to the conference; only three British women, already on the Continent, could attend.[67] Schreiner sustained her international peace commitment by sending to *Jus Suffragii*, the main organ of the International Congress of Women, occasional articles in which she hammered her basic theme of the need to transcend the boundaries of nation and race to create a genuine peace. Besides her contribution to the UDC and various other efforts with peace-minded women, her activism included an address on conscientious objection for the *Labour Leader* in 1916 and participation in a deputation of roughly sixty people who went to the House of Commons to lobby against conscription.

A dimension of political ethics and strategy that Schreiner (and pacifists generally) ignored was the complex issue of whether refusal to inflict injury on certain threatening or attacking individuals or groups was a moral act insofar as it endangered potential or actual victims. This tragic dilemma, the necessary choice between two possible evils, never complicated Schreiner's thinking as she resisted weighing, for example, the effects of a black uprising in South Africa against the effects of continued white oppression. Her only fictional episode that even approaches addressing this dilemma is in *African Farm*. Waldo and Em resent Lyndall's departure from the homestead because she provides a measure of protection for them from the cruel actions of Bonaparte Blenkins. Their resentment appears selfish and weak, but the larger issue is shallowly explored, since they, too, are as free to escape as Lyndall.

Though she could affirm the violence of honorable soldiers and suffragettes in her political writing, Schreiner could not practice such tolerance in her fiction. Her revulsion from violence, no matter whom it protected, prevented her from creating characters who could be both "good" and violent. Apart from her pro-Boer short story "Eighteen-Ninety-Nine," none of her well-meaning figures ever resorts to violence; it remains exclusively associated with malicious folk, who brutalize animals and human beings. Since her more virtuous characters must not use physical force, the unjustly oppressed never organize to rebel or even seek individual revenge. Generally at the mercy of the more powerful, they resolve their victimized situation most often through flight, only to find themselves in a situation no less vicious. Rebekah alone manages to escape somewhat successfully, when her self-owned and self-operated farm becomes a refuge from her husband's psychological cruelty to her. Occasionally, however, Schreiner's characters exert nonviolent forms of protest. Peter Halket is unable to ignore Africans soon to be shot, but he himself is shot as a result. More successful is young Lyndall, whose piercing gaze is all that halts the tyrannical behavior of Bonaparte Blenkins and stems the rage of Tant' Sannie. Though Schreiner admitted that the underdog might succeed in effecting social change through collective nonviolent actions, she did not illustrate this dynamic in her fiction. The simplistic elements of Schreiner's pacifism were typical of modern pacifist thinking. Fortunately, these elements were offset by her exceptional psychological realism. She realized how deep the pacifist's conviction must be if it was to withstand social persecution and relentless human proclivities to violence. In Schreiner's case, the depth of her conviction had to overcome, too, the incomprehension of her prowar friends and kin.

In the context of her time, Schreiner's pacifism was unique. Before World War I, all prominent British pacifists were allied to a Christian denomination, usually Quaker, and they marshaled both religious and secular arguments to support their beliefs. When, during the war, a more complex secular pacifism began to develop, it was grounded in democratic and/or socialist ethics and politics and sometimes in the moral philosophies of G. E. Moore and Bertrand Russell. By contrast, Schreiner's pacifism was a singular blend of moral and spiritual intuitions with secular logic, further heightened by strong Buddhist elements. It would become less unique in the 1930s when many varieties of nondenominational religious pacifism emerged. In many respects, her pacifist outlook anticipated that of two prominent pacifist writers of the thirties, Aldous Huxley and Gerald Heard. She would have differed with Huxley and Heard, though, over their neglect of gender, race, and class considerations for a durable peace.[68]

Though it forms a quiet obbligato to her overall philosophy, Schreiner's pacifism amply conveyed the distinctive character of her alienation from dominant modes of British thought and feeling. Her nonpacifist contemporaries viewed conflict as necessary and potentially ennobling. Their affirmation of force and violence reflected the confluence over many decades of evangelical, masculinist, Social Darwinist, capitalist, and imperialist assumptions about the formation of strong nations and individual characters. The concepts of manliness, patriotism, and security saturated the language of nineteenth-century intellectual discourse.

How clear, then, Schreiner's anti-Victorian sensibilities. She rarely employed military imagery and terms; instead, as we have seen, her imagination was alive with medical metaphors, images of disease and healing, rifts mended, organic wholes reconstituted. At the very marrow of her being, she abhorred a society in which any group coercively imposed its leadership and values upon others. With countless other feminist pacifists, she favored consensual democratic processes for change rather than policies resting on brute force. One can imagine how she might prize the mythic transformation of Athena from a goddess of war to a patroness of learning and guardian of peace, adorned with the branches of her favorite tree, the olive.

8

*". . . flew the bees, the wild bees"**

THE AESTHETICS OF LITERARY MISCEGENATION

> I think no artist need fear to give his work to the world
> because there are none who can understand. No human
> soul is so lonely as it feels itself, because no man is
> merely an individual but is a part of the great body of life;
> the thoughts he thinks are part of humanity's thoughts,
> the visions he sees are part of humanity's visions; the
> artist is only an eye in the great human body, seeing for
> those who share his life.
>
> Olive Schreiner, *From Man to Man*

THE PLURALIST, HARMONIZING, and healing impulses that shaped
Schreiner's social and political thought suffused her aesthetics. As with her
spiritual and philosophical concerns, her views on artistic creativity often
incorporated antithetical approaches: She affirmed unconscious and conscious inspiration, physiological and spiritual roots of intuition, and blended
romantic and realistic literary styles and criticism. Her novels fused diverse
literary genres—allegories, philosophic disquisitions, and narrator reflections, all of which interrupted linear plot development. She felt no problem
with such literary miscegenation. For her, artistic coherence required homogeneity of genre no more than national unity presumed racial uniformity.
With uneven success, she cross-fertilized techniques and experimented with
literary hybrids, much like a gardener in an inventive nursery. Her aim was to
discover what techniques most effectively enabled her to express reality in all
its guises, actual and ideal. As a result, her fiction refuses classification
according to the customary categories of nineteenth-century literature: romantic, realistic, naturalistic, symbolic. She wrote in all of these veins and on

*"A Dream of Wild Bees," in *Dreams*, 73.

occasion adopted what would become central twentieth-century antirealist and stream-of-consciousness devices.

Given the controversial character of Schreiner's social and philosophical values, critical response to her fiction during and after her lifetime corresponds closely to each critic's political and social attitudes. Among her contemporaries, critics who were progressive-minded, particularly religious skeptics uneasy with conventional social and political practices, hailed Schreiner's fiction as rich in moral insight and artistry. Her admirers included such eminent thinkers and writers as William Lecky, Sir Charles Dilke, Rudyard Kipling, George Meredith, George Bernard Shaw, Arthur Symons, John Galsworthy, Stephen Crane, and D. H. Lawrence.[1] Beyond elite literary circles, less illustrious folk also acclaimed her fiction, such as members of the Women's Cooperative Guild as well as a Lancashire working-class woman who wrote Schreiner, "I read parts of it [*African Farm*] over and over. . . . About yon poor lass [Lyndall] . . . I think there is hundreds of women what feels like that but can't speak it, but *she* could speak what we feel." In sharp contrast, critics committed to Christianity and Victorian social mores found Schreiner's fiction offensive. An anonymous writer for *Church Quarterly Review* declared that *African Farm* revealed a "mind that seems hopelessly diseased" and proceeded to lambaste both its style and its content.[2]

Until recently, twentieth-century literary critics outside South Africa tended to ignore Schreiner's writing. When they treated her work at all, they faulted its artistry, focusing primarily on its weak character development, uneven quality of prose, fragmentation of plot, and heavy didacticism. Although Schreiner's inventiveness was both deliberate and spontaneous, critics, with few exceptions, labeled her as an intuitive writer with little regard for conscious crafting and rigorous revising.[3]

Since Schreiner is unquestionably the first major South African novelist, twentieth-century South African critics, even before the current Schreiner boomlet of interest, were far more attentive to her writing. Although they often share the negative criticism cited above, they willingly acknowledge the immense influence she exerted on white South African prose. Of course, South African liberals and radicals tended to idolize her. Literary critic Ruth Alexander recalled her father, Dr. Solomon Schechter, himself an illustrious Hebrew scholar, recounting how he and his friends identified with Waldo in *African Farm* and were stirred by the novel's moral force. A subsequent generation of young poets and novelists, such as Roy Campbell, William Plomer, Alan Paton, and Isak Dinesen, who lived many years in Africa, testified to the "magic quality" (Dinesen) of Schreiner's ability to evoke the very air of the South African environment.[4]

Among current writers and critics, Schreiner's fiction is finally receiving the serious scrutiny it deserves. Opinion continues to reflect the critic's artistic and political biases, but with new concerns and new balances. Whereas the well-known South African novelist and short-story writer, Nadine Gordimer, among those distressed by Schreiner's inadequate treatment of race relations, emphasizes the limits of Schreiner's propagandistic "liberal" imagination, Gordimer nonetheless lauds the questioning, exploratory spirit of *African Farm* and calls it a challenging standard for present-day South African artists. More sensitive to Schreiner's time period and deeply indebted to her literary inspiration, no less distinguished a South African writer, Doris Lessing, extols the emotional and moral depth and daring of Schreiner's prose. The prolific South African literary scholar Stephen Gray exemplifies current enthusiasm for Schreiner in deeming her "the first author to think out a blow-by-blow answer to the question: what can South African literature be?"[5]

Contemporary European and American feminist critics are far from unanimous in their response. They range from the harsh assessments of Elaine Showalter ("The labors of construction and plotting were beyond her; . . . the novels are depressing and claustrophobic . . . she was not a productive or self-disciplined writer") to the far more sympathetic treatment by Liz Stanley. She charges those who deem Schreiner's allegories mere romantic and neurotic escapism as guilty of a narrow materialist critique that "excludes from it dreams, parables, fantasies and the like." The assessment of Schreiner's fiction in her most recent biography by feminists Ann Scott and Ruth First, though moderately critical, is not as negative as Showalter's, tending toward the position held by Gordimer. Only very recently do twentieth-century critics begin to look more favorably on Schreiner's philosophical digressions and argue a coherence to her style.[6]

Without denying significant flaws in her artistry, my study of Schreiner's fiction accords with the current, more positive evaluations. I am taken with the evocative power of the diverse forms of her prose and value its roots in her openness to unconscious sources (her personal mulch, so to speak). Contrary, though, to those who designate Schreiner a simplistically intuitive writer, I find her intuition wedded to a disciplined, painstaking self-criticism, a careful process of "writing it out," as she defined it.[7]

In grappling with deeply disturbing existential, psychological, and social experiences, Schreiner was prepared to use or devise whatever stylistic methods would help her achieve her ends. She modified traditional forms, such as allegories, and created new literary hybrids, such as *Trooper Peter Halket of Mashonaland,* an allegorical novella. She resorted to familiar classical and Christian imagery and introduced her own original forms of metaphor and analogy. Above all, she allowed both her passions and her intellect freedom to roam, which enabled her writing to sing and brood and to touch many a reader's deepest self.

At times Schreiner's efforts faltered. Her confusion over her literary audience led her to inconsistent statements about her artistic goals. On occasion her symbolic vocabulary reflected the dualistic structures of Victorian discourse and undermined her efforts to deconstruct moral and social dichotomies and hierarchies. These lapses brought to the fore the tensions in her life between her unconventional idealism, which alienated friends and kin, and her realism, which sought change incrementally and in ways familiar to most of her contemporaries. Her dilemma as a writer was not unlike that of a doctor, who, despite professional knowledge and vocabulary, must be accessible to patients if she is to heal their wounds. The inconsistent yet challenging, fertile and protean character of Schreiner's imagination emerges most clearly if we examine first her views on the creative process; then move on to her self-criticism and criticism of other writers; proceed to her most distinctive fictional mode, dreams; and, finally, treat her literary techniques.

The Creative Process

As a highly conscious artist, Schreiner was intrigued by the creative process and explored it in her various writings. In *From Man to Man* she offered her most systematic presentation. She identified three stages in the production of a work: the period of spontaneous, irresistible flashes; the time of deliberate crafting of these perceptions; and the point of decision making as to the fate of the work once finished. She set forth these stages in the form of a conversation between Rebekah and Mr. Drummond on the veranda of Rebekah's Cape Town home.

Drummond introduces the first stage—the sudden flash of inspiration—with an account of the origins of his manuscript on African landscape and peoples. He had traveled for a year and a half all over Africa in his wagon during a time of personal stress when he was particularly susceptible to the impact of nature's phenomena. While he was immersed in these sensations he did not write about them, but during his four-month stay in England an illumination struck him. He had been feeling depressed and was busily writing descriptions to accompany various specimens he was cataloguing when suddenly he found himself flooded with African images, flashing one after the other. Immediately he wrote them down, working through the night, propelled as though by a power beyond himself.[8]

Rebekah, in turn, recalls incidents from her childhood when, after an inexplicable depression, she experienced "some sudden flash of perception." She dubs such a mental burst "intuition" and reasons that such in fact was Socrates' demon. Like Rebekah, Schreiner alluded to a number of her stories, allegories, and parts of her novels sweeping before her mind to introduce themselves to her in this way.[9]

In addition to sudden flashes, the unconscious bursts into Schreiner's consciousness through dreams and fantasies. She called dreams "brain pictures," a term that merged visual flashes with more extended symbolic content. Brain pictures were particularly apt to occur during states somewhere between wakefulness and full sleep, that is, when, in Rebekah's voicing of Schreiner's experience, "the brain is too busily secreting to rest" and pictures and sound automatically succeed each other. Images would flow randomly, in a montage of free association. Sometimes these moments stirred conscious fantasizing, such as in "self-to-self" stories.[10]

Schreiner was certain that creative flashes sprang primarily from unconscious processes. Her fullest statement of this idea appeared in a letter to Ellis concerning a particularly eerie episode: One sunny, peaceful afternoon she had gone for a walk in the veld, feeling very happy, taking a book by Ruskin she was in the midst of reading. Suddenly she found herself crying, "Not quietly but in a wild convulsive agony." What struck her as especially odd was her detachment from her crying; "And yet *I* wasn't crying. . . . It was as if some terrible thinking, quite beyond the range of my *conscious consciousness* were affecting me." She speculated that "it is a new strange evidence of that double consciousness which I am sure exists in the brain, at least in mine." She linked this experience to her inspiration for the first section of *From Man to Man*, "The Prelude," which soon followed the crying spell; "in *one instant* the whole of my Prelude flashed on me." A related episode inspired her writing of *Peter Halket*. After awakening abruptly from a deep sleep, she told Cronwright the story as it was to be.[11]

Schreiner's explanations for these flashes were both physiological and metaphysical in character. Averse to notions of divine revelation, she has Rebekah, in *From Man to Man*, turn informal scientist: "some part of one's brain we are not conscious of has been working intensely, so that the part we are conscious of is ill supplied with blood; then something bursts and it comes into consciousness." Drummond, carrying forward Rebekah's speculation, proposes that the irresistible activity may not be cerebral so much as spinal and visceral. As in Drummond and Rebekah's exchange, Schreiner insisted that her artistic flashes arose from "absolutely unconscious cerebration that had been going on in my brain."[12] She argued that impressions and observations germinate in the mind, unknown to our conscious mind until a moment of maturity when, as with a butterfly bursting through its chrysalis, they invade our consciousness. The invasion is literally felt as a flood of light.[13]

In her probing of unconscious flashes, Schreiner, in common with a small coterie of progressive Victorian thinkers, stressed the erotic content of the unconscious. Indeed, she regarded sexuality as the fount of all artistic and intellectual inspiration, though she would not go as far as her friend Edward Carpenter, who claimed the energy that united the universe was desire. Schreiner, for all her belief in the erotic, charged that he too greatly devalued the rational side of the cosmos.[14] Although she did not flesh out her concept of the erotic content of the unconscious, she refused to assign it, anymore than she did the soul, gender attributes. Though historically acquired gender traits commingle in the artistic imagination, she invoked no a priori female sensibility, the rush of erotic/artistic energy essentially identical in both sexes.[15]

To be sure, Schreiner's interest in the physiology of unconscious processes and their relation to artistic imagination was hardly unique in her time. A cluster of Victorian scientists and philosophers, intrigued by the unconscious, foreshadowed the development of modern psychology and psychoanalysis. In 1872 Frances Power Cobbe had written about dreams in terms akin to Schreiner's. Cobbe's essay "Dreams and Illustration of Unconscious Cerebration," published in *Darwinism in Morals and Other Essays* (1883), was perhaps the source of Schreiner's term "unconscious cerebration." Cobbe cited the research of other investigators of the unconscious, most notably Dr. W. B. Carpenter, whom she credited with first coining "unconscious cerebration" in a lecture to the meeting of the Royal Institution on March 1, 1868, and with whose writing Schreiner was also familiar. Cobbe noted a long-standing British empirical interest in dreams, stemming from British interest in Leibnitz's writing on "latent thoughts" and "preconscious activity of the soul." Cobbe could have as easily referred to British Enlightenment inquiry into nonrational processes in the work of Hobbes, Locke, the Associationists, and Hume. Samuel Johnson's perceptions of the fluidity among impulse, instinct, passion, and imagination were particularly farseeing. British empirical analysis of the unconscious reached a nineteenth-century climax through the formation in 1882 of the Society for Psychical Research, which included such eminent figures as Frederic Myers, Samuel Butler, George Romanes, and Schreiner's friends Arthur Symons and J. A. Symonds. These men were all in active correspondence with William James in the United States and with Henri Bergson in France. The society drew no limits to its investigations of the unconscious, sharing in such fashionable pursuit of supernatural phenomena as communication with the dead.

No doubt Schreiner's intimate friendship with Havelock Ellis encouraged her scientific approach to unconscious flashes. Ellis's physical interest in the unconscious, his proclivity for naturalist and empirical explanations, led him to experiment with mescal in the 1890s to induce visions. No evidence exists to suggest that he and Schreiner attempted drug-stimulated visions earlier, in the 1880s, or even that they discussed such experiments, though Schreiner's heavy use of drugs for health reasons no doubt prompted her consideration of connections between drug and dream states.[16] More pertinent, through Ellis's publication in the 1880s and 1890s of scientific studies (the Contemporary Science Series), Schreiner read Albert Moll's *Hypnotism* (the most popular book of the series) and Mercier's *Sanity and Insanity,* which familiarized her with current theories on unconscious activity. She did not care for either of these books, preferring Ellis's *Criminal* and Geddes and Thompson's *Evolution of Sex* as more illuminating. Evidently, the supernatural directions of much of psychical research alienated her.[17]

Despite Schreiner's search for scientific explanation of creative flashes and dreams, she could not settle for purely physiological theories. When she was particularly awed by the mystery of a flash or dream, she wrote about the unconscious in semispiritual terms. According to Symons, she claimed "a force works in us such as works in nature, and if we follow that we must be right." Though the accuracy of Symons's reporting is doubtful, Schreiner's view of the artistic unconscious did coincide with her sense of the individual soul, at once unique and yet a microcosm of the cosmos' creative energies. Through Drummond and Rebekah, in terms akin to those of German and English romantic writers and theorists, she speaks of the flash as both universal and individual in time and place. Though the substance of an intuition is construed from an artist's lived experience, "himself-of-himself," Drummond and Rebekah philosophize, it represents more than that artist's particular life. The ability to dream, hear, see objects unknown to the artist's actual life arises from "the accumulated life of his race, of the millions of human creatures who have been his ancestors," to which he adds his unique ability, organically connected with the entire complex of human experience, to paint the future.[18] In short, the creative force bears both spiritual and material characteristics.

Schreiner, then, oscillated between naturalist and supernaturalist perspectives on unconscious activity. When eschewing supernatural angles, she advised that though dreams are revealing they are neither divine nor premonitory. When she considered possible links between her attraction to Buddhism and psychical research, she spoke of writing a story based on a *conscious,* not supernatural, migration of the soul.[19] Still, her belief in a form of collective unconscious, as well as her mystic illuminations of the fusion of individual soul and cosmic truths, inclined her toward a more romantic outlook on unconscious creativity. When, in her allegories, she imagined a synthesis of natural and transcendental reality, she heard, as did Keats and Shelley, the music of the spheres.

Schreiner's comments on artistic flashes raise a number of unresolved questions about the imagination which romantic thinkers bequeathed later theorists. Two among these bear directly on Schreiner's writing: (1) Were spontaneous flashes an expression of only beneficent nature? (2) Was the artist a passive vessel for the bubbling up of creative ideas, or did the artist control in some way the seemingly spontaneous inspiration?

Contrasting views of the morality of imagination flourished in the early nineteenth century. Theorists such as Shelley and Fichte upheld the imagination as the reservoir only of truth, good, and beauty, integrated exclusively with positive cosmic patterns and energy, whereas Johnson, Goethe, and later Keats acknowledged the imagination's destructive potency. For Goethe, whom Schreiner revered, the imagination could not regulate itself; it required the tether of hard facts and informed judgment. Schreiner's own position was inconsistent. Despite her frequent affirmation of the correspondence between artistic inspiration, the higher laws of the brain, and cosmic laws, she did not minimize the destructive sides of fantasy and imagination.

Schreiner's most comprehensive treatment of the ambiguity of imaginative activity was *African Farm,* in which the major characters and several of the minor ones are partly or wholly dreamers. She presented the dreamer as both tyrant and victim. Dreaming is juxtaposed at various points with realistic sensibility. The line between mere innocuous dream and possibly harmful illusion is blurred. The demonic nature of the dream is personified by Bonaparte Blenkins, modeled after the historic Bonaparte with his own grandiose fantasies. Blenkins envisions dominion over Tant' Sannie's farm, but consumed by his fantasy he loses his realistic grip, which ultimately leads to his downfall. A contrasting dreamer, Old Otto has such illusions of the goodness of human nature that he falls prey to Bonaparte Blenkins's machinations. Otto's son, Waldo, shares his father's gentle dreaming propensity, though his dreams are mixed with nightmarish terrors of the cruelty of God and nature. Although Waldo never forsakes dreaming (paradoxically, it is his primary link with sanity and love), he learns the danger of illusions, most painfully when he discovers that his adored Stranger (the teller of the Hunter allegory) participates collusively in an insensitive, snobbish, and oppressive social world.

It is Lyndall who can see through the illusions that deceive others. Most indicative of Schreiner's command of ambiguity, Lyndall-the-realist, who carefully plots her departure from the farm, has her own youthful fantasies about education, independence, and success, all of which dissolve in the face of actual experience. She dreams of someone who will deliver her from cynicism and hopelessness, her inability to affirm life—the fruits of her disillusionment. (Waldo, by contrast, swings from his own states of cynical despair to comforting and creative dreams.)

Schreiner's question of passive or active artistic receptivity was no less perplexing than that of the benign or malignant character of unconscious fantasies and dreams. Although she tended toward Schiller's and Emerson's views of the involuntary, passive character of at least initial artistic inspiration, she argued that, although a writer could not determine that flashes come or what their nature would be, she could prepare for their coming: "One lays oneself open," as Drummond explains; "You may put yourself into the condition in which they *may* come." In what resembled traditional Calvinist conceptions of opening oneself to the operation of God's grace, Schreiner dwelt on the need for active meditating, removed from distraction and requiring those same conditions conducive to her mystic vision.[20] Perhaps the key difference between preparing for spiritual visions as opposed to artistic illumination related to the greater physical activity stirring Schreiner's creative flow. Though sleep and rest were stimulants, no less was vigorous pacing, whether indoors or out. Since childhood, Schreiner had found that rhythmic walking could spark images and stories.[21] Proximity to landscape comparable to what she had known in her South African youth was vital. In Alassio, Italy, where she wrote many of her finest allegories, the colors and sky resembled those of South Africa, and, wandering the countryside, she found herself keenly receptive to both natural impressions and artistic flashes.[22]

For Schreiner, the unconscious not only gives birth to a literary work but to some extent influences its style. Just as her pacing evoked stories, so too did it shape her rhythmic diction. She spoke of "plain" or "ribbed" writing options, noting that these modes were unwilled and spontaneous. Her terms, *plain* or *ribbed*, were taken from knitting where "there are two stitches, one makes a plain surface and the other makes ribs. Ribbed knitting goes up and down, up and down." When she wrote description she tended to write plain, but when she philosophized or "painted thought" (her metaphor) she wrote ribbed, neither a deliberate choice. Both styles, she felt, involved deeper structures and laws than she could consciously grasp, laws as compelling as genetic structure. When Carpenter criticized her long sentences, she replied, "No, I like my long sentences—*when they come!* There are things you want to present short off and blank; and there are other things don't present themselves to your mind so. Their tails are part of their nature—like my little grey Persian cat's tail. My dog has no tail hardly—that's his nature."[23]

Sometimes Schreiner wished that she could exercise more control over basic form. Her allegory "The Sunlight Lay across My Bed" came to her in blank verse. She wished it had arrived in plain prose, for as a result she was "drawn unconsciously into doing the very thing I hate." "The very thing" was the lilt in her sentences, though she admitted she could not escape the power of the lilt, which produced "such a delicious sensation going all through your body."[24]

Whichever form and style was in command, Schreiner trusted her adherence to its inner structures and laws. She spoke of intuiting what is aesthetically right, sensing when a word or sentence violated the law and feeling the agony that violation caused.[25] Statements such as these were what led scholars to dub her strictly intuitive. And such would be a reasonable judgment were it not for her equal concern for the second stage of the creative process—that of crafting.

The transition to artistic stage two—the decision to give outward expression to the inspiration, flash, dream—could be either a conscious or an unconscious decision. Sometimes the claim of the unconscious image was so urgent, Schreiner explained, that the act of writing it out was comparable to the instinct that impelled birds to make nests. At other times, the artist chose to flesh out an idea more deliberately. Whether the decision to write be conscious or unconscious, Schreiner viewed personal desires—self-expression for its own sake and for one's own growth, to "see more"—as paramount in the decision's occurrence.[26] Social aims entered only with the third stage, the decision to publish.

Having willed to incarnate a story born of the unconscious, the artist must turn to issues of craft. In *From Man to Man*'s aesthetic dialogue, Rebekah maintains that the artist's only urge should be fidelity to the original intuition and finding the most effective techniques to express it. Schreiner, elsewhere in a letter, went so far as to say, "If I feel I have not expressed the exact truth that is in me in any line or sentence or book, it shall be destroyed." Consequently, after the first "inspired" draft, the writer must "turn a fierce, unblind criticism on it" and embark on needed revisions. This activity demanded the writer's finest energies. Schreiner told Cronwright that she could revise only when her "nature is alive and intense," adding "I dare not touch my work at a lower mood than the mood I wrote it in, or I shall spoil it."[27] She implied a two-phased crafting process. After the initial writing and revising, a finished work should undergo yet another revision. She deemed "distance" a crucial requirement so that artists "may judge of it [their work] in a manner which was not possible while the passion of creation and the link of unbroken emotion bound them to it." To the understanding of a person or object that springs from love and passion, the artist must add the understanding derived from cold criticism.[28] Evidently, Schreiner did not view such psychic sobriety as being at odds with the elevated mood she needed to revise.

Schreiner found the writing out and revising of her work a painful struggle. She contrasted her own slow, bleeding efforts with that of superficial artists who "write in water three novels a year!"[29] She told Symons that she had agonized over her allegory "The Sunlight Lay across My Bed" for three months in order to form it musically and pictorially. She was never satisfied with *From Man to Man*, which, like many other of her works, underwent innumerable revisions.[30] Although Schreiner usually felt that she was loyal to her inner inspiration, she hungered for perfect artistry. In a disconsolate moment, she wrote: "all I have done I hate. It is *true*, but there is perfect beauty *and* truth." Her dual commitment to truth and beauty (her Platonic belief that they were essentially compatible) was lifelong, early appearing in the words of the Stranger in *African Farm*. When the Stranger praises the truthfulness of Waldo's woodcarving, he adds, "What your work wants is not truth, but beauty of external form, the other half of art." He gently assures Waldo that with hard work and an inborn passion for beauty, skill will gradually follow.[31]

Schreiner's scrutiny of her writing, whether in initial or later revisions, could be so devastating that she would partially or entirely destory a manuscript. In July 1884, she had cut up and altered *From Man to Man* to such an extent that she plunged into despair: "There is hardly anything left and I don't know how to put it together. This afternoon I nearly got up and burnt the ms." She managed to persist with the novel, hoping to produce a better version. The following year she wrote nine drafts of one chapter of it, ultimately concluding that the preferred draft was her first draft.[32] Though she did not labor so extensively over all her works, a question must be raised: Was it reasonable self-criticism or neurotic perfectionism that aroused such sustained revising and self-deprecation? Or was it overweening ambition to produce a masterpiece? Certainly her critics' impression of Schreiner-the-pure-intuitive can be laid to rest.

Much of Schreiner's revising focused upon condensing. This she found "the most mentally wearing work." Though condensing consumed time significantly, her revising process spanned the gamut of stylistic concerns.[33] South African literary scholar Ridley Beeton studied her three drafts of a chapter of *From Man to Man* with exceptional care and concluded that her changes revealed "a grasp of nuance and a sensitivity to diction that (wrongly, I think) we have not always associated with Olive Schreiner." Her corrections showed an earnest eye for precision, complexity, and felicity, though occasional improvements were at the cost of boldness of statement.[34]

Schreiner's comments about revising are scattered through her correspondence. She was not more systematic in setting forth her criteria for effective writing than in explicating her social theories. Her views must be gleaned indirectly through her criticism of her own writing and that of others. Such an examination reveals a consistent set of literary values throughout her adult years, values consonant with her motives for incarnating her "flashes" as she did.

With regard to her own works, Schreiner judged *African Farm* crude and youthful. The novel, she admitted, contained "too much moralizing." She considered that fault a consequence of her solitary life, which made the novel "an outlet for all one's superfluous feelings, without asking too closely whether they can or cannot be artistically expressed there."[35] *African Farm* was specifically crude in its one-dimensional portrait of the confidence man Bonaparte Blenkins. Though "drawn closely after life," he lacked, Schreiner agreed with a criticism she had received from Ellis, sufficient artistic shading. Instead of painting him from the outside, she should have depicted him from within, "showing the how and why of his being the manner of sinner he was. . . . I should have entered into him and showed his many sides, not only the one superficial side that was ridiculous; then he would have been a real human creature to love or to hate, and not farcical at all."[36]

In her drive to move beyond parody and caricature, Schreiner was invoking the Victorian standard of character development, the central pillar of her and other Victorian writers' commitment to realism. She credited Goethe, especially *Wilhelm Meister*, with influencing her realistic approach to character, considering Goethe's effort to understand evil and paint life as it is, rather than hate and deny unpleasant truths, a model for her own work.[37]

Schreiner's sensitivity to charges of inadequate character dimensionality, as with Bonaparte Blenkins, aroused her own criticism of those writers with similar lapses, especially of subjective sympathy. Accordingly, Ibsen's characters, with the exception of Mrs. Alving (*Ghosts*), were "not real" because, Schreiner presumed, Ibsen never loved any of them and so they became "only pegs on which to hang actions and ideas." She criticized Shaw, Samuel Butler, and Hardy for the same deficiency.[38] By contrast, she applauded Shakespeare, and still more Euripides, for deeply caring for their characters. She also considered Dickens's and Balzac's strength in realistic characterization as originating in the way ordinary details of life had "eaten" emotionally into their own psyches.[39]

Schreiner extended her critical standard of realism beyond characterization to all literary phenomena. Indeed, her preface to *African Farm* is a realist manifesto. In it she contrasted her novelistic intent with the standards of idealized romances, literary expectations of which as applied to the realistic novel did the novel a disservice: "The canons of criticism that bear upon the one cut cruelly upon the other."[40] To paint life as it is, not as the romance would color it, demanded the artist depict foul as wholly as fair, nature's sinister and bloody claws as vividly as gorgeous wings. Like most Victorian exponents of realism, Schreiner held that where facts require that writing convey drab and grim experience, the artist must "squeeze the color from his brush and dip it into the gray pigments around him."[41]

In depicting life "as it is," Schreiner shared the Victorian assumption that an autonomous objective reality exists that interrelates seemingly diverse, discontinuous phenomena in meaningful patterns that have simply to be discovered, as a scientist discovers what the microscope makes plain, a discovery unshaped by the eye and perspective of the beholder. Like other Victorian writers, Schreiner used her fictive narrator to act as objective historian, whose omniscience interconnected simultaneous events as well as past, present, and future. In accordance with this convention, the narrators in her novels speak in the third person and in the past tense. With the familiar voice of the Victorian historian, the narrator in *From Man to Man* lifts the curtain on each mystery: "Now, what really happened to Baby-Bertie was this: . . ." Typical, too, of realist fiction, Schreiner's narrators, if not omniscient (at times explicitly limited), possess a distance from the events of the story that enables a wider angle of vision for the reader than that accorded individual characters.[42] The narrator enlists the reader's memory to perceive causal relations and ironies. Further, the panoramic vision separates the reader from single identification with a particular character's thought or feelings. For example, in *From Man to Man*, during the narrator's lengthy conveying of Rebekah's ruminations, the flow of Rebekah's thought is period- ically interrupted by narrator references to her gestures, her vocalizing, the rain outside, and household concerns. Gone is the philosophical narrator of *African Farm* who uses characters' inner monologues as a springboard for offering general truths about the human condition. Schreiner deliberately followed the realist novelists' efforts to remove the narrator's obtrusiveness but preserve the reader's distance from the characters' inner wrestlings through keeping a narrative eye on nonverbal behavior and external condi- tions: "She paced up and down quickly and more quickly with her hands behind her, still holding the pen, and went on in her thought to illustrate her view."[43] A variant form of such authorial intervention is the narrator's com- mentary on Rebekah's dream in which she shifts from being wife to being husband. The narrator informs the reader of the shift through a parenthetical sentence: "(She was him now, not herself any more.) And such a great tenderness came over him." The parenthesis makes a second appearance in the dream as Rebekah again shifts personae, this time from husband to newborn female child: "put his lips to its soft tiny lips (she felt the lips touch hers), and then he . . ."[44]

Schreiner's premise of a shared objective reality led to her narrator's presumptuous use of *we* and *our* to generalize her characters' experience as that of her readers. This tendency was evident as early as *African Farm* when, for example, in Part 2 (the psychospiritual stages of a soul's progression from infant consciousness to that of adolescence) the sequence is assumed to be collectively human, despite acknowledged individual differences.

Nevertheless, Schreiner and her fictional narrators were uneasy with prof- fering even their partial visions as reality's essence. Extending her realism to include life's mysteries, Schreiner, much like Eliot in her later writings, viewed elusive, subjective, and intangible facts as likewise worthy, empirical, and artistic subjects. Schreiner held that "the method of life" defied predic- tion, known causal explanations, and a sense of neat coherence. On life's stage, she expounded, "There is a strange coming and going of feet. . . . When the crisis comes the man who would fit it does not return. When the curtain falls no one is ready. When the footlights are brightest they are blown out; and what the name of the play is no one knows." These mysterious facts of existence are what enabled her, as I shall elaborate shortly, to deviate from the conventional realist fiction she prized.[45]

Schreiner experimented with a variety of techniques that would express elusive psychic and transcendent reality. A minor example is Rebekah's extended letter to her husband, an essay Schreiner admitted could not be composed in the one night Rebekah claimed to have written it. But such a lapse in credibility was acceptable, Schreiner felt, since her primary goal was the full externalization of Rebekah's feelings. More striking an example is her use of allegories, whether in the form of dream tales or as segments of her novels and stories. According to Symons, Schreiner regarded her allegories as "the very essence of art"; she deemed all art symbolic and allegories a pure symbolic form. Insofar as the artist was the vessel of the collective unconscious, allegories could carry a truth further than ordinary realism, a conviction that led Schreiner to assert that her allegories had "a deeper value" than *African Farm*.[46]

Moving toward alliance with realism's staunchest opponents, Schreiner disdained photographic representation as not true art. Despite the detailed veracity of passages in *Undine*, they were for her no more art than a diary. She often spoke of suggestiveness as a cardinal quality of true art. The Stranger in *African Farm* declares, "[Art] says more than it says, and takes you away from itself. It is a little door that opens into an infinite hall." In this regard, Schreiner particularly cherished poetry: "As soon as there is the form and the spirit, the passion and the thought, then there is poetry, or the *living* reality."[47]

In considering questions of craft relevant to conveying subjective reality, Schreiner was unable to maintain her self-defined borders between the second stage of creativity, the artist's writing for herself, and the third stage, audience considerations and issues of publication. Indeed, Schreiner's tidy separation of personal and social aims was deceptive and reflected her deep confusion over artistic aims. She argued that the artist's task must go beyond incarnating an insight for herself to where she made the image real to someone else: "If I tell you that John Smith was sitting at this table, *I must make you see him there.*" Virginia Woolf, though far from enthusiastic about Schreiner's writing, credited her with achieving this goal. When encountering Schreiner's writing, she felt "in the presence of a powerful nature which can make us see what it saw, and feel what it felt with astounding vividness."[48]

Schreiner's foremost critical criterion, which united both romantic and realist aesthetic ideals, was a passionate devotion to truth telling. To her favorite writers she attributed such passion, which penetrated into the deepest strata of reality and re-created its complexity with a direct, unadorned, yet graceful sytle. Among those she most acclaimed for this accomplishment were Euripides, Shakespeare, Milton, Shelley, Heine, Turgenev, Goethe, Sand, Emily and Charlotte Brontë, Austen, and to some degree Dickens.[49] Above all others, Heine, whose grave "was the most sacred spot to me in Europe," elicited her esteem.[50] She identified with his writing more closely than with any other artist, informing Ellis, "I know how and why he wrote every line he did write. There is more depth and passion in one of his sneers, more quivering tenderness veiled under it, than in the outcries of half the world."[51] In later years she treasured Euripides almost as highly, judging him a far superior playwright to Shakespeare, admiring his "fierce, unrestrained questioning of the mystery of existence, and also his deep understanding of woman's position."[52]

The passion and depth of her beloved writers were able to stimulate thoughts and feelings that extended beyond each specific work of theirs: "I like a book you can only read a few pages of and then you have to throw it down you have so many thoughts of your own." She singled out Goethe, Whitman, and Robert Browning as artists with this gift of stimulation. By contrast, she found Tennyson, though a master of sweet and tender poetry, unable to spark her thought. That was because Tennyson (as well as Schiller) lacked sufficient intellectual range and emotional intensity. Even less stimulating was Zola, whose work and "that school" (naturalism, one assumes) she "hated," though what exactly repelled her, and how she distinguished naturalism from realism, she never explicated.[53]

With the third stage of literary production—the decision to publish—her artistic objectives became more complex. According to Rebekah in her conversation with Drummond, the decision to make a work public, that is, to remove it from the artist's self, is a fully conscious act, much like weaning a child. In considering an array of honorable and dishonorable motives for publication, Rebekah predictably dismisses as true art work that originates in the thirst for money or fame.[54] The honorable motives, ones that Schreiner personally claimed activated her, are essentially three: (1) the simple desire to re-create for others the writer's perception of beauty and truth; (2) the yearning to alleviate human isolation and suffering; and (3) the urge "not to let the thing die!" Schreiner asserted that the first motive was foremost in her mind when she decided to publish *African Farm*, but more commonly she emphasized the second motive. For all her prizing of private art, she needed to write for others to escape her own isolation: "Art is the little crack in the iron wall of life which shuts one in awful isolation through which the spirit can force itself out and show itself to its own like-minded fellow spirits outside; or rather creep in through the cracks in the terrible walls that shut in the individual life."[55]

Schreiner hoped that by showing that another person felt as her readers did, and by fostering human understanding and tenderness, her writing could decrease the suffering that loneliness brings, especially for women and for social outcasts of either gender. With specific relation to *From Man to Man* she proposed that, "if only one lonely struggling woman read it and found strength and comfort from it, one would not feel one had quite lived in vain."[56]

Schreiner felt her writing would relieve loneliness by articulating (to paraphrase Alexander Pope) what others deeply felt but did not have the talent and skills to express.[57] Here, she is in harmony with Novalis's (late eighteenth century) and Keats's (early nineteenth century) view of the poet as psychic physician. Unlike George Eliot, who validated art as a means to create a larger and more humane community through extending the boundaries of readers' collective sympathy, Schreiner saw her fiction as fostering at best specific interpersonal sympathy. The closest she came to Eliot's outlook was in her justification for publishers' charging a higher price for her *Dreams* than for *African Farm*. Whereas the latter was written for the comfort of poor and lonely souls, the former was intended to ignite the conscience of the rich and powerful.[58]

Despite the confidence with which Rebekah can set forth the honorable reasons for publishing, Schreiner's acute sense of privacy and her sensitivity to misinterpretation frequently undermined her belief in any publication's social usefulness. In a most undemocratic mood she wrote that the mass audience would inevitably misunderstand and desecrate her work. From childhood, when she would tear up a story that Will had managed to find and read, to her adult years when the sheer sight of *African Farm* in a store window felt like a knife in her heart, she felt both violated and morally promiscuous in the act of sharing deeply personal thoughts. Regarding *From Man to Man* she asked Ellis, "Do you think I could write Bertie's death scene, do you think I could show all the inmost working of Rebekah's heart, if I realized that anyone would ever read it?"[59] The novella *Peter Halket* provides an unusual instance of where Schreiner could risk the outrage of family and friends and yet not feel psychic violation. Although she devoted much care to the artistry of the composition, and interspersed dreams and personal experiences throughout, the novella never plumbed her inner depths and thus, as a published work, never threatened to expose her most personal experience.

Various feminist literary scholars have treated the conflict between the demands of art and female anxieties over self-disclosure.[60] Clearly, though Schreiner shared these anxieties, feminine acculturation was unlikely their primary source since she readily violated so many canons of feminine propriety. The frequency with which her writing actually was misunderstood and attacked by her family and friends seems a more salient source. One of many such difficult occasions was her discovery, not long after her return to South Africa in 1890, that her family and friends were horrified by Ellis's essays and could neither understand nor accept her allegories. It stung her that her allegories were disliked even by one of her closest friends, Erilda Cawood. Schreiner treasured individual, positive responses to her writing, particularly her allegories. On the whole, despite her eagerness to reach out to the Waldos and Lyndalls of the world, she sensed that much of her work was unpopular. At times, she defined her audience in such a way as to mitigate her awareness of this. She spoke of writing for her husband, close friends, and a more sympathetic posterity.[61]

In general, as distinct from her nonfiction or *Peter Halket*, where she knew exactly which audience she wished to convert, Schreiner's sense of audience grew confused when she wrote her fiction. Not only was she unclear whether she wrote for her present or a future generation, or whether she wrote for herself only or for others, she also had to deal with the incompatibility of colonial and noncolonial, Boer and English South African readers. Their differing values, family life, and even geographical experience complicated Schreiner's struggle for both material and subjective realism. Consider, for example, her fictional landscapes. For South African readers the desert terrain of her novels as well as Cape Town and other South African towns and villages were familiar. By contrast, for the English reading public, these settings were alien and exotic. They were accustomed to novels set in country villages amid green, undulating hills and valleys or in the hurly-burly of industrial and commercial centers. If one of the goals of realism, and a goal of Schreiner's, was that of uncovering the significance of the ordinary and the familiar as breathtaking, then Schreiner's fiction was bound to have drastically different results for metropolitan and colonial readers. How could a British reader respond to Waldo's gaze at a little ice plant, whose crystalline pattern and beauty he discerns, with the same shock of recognition as a South African who is reveling in a familiar object endowed with fresh significance?[62]

It may well be that just this complexity of readership accounts for Schreiner's alacrity in combining diverse modes of writing within and among her works. In this fashion, whatever the readers' backgrounds, parts of

Schreiner's work will seem written specifically for them. When Rebekah enters into a long, sophisticated, theoretical digression, for example, those among Schreiner's readers who were the advanced thinkers of their time would find in Rebekah's astonishing intellectuality their instant kin, though it is hard to imagine those less educated than Rebekah remaining engaged. On the other hand, "The Prelude," which begins *From Man to Man*, could easily attract the ordinary, conventional reader, charmed by its fairy tale quality. What appealed to the widest array of Schreiner's readers, despite the mystified comments of some of her relatives and friends, were her dreams and allegories. Removed from highly specific, detailed, earthly terrain, these elicited praise from a widely heterogeneous public, from working-class women in cooperatives to wealthy entrepreneurs. The dreams and allegories appeared in countless editions, including tiny pocket-size versions, popular throughout England and the United States.

The Medium of Dreams

Dreams form the most prevalent and distinctive motif in Schreiner's fiction. Though many nineteenth-century writers incorporated dreams into their writing, Schreiner accorded them a singular primacy. Many of her allegories and short stories were cast almost wholly as dreams. Indeed, her first published collection of allegories was titled *Dreams*. Dreams graced her novels, and even in her nonfiction she inserted dreams to advance and enrich her arguments.

Schreiner's dreams assumed myriad forms: sleep dreams, daytime fantasies, political satires, utopian visions, and more. They served multiple purposes. Crucially, they freed her from the constraints of conventional, linear realism and allowed her to enter the realm of fluid time and space. Past, present, and future could merge, transcending the boundaries between rational and nonrational, conscious and unconscious phenomena. Dreams offered her ways of bridging actual and ideal reality, mythic and spiritual perceptions, with material existence (the flash became flesh). Serving as vehicles to express her moral, political, and social ideals, pointing to ways to heal divisions of race, class, and gender, her dream images no less importantly were able to transform and transfigure her own and, she hoped, others' perception of the seeming inevitabilities of their immediate, often mundane lives.

Particularly in light of the wide readership for *Dreams*, I find considerable merit in Jane Marcus's argument that, whereas irony mocks the ordinary reader, allegories are direct, naked, the universal language of archetypal image accessible to all. Dreaming was an effective strategy for nineteenth-century women, especially writers, to move beyond the social restraints on their autonomy. Read in conjunction with her more earthy, concrete, social and political treatises as well as her narrative verisimilitudes, Schreiner's literary use of dreams can be seen to serve a crucial and complementary function, that of arousing in her readers the passionate idealism and optimism requisite to positive actions detailed elsewhere in her writing.[63] In sum, dreaming was for her not primarily escapist activity but an instrument for reconceiving and changing the present.

Of her varied fictional writing, Schreiner's allegories embodied the most diverse functions of her dreams.[64] For that reason I will treat her allegories first and follow with an analysis of other of Schreiner's fiction in which dreams play a formative role.

Chief among Schreiner's allegorical ingredients was the dissolving of Victorian oppositions between actual and ideal reality. In "The Sunlight Lay across My Bed" the narrator, through two extended night dreams, is able to move back and forth between the mundane and the transcendent. The "I" of the story, in despair over human nature, leaves grimy, noisy London where he felt suffocated. He undertakes a journey to Hell and Heaven and, while in Hell, discovers the symbiosis, discussed previously, between the exploitative upper classes and oppressed workers. During the narrator's time in Heaven, he beholds visions of androgyny and genderlessness, and the commingling of music, light, God, self, and collective humanity. The dream is preeminently transformative, for when the illumined narrator awakens, instead of the familiar sordid character of London, he finds ordinary life radiant. Diverse individual souls, no longer choked by urban dust, cry out for truth and beauty.

With "Three Dreams in a Desert" Schreiner introduced another form of boundary transcendence. This allegory telescopes the collective history of women—past, present, and future—climaxing in an evocative vision of androgyny and female autonomy as well as male–female and female–female equality, comradeship, and affection. Yet another form of exceeding limits occurs in the most abstract of Schreiner's dream allegories, "A Dream of Wild Bees," where bees metamorphose into humans and, as in traditional allegories, abstract values take on human shape as well. The Ideal, for example, appears as a sallow-faced, hollow-cheeked figure with a quivering smile. A startling feature of this allegory is its fusion of the Ideal and the Real in the form of a dreaming fetus within its dreaming mother!

The least stylistically inventive, though in certain respects the most original of Schreiner's dream allegories was her political satire "The Salvation of a Ministry," originally titled, simply, "Dream."[65] As noted previously, the stimulus for this allegory was her outrage at Rhodes's support for the strop bill. The narrator of the allegory has a dream that pits Christian ethics against the political behavior of the ministers of the Cape Colony government. Various members of the Ministry come before God's throne to face judgment as to their fitness to enter Heaven. The strop bill and other government policies are indicted. The dream culminates in God's sentencing of Rhodes. Although one of Schreiner's most comic literary pieces, a bagatelle of sorts, it makes no particularly imaginative boundary leap. Its originality lies in its goal. Except for such early modern allegories as Erasmus's *Julius Exclusus,* modern allegories have not targeted specific individuals and political policies. In fact, allegorical writing was uncommon among nineteenth-century British writers. According to literary historian Paul Piehler, romantic distrust of the universalizing of individual experience, along with scientific empiricism and social realism, rejected the allegory as mere artifice.[66] If we consider the dreams and allegories of other mid- and late-Victorian writers, for example William Morris and the pre-Raphaelites, we find brilliantly painted visions of alternative worlds, but worlds projected so far into the past or future that no bridge appears between present conditions and the allegorical utopia. Not only, then, was Schreiner an uncommon allegorist, but she was singular for her time in transforming the allegorical mode into political and social criticism, satire, and exhortation. In effect, she took the moral allegorical mode of *Pilgrim's Progress,* a work she knew well, and secularized it, emphasizing social redemption and propaganda among the aims of moral instruction.

Among Schreiner's short stories, two are woven virtually as dreams, "The Great Heart of England" and "Who Knocks at the Door?" They differ markedly from her allegories in their pessimism. Composed during World War I, they are essentially nightmares. The first line of "The Great Heart of England" reads: "I have had a dream, and again it comes to me till I fear the night for its return."[67] Both dreams, to the degree that we can verify their social intent, seek to awaken war-hungry and power-intoxicated Britons to the horror of their government's policies, but both dreams may simply embody Schreiner's personal testimony of the world's evil.

"The Great Heart of England" is very brief and laden with vivid psychological imagery. The narrator dreams that she has lost all of her clothes; even her beloved dress is "shot to pieces." She arranges for a new dress to be made, but the only materials available are in garish colors, combining a clashing red, white, and blue (of the Union Jack) with green (of the Irish nationalist movement?). Having no other choice, she wears her patchwork dress and, with a broken heart, dances down the street while passersby taunt her about her dress's colors and her dancing. Ominously, she hears a familiar old song about the hanging of men and women who wear green. Quick upon this she sees the gleam of bayonets, and guns begin to fire. The story ends with her yearning to hear once again the heartbeat of England's idealistic love of justice.

By casting this story into a dream form, Schreiner achieved several purposes. Able to avoid distracting realistic questions about her specific female character, she afforded herself the license to present a single, powerful image of a brokenhearted woman, who appears to embody the blasted illusions of the Irish nationalist movement, the prewar Liberal government's promise for a united, free Ireland, and also the emerging conflict-ridden, patchwork, divided Ireland. Through the woman's dance, Schreiner combines an array of feelings—anger, sadness, wistfulness—with the resolve to survive, no matter in what disheveled or manic state.

"Who Knocks at the Door?" also bears allegorical overtones. The narrator, incited by the death and destruction of World War I, dreams of being in a stormy, dark, primeval forest. She comes upon an opulent and elegant banquet hall, its tables spread with rare meat and wines, suggestive of European society just before and during World War I. The bejeweled people in the hall, for all their individual differences, share much in common as the men fall into vicious, demented battle, with the women spurring them on. Destruction and death ensue on a grand scale, the belligerents unaware of three knocks on the banquet hall door by some indefinable human force. The narrator leaves the scene, overcome by its madness, as she awakens. As with her allegories, this story freed Schreiner to roam beyond literal time and space and to employ expressionistic techniques to crystallize prime features of European political and social history, particularly—as with George Bernard Shaw's *Heartbreak House*—the lunacy of war and the tragic obliviousness of the privileged to its nature and consequences.

The ambivalent impact of dreaming, at once creative and destructive, was an important feature of Schreiner's early short story "Dream Life and Real Life: A Little African Story," which in this regard prefigured *African Farm*. This story incorporated two dreams, both rich in social and psychological insight, one with a decisive impact on the plot. Janita, a poor, indentured orphan child lives with an abusive Boer family, for whom she herds Angora goats. One day while herding, she feels depressed and tired and falls asleep. She has a "beautiful dream" that transmutes all the unpleasant facts of her

The Aesthetics of Literary Miscegenation

life: The "kraals" for the sheep change from drab red stone to lilac trees, and the goats, upon their return from grazing, leap over a blossoming lily rod instead of a bare stick. Her ordinarily cruel, callous, stingy masters now smile at her, are polite, and feed her well. As her dream unfolds, she is no longer a vulnerable orphan: Her father is alive, kisses her, and carries her away to Denmark in his strong arms.

The story's title, "Dream Life and Real Life," keeps its promise: While Janita sleeps and dreams, one of her goats is stolen. For this calamity, when she awakens, she is deprived of dinner and whipped, one of her hands cut open. In her hurt and despair she runs away, savoring her freedom and in time creating a feathery wild asparagus and rock hideaway. On the second night of her flight she has her second dream, again resurrecting her father. Daughter and father, their heads crowned with wild asparagus, walk together, hand in hand, while passersby smile, kiss her, and bestow upon her flowers and food. Waking up, she overhears two robbers planning to burn down the Boer family hut. She flees back to the Boer home to warn the family, but in vain, and only to be killed by the two robbers.

These two dreams disclose various meanings. If Janita had not dreamed on the job, she might have spotted the robbers earlier, warned the Boers in time, and saved her own life. Dreaming, in this light, is dangerous, indeed fatal. Yet it is dreaming that enables Janita to endure her daily ordeals. Dreaming nourishes her with beauty and affection. Her fantasies become, as with countless oppressed peoples who have no other viable recourse, her instrument of survival, even though in this case they indirectly lead to her death. Both dreams also heighten the readers' perception of the cruelty and ugliness of Janita's actual circumstances through juxtaposing the details of her suffering with alternative, imagined possibilities. Poignantly, the fact that her father performs the deliverance role and that her mother is never mentioned reveals Victorian social patterns and Janita's (possibly also the young Schreiner's) gender acculturation.

Midway between Schreiner's short stories and novels lies *Peter Halket*. I explore its social and political content elsewhere. Here I want to examine the way dreams shape it. An extensive dream of moral conversion and psychological healing forms the axis of the novella's first half. This dream inspires Peter in the second half of the story to act out his transformed convictions. Unlike the role of dreams in Janita's experience and in *African Farm*, Peter's dream has a clearly positive impact, facilitating his moral maturation, though the dream's aftermath culminates, too, in Peter's heroic, albeit futile, death.

As in the allegories, the dream in this novella obliterates realistic historical and scientific causality. Its subjecting Peter to critical questioning is obviously an expressionistic externalization of Peter's inner conflict, his repressed guilt over his behavior, in view of his moral upbringing by his mother. As such, the dream offers a more dramatic and engaging way for the reader to confront that conflict than, say, through extended narrative exposition of Peter's inner reflections. As in many classical and medieval allegories, the dream dialogue permits the reader to identify with both contending parties; in effect, the reader vicariously undergoes Peter's conversion to his questioner's point of view. Further, as Stephen Gray has brilliantly set forth, the dream mode offers Peter a way of releasing sexual anxieties and coming to terms with his specific childhood traumas, for example, Peter's missing father, poverty, and the humiliation of class inferiority.[68]

It is in Schreiner's novels that dreams appear in their greatest complexity, taking on a multiplicity of forms, unveiling character, influencing plot, and offering societal visions. In *African Farm*, although most of the characters in the novel dream—including Waldo's dog, Doss—the principal dreamer is Waldo, who is subject to "dreaming fits." As a child and adolescent he had both nightmares and soothing dreams, which reflected his spiritual doubts and hopes. His most significant dream happens late in the novel, in chapter 13, "Dreams." The dream follows upon Gregory Rose's account of Lyndall's death and precipitates Waldo's heart attack. Until the very end of the dream, the fantasy is elegiac; Schreiner paints a sensuous landscape wherein interpersonal behavior is romantic and impressionistic. The entire dream canvas is bathed in sunshine, the setting one of high mountains with snowy peaks and steep sides covered with bush. Between the foot of the mountains and an unearthly blue and breezy sea stretches a narrow forest. Aromatic honeycreepers hang from its dark green bushes, and streams purl through velvety grass down to the sea. Waldo and Lyndall (appearing as a child) sit together amid the bushes on a high, square rock. Suddenly, Lyndall disappears. Waldo follows her little footmarks, eventually seeing her in the distance gathering shells. She is now a woman. She awaits his coming, and they walk together over the sand and shells, listening to the music of leaves, streams, and sea. On an expanse of white sand, Lyndall pauses, drops each shell, gazes into Waldo's face. She lifts one hand and lays it "softly on his forehead; the other . . . on his heart." With that action, the serenity is broken. Her touch cuts through him like a knife, and he awakens in agony.[69]

The expressionistic techniques of this dream dramatize Waldo's passion for Lyndall, his broken heart over her death, and his coming heart attack, with graphic economy. A remarkable feature of this dream is Schreiner's transmutation of who is alive and who is dying. Contrary to reality, Lyndall is fully alive as the dream ends whereas Waldo is fatally stricken by Lyndall's touch. Perhaps the dream expresses Waldo's longing to die in Lyndall's place, if by so doing she would still live.

The most famous and compelling dream, a daydream, in the novel is the Hunter allegory (treated in Chapter 2 for its philosophical content). Not only does the allegory permit Schreiner to express her basic philosophical beliefs, it also serves as a delicate and decisive moment in Waldo's character development as it releases him for a time from the weight of loneliness and despair and advances his pondering on the nature of life. Coming at a vital moment in Waldo's life, it smacks of a dream come true. The brief appearance from some unknown terrain of a figure, never named, who understands and addresses one's most secret and convulsive feelings is surely a quintessential and widely shared fantasy.[70]

What is striking is Schreiner's readiness to use an extended allegory to interrupt the novel's narrative flow. Her decision is wholly consonant with the texture of Waldo's consciousness, his brooding as a young child over the souls slipping off the edge of the world into Hell, his dreams a little later of the sweet Rose of Heaven, and his spurning of supernatural illusions. He shares with the narrator the ironic view that religious beliefs are dreams and that "without dreams and phantoms man cannot exist." The narrator observes that each generation creates its own dreams of existential meaning.[71] "The Hunter" is just such a dream, of a more secular-minded generation.

Because in Schreiner's last and unfinished novel, *From Man to Man*, she subordinated existential crises to pressing questions of gender and, to some degree, race and class, the novel's fantasies consequently serve as modes of feminist, antiracist, and antiimperialist instruction and inspiration. Occasionally, as in her other writing, Schreiner uses dreams to expose personality dynamics. New kinds of fantasizing also appear. The primary dreamers are the two sisters, Rebekah and Baby-Bertie.

A dream motif in *From Man to Man* that is absent in her other writing is the rambling imagery, the fleeting impressions, of semisleep states. At one point, Rebekah, nearly asleep, experiences a flow of pictures conveying her daily pressures and pleasures. She sees pictures of household items—the rows of tins on her kitchen shelf needing dusting, the large bag of wash-clothes needing counting—and also pictures of impersonal items—the curious moss to be examined under her microscope, "Kaffir" bean trees, rock piles—as well as, finally, the site where her husband, Frank, first embraced her. A more complex expression of Rebekah's subjective consciousness is her transsexual dream, the product too of a half-asleep state.[72] She fantasies being a man with a strong, hard body and revels in his life opportunities and his ability to protect weaker and smaller beings. In the dream she becomes the husband of a pregnant wife. He is lying on a mat in a hut, and his wife's head rests on his shoulder. He lovingly enwraps her with his limbs. The dream proceeds to the birth of their infant. At this point Rebekah becomes the baby and thrills to its father's kiss. In this dream Rebekah is both the giver and the receiver of male tenderness. This fantasy epitomized not only Rebekah's but Schreiner's longings for male/female nurturance and sensuous gentleness. To what extent it also served as wish fulfillment for readers cannot be known, but given the rigidly bound constraints on gender in nineteenth- and twentieth-century Europe, the dream's freedom of role playing and gender transmutation would no doubt gratify many of Schreiner's female readers.

More explicitly feminist and didactic is five-year-old Rebekah's elaborate daydream, which acts as the core of chapter 1, "The Prelude." As I suggested in Chapter 5, the fantasy provided bewildered, lonely, and persecuted Rebekah with hope, companionship, and inner freedom. It was the counterpart to her audible conversations with a made-up male friend, Charles. Replete with expressionistic strokes, the fantasy enables young Rebekah to be an ideal mother, full of love, perfect understanding, and guidance for her baby. It provides solace to Rebekah, confused by her coming upon the one dead infant of the twins recently conceived by her mother. To some extent, it foreshadows Rebekah's nurturance of the live twin, Baby-Bertie, and of her own children. Characteristic of most of Schreiner's dreams, the fantasy incorporates details of South African landscape and people, mingled with non-African settings the dreamer has never seen. In this fantasy Rebekah travels to an island, where swans swim on still waters, though she has never seen an island or real swans. On this island, too, are South African flora and fauna, including mimosa trees and cock-o-veets. This suspension of realism that permitted Schreiner to interlace fantasied and actual experience extends to the various lyrics that dot "The Prelude": quotations from classic poetry, folk limericks, and comic doggerel on the order of "You tell tale tit, / your tongue shall be slit, / And every dog in the town, / Shall have a little bit!"[73]

Whereas Rebekah's dreams are usually sanguine, Baby-Bertie's fantasy life, like her physical life, is decidedly the opposite. Bertie's saga of sexual seduction and betrayal and her ultimate desperate succumbing to prostitution endow her dreams with a richness of unconscious erotic imagery rare in Schreiner's writing. As but one example, after Bertie hears rumors of her fallen state at a Cape Town dance, she dreams she is seated in a round circuslike theater, filled with people in tiers of seats from floor to ceiling. Scattered in the center of the circular stage is white sand on which women in white dresses dance. Suddenly the crowd stops watching the dancers, and their eyes search the theater until they fix on Baby-Bertie, her presence spotted by a man "with a great red fat face" who points at her with his "great red fat finger." The audience rises, staring at her, as the man cries out, "That is she!" She tries to flee but cannot. The staring faces include those of her family and its servants, everyone she has ever known. The dream climaxes when one dancer's white dress gets torn. It leaves a long white trail which, as the dancer twirls, whirls and grows fuller until it billows out to where Bertie sits, enveloping her and the audience so that "they [are] all suffocating."[74] As in other character-revealing dreams, Schreiner wove into this account details from the precipitating predream episode. At the Cape Town dance, Bertie is twirling rapidly when someone treads on her dress. This tears the white gauze, which covers the silk skirt from waist to hem, leaving a streamer of long gossamer flounce. It is when she is pinning it back in place that she overhears the women gossiping about her. As she runs in the rain to her sister's home, the gauze train slips from her arm and billows out behind her, trailing in the mud puddles and dead leaves. Schreiner's care in situating this dream in physical circumstances underscored her refusal to have dreams replace realism altogether.

Multiple layers of meaning are embedded in Bertie's frightening dream, though its overall plot and character function are to deepen the reader's subjective awareness of Bertie's terror and the desperation that soon impels her to flee Rebekah and Cape Town. Sexual implications are evident in the ruin of the virginal white train, in the man with the fat, red face and finger, and even, perhaps, in the tumultuous round and deep theater with its circular stage of frenzied dancing. Bertie's sense of herself as a circus freak, exposed by gross, vulgar men, certainly underscores the position of women once reputable, now socially stained.

Literary Techniques

In crafting her allegories, dreams, and expository passages, Schreiner deployed techniques that, sometimes intuitive, sometimes deliberate, were consonant with her visionary impulses. Though seeking to reconstruct the conventional ways of seeing and feeling of a broad audience, she frequently adopted the symbolic vocabulary of her upbringing, a language that included traditional symbolic dichotomies at odds with her desire to dissolve dualistic mentalities. To some extent her predicament was unavoidable. If she had utilized imagery and rhythms unfamiliar to her readers, she certainly risked their refusal to read further and grapple with her ideas. Her choices, however, might have been less conscious than this interpretation conveys. The discrepancy between her symbolic language and her conscious sensibilities certainly points to deeper recesses of conflict within her which contributed to other occasional inconsistencies and contradictions in her writing and behavior. Although this tactic may have won her a responsive readership in her own time, it did so at a cost both to her own creativity and to later twentieth-century critical respect for her work.

As one would expect from a writer who relied upon unconscious "flashes," light was the paramount symbol in Schreiner's writing. Her use of light was conventional, easily resonating with her readers' experience with other literature: the Bible, religious sermons and iconography, oral traditions, classic mythology, Platonic dialogues. Nineteenth-century poets commonly depicted the imagination as an overflowing fountain of light—the radiating sun. The spirit of man was termed a candle, the mind a lamp.[75] At the time Schreiner was writing her first works, Max Müller published his interpretation of myth in terms of solar symbolism. His readers heralded the volume as authoritative. Concurrently, nineteenth-century scientists contributed to intellectual interest in light through their probing of light as intense, refined energy.[76]

The classic and common duality of light versus dark permeated Schreiner's writing. Despite her penchant for undermining polarities, she never suggested that some blend of the two elements, such as dusk, might serve as a more reflective setting than full light or that the dark might hold incomparable truths and beauty. Unlike most romantics, she was not attracted to transitional light. She describes death in *African Farm* as "The Gray Dawn," evoking popular dread of liminal states.[77] In general, her verbal painting selected starkly contrasting colors and forms: not only dark versus light, but red or black versus white, huge versus tiny, inside versus outside. She was clearly oblivious to the racist overtones of equating darkness and blackness with negative reality.

In Schreiner's various allegories of moral and spiritual instruction, positive experiences, ideals, and figures are bathed in light. Several examples can suffice. In *African Farm*, when Old Otto feels Jesus' presence, he experiences his room full of light. The narrator describes Otto's bearded face as "illuminated with a radiant gladness." Otto senses "that at almost any moment the thin mist of earthly darkness that clouded his human eyes might be withdrawn." Similarly, in the novel's chief allegory, after the Hunter passes through the dark valley of superstition, he follows a faint light along the horizon that leads him to the mountain of Truth upon which "the merry sunshine" plays.[78]

Truth, purity, and light are virtually synonymous. In "A Dream of Wild Bees" truth enters the dreaming fetus as a sensation of light. When in "In a Ruined Chapel" the seeker finally discerns the essential soul of the individual whom he cannot forgive, his eyes radiate light so intensely that the guiding angel "shaded his own face with his wing from the light." The allegory in which Schreiner used light most evocatively is appropriately titled "The Sunlight Lay across My Bed." It can be visualized as an impressionistic canvas. To the narrator who ascends the levels of Heaven the inhabitants there glow. They shine on plants to make them grow. The small stones of truth that they garner are so bright that God must touch the narrator's eyes in order for him to see them. When the ultimate enlightenment of universal oneness bursts into being, the scene dazzles "so bright I could not see things separately. . . . we were all blended."[79]

The power of sunlight to lay reality bare pervades all of Schreiner's writing. Sun shining through a little leaf of an ice plant enables Waldo to "see every little crystal cell like a drop of ice in the transparent green, and it thrilled him." Here, light serves Waldo's scientific impulse. In a more metaphysical vein, when Waldo, forlorn, basks in a lovely, sunny day, his despair brightens: "There will always be something worth living for while there are shimmery afternoons."[80]

Schreiner's use of sunlight would be simplistic were it not for her recognition of the sun's deadly power. In *African Farm*, the parched desert landscape forms a backdrop to the brutal events on the farm. The sun's merciless heat shrivels plants, causes drought and starvation, and melts the mutton chops of Waldo's futile sacrifice to God. Schreiner's depiction of the awesome impact of sunlight upon arid and semiarid terrain lends her writing an oft-noted, timeless, biblical quality.[81]

Firelight ranks second to sunshine as a source of enlightenment. When Peter Halket looks into the blaze of his campfire, the flames set him thinking, kindle his conscience, and prepare him for the arrival of the Stranger from Palestine. During the dialogue that ensues, the Stranger adjusts the logs, making the flames soar, much to Peter's amazement. The flames correspond to Peter's inner surge of conscience, just as they do for the Hunter in the Stranger's allegory when, as he beholds the white bird of Truth, "a great fire burned within his breast to find the bird."[82]

An adroit variation of firelight is Schreiner's decision to cast fireflies in

From Man to Man as heralds "of the coming dawn after the dark." It is at the end of the chapter "Fireflies in the Dark" that Mr. Drummond, the precursor of Rebekah's "new man," enters the story. Schreiner's cornucopia of luminous sources includes the lighthouse (the Stranger from Palestine would have Peter Halket be a moral beacon for others) and glow-worms, which become another image for the potential proselyting role of the righteous on earth. The minister in *Peter Halket* justifies his speaking out against evil with the comment, "Shall the glow-worm refuse to give its light, because it is not a star set up on high?"[83]

Like sunshine, other light sources are not always positive. There are deceptive lights: When the Hunter suffers in the dark and rainy Land of Absolute Negation and Denial, two merry wisps of light dance like "stars of fire" to beckon him to abandon his quest for truth. A particularly and traditionally ambiguous source of light for Schreiner is the moon; its dark side and its association with night lend it a sinister power. If *African Farm* ends serenely with the landscape awash in sunlight, the novel begins with a moondrenched scene mingling restfulness with dread. Casting a weird and oppressive beauty, the moonlight benignly conceals defects in faces and objects, yet stirs Tant' Sannie's nightmares and Waldo's night fantasies of death and damnation. When the moon shines on the prickly pear, Waldo sees the light identical to the cold glint of his heart.[84] Intense lunar light can also disclose awful truths, as when Rebekah watches her husband beneath the dazzling moon enter their servant girl's room. Whereas sunlight is frequently golden, moonlight is white and carries both the deathly and the pure connotations of that color.

In contrast to all forms of light, darkness for Schreiner is always negative in both its external and its subjective manifestations. The soul's despair is dark and "cannot see the sunlight shine." In darkness of night, Waldo's spiritual and self doubts torment him. When Rebekah plunges into despair over her husband's furtive affairs, she laments the dark closing in on her and refers to her hours of great darkness.[85] Nighttime is ominous; it is at sundown that Bonaparte Blenkins arrives at the farm and begins to insinuate himself into the gullible good graces of Tant' Sannie and Old Otto. Harmful plots are hatched at night: Bonaparte Blenkins lays his trap for Old Otto, and the following night Otto dies.

Closely connected with the absence of sunlight is rain. Many of Schreiner's scenes depicting intense psychological oppression feature relentless rain. Two chapters in *From Man to Man* include rain in their titles. It is in chapter 7, "Raindrops in the Avenue," that Baby-Bertie overhears the women gossiping about her fallen state and has the suffocating dream earlier depicted. That stormy night is painted as "inky blackness." The entire chapter 11, "How the Rain Rains in London," focuses on Bertie's stifled, guilt-ridden London life. A moist, clammy darkness permeates the city when she arrives, and the following day, "gray damp was everywhere. It seemed to ooze out of the walls."[86] The rain falls nearly daily during Bertie's months in London. As a psychic equivalent, she cries almost daily too. When her unnamed Jewish protector casts her from his home because of his unwarranted belief that she is having an affair with his cousin, it is raining heavily, though the storm eventually lets up into a "slight mizzle."[87]

Rain is lethal for Lyndall in *African Farm.* It is a drizzly day when she sits at the graveyard mourning the death of her newborn infant and contracts a fatal illness. In the final weeks of her life, a "mist" clouds her mind, but as death approaches, the mist rolls back and her intellect awakens from "its long torpor." The mist reappears in new guise as the "veil of terrible mist over the face of the Hereafter."[88]

Although Schreiner generally used rain to accentuate despair, danger, and oppressive situations, occasionally she did cast rainfall as positive. Just as intense heat and light could spell destruction, so too intense rain might signal welcome nourishment. The setting that unleashes the flow of Rebekah's philosophical thoughts is torrential rain. She finds the sound "delicious." The force of the rain is protective, comforting; it "made her feel as though great strong arms were folding themselves about her, and a great strong hand were stroking her down softly."[89]

In contrast to rain and mist, dew is associated with light, dawn, morning. It heightens the sparkle and color of leaves. The moist earth seems fertile, not sodden. Correspondingly, Rebekah, feeling hopeful after tortuous thoughts, can muse that she feels "as if a soft dew were falling on her mind."[90]

Schreiner's nimble imagination took these hackneyed symbols of light and dark and turned them fresh and versatile. Her success derived, in part, from the lyric force of her prose but, more crucially, from hooking the symbols to challenging intellectual ideas. Whereas most readers equated the light of spiritual truth with some form of traditional creed, Schreiner saw religions as breeders of darkness. The shining figures in Heaven whom the seeker meets in "The Sunlight Lay across My Bed" reveal a world without the gender, race, and class distinctions commonly held by her readers. In this way, familiar symbols can achieve radical, subversive effects.

Although no other symbolic pattern saturated Schreiner's writing so fully as light and dark, her choice of descriptive colors showed both consistency and similar attraction to stark contrasts. While the most obvious fact about her verbal paintbox was its confinement to primary colors—as she most often juxtaposed red and white, black and white, and somewhat less frequently green, blue, and yellow—she was willing to mute them to lighten red to pink and black to grey. As with her aversion to transitional light, she avoided intermediate, mingled, "secondary" hues, such as aqua, orange, lavender, olive. Brown was her major exception, and on rare occasions she introduced a complex pigment as when Bertie dons a "dark puce-colored silk dress" for a country walk.[91] The effect is jolting, much like Bertie's request to leave her London residence for an outing.

Schreiner's selection of forceful, vivid colors is consonant with the overall dramatic intensity of her personality and writing style. The propulsive energies of her writing spring from elemental, passionate, childhood experiences, often heightened rather than mellowed by her adult encounters. Though her intellect was capable of fine nuance, her feelings, as her detractors often charge, were rarely subtle. Further, there was a sharp affinity between her inclination to write allegories, parables, visions and her primary-color choices. Such a basic mode evoked universal, biblical, mythic truths for her. We can imagine *Red* capitalized but not *maroon*. Indeed, dictionaries of symbols list only primary colors. Perhaps no better example of the dominance of her dream style and her refusal to capitulate to realism even in her most realistic narratives was the overwhelming presence of sharp color and light contrasts in her work.[92]

Schreiner mined many other images rich in mythic content, such as the rose, mountaintops, gardens, jewelry boxes. She rendered these with realistic particularity, much as she clothed ordinary details with symbolic significance. Within her symbolic nursery, her multiple treatments of the rose, classic symbol of love, represent her most complex grafting.

Although in England roses grew in profusion, on the South African karroo and in up-country villages of Schreiner's childhood they were rare and highly prized. Their rarity informs the extended and varied rose metaphor in *Undine.* Lonely, hungry, barely employed, the eponymous heroine of this novel wanders about the sandy diamond fields of Kimberley and comes upon the first flower she has seen growing in the area. It is a tiny rose slip that the crippled girl, Diogenes, rescued from a stem of a withered rose tossed away by some gentleman (as men discard women once they have been, like Undine, sexually used). Diogenes plants the fragile rose slip in a broken pot and diligently nurses it until it blossoms "with one deep-bosomed red rosebud"— all the more precious because it is only one. Meanwhile, her friendship with

Undine has blossomed too, and one day Diogenes picks the rose and lovingly places it in Undine's hair, declaring that her love for Undine surpasses her devotion to her rose bush. Several nights earlier, Diogenes had dreamed that her rose bush was flowering with a great white rose that Undine wore in her hair, the whiteness linked to loss and death. For Diogenes the dream suggests that Undine is planning to sail away and foreshadows her actual imminent death. Meanwhile, with the red rose in her hair, Undine comes upon a young boy who appears to be the son of Albert Blair, who long ago jilted her. The boy demands the rose, and Undine obliges. When the child passes his mother, Mrs. Albert Blair exclaims over the beauty of the rose. The gentleman accompanying her, who is not her husband, takes the rose from the reluctant boy and lays it on the woman's breast. The mother acquiesces to the gentleman's request to leave her husband for a bit and join him at a ball where she becomes "the loveliest of all women there, with that bright flower at her heart." That night Albert Blair dies.[93]

Clearly, the rose in *Undine* has multipetaled meanings. Among innumerable possibilities, it represents: the singular spirits of Diogenes and Undine (rare souls among the motley folk who flock to find rare gems in Kimberley but are blind to genuine human diamonds); the precious love between the two women; the lingering love of Undine for Albert Blair; the fragility and unfixed nature of love, so easily discarded or, as with Blair's wife, shifted to another man. The female erotic connotations of the rose are obvious: Schreiner refers to it as "deep-bosomed" and places it on the breast of the mother/adulteress.

The unusual appearance of roses in South Africa and their association with female passion contributed, as well, to Schreiner's short story "The Woman's Rose." The narrator of this story recounts the tale of the white rose she placed in her box of treasured items twelve years before. The flower was the sole rose growing in a village she had visited. It was given her by a woman whose status as the courted beauty of the village the narrator had supplanted. Feeling no animosity or jealousy, the woman, at a farewell party for the narrator, placed the rose in her dark hair. The rose consequently symbolizes for the narrator the possibility of love and magnanimity between potentially rivalrous women.

A white rose appears again in *From Man to Man* as a symbol of the future, of the ideal. When Rebekah and Drummond pass a tall pink rose bush in Rebekah's garden, Drummond notes one white rose, a particularly healthy and perfect rose, in the midst of all the pink ones. For obvious autobiographical reasons, singularity and oddity are crucial to Schreiner's symbolism. Rebekah responds that this bush has always had such a single white rose, thereby arousing Drummond's scientific interest. Rebekah cuts the rose for him to examine. This incident hearkens back to an earlier point in the novel when Rebekah refers to rose shoots as she draws an analogy about the relationship between the individual pathfinder and the masses.[94] Drummond's personality as prototype for the new man, the pure and uniquely budding relationship between him and Rebekah, and their shared interest in both beauty and science are captured in her offering him the rose.

Among the many other rose references in Schreiner's writing, one other rose deserves special comment, and this is the character Gregory Nazianzen Rose in *African Farm*. Here, Schreiner uses the rose for comic effect. Gregory, in many ways effete and pretentious, takes pride in his aristocratic lineage stemming from the English War of the Roses. He succumbs to sentimental infatuations and views his life through rose-tinted glasses. Yet, in the course of the novel, the doltish, puerile Gregory, through his exemplary love and devotion to Lyndall, rises to the nobility of his name.

Schreiner's love of imagery became still another release for her romantic passion for patterns of correspondence. In her nonfiction and in the philosophical digressions of her novels, her delight in the patterns of analogy among diverse forms of life and between external forms and subjective, psychological states tended to become excessive. Prone to follow Gibbon's style, which she greatly admired, she amassed numerous comparable examples from diverse cultures to illustrate one particular opinion. This was a very Victorian impulse, epitomized in the work of Darwin. It fused the positivist search for general laws from accumulated data with a romantic poetic engagement with the hidden symmetries of nature.

Thriving on multivalent symbols, the visual, cinematic quality of Schreiner's prose, whether in realistic or allegorical narratives, reflected her sense of herself as a painter. Quite deliberately, Schreiner assigned Farber as Waldo and Otto's surname (*Farber* meaning *painter* in German): Both father and son have artistic souls. In London and when traveling in Europe Schreiner visited galleries and commented upon what she saw. She enjoyed dreaming over pictures, as when she attended a Holman Hunt exhibit in London. Paintings in two of her novels kindle stories for her characters. When Undine visits the Blair home at Greenwood, she muses over the content of a canvas on the wall. Likewise, young Rebekah delights in inventing stories for her favorite pictures in an alphabet book.[95]

Nonetheless, the evocative power of Schreiner's writing conceivably arose less from her brushworklike prose than from her musicality. Isak Dinesen likens Schreiner's spirit to an "aeolian harp," on whose strings African days and nights are singing. Earlier I referred to Schreiner's remarks on the unconscious, irresistible, rhythmic nature of writing. She credited two primary influences on her rhythmic lyricism. The foremost was religious: the hymns of her childhood beautifully sung by her father and the cadences of the Old and New Testaments. These drew her to the poetry of Robert Browning. She told Symons that, as she read "Grammarian's Funeral," "Abt Vogler," and "Holy Cross Days," she heard them performed on a great organ.[96]

Steeped in biblical syntax, Schreiner employed repetition in diverse ways. She frequently began and concluded a sequence of sentences or paragraphs with the identical word or phrase doubly or triply repeated.[97] One of many examples: Through a syncopated mix of repetitions and stark color contrasts, Schreiner created in "The Sunlight Lay across My Bed" a vivid sensation of creeping blood: "slowly the thin, red stream ran across the white marbled floor; it reached the stone steps; slowly, slowly, slowly it trickled down, from step to step, from step to step: then it sank into the earth. A thin white smoke rose up from it." She also used repetition in the very structure of her literary work: A classical minuet shapes her allegory in "In a Ruined Chapel." The use of echo or refrain technique characterizes many of her dialogues, with one of the conversants repeating part of the answer or question stated by the other. Finally, Schreiner's love of repetition led her to rely heavily upon rhyme, alliteration, and vowel assonances, as in "for Love and Life must through strange drear places—there, where all is cold, and the snow lies thick, he took their freezing hands and held them against his beating little heart."[98]

The second major influence upon Schreiner's lyricism drew upon "Kaffir" and Boer speech, including folk tales and songs. She learned particular tonalities from "Kaffir" inflections, which struck her as unusually harmonious. From Boer speech she adopted an array of flowing and comic rhythms.[99] This multicultural blend of sounds, its mingling of familiar and unfamiliar tones and beats, lent her diction an intangible and haunting freshness that inspired the affection so many of her readers have for even her most flawed writing.

Schreiner's sensitivity to metric beat deserves note as one last component of her lyricism. In a footnote in chapter 2 of *From Man to Man*, Cronwright refers to a brief paragraph in the chapter that Schreiner explicitly alluded to as poetic. It appears in the text in regular prose form, but Schreiner heard it with staggered dactylic scansion: "Her father, as he passed her / On his way back from the sheep kraals, / Laid his hand upon her shoulder: / 'It grows late and cold,' he muttered."[100]

As with her dark/light and color/object imagery, Schreiner's lyrical elements are scarcely distinctive in themselves. Again, what makes her work singular is her wedding of these familiar sounds with unorthodox ideas in a prose style that is elemental, incantatory, hypnotic. Her ear, eye, mind, and voice grafted onto familiar images and tonalities new and at times radical content, which, despite her reliance upon certain symbolic dichotomies, challenged the social divisions and mental dualisms of her time.

CONCLUSION

PARADOXICALLY, SCHREINER'S PASSION to cure the intellectual and social maladies of her time was her preeminent intellectual contribution to posterity as well as her key weakness. The strengths of her passion are prodigious. Surpassing her contemporaries she, like current poststructuralists, was bent upon exposing culture-bound binary oppositions, locating their roots in the errors of religion and science which reflected and upheld Victorian power relations in private and public spheres. Unlike present-day thinkers, who can marshal a plethora of twentieth-century scientific, historical, and philosophical evidence for their views on the cultural construction of gender, class, and race, Schreiner attacked widely held assumptions about human differences without such scholarly support. Unlike many of today's deconstructionists, she not only challenged these assumptions but was also an activist who strove to alter the political relations that gave rise to them. With regard to certain Victorian antitheses, for example, religion versus science, mind versus matter, she was less isolated (though for years she scarcely knew anyone to whom she could convey her views). A dissident stream of intellectuals shared her organic view of the wholeness of reality and probed the interpenetration of body and spirit, of conscious and unconscious behavior. Similarly, her critique of capitalism and social class differences found allies, except insofar as her antiracism and feminism highlighted the inadequacies of reigning socialist theories and practice. Until her final treatise, *The Dawn of Civilization*, Schreiner's case against war and violence, though clearly unpopular, was compatible with nineteenth- and early-twentieth-century feminist pacifism. And, though they were rare, artists who, like Schreiner, spurned the rigid literary canons of the time and intermixed literary genres and styles did exist.

By contrast, the scope of Schreiner's assault upon scientific rationale for Victorian racial prejudices and the rigor of her deconstruction of presumed gender differences were without parallel. With regard to the latter, she elicited praise from feminists, even when they clung to their beliefs (as most did) in certain natural, universal differences in gender identity and roles. With regard to the former, she fought virtually unaided; socialists and feminists did not usually question the racist bigotry of their times. What is most significant in her culture criticism, what sets her vastly apart from all of her contemporaries, is her inclusion of all of these categories of analysis. She was unique in the extent of her diagnosis into how cultural prejudices infected all categories of social organization and intellectual endeavor and, further, how these prejudices spread their toxins into each other's domain.

To be sure, Schreiner did not wholly transcend the cultural premises of her time. She was more thorough and consistent in her feminist analysis of gender than of race. Though uncommon in her espousal of racial and ethnic diversity and pluralism, she could not free herself from Victorian tendencies to typologize, nor could she resolve her ambivalence toward interracial mating. Similarly, she lacked a vocabulary to articulate her alternative visions, as in her fluctuations over the use of "God" and in her inability to signify precisely her definition of erotic passion and love. More than occasionally, she succumbed to conventional literary modes—images of light versus dark, biblical cadences, and excess plotting—to render her subversive ideas accessible to ordinary readers. Even so, her fiction puzzled and alienated many readers, which led to her confusion over her intended audience and over her role as artist. Despite these and other ways that her thought and writing reflected her historical circumstances, she stalked the frontier of South African and English culture. From that vantage point she examined the conflicts and diseases of her age with rare acuity and offered inspiring visions and concrete proposals for healing the rifts that divided human beings from each other and fragmented their sense of self.

Unfortunately, the same healing passion that impelled Schreiner to such achievements impeded her facing the intransigence of cultural divisions. Although her optimism about eventual worldwide racial pluralism, democracy, and peace did wane as South Africa's racist political framework found its legs in the early twentieth century and as World War I unleashed hitherto unimagined slaughter and destruction, most of her writing emerged during the more politically inchoate period prior to 1914 when her optimism could ride roughshod over nails. Though bearing the imprint of World War I, even *Dawn of Civilization,* her most pessimistic statement on human nature, sustained her belief in the possibility of ultimate human conversion to a pacifist stance. Though she examined more deeply than most of her contemporaries the vigor of cultural prejudices regarding race, gender, and class, and though she exhorted writers to grapple with and express unstintingly all aspects of reality, she did not consistently heed her own advice. Her lapses are most evident in her approach to racism in South Africa. She harbored more faith in white South African liberals and radicals than their inadequate numbers and racial attitudes warranted. Though she predicted racial violence unless whites moved toward a pluralist democracy, she did not explore whether a black revolution might be a necessary approach to empowering psychologically as well as politically the mass of colonized Africans. In her innocence, she was surprised and stung when the Boers, for whom she suffered internment during the Anglo–Boer War after years of championing their rights, turned against her because of her support for racial equality.

A telling pattern in Schreiner's thought was to present contradictory explanations as complementary—her counting altruistic and ideal-making impulses as vital to animal and human evolution as competitive and aggressive ones—yet not clarifying systematically the rivalrous interplay of the two. This conflict avoidance curbed the persuasiveness of her otherwise brilliant conjuring of the comradeship of the "new woman" and "new man." Though Schreiner granted the difficulty and painfulness of societal and psychological transformation, she never fully delineated the magnitude of male privilege, violence against women, and aversion to change. At times she sensed the severity of sex antagonism, as when, despite her pacifism, she justified recourse by English suffragettes to militant tactics. Generally, however, she muted the sharpness of sexual animosities in the interest of her vision of ennobled comradeship. Even as she advocated the dismantling of class hierarchy and the benefits of labor strikes, she never entertained the possibility that, in given settings, violent class struggle might provide the only means to uproot capitalism and social inequality.

Unwilling to buy into the dialectic of materialism versus idealism, Schreiner posited a blending of spiritual and material, and of conscious and unconscious, phenomena without exploring the precise and often dissonant nature of this problematic relation. At times she described a complementarity, other times integration, and still other times a transfiguration of all components. A similar blurring of alternatives weakened her advocacy of androgynous identity. Throughout her writing she never doubted the existence of a self, as well as of an unprejudiced mind able to grasp and express objective rational and irrational reality. This faith corresponded to her trust in her creative flashes and basic emotions. The unconscious was not for her a terrain of clashing creative and destructive impulses. Despite her lifelong effort to balance and combine service to others and self-development, she did not explicitly discuss that tension as not only revelatory of the struggles of individual willpower that many might wage but endemic as well to the human condition, albeit a conflict heightened for women acculturated into self-denial in a patriarchal society. In sidestepping these questions she evinces both the impact of her times and the limits of her inquiry into conflict.

It is easier to explain Schreiner's pluralist-integrationist approach than her resistance to dialectical analysis. No doubt the ferocity she needed to rebel against the Victorian conflict model of reality disinclined her to cede any quarter to those thoughts within her sympathetic to the dominant rhetoric of her time. Better to defer these thoughts than to let them undermine her belief in the power to cure. Her female upbringing and feminist position placed a premium on peacemaking and forming bonds of connection as opposed to encouraging ample recognition of separate and competing interests. If mending bones or acting as a midwife was her vocation, healing the ruling metaphor, then letting certain social bones, so to speak, remain broken and society crippled was anathema.

Indeed, the deeply personal background for Schreiner's brave and lonely convictions enhances our comprehension of their limits. For someone as reform-minded and compassionate as Schreiner, a wholly uninhibited exploration of the intractable quality of various intellectual and societal divisions would require a supportive environment of others who shared her values yet were prepared to consider unsparingly, as she finally did in *Dawn of Civilization*, the anxieties and ambitions that militate against radical change in gender, class, international and race relations. Such a network of friends and allies was clearly nonexistent. In her striving to face, understand, and surmount her psychological conflicts she was also alone. Unquestionably, she benefited from the concern and partial understanding of close friends and her husband, but living when she did she lacked, to use a contemporary term, an appropriate therapist, someone fully capable of understanding her problems and impersonally validating her self-worth. (An appropriate therapist, however, if unfriendly to her freethinking, social, and political views and if inclined toward individualistic as opposed to societal analysis and strategies of change, would have retarded Schreiner's self-affirmation, autonomy, assertiveness, and range of political and literary activity.) Despite the absence of such a wise and supportive figure and despite the incompatibility between her views and dominant Victorian values and social patterns, she made remarkable progress toward the resolution of her psychological conflicts.

We can see, however, how this progress hinged upon a bold but incomplete encounter with her psychological issues that mirrored and possibly reinforced the way she grappled with philosophical and societal conflicts. As Chapter 1 set forth, Schreiner faced the traumatic deaths of her younger sister and her own daughter, the physical agonies of asthma and, later in life, kidney and heart disease, numerous miscarriages, frustration in securing heterosexual friendship and love (even her marriage, which initially met many of her needs and wishes, withered in her later years), the loss of her voluminous notes for her "sex opus," the failure to finish *From Man to Man*, and countless setbacks in effecting political and social change. Yet, with the help of offsetting experiences, including her ability to vent her misery freely with friends, she did not sink into bitterness and despair. Instead, she developed positive, creative, energetic responses to her plight, producing works to move to thought and feeling generations to come. Her optimism was her lifeline. To sustain that optimism she could not bear the full weight of her unresolved conflicts. As early as postadolescence, she no longer suffered keenly the tension between her view of nature's caprice and malice and its sacred beauty; her dulling of this conflict is reflected in her self-styled mysticism and her failure to probe systematically the relation between altruistic and competitive forces in evolution. Within the context of her colonial birth as well, she resolved her conflicting national identity as both South African and English by asserting a global citizenship, idealizing her role as both an insider and an outsider in South African political life. Inadequately exploring this conflict, she overestimated her ability to convert English men and women to her antiimperialism and to convert liberal white South Africans to her constitutional proposals. There is no doubt but that she and we benefited from her optimism, whatever its cost, for it enabled the treatises and fiction that have inspired subsequent generations of critics of South African capitalism and racism.

DURING THE DECADE and more that I have studied Schreiner's life and work I have shifted back and forth in my enthusiasm for her rebellion against the Victorian—or, as more recently termed, the EuroAmerican white male— conflict model of reality. My oscillation reflects a lifelong ambivalence toward the philosophy of nonviolence. When awed by the brilliance of Schreiner's deconstruction of cultural dichotomies and the breadth and creativity of her healing imagination, I regard her analytic lapses as not only historically explicable but essential to her sanity and intellectual and political courage. At such times I view the competitive, aggressive, and polarizing mentality of Victorians as justifying as powerful a counterpoise as possible. At other times,

I worry about feminist eagerness to create bonds of human solidarity founded upon an ethic of compassion and gentleness, faith in nonviolent conflict resolution and the potential harmony of all creation. I fear this outlook underestimates the power of egoism and the need for tough confrontation, including on occasion violence, to advance freedom and justice for individuals and groups. I then cast a colder eye on Schreiner's pluralist-integrationist proposals.

I suspect that my shifting perspective with its implicit tensions echoes that of many contemporary idealists and forms part of an explanation for the current extraordinary burgeoning of interest in Schreiner's writing. Many of us share her revolt against long-dominant cultural constructions of race, class, and gender and their underlying hierarchical and dualistic mentality. We are drawn to her visions of egalitarian, culturally pluralist harmony, but we fear being seduced too easily. The enduring quality of *African Farm* resides in part in its contradictory messages of intellectual and moral progress on one hand and on the other the futility of human endeavor in the face of nature's malice and human cruelty. The evocative power of the corpus of Schreiner's writing is that, whereas in one work the reader encounters positive, optimistic proposals for change, in the next the power of the privileged to abuse women, children, racial minorities, and poor people looms insuperable. If she did not resolve this contradiction, neither have we. There is a wonderful truth both in her desire and effort to resolve it and in her inability to do so.

APPENDIX A: OLIVE SCHREINER CHRONOLOGY

In South Africa

1855 March 24, Olive Emilie Albertina Schreiner born at Wittebergen Mission Station, District Albert, Cape Colony.

1861 Family moves to Healdtown where Gottlob Schreiner directs a missionary training institute.

1865 Suffers traumatic death of younger sister, Ellie. Wesleyan Missionary Society dismisses Gottlob Schreiner for violating regulations against trading.

1867 Joins her brother Theo and sister Ettie in Cradock. The following year Will joins her. Begins writing stories and first novel, *Undine*.

1870 Visits various relatives and family friends. Stays over a year with Zadoc Robinson family in Dordrecht, where she reads voraciously and meets Julius Gau.

1872 After abortive engagement to Gau, joins Theo and Ettie in New Rush (later named Kimberley) diamond fields.

1873 Visits her sister, Alice Hemming, in Fraserburg. Meets John and Mary Brown, who support her medical and literary ambitions.

1874–81 Governess: Weakleys (Colesberg); Fouchés (Klein Ganna Hoek, Leilie Kloof); Martins (Ratel Hoek); Cawoods (Ganna Hoek).

In England

1881 Sails to England. Abortive attempt at nursing training at Edinburgh Royal Infirmary.

1882 Meets Eleanor Marx.

1883 *The Story of an African Farm* published.

1884 Meets Havelock Ellis and Edward Carpenter.

1885 Meets Karl Pearson. Joins Men and Women's Club.

1886 First references to research and writing for "sex book." Dr. Bryan Donkin proposes marriage.

1887 Until June, recuperates from physical and emotional stress in Europe, residing for most of the time in Alassio, Italy. In England from June to November, when she returns to Italy.

1888 In Mentone, Italy, until April 1889.

1889 In England from April to October.

In South Africa

1889 October 11, sails to South Africa.

1890 Settles in Matjesfontein. Begins series of articles on South African life. Meets Cecil Rhodes; forms friendships with a number of prominent Cape women and men. *Dreams* published.

1892 December, meets Samuel Cron Cronwright.

1893 Travels to England; rents cottage in Millthorpe. *Dream Life and Real Life* published.

1894 February 24, marries Cronwright, lives briefly at his farm near Cradock, then moves with him to The Homestead, Kimberley.

1895 April 30, birth of daughter. Death of daughter, May 1.

1896–1900 Six to seven miscarriages.

1896 Jameson Raid. *The Political Situation* published.

1897 Sails to England. *Trooper Peter Halket of Mashonaland* published. March to May, traveling in Europe. August 21, departs for South Africa.

1898 Brother Will becomes prime minister of Cape Colony. Schreiner moves to Johannesburg.

1899 Anglo–Boer War erupts. House looted, almost all papers destroyed. *An English South African's View of the Situation*, also published in Cape Town and Chicago under the title of *The South African Question.*

1900 Antiwar speeches and campaigning. Interned in Hanover, where in December martial law is proclaimed.

1902 Peace of Vereeniging.

1905 Letter on Johannesburg Shop Assistants' Union demonstration. May 10, Letter on "The Taal" (Afrikaans).

1906 *A Letter on the Jew* published.

1907 Cronwright sells Hanover business and moves to De Aar, where Schreiner joins him for cooler months of the year.

1909 *Closer Union* published. Continues agitation for a federal constitution based upon sex and race equality.

Chronology

1910   May 31, Union of South Africa.

1911   *Woman and Labour* published.

1913   Resigns as vice-president of the Cape Women's Enfranchisement League. Marital strains. December, sails to England.

In England

1913–14   After brief stay in London, travels to Europe, returns to London in April 1914; travels again in June to Europe, remaining until August 2, 1914.

1914–18   World War I. Engages in various public and private efforts to end the war and promote women's suffrage. Begins *The Dawn of Civilization.*

In South Africa

1920   June, Cronwright sails to England to join his wife after six-year separation. August 13, Schreiner sails to South Africa with her nephew Oliver and family. Resides at Oak Hill, Wynberg, until her death during night of December 10–11.

1921   August 13, reinterred at Buffels Kop, Cradock.

Posthumous First Printings

1923   *Thoughts on South Africa*
         Stories, Dreams, and Allegories

1926   *From Man to Man*

1929   *Undine*

APPENDIX B: OLIVE SCHREINER'S FAMILY

Gottlob Schreiner   m.   Rebecca Lyndall
(1814–76)   11/7/1837   (1818–1903)

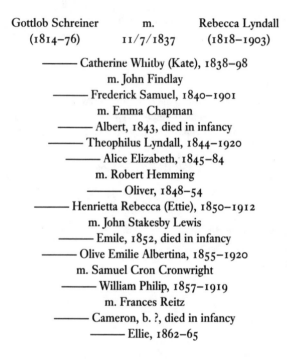

———— Catherine Whitby (Kate), 1838–98
m. John Findlay
———— Frederick Samuel, 1840–1901
m. Emma Chapman
———— Albert, 1843, died in infancy
———— Theophilus Lyndall, 1844–1920
———— Alice Elizabeth, 1845–84
m. Robert Hemming
———— Oliver, 1848–54
———— Henrietta Rebecca (Ettie), 1850–1912
m. John Stakesby Lewis
———— Emile, 1852, died in infancy
———— Olive Emilie Albertina, 1855–1920
m. Samuel Cron Cronwright
———— William Philip, 1857–1919
m. Frances Reitz
———— Cameron, b. ?, died in infancy
———— Ellie, 1862–65

NOTES

Introduction

1. Schreiner to Havelock Ellis, January 30, 1885, *The Letters of Olive Schreiner, 1876–1920*, ed. Samuel Cron Cronwright Schreiner (London: Unwin, 1924), 57–58 (hereafter cited as SCCS *Letters*, Havelock Ellis as HE, and Olive Schreiner as OS).

2. OS to Sarah Ann Tooley, June 1897, in Samuel Cron Cronwright Schreiner, *The Life of Olive Schreiner* (London: Unwin, 1924), 295–97 (hereafter cited as SCCS *Life*). See, too, OS to J. T. Lloyd, August 1896, SCCS *Letters*, 222. Cronwright excused his biography of his wife with reference to a conversation he had with her when she was in her midfifties. Apparently, she realized that someone would probably write about her life, and if a biography was to be written she preferred Cronwright to undertake it or, if he could not, her close friend Havelock Ellis. See Preface, vii, to SCCS *Life*.

3. OS to HE, June 1916, July 4, 1916, Schreiner Collection, Harry Ransom Humanities Research Center, University of Texas at Austin (hereafter cited as HRC); Havelock Ellis, *My Life: Autobiography of Havelock Ellis* (Boston: Houghton Mifflin, 1939), 187–88; for Cronwright's account of Ellis's ordeal in burning Schreiner's copious letters to him, see his note in SCCS *Letters*, 202–3; OS to Karl Pearson, November 11, 1890, *Olive Schreiner: Letters*, vol. 1, *1871–1899*, ed. Richard Rive (Oxford: Oxford University Press, 1988), 177. In my citations of Schreiner's letters to Karl Pearson, I have wherever possible referred the reader to the Rive edition. In 1979, Betty Fradkin Tetlow, who introduced scholars to the significance of the Pearson Collection, loaned me a copy of most of the Schreiner-related items in that collection. Until the Rive edition of Schreiner's correspondence, scholars could have access to the Pearson–Schreiner letters only by visiting the collection held at University College, London, donated by Pearson's daughter, Helga Sharpe Hacker. Rive's second volume of letters is forthcoming. More than a thousand Schreiner letters appear in these two volumes. See Rive's discussion of Schreiner's correspondence in his preface.

4. OS to Sarah Ann Tooley, June 1897, SCCS *Life*, 295–97.

5. Schreiner's most recent biographers, Ruth First and Ann Scott, in *Olive Schreiner* (London: Andre Deutsch, 1980), offer the first substantive probing of Schreiner's

writings and "abstract opinions." Even they, however, slight certain of her works and neglect key dimensions of her intellectual activity, favoring instead provocative psychoanalytic and insightful social-historical discussions of her physical health and sexual relationships.

6. Jeffrey Weeks, *Sex, Politics, and Society: The Regulation of Sexuality since 1800* (London: Longman, 1981); Michel Foucault, *The History of Sexuality*, vol. 1, *An Introduction* (London: Allen Lane, 1978).

7. Thomas Hughes, *Tom Brown's School Days* (Philadelphia, 1868), pt. 2, chap. 5.

8. Needless to say, Victorians were not alone in conceiving reality as an arena of conflict. Dualistic and hierarchical philosophical and social frameworks shaped European thought and experience for centuries. This tradition remains, in fact, vigorous in the twentieth century, as with the Freudian dialectic of Eros and Thanatos, not to mention Lévi-Strauss and his structuralist followers' emphasis upon universal binary formulations, e.g., the raw and the cooked, clean and unclean, sacred and profane. Still, the twentieth century has also witnessed powerful countercurrents in systems theory, in the growing popularity of Eastern and Western holistic philosophies and in poststructuralist deconstructionist theory. To be blunt, however, the Victorians were exceptional in the breadth and intensity with which they framed relations dualistically and hierarchically. For a discussion of this mental proclivity of warring forces as it bore on the Victorian conflict between science and religion, see James R. Moore, *The Post-Darwinian Controversies: A Study of the Protestant Struggle to Come to Terms with Darwin in Great Britain and America, 1870–1900* (Cambridge: Cambridge University Press, 1979); as it bore on race, see Nancy Stepan, *The Idea of Race in Science: Great Britain, 1800–1960* (Hamden, CT: Archon Books, 1982); as it bore on gender, see Cynthia Russett, *The Scientific Construction of Womanhood in the Late Nineteenth Century* (Cambridge, MA: Harvard University Press, forthcoming).

9. Olive Schreiner, *The Dawn of Civilization*, A MS with A Revisions (1920), 12–13, HRC.

10. Diane Postlethwaite, in *Making It Whole: A Victorian Circle and the Shape of Their World* (Columbus: Ohio State University Press, 1984), opposes the scholarly tradition that describes Victorians as thoroughly opposed to holistic thinking. She points out a significant alternative rivulet of thinkers—Harriet Martineau, John Stuart Mill, G. H. Lewes, George Eliot, Charles Bray, Herbert Spencer—eager to synthesize and banish dichotomies. She makes no claim for the cultural dominance of their outlook. By contrast, Jonathan Rose argues in *The Edwardian Temperament* (Athens: Ohio University Press, 1986) that a majority of Edwardians were similarly eager to dismantle binary oppositions. Given the realities of growing numbers of paramilitary organizations, heightened racism and anti-Semitism, the growing militance of labor and women, I find his thesis unconvincing. Indeed, Stepan and Russett portray the Edwardian intellectuals' construction of reality as decidedly dichotomous.

11. Regina Markell Morantz-Sanchez, *Sympathy and Science: Women Physicians in American Medicine* (Oxford: Oxford University Press, 1985); Barbara Alpern Engel, *Mothers and Daughters: Women of the Intelligentsia in Nineteenth-Century Russia* (Cambridge: Cambridge University Press, 1983), 156–57.

12. To be sure, awareness of the interdependence of individual and collective well-being can spur conservative as well as liberal and radical prescriptions. The eugenics movement is a prime example of the former, as was fascism, whose rhetoric made extensive use of disease analogies. Moreover, just as some doctors are content to apply Band-Aids and balm whereas others seek to eradicate an ailment's causes, so, too, social prophylaxis encompasses a spectrum of moderate to radical curatives.

13. Richard Stites, *The Women's Liberation Movement in Russia: Feminism, Nihilism, and Bolshevism, 1860–1930* (Princeton, NJ: Princeton University Press, 1978), 83–84. Stites generalizes from Russian experience, arguing that in "backward" societies medical education and practice often serve as introductions to social maladies and, hence, are formative in the development of an individual's social conscience and compassion. In America, Jane Addams represents a notable example of this.

14. Mary Poovey is cited by Judith Newton and Nancy Hoffman, "Preface," *Feminist Studies* 14, 1 (Spring 1988): 7. This issue of *Feminist Studies* is devoted to essays exploring the implications of deconstructionism for feminism.

15. OS to HE, July 25, 1899, SCCS *Letters*, 226–27.

16. Olive Schreiner, *Woman and Labor* (New York: Frederick A. Stokes, 1911), 23. In my discussion of this work I will identify it as Schreiner did for its British publishers, *Woman and Labour*, but since I relied upon this American edition, I will retain its spelling in my notes.

17. See Appendix A for an abbreviated chronology of Olive Schreiner's life.

Chapter 1

1. Olive Schreiner, *The Story of an African Farm* (New York: A. L. Burt, n.d.; originally published in London under the pseudonym Ralph Iron, Chapman and Hall, 1883), 245–46, 295.

2. SCCS *Life*, 67, quoted from a letter from Schreiner to Havelock Ellis. As Schreiner matured she was able to declare, "I don't hate myself quite so much as I used to"; Journal entry, April 8, 1874, quoted in SCCS *Life*, 97–98.

3. See Appendix B for Schreiner's immediate family tree.

4. OS to Dr. Alice Cothorne, March 2, 1894, "I'm glad I'm still OLIVE SCHREINER. I couldn't have borne to give up my name"; quoted in D. L. Hobman, *Olive Schreiner: Her Friends and Times* (London: Watts, 1955), 101.

5. Mrs. E. J. Stanley (the eldest daughter of Erilda Cawood) to Cronwright, quoted in SCCS *Life*: "At the Fouchés [a family for whom Schreiner worked as a governess prior to the Cawoods] she wouldn't have a mirror in her room and never looked at

herself in one if she could help it. She told my mother she was too ugly," 113. As photographs attest, Schreiner possessed considerable beauty but perhaps feared her impulses toward vanity.

6. During Schreiner's youth, South Africa was more a geographical than a political entity. It encompassed a congerie of agrarian African and European societies. The largest state was the Cape Colony, a self-governing colony of the British Empire.

7. SCCS *Life*, 139. Schreiner's refusal to "be still" has led some scholars to accuse her of wallowing in self-pity; e.g., Yvonne Kapp in her study, *Eleanor Marx* (London: Lawrence and Wishart, 1976), 2:24–28, attacks Schreiner's emotional openness as inviting Marx's own "incontinence" in bemoaning her marital distress. I find this scholarly response unfortunate.

8. OS to HE, May 2, 1884, SCCS *Letters*, 17: "The dream of my life was to be a doctor: I can't remember a time when I was so small that it was not there in my heart. I used to dissect ostriches, and sheeps' hearts and liver, and almost the first book I ever bought myself was an elementary physiology."

9. SCCS *Life*, 13. Schreiner's passion for a medical career formed part of her general devotion to scientific inquiry. In her fiction her major female protagonists are amateur naturalists, with particular interest in physiology and botany; see *Undine* (New York: Harper and Brothers, 1930), 10, 18, 53; *African Farm*, 193–94; *From Man to Man* (New York: Harper and Brothers, 1927), 31, 37, 40, 49, 92–94, 146–48, 155, 220.

10. OS to HE, July 12, 1884, SCCS *Letters*, 28–29; OS to HE, April 20, 1887, ibid., 138. See also OS to HE, July 22, 1888, ibid.

11. OS to Mrs. Francis Smith, October 22, 1907, SCCS *Letters*, 274; Schreiner, *African Farm*, 227; OS to HE, July 12, 1884, SCCS *Letters*, 28–29; OS to Rev. John T. Lloyd, October 29, 1892, SCCS *Life*, 218.

12. I derive the estimate of the number of Schreiner's miscarriages from allusions to pregnancies and miscarriages in her letters, primarily to Mary Sauer, in Rive, *Schreiner: Letters.*

13. OS to SCCS, July 4, 1903, SCCS *Letters*, 237.

14. OS to SCCS, January 26, 1919, SCCS *Letters*, 361; OS to Rev. J. T. Lloyd, 1892, quoted in SCCS *Life*, 219.

15. OS to HE, October 19, 1918, SCCS *Letters*, 358–60; OS to Sir George Grey, February 4, 1897, "Olive Schreiner: A Selection of Letters," in Cherry Clayton, ed., *Olive Schreiner* (Johannesburg: McGraw-Hill, 1983), 120; *The Findlay Letters, 1806–1870*, ed. Joan Findlay (Pretoria: L. Van Shaik, 1954), 116 (hereafter cited as *Findlay Letters*).

16. OS to HE, November 2, 1888, SCCS *Letters*, 144. Note my discussion in Chapter 3 of Schreiner's use of the term *Kaffir.*

17. OS to Mrs. Francis Smith, September 1908, SCCS *Letters*, 282.

18. Schreiner's recent biographers are convinced of the psychogenic origins of her

asthma, attributing its onset to the sexual turmoil unleashed by an abortive love relationship in her late adolescence. Although I concur that psychological stress exerted an influence, I see its role as secondary and am struck by current medical theory which maintains asthma is not psychogenic. See the statement of Dr. Robert Strunk and Joyce Walker Boyd, National Asthma Center in Denver, Colorado, in *Today's Education: Journal of the National Education Association,* November–December 1980, 66–67: "Asthma begins in the lungs, not in the head. No amount of emotional stress will cause asthma unless the child already has the abnormal lung characteristic of the disease." Clearly, Schreiner's early lung inflammations prepared for her asthmatic response to various allergens. The initial occasion of Schreiner's asthma is unclear—either at eighteen following a journey to her sister Alice Hemming or on another journey with her aunt, Mrs. Rolland, and a second woman, probably a cousin. Admittedly, on both journeys, insensitive treatment from relatives compounded Schreiner's physical stress (during the former, starvation and the onset of menstruation; during the latter, rain dripping down her neck).

19. Pharmaceuticals were readily available to the public throughout most of the nineteenth century. Schreiner's close friendships in England with a medical student, Havelock Ellis, and an accredited physician, H. Bryan Donkin, further eased her access to medicines. Though some scholars attribute Schreiner's writing difficulties in England primarily to psychological stress, Yaffa Draznin, in "Did Victorian Medicine Crush Olive Schreiner's Creativity?" *Historian* (February 1985): 196–207, alleges that the medicine Schreiner adopted to relieve her asthma "inadvertently but undeniably" undermined her creative genius. Prior to Schreiner's move to England, we have very little evidence of drug use (a passing reference to carbolic acid appears in her Journal; see SCCS *Life,* 115), but subsequently there are frequent allusions. A number of scholars allege that Schreiner's dependence upon large doses of potassium bromide during her early years in England not only increased her restlessness and sieges of depression and irritability but, by muting the functions of her central nervous system, diminished, if not suspended, her genital excitement. They surmise that a sexually conflicted Schreiner may have chosen this medication for reasons additional to asthma, a conjecture I do not share. Schreiner experimented with a range of prescribed (but sold over the counter) medicines: quinine, nux vomica, chloral, glycerine, strychnine, chlorodyne, morphia, and Tucker's Asthma Remedy. Smoking tobacco also soothed her. Given contradictory medical advice, her empirical approach to drug choice was inevitable. Of course, none of these drugs brought more than temporary relief, and many had toxic effects: hallucinations, depression, headaches, gastrointestinal distress, weakness in the limbs, overstimulation, lethargy.

20. SCCS *Life,* 268.

21. Though Gottlob Schreiner worshiped his wife, he could neither provide reliably

for his family's material needs nor face many of life's unpleasant truths. Schreiner attributed their family's economic difficulties to her father's incompetence and gullibility. Only during her early years did her family have sufficient material comforts. The situation changed when she was six and her father was assigned to the Wesleyan Training Institute in the Eastern Cape. The move to Healdtown required that the Schreiners sell all their property and return to the state of marginal subsistence that had characterized the family's economy in the years prior to Schreiner's birth. Insufficient food caused her to suffer from occasional acute bouts of hunger, manifest in her fiction in images of food deprivation and in her nonfictional identification with the unpropertied. For unclear reasons, Gottlob Schreiner failed in both his missionary and institute duties at Healdtown. Compounding this failure, he broke strict missionary regulations against trading, to which he resorted to alleviate his family's economic straits. For this infraction, after twenty-seven years as a missionary, he was expelled. His reckless, often naive, economic practices also undermined his subsequent business ventures. With the family bankrupt and destitute, Schreiner's mother, Rebecca, moved into a village outhouse where she was cared for by neighbors; Olive, Will, and Ettie (the three children still living at home) went to live with their brother Theo, a headmaster of a school in Cradock; and Gottlob, with financial assistance from his older children, eked out a living by trading on horseback throughout the district.

22. SCCS *Life,* 188: eminent Victorian and poet Arthur Symons's interview with Olive Schreiner, June 10, 1889. See also OS to HE, February 25, 1885, SCCS *Letters,* 61.

23. SCCS *Life,* 250.

24. Ibid.

25. Rebecca Schreiner to her children Kate and Fred Schreiner, 1848, *Findlay Letters,* 94–95; OS to Mrs. Francis Smith, July 25, 1909, SCCS *Letters,* 287; Rebecca Schreiner to John Findlay, n.d., *Findlay Letters,* 150.

26. OS to HE, May 30, 1884, SCCS *Letters,* 21. *Koppig* is a Cape Dutch word that literally means *heady* (headstrong, perverse). It derived from the behavior of a horse's head, which when reined in one direction resists and seeks to move in reverse.

27. Lyndall Gregg, *Memories of Olive Schreiner* (London: Chambers, 1957), 17.

28. OS to Mrs. Francis Smith, May 13, 1912, SCCS *Letters,* 307. Through church sermons, hymns, parental warnings, the reading of religious literature and didactic, evangelical fiction, Schreiner was brought up to view the human world as divided between the multitude damned and the minority saved. The early inculcation of the fear of damnation embittered the lives of countless Victorians. David Grylls, *Guardians and Angels: Parents and Children in Nineteenth Century Literature* (London: Faber and Faber, 1978), 23.

29. SCCS *Life,* 219.

30. Ibid., 186. I wonder, too, whether Rebecca's sobbing at Schreiner's bed may not have entailed her awareness that the family's poverty prevented her precocious

daughter from gaining the education and cultural opportunities greater economic well-being might have afforded.

31. When Will overheard his sister, he would embarrass her by telling her story to everyone. Schreiner would be furious but, repressing her anger, would dance and bite her hands rather than strike out at her brother. Rebecca, however, would spank or scold Will on her daughter's behalf. Ibid., 67.

32. Ibid., 22.

33. Of course, such sympathy for her mother was not fully developed until after childhood. Schreiner, "Reminiscences," in ibid., 13.

34. OS to SCCS, January 13, 1893, ibid., 245; OS to SCCS, December 5, 1918, SCCS *Letters*, 360–61.

35. SCCS *Life*, 16, 170–71. Until Schreiner became a freethinker at age ten, Theo was very affectionate. Not until 1884 did Schreiner again receive a tender letter from him. Although Fred found many of Schreiner's ideas offensive he gave her an annual allowance of fifty pounds until her marriage. OS to HE, December 22, 1884, and OS to Karl Pearson (KP), May 21, 1886, Rive, *Schreiner: Letters*, 61, 80.

36. SCCS *Life*, 142: Olive Schreiner Journal, January 3, 1881. See too OS to Mrs. Francis Smith, January 9, 1911, SCCS *Letters*, 297–98; OS to SCCS, January 11, 1911, ibid.

37. It is something of a mystery how Schreiner came upon these works. She recorded purchasing certain books in Cape Town, reading others in church libraries, and in certain cases a chance encounter introduced her to a significant work. When in 1871 Schreiner was visiting her cousin Emmie Rolland at Hermon, a mission station in Basutoland, a stranger, Willie Bertram (model for Waldo's Stranger in *African Farm*), an official in the Native Affairs Department of the Cape Civil Service, loaned Schreiner Herbert Spencer's *First Principles*. SCCS *Life*, 81–82.

38. Schreiner Journal, April 8, 1874, SCCS *Life*, 97–98.

39. "You ask me whether Spencer is to me what he was. If one has a broken leg and the doctor sets it, when once it is set one may be said to have no more need of the doctor, nevertheless one always walks on his leg. I think that is how it is with regard to myself and Herbert Spencer." OS to HE, April 8, 1884, SCCS *Life*, 82; OS to J. T. Lloyd, October 29, 1892, ibid., 219–29.

40. In a most informative essay, A. E. Voss examines *African Farm* for its clues to Schreiner's reading. In addition to poets, playwrights, philosophers, and historians, he stresses her familiarity with biblical critics, represented in South Africa by John William Colenso. "'Not a word or a Sound in the World about Him that is not Modifying Him': Learning, Lore, and Language in *The Story of an African Farm*," in Clayton, *Olive Schreiner*, 170–81.

41. SCCS *Life*, 78; Schreiner, *From Man to Man*, 4–6.

42. SCCS *Life*, 103, 100, 116, 118, 139.

43. OS to Mrs. Cawood, January 17, 1878, January 9, 1879, February 26, 1879, March 1888, SCCS *Letters*, 3, 6, 8, 133; e.g., "I should love to come and rest with you for a

week and tell stories to the children, the new little ones, and look at your face." According to one of Erilda Cawood's daughters, when her brother was asked what he prayed for, the young lad replied, "*All* of Olive Schreiner." SCCS *Life*, 113.

44. Boers (Afrikaners) descended from Dutch, German, French, and other northern Europeans who settled at the Cape of Good Hope under the auspices of the Dutch East India Company in the seventeenth and eighteenth centuries. The term *Boer* means *farmer*. The language of the Boers—the Taal—constitutes a mix of Dutch and French with some African.

45. Olive Schreiner, *Thoughts on South Africa* (New York: Frederick A. Stokes, 1923), 19. This book consists of a series of articles published in various periodicals between 1891 and 1900. First and Scott, *Olive Schreiner*, 78. Schreiner learned oral Afrikaans (the Taal) during these years, though she continued to have difficulty in writing it. SCCS *Life*, 120.

46. Schreiner, *Thoughts*, 202–21, 266–70.

47. Schreiner Journal, May 23, 1875, SCCS *Life*, 115; OS to HE, Christmas Eve, 1884, SCCS *Letters*, 52.

48. First and Scott, *Olive Schreiner*, 69–70; SCCS *Life*, 97, 96.

49. Ad Donker, "English-Language Publishing in South Africa," in Susan Gardner, ed., *Publisher/Writer/Reader: Sociology of Southern African Literature* (Johannesburg: University of Witwatersrand Press, 1986), 19.

50. The nature of Schreiner's breakdown remains murky. Despite her insistence that it was only physical, the result of malnutrition, overwork, and bronchitis, she also granted the influence of emotional conflicts. See OS to KP, January 30, 1887, Rive, *Schreiner: Letters*, 120–23. A reading of Schreiner's correspondence during the fall of 1886 reveals that scholars have overstated the severity of Schreiner's nervous collapse. Her letters are consistently articulate, clear-headed, sensible.

51. OS to Mrs. J. H. Philpot, Christmas Eve, 1885, SCCS *Letters*, 88; to HE, November 16, 1885, ibid., 86; to HE, March 10 and 31, 1886, March 22, 1887, November 24, 1887, ibid. See also OS to William Stead, 1891, ibid.

52. OS to HE, November 24, 1887, ibid., 124. See also OS to Edward Carpenter, April 23, 1888, Carpenter Collection, Sheffield City Libraries Archives Division, Sheffield (hereafter cited as CC): "human creatures need to be taught selfishness."

53. Judith R. Walkowitz, "Science, Feminism, and Romance: The Men and Women's Club, 1885–1889," *History Workshop* 21 (Spring 1986): 37–59; and Betty Fradkin, "Olive Schreiner and Karl Pearson," *Quarterly Bulletin of the South African Library* 31, 4 (June 1977): 83–93.

54. The other six were: Monica (mother of Saint Augustine), Sappho, Joan of Arc, Saint Catherine of Siena, Mary Wollstonecraft, and Mme. Roland. SCCS *Life*, 181.

55. Ibid. 151. Edinburgh Royal Infirmary was one of the three British hospitals to initiate professional training in the midseventies. Its regime was formidable. Nurse probationers were warned that their training required "a very great outlay of health

and strength" as well as tough nerves and emotional endurance to cope with the gamut of trying experiences such as surgery and deathwatch. To add further stress, nurse probationers were under constant supervision, off duty as well as on. First and Scott, *Olive Schreiner,* 113.

56. os to Edward Carpenter, September 4, 1889, CC; os to Carpenter, June 11, 1888, CC; Mrs. John Brown, "Memories of a Friendship," in Zelda Friedlander, ed., *Until the Heart Changes: A Garland for Olive Schreiner* (Cape Town: Tafelberg, 1967), 25–41; Hobman, *Olive Schreiner,* 44; Vera Buchanan-Gould, *Not without Honour: The Life and Writings of Olive Schreiner* (London: Hutchinson, 1948), 93.

57. os to HE, November 16, 1885, SCCS Letters, 86–87; to HE, January 20, 1886, ibid., 92; to HE, November 9, 1888, ibid., 146.

58. os to KP, November 11, 1890, Rive, *Schreiner: Letters,* 179.

59. Havelock Ellis's recollection of Schreiner's words in his letter, cited by Phyllis Grosskurth, *Havelock Ellis: A Biography* (New York: Knopf, 1980), 323. For Schreiner's views of sexual passion, see: *Minute Book,* Men and Women's Club, October 12, 1885, 133, Pearson Collection, University College Library, London; os to W. T. Stead, January 10, 1896, and Summer, 1896, SCCS Letters, 217, 220–21; to HE, July 16, 1884, ibid., 31–32; and discussion of sexuality in Chapter 6, herein.

60. os to KP, April 4, 1886, May 21, 1886, Rive, *Schreiner: Letters,* 79–80, 300–3.

61. os to HE, December 7, 1886, SCCS Letters, 105–6.

62. Ellis's sexual needs, e.g. his urolagnia, a consummate delight in women urinating in his presence, countered by his reluctance to proceed sexually to the point of coitus disturbed Schreiner. Grosskurth, *Havelock Ellis,* 90–93. On one occasion Schreiner wrote Ellis that there was something "morbid" in his approach to sex. She found him preoccupied with the abnormal and diseased. os to HE, March 27, 1887, HRC. See illuminating discussion of Schreiner's and Ellis's sexual relationship in Betty McGinnis Fradkin, "Havelock Ellis and Olive Schreiner's 'Gregory Rose,'" *Texas Quarterly,* Fall 1978, 145–53.

63. SCCS Life, 97.

64. Schreiner biographers suspect that Gau promised to marry her if she proved to be pregnant. Because the two had discovered their mutual unsuitability, when Schreiner realized she was not pregnant she ended the engagement. The ordeal left her almost suicidal. Events in her novels *Undine* and *African Farm,* begun shortly after her severance of her ties to Gau, lend plausibility to this hypothesis. Indeed, all three of her major novels treat the plight of "fallen women." First and Scott, *Olive Schreiner,* 61–63; Buchanan-Gould, *Not without Honour,* 39; Johannes Meintjes, *Olive Schreiner: Portrait of a South African Woman* (Johannesburg: Keartland, 1965), 21.

65. First and Scott, in *Olive Schreiner,* present this theory skillfully. The authors further assert that such an ideal is unhealthy, reflecting Schreiner's inability to affirm sexual pleasure in and of itself. Here I profoundly differ. Schreiner's sexual

ideal seems valid to me; and, further, I note various occasions when she celebrated erotic desire and pleasure.

66. For evidence of Schreiner's attraction to men stronger in mind and body than herself, see OS to HE, January 5, 1886, and January 19, 1906, SCCS *Letters*, 90, 253; to Mrs. J. H. Philpot, March 17, 1889, ibid., 157. For evidence of her attraction to a more balanced relationship, see OS to W. P. Schreiner, February 20, 1894, in Clayton, *Olive Schreiner*, 118. Her ambivalence toward both strength and weakness in men is evident throughout her correspondence with Ellis and in her novels.

67. SCCS *Life*, 232–34, 241, 246, 350–53; OS to HE, February 16, 1894, SCCS *Letters*, 213; OS to Carpenter, August 1, 1893, Rive, *Schreiner: Letters*, 222–23; to Carpenter, November 9, 1895, ibid., 225; to Will, April 11, 1894, ibid., 236–37.

68. OS to Louie Ellis, March 1894, SCCS *Letters*, 214; SCCS *Life*, 263.

69. OS to Mary Brown, January 1895, SCCS *Life*, 274.

70. OS to Mrs. John Brown, September 24, 1894, HRC. Knowledge about Schreiner's sexual experience with Cronwright is virtually nonexistent. In contrast to her correspondence with Ellis concerning individual sexual needs and activity (e.g., masturbation) and with members of the Men and Women's Club about gender and sexuality, we have no record of the sexual sphere of her marriage. Conceivably, she discussed it in her correspondence with Ellis, but she and Ellis destroyed almost all their letters written between 1893 and 1899. As a result, we do not even know whether she practiced birth control. (In theory, she favored the use of contraceptives.) We know nothing about how menopause affected her and, crucially, whether her marital erotic experience influenced her views on sexuality.

71. Schreiner and her husband did hire domestic help. Gandhi, commenting on his visit to their home, praised the absence of class boundaries between Schreiner and her servants. Mohandas Karamchand Gandhi, *Satyagraha in South Africa*, translated from original in Gujarati by M. Desai (Madras: S. Ganesau, 1938), 37.

72. SCCS *Life*, 272.

73. OS to HE, July 25, 1899, SCCS *Letters*, 226–27; to SCCS, February 25, 1907, ibid., 263; OS to Betty Molteno, Johannesburg, October 4, 1898, in First and Scott, *Olive Schreiner*, 234, 230.

74. Schreiner and Cronwright belonged to a small group of whites whom contemporaries and later scholars designated "friends of the natives." Black esteem for Schreiner and Cronwright is exemplified in the decision of the distinguished black leader of South African nationalism, Sol Plaatje, to name his daughter, born in 1903, Olive. Brian Willan, *Sol Plaatje: South African Nationalist (1876–1932)* (Berkeley: University of California Press, 1984), 134–35. See also Stanley Trapido, "'The friends of the natives': Merchants, Peasants, and the Political Ideological Structure of Liberalism in the Cape, 1854–1910," in Sheila Marks and Anthony Atmore, eds., *Economy and Society in Pre-industrial South Africa* (London: Longman Group, 1980).

75. Gregg, *Memories of Schreiner*, 32–34; SCCS *Life*, 322; Schreiner, *Woman and Labor*, 11; OS to SCCS, August 26, 1902, SCCS *Letters*, 233.

76. SCCS *Life*, 353.

77. Schreiner's deep attachment to her fox terrier "Nita" led her to request Nita's burial beside her and her infant daughter. Each mierkat had a name, often comic, e.g., "Inbred Sin." SCCS *Life*, 341–47. Schreiner's affection for her pets is lovingly captured in Stephen Gray's insightful one-woman play based upon her life: *Schreiner* (Cape Town: David Philip, 1983), 42–43.

78. For a full exposition of this matter, see First and Scott, *Olive Schreiner*, 315–19, and Cherry Clayton, "Olive Schreiner: Life into Fiction," *English in Africa*, 12, 1 (May 1985): 37, which indicates that Cronwright entered into flirtatious relationships with Ethel Friedlander as well as Isaline Philpot.

79. Besides these few very close female friends, Schreiner formed meaningful connections with many other reform-minded women, e.g., Beatrice Potter Webb, Mrs. C. A. F. Rhys Davids, Isaline Philpot, Charlotte Wilson, Henrietta Muller, Margaret Elise Harkness, Elizabeth Cobb, Caroline Haddon.

80. OS to HE, October 1888, SCCS *Letters*, 243–44. Also cited in Doris Langley Moore, *E. Nesbit: A Biography* (Philadelphia: Chilton, 1966), 110.

81. Elizabeth M. Molteno (1852–1927), the eldest daughter of Sir John Molteno, the first prime minister of the Cape Colony, was headmistress from 1890 to 1899 at Collegiate Girls School in Port Elizabeth where Alice M. Greene (1858–1920) served as vice-principal. I am indebted to my former graduate student Ellen Ziff, who provided me with the copies of Schreiner's letters to Aletta Jacobs held in the International Archives of the Women's Movement in Amsterdam (Intern. Archief Vrouwenbeweging Amsterdam).

82. OS to T. Fisher Unwin, September 26, 1892, SCCS *Letters*, 209: "I insisted on *An African Farm* being published at 1/– because the book was published by me for working men. I wanted to feel sure boys like Waldo could buy a copy, and feel they were not alone. . . . *Dreams* is not published by me with the special intention of reaching the poor. I would prefer the rich to have it. If I dedicated it to the public, I should dedicate it 'To all Capitalists, Millionaires and Middlemen in England and America and all high and mighty persons.' It is a book which will always have its own public of cultured persons who will have it at any price."

83. OS to HE, January 24, 1886, HRC.

84. OS to HE, January 24, 1888, SCCS *Letters*, 126–28.

85. Rhodes remained prime minister until January 1896. Sir John Gordon Spriggs succeeded him from 1896 to 1898. Schreiner's brother Will, initially a Rhodes protégé, had broken from Rhodes by the time he succeeded Spriggs as premier from 1898 to 1900. After the formation of the Union of South Africa in 1911, Will became high commissioner to London until his death in 1919.

86. She became particularly close friends with Lady Constance Lytton and Miss Adela Villiers (later Mrs. Francis Smith), nieces of Governor and Lady Loch.

Schreiner's circle of friends in Cape Town also included such prominent political figures as Mr. Seymour Fort (secretary to the governor), John X. Merriman, Sir James and Lady Rose-Innes, J. W. and Mary Sauer, and Mrs. Marie Kuipmans de Wet.

87. OS to Erilda Cawood, October 5, 1885, SCCS *Letters*, 83: "our old Africa beats this old country through and through." See similar expressions in OS to HE, February 25, 1884, August 6, 1884, March 19, 1886, April 12, 1886, ibid., 12–13, 38, 95, 114, and to Cawood, March 19, 1886, ibid., 95.

88. OS to HE, April 15, 1890, June 25, 1890, August 30, 1890, SCCS *Letters*, 182–83, 190, 196; to HE, March 25, 1890, April 6, 20, 25, 28, 1890, ibid., 182, 183, 184, 184–85. See also Schreiner, *Thoughts*, chap. 1.

89. OS to Louie Ellis, April 19, 1887, SCCS *Letters*, 115. Schreiner desired these words inscribed on her gravestone.

90. Some years prior to her death, Schreiner had written: "Is it strange that when we are in other lands and we fear that death approaches us, we say: 'Take me back.' We may live away from her, but when we are dead we must lie on her breast. Bury us among the kopjes where we played when we were children, and let the iron stones and red sand cover us." Olive Schreiner, *The South African Question* (Chicago, Charles H. Segel, 1899), 9. Schreiner's image of the karroo as a mother's breast underscores the succor it offered her during periods of childhood loneliness.

91. OS to W. T. Stead, October 12, 1892, SCCS *Letters*, 209.

92. OS to W. P. Schreiner, June 29, 1898, quoted in First and Scott, *Olive Schreiner*, 231. See also Rive, *Schreiner: Letters*, 332–33 for full letter. There is an extensive debate among Schreiner's contemporaries as well as subsequent Schreiner biographers and literary critics about the merits of *Trooper Peter Halket of Mashonaland*. Very recent literary critics are more favorably disposed toward the novella than those of previous decades, e.g., Stephen Gray, "The Trooper at the Hanging Tree," in Clayton, *Olive Schreiner*, 198–208. See my discussion of the novella in Chapters 4 and 8, herein.

93. OS to W. P. Schreiner, May 20, 1908, quoted in Clayton, *Olive Schreiner*, 125.

94. "Speech on the Boer War, at the Public Meeting in Cape Town, 9th July, 1900," SCCS *Letters*, App. A, 374.

95. OS to SCCS, March 25, 1908, SCCS *Letters*, 277.

96. Schreiner, *Woman and Labor*, 23.

97. Alfred Cronwright to SCCS, November 26, 1920, SCCS *Life*, 379; Ethel Hermann, "Personal Recollections," in Friedlander, *Until the Heart Changes*, 50–52.

98. Ben Farrington in an interview with Ruth First in 1969, quoted in a footnote in First and Scott, *Olive Schreiner*, 322. See too Lyndall Gregg, "Memories of Olive Schreiner," in Friedlander, *Until the Heart Changes*, 21–41, esp. 40.

Chapter 2

1. SCCS Life, 289–90. Madeleine Cazamian, Le roman et les idées angleterre, 1860–1914 (Paris: Société d'Edition, 1955), 3:351. See too the acclaim for her spiritual inquiry by Laurence Housman, The Unexpected Years (London: J. Cape, 1937), 135, 139; Herbert Gladstone and Sir William Lecky in SCCS Life, 158, 162; Herbert Spencer in OS to SCCS, January 16, 1911, SCCS Letters, 298–99; Ellis, My Life, 184; Arthur Symons, notes on meeting with OS on June 10, 1889, in SCCS Life, 184–90.

2. OS to KP, October 23, 1886, Rive, Schreiner: Letters, 108–110. Mary A. Hill, Charlotte Perkins Gilman: The Making of a Radical Feminist, 1860–1896 (Philadelphia: Temple University Press, 1979), 176–77, 221, 186; Charlotte Perkins Gilman, "Woman and Labor," Forerunner 2, 7 (July 1911): 197–98. Ruth Alexander, "Olive Schreiner: A Study of Her Amazing Personality," Cape Times, April 26, 1930.

3. An important exception is Jane Marcus's "Olive Schreiner: Cartographer of the Spirit/A Review Article," Minnesota Review, Spring 1979, 58–66.

4. Postlethwaite, Making It Whole, passim.

5. Schreiner, Undine, 112. Franklin L. Baumer, Religion and the Rise of Scepticism (New York: Harcourt, Brace, 1960), 132, 136–38.

6. Schreiner, African Farm, 118.

7. Ibid., 119–20.

8. Ibid., 120, 121.

9. Schreiner experienced a similar parental rejection; SCCS Life, 67.

10. Schreiner, African Farm, 121, 122.

11. The literature of Hell and damnation pervaded all Christian denominations and formed a part of Victorian childhood in a manner inconceivable in the twentieth century. See Ian Bradley, The Call To Seriousness: The Evangelical Impact on the Victorians (New York: Macmillan, 1976); and Grylls, Guardians and Angels.

12. The reader will recall these years as coinciding with the death of her beloved younger sister, her loss of faith, her father's professional and economic travails, and her leaving home to live with her brother and sister, Theo and Ettie.

13. Schreiner, African Farm, 123, 122.

14. Compare image of the clock discussed by Baumer in Religion, chap. 2, "The Strasbourg Clock," and portrayed by Ingmar Bergman in his film Wild Strawberries.

15. Schreiner, African Farm, 3–5.

16. Ibid., 7. Schreiner has Undine undergo a comparable experience; Undine, 88–89. Evidently, such Victorian testing of God's response was not uncommon. See Edmond Gosse, Father and Son (New York: Scribner, 1916).

17. Schreiner, African Farm, 11. Adults offer no comfort; rather, as in the case of ten-

year-old Undine, they rebuke her for challenging God's benevolence. When she declares that the devil is not as cruel as God since he did not make Hell, she is locked in her room for the day and denied dinner. Despite her momentary joy in venting her anger she soon feels guilty, incorrigibly evil, and desperately alone. Her tears, the narrator comments, are like drops of blood congealed beneath the eyelids. *Undine,* 18–21, 25–26, 69–70.

18. Schreiner, *African Farm,* 126.

19. Schreiner, *African Farm,* 127. For a classic presentation of the sequence of religious suffering and rebirth, see William James, *The Varieties of Religious Experience* (1902; rpt., New York: New American Library, 1958), 208.

20. Schreiner, *African Farm,* 128.

21. Ibid., 131. See also Schreiner, *Undine,* 40, 58–60.

22. Schreiner, *African Farm,* 132.

23. In almost all of Schreiner's fiction we meet destructive individuals disguised as sincere Christians. Throughout we find the longing for an essentially beautiful and good universe colliding with the blatant cruelty of nature and human behavior. The reader will recall that Schreiner's family's desperate economic circumstances were in part a consequence of her father's credulity, his erratic shifts from worldly, business affairs to dreamy otherworldliness.

24. Ibid., 134, 135, 136, 138–39.

25. OS to SCCS, January 16, 1911, SCCS *Letters,* 298–99.

26. SCCS *Life,* 70, 121, 126, 147.

27. Karl Pearson, *The Ethic of Freethought* (1888; rpt., London: Adam and Charles Black, 1901), x.

28. Schreiner, *From Man to Man,* 151.

29. Baumer, *Religion,* 140. Baumer lists six basic Victorian objections to a belief in God, which he labels the utilitarian, the scientific, the anthropological, the psychological, the economic, and the historical. The last three arguments reflected new intellectual currents of the nineteenth century.

30. On various occasions Schreiner cited the writing of Ernest Renan and David Friedrich Strauss, formative Higher Critics. OS to HE, April 8 and 21, 1884, SCCS *Letters,* 14–15, 15–16: "Strauss's *Life of Jesus* is very different from Renan's, I think better; though I like Renan." Gibbon's writing was also decisive in the loss of belief of many Victorians, e.g., Frances Power Cobbe and Samuel Butler. See Frank Turner, *Between Science and Religion* (New Haven: Yale University Press, 1974), 170. Although some freethinkers fiercely opposed existing systems of belief, others considered current religions as curious mixtures of falsehoods and real knowledge and rejected the simple scoffing at inherited beliefs. Acknowledging the bigotry and superstition contaminating all Christian denominations, Schreiner nonetheless had kind words for the Dutch Reformed Protestantism of South African Boers. Most religions she deemed dead or "more or less moribund [which,] like decaying flesh, corrupt the atmosphere, and render putrid the whole

environment of those who bear it," but the Boers' religion struck her as alive, in harmony with their needs, knowledge, ideals, and aims. Basic to Schreiner's appraisal of Boer religion was her conviction, quite typical of freethinkers, that "There is perhaps no life quite worth living without a living religion, under whatever name or form it may be concealed." Schreiner, *Thoughts*, 284–85, 179.

31. Susan Budd, "Reasons for Unbelief among Members of the Secular Movement in England, 1850–1950," *Past and Present* 36 (April 1967): 106–25, esp. 111–16, 120; Howard R. Murphy, "The Ethical Revolt against Orthodoxy in Early Victorian England," *American Historical Review* 60 (1955): 800–17; Peter Rowell, *Hell and the Victorians* (Oxford: Oxford University Press [Clarendon Press], 1971), 2–3, 29–30; A. O. J. Cockshut, *The Unbelievers: Early Agnostic Thought, 1840–1890* (New York: New York University Press, 1966); Bernard Lightman, *The Origins of Agnosticism: Victorian Unbelief and the Limits of Knowledge* (Baltimore: Johns Hopkins University Press, 1987), 112.

32. Rowell, *Hell and the Victorians*, 137–38, 147. Typifying the shift toward an ethic of compassion and forgiveness, nineteenth-century reformers promoted new attitudes toward the punishment of criminals. The traditional approach of retributive punishment succumbed to a penal theory popularized by Utilitarians, which validated punishment only insofar as it deterred crime and reformed the criminal. Retribution accomplished neither. Moreover, it did not take into account the intentions and understanding of the offender. Inevitably, the debate about penal theory in the social realm had repercussions in the spirited theological debate about divine retribution.

33. OS to HE, September 23, 1884, HRC. Front cover of Schreiner's Journal, 1881–86, SCCS *Life*, 159. Schreiner refers to the doctrine of vicarious atonement in her discussion with Arthur Symons and in her letter to Mrs. Francis Smith. Symons recorded that she stated this doctrine darkened and embittered her childhood. SCCS *Life*, 187. See OS to Mrs. Francis Smith, May 13, 1912, SCCS *Letters*, 307.

34. Schreiner, *Undine*, 84–85, 137–38, 147.

35. Bradley, *Call to Seriousness*, 180–81.

36. Margaret Maison, *Search Your Soul, Eustace: Victorian Religious Novels* (London: Sheed and Ward, 1961), 218–22.

37. Valentine Cunningham, "Mad Pilgrimings, Aimless Discontinuities, Painful Transitions, Faith and Doubt in Victorian Fiction," *Victorian Studies* 22, 3 (September, 1979): 321–34, esp. 334. See also Cunningham, *Everywhere Spoken Against: Dissent in the Victorian Novel* (Oxford: Oxford University Press [Clarendon Press], 1975).

38. Olive Schreiner, "The Sunlight Lay across My Bed," in her collection of allegories, *Dreams* (Boston: Little, Brown, 1916), 156–57. Elizabeth Cady Stanton, *The Original Feminist Attack on the Bible* (originally published in 1895 as *The Woman's Bible*; rpt., New York: Arno Press, 1974), x.

39. In more recent feminist spiritual thought, androgynous constructions are rivaled

either by neuter concepts akin to Schreiner's or by espousal of a simply feminine godhead. Carol Ochs, *Behind the Sex of God* (Boston: Beacon Press, 1977); Carol P. Christ, "Why Women Need the Goddess: Phenomenological, Psychological, and Political Reflection," in Carol P. Christ and Judith Plaskow, eds., *Womanspirit Rising* (San Francisco: Harper and Row, 1979), 273–87.

40. A quintessential example is June Singer, *Androgyny: Toward a New Theory of Sexuality* (New York: Doubleday [Anchor Books], 1977), chap. 3.

41. Olive Schreiner, *Mary Wollstonecraft: Rights of Women*, 4, unfinished manuscript held in the Albany Library, 1820 Settlers Memorial Division, Grahamstown. I am grateful to Betty Fradkin Tetlow for copying it for me.

42. SCCS *Life*, 218.

43. I. M. Lewis, *Ecstatic Religion* (Middlesex: Penguin Books, 1971), 31, 34. OS to Mrs. Francis Smith, October 16, 1909, May 8, 1912, SCCS *Letters*, 289–90, 305–6.

44. Schreiner, *Thoughts*, 291.

45. Ibid., 289–90, 284.

46. Jane Marcus, in "Olive Schreiner," 63, contrasts the primitive pastoralism and egalitarianism of Schreiner's imagination with Virginia Woolf's Quaker and Clapham sect restraint, rationality, and asceticism. She describes Schreiner as broadly baptist, Bunyanesque.

47. Schreiner, *From Man to Man*, 153, 155. Schreiner, *African Farm*, 158. Deviating from most freethinkers, Karl Pearson questioned the certainty of correspondence between mental discoveries and objective reality: *Ethic of Freethought*, 15, 20.

48. Schreiner, *From Man to Man*, 219, 155–56.

49. SCCS *Life*, 219.

50. Schreiner, "In a Ruined Chapel," in *Dreams*, 94.

51. Schreiner told Arthur Symons that Emerson, although he did not express all her feelings, "has never said, not even a half sentence that she doesn't absolutely agree with and feel." SCCS *Life*, 187–88. The affinity between Schreiner's views and Emerson's is strikingly evident in Emerson's pronouncement that "The true doctrine of omnipresence is that God reappears with all his parts in every moss and cobweb." *The Works of Ralph Waldo Emerson* (Boston: Houghton Mifflin, 1883–87), 2:101.

52. SCCS *Life*, 220; Schreiner, *African Farm*, 301, 302; SCCS *Life*, 219.

53. SCCS *Life*, 220; Schreiner, *From Man to Man*, 155; SCCS *Life*, 220.

54. Turner, *Between Science and Religion*, 133, 195–97.

55. OS to HE, July 13, 1884, SCCS *Letters*, 30.

56. OS to HE, March 26, 1889, ibid., 159; OS to Carpenter, February 4, 1888, CC.

57. OS to Mrs. Francis Smith, May 13, 1912, SCCS *Letters*, 306–7; SCCS *Life*, 220; OS to HE, November 3, 1888, SCCS *Letters*, 145.

58. SCCS *Life*, 270. Schreiner's fastening upon Jesus' identity formation may well have accounted for her recurrent desire to create a play about Jesus. I do not conclude,

however, as First and Scott do, that this projected play indicates Schreiner's latent reverence. In light of all her criticisms of Jesus and her regard for other religious leaders, her hopes to write about him simply reveal her regard for his genius and an interest in imaginatively fleshing out his hidden personality.

59. SCCS *Life,* 7; OS to Mrs. Francis Smith, April 9, 1908, SCCS *Letters,* 277.

60. Too much can be made of Schreiner's frequent reliance upon the Bible. There is no question that the Bible nourished her idealism; its cadences flowed through her prose. But it did not serve her as a source of awesome truths. Schreiner impishly enjoyed turning biblical phrases against Christians, boasting, "I am always quoting from the Bible, sometimes for the Devil's own purposes." OS to Mrs. Francis Smith, November 3, 1888, SCCS *Letters,* 145. Her niece, Joan Hodgson, recalled "the mixture of wicked joy and aesthetic appreciation [Schreiner] put into the recitation of denunciatory passages from the Bible. 'I could always beat them when it came to quoting,' she chuckled." SCCS *Life,* 370.

61. SCCS *Life,* 6–7.

62. SCCS *Letters,* App. F, "A Letter on the Jew" (extracts from), 392–95. OS to Mrs. Francis Smith, May 13, 1912, ibid., 306–7; OS to Ruth Alexander, 1915, in Ruth Alexander, "Olive Schreiner's Letters," *Cape Times,* December 1944; Schreiner, *Woman and Labor,* 94–96, 144–45, 167; Schreiner, *Thoughts,* 287, 344.

63. Schreiner to Mrs. Francis Smith, May 13, 1912, SCCS *Letters,* 306–7; Schreiner, *Thoughts,* 287; Schreiner, *South African Question,* 92. See also Ochs, *Behind the Sex of God,* 132–33, 136–37, for Spinoza's role in opposing mind/body dualism.

64. Havelock Ellis, *My Confessional: Questions of Our Day* (Boston: Houghton Mifflin, 1934), 182. Ellis writes about his reading Spinoza at the age of twenty and revering his writing, then, later, learning of Schreiner "affectionately hugging Pollock's *Spinoza* . . . and eagerly talking about it." Ellis and Pearson, perhaps Schreiner too, may have been familiar with George Henry Lewes's groundbreaking essay, "Spinoza's Life and Works," in the *Westminster Review* (1843), which appeared at a time when Spinoza's writing was not yet translated into English. Spinoza's earliest English champion was Coleridge.

65. OS to Carpenter, March 1908, SCCS *Letters,* 276.

66. Typical of Victorians who turned toward the Orient during a religious crisis was Beatrice Potter Webb. In 1876 she found herself drawn to Buddhism, viewing it as logically and ethically superior to Christianity. So, too, Charles Darwin regarded Buddhist ideas as deeply challenging to Christian belief. Owen Chadwick, *The Victorian Church* (Oxford: Oxford University Press, 1966–70), 2:35–37; Deborah Epstein Nord, *The Apprenticeship of Beatrice Webb* (Amherst: University of Massachusetts Press, 1985), 42.

67. Mrs. Rhys Davids, *Buddhism: Its Birth and Dispersal* (London: Thornton Butterworth, 1912), 15–17. Various letters to Mrs. Rhys Davids, e.g., OS to Mrs. Rhys Davids, August 20, 1909, SCCS *Letters,* 287–88: "Thank you for the pamphlet;

and thank you much more for your wish to dedicate the book to me. In two ways I shall feel it an especial gift. In one, because of my strong feeling about Buddha's teaching, that it was of a higher grade in many directions than that of any other religious teacher."

68. Ellis, *My Life*, 153; Pearson, *Ethic of Freethought*, 9.

69. Sheila Rowbotham and Jeffrey Weeks, *Socialism and the New Life: The Personal and Sexual Politics of Edward Carpenter and Havelock Ellis* (London: Pluto Press, 1977), 40. In 1890 Carpenter traveled to Ceylon and India, meditating with an Eastern religious teacher (a gnani). It was through Carpenter's elder brother who worked in India and an Indian college friend, P. Arunachalam, that he developed his opposition to the Empire, identified with Indian nationalist strivings, and learned how to make the sandals he wore and made for Schreiner and other friends of the "simple life."

70. Schreiner, *African Farm*, 213. Betty Fradkin Tetlow argues in her unpublished essay, " 'Seek, Then, and Be Lost in the Quest . . .' Farid ud-Din Attar," that Doris Lessing's hunch about Schreiner deriving the Hunter allegory from reading Attar's *Parliament of the Birds* (a foremost Sufi document) is highly plausible. However, Schreiner alludes nowhere in her writing to Persian or Sufi philosophy.

71. Pearson, *Ethic of Freethought*, 9.

72. OS to Carpenter, March 1908, SCCS *Letters*, 276.

73. Her allegories and even her political treatises ring with Old and New Testament cadences and vocabulary. Consider the peroration from *Woman and Labor*: "The ancient Chaldean seer had a vision of a Garden of Eden which lay in a remote past. . . . We also have our dream of a Garden, but it lies in a distant future. We dream that woman shall eat of the tree of knowledge together with man, and that side by side and hand close to hand . . . they shall together raise about them an Eden nobler than any the Chaldean dreamed of; an Eden created by their own labor and made beautiful by their own fellowship." Schreiner, *Woman and Labor*, 298.

74. Elizabeth Alvilda Petroff, *Consolation of the Blessed* (New York: Alta Gaia Society, 1979), 195.

75. See Chapter 8 for a discussion of the central role of light in Schreiner's aesthetics. Mercea Eliade, in *The Two and the One* (Chicago: University of Chicago Press, 1965), chap. 1, "Experiences of Mystic Light," discusses the cross-cultural experience of resplendent illumination accompanying certain ecstatic moments.

76. Abraham H. Maslow, *Religions, Values, and Peak Experiences* (Columbus: Ohio State University Press, 1964); Marghanita Laski, *Ecstasy: A Study of Some Secular and Religious Experiences* (Bloomington: Indiana University Press, 1961); Lewis, *Ecstatic Religion*.

77. SCCS *Life*, 223; Schreiner, *African Farm*, 312; Schreiner, *Thoughts*, 285.

78. Maslow writes in *Religions*, 63, that "The person in the peak-experience may feel a day passing as if it were minutes or also a minute so intensely lived that it might feel

like a day or a year or an eternity. He may also lose his consciousness of being located in a particular place." Such was Schreiner's experience.

79. SCCS *Life,* 219. In Schreiner's own time, the more scientific-minded, along with her freethinking and rationalist allies, might well agree with her contemporary, Henry Maudsley, that such experiences could not serve as a basis for truth since they could not be examined by objective scientific methods. For him they were best explained as hallucination or illusion. The freethinking Samuel Butler, who shared Schreiner's emphasis upon the insufficiency of purely rational knowledge, nevertheless felt that human feelings corresponded to ultimate reality no more than human reasoning. Turner, *Between Science and Religion,* 33, 180. Among Schreiner's other contemporaries, the American William James, whose writing she does not appear to know, furnished the most sympathetic analysis of her experience, an analysis later modified and expanded among psychoanalysts such as Carl Jung and Erich Fromm. James and Jung viewed the resolution of mundane dichotomies and fragmentations as a process of reintegration with the riches of the unconscious, a realm they regarded as fertile with sacred energy. James, *Varieties of Religious Experience,* 371–72, 378–79. In a more matter-of-fact way, Fromm, in *Psychoanalysis and Religion* (New Haven: Yale University Press, 1958), 94, typical of other analysts positively disposed toward religion, regarded ecstatic experience— as have Maslow and others—as the mature personality's creative "reconnection of the ego—with the disassociated world of the unconscious, replacing repression by permeation and integration."

80. SCCS *Life,* 70.

81. Ibid., 220–22; OS to HE, April 20, 1890, SCCS *Letters,* 183–84; OS to KP, November 1886, 455–56, Pearson Collection; Schreiner, *Undine,* 96–97, and *African Farm,* 312; OS to HE, March 23, 1885, SCCS *Letters,* 65.

82. Her statement of the need for psychological detachment is eloquently set forth by the narrator in *African Farm,* 312: "Go out if you will and walk alone on the hillside in the evening, but if your favorite child lies ill at home, or your lover comes tomorrow, or at your heart there lies a scheme for the holding of wealth, then you will return as you went; you will have seen nothing."

83. Schreiner, *Thoughts,* 285.

84. Ibid., 290–91; SCCS *Life,* 222. Scholars of mystical experience often discriminate among levels of mystic awareness. Laski, for example, distinguishes Adamic experiences from more developed visions. The Adamic experience is a predominantly emotional intuition of oneness with transcendent energy similar to Freud's oceanic, primitive infantile unity with the mother, whereas, according to Laski, the more developed ecstatic experiences include significant ideational and moral content. The vision precipitates a new cognition of reality or a change of personal values and behavior. Petroff, likewise, articulates seven stages in visionary expansion, the unitive visions of the sixth stage preceding the highest visionary stage, the intuition of divine or cosmic order. See Laski, *Ecstasy,* 49, 106; Petroff, *Consolation*

of the Blessed, 78–79, 198. Schreiner's experiences usually reflected a combination of Petroff's sixth and seventh stages. Just before a vision occurred, she would often feel intellectually, morally, and emotionally bewildered by human oppression and cruelty. Her vision would offer her both a psychic release and deepened understanding.

85. Schreiner, *African Farm,* 312, 313; SCCS *Life,* 98; OS to SCCS, April 1893, SCCS *Life,* 252–53. Note, too, that in Schreiner's novella *Trooper Peter Halket of Mashonaland* (Boston: Roberts Brothers, 1897), 32, Jesus' gaze reminds Peter of his mother's.

86. Petroff, *Consolation of the Blessed,* 78. See also Caroline Walker Bynum's study of thirteenth-century nuns of Helfta, in *Jesus as Mother: Studies in the Spirituality of the High Middle Ages* (Berkeley: University of California Press, 1982), 245. Bynum also notes a decline in a view of cosmic conflict when Jesus is perceived as mother.

87. Nancy Chodorow, in *Reproduction of Mothering: Psychoanalysis and the Sociology of Gender* (Berkeley: University of California Press, 1978), maintains that women have less need to separate themselves from erotic and affective bonds with their mother. Consequently, the boundaries between mother and daughter are more permeable and more continuous into adulthood than between mother and son. According to Philip M. Halfaer, *The Psychology of Religious Doubt* (Boston: Beacon Press, 1972), 72, "the symbolism of God the Father is a defense against maternal engulfment."

88. Petroff, *Consolation of the Blessed.* Bynum, however, finds that certain male mystics also conceived of Jesus as mother, e.g., Anselm of Canterbury, Bernard of Clairvaux, and Gueric, abbot of Igny. Bynum, *Jesus as Mother,* 110–11.

89. Mary Daly, *Gyn/Ecology: The Metaethics of Radical Feminism* (Boston: Beacon Press, 1978), 49, 67. Schreiner, as did Pearson, regarded the bo tree as a superior symbol to the cross. The bo tree was the tree of knowledge, the quest for truth, and the individual's supreme mission. It resonated with the sacred tree symbol of multiple cultural traditions. Mercea Eliade explains that one of the various modalities of the cosmic tree is its connecting of Earth, Heaven, and Sky. By so doing it signifies "living, sacred and inexhaustible reality." Eliade, *The Two and the One,* 196–98. By contrast, the cross bore for freethinkers the dubious ethics of the doctrine of atonement as well as belief based upon faith and the suppression of critical judgment. Furthermore, to Schreiner at least, the attraction of the tree over the cross may relate to its female connotations. Mary Daly, tapping the insights of Diner's *Mothers and Amazons,* dwells upon the transformation of the tree of life into the cross, arguing that this represents the supplanting of the goddess, the organic life of vegetation, with patriarchal religious conceptions.

90. Baumer, *Religion,* chap. 3, "The Death of God"; Walter E. Houghton, *The Victorian Frame of Mind, 1830–1870* (New Haven: Yale University Press, 1957), chap. 10, "Earnestness"; Lightman, *Origins of Agnosticism,* chap. 6, "The New Natural Theology and the Holy Trinity of Agnosticism."

91. Schreiner, *African Farm*, 160.
92. OS to HE, July 4, 1903, SCCS *Letters*, 237; to HE, February 10, 1885, ibid., 59; to Mrs. Francis Smith, May 13, 1912, ibid., 306–7. Schreiner, *African Farm*, 160.
93. Schreiner, *African Farm*, 161.
94. Schreiner, *From Man to Man*, 157, 160, 159.
95. OS to SCCS, July 16, 1903, SCCS *Letters*, 238–39.
96. Schreiner, *African Farm*, 291.
97. Schreiner, *Thoughts*, 287–88.
98. SCCS *Life*, 370.

Chapter 3

1. Baumer, *Religion*, 177–84, 149, 162–64; Houghton, *Victorian Frame of Mind*, 13–14; Rowell, *Hell and the Victorians*, 180.
2. Schreiner, *Woman and Labor*, 23.
3. Marvin Harris, *The Rise of Anthropological Theory* (New York: Crowell, 1968), 122–24.
4. For all her quarrels with Darwin, Schreiner had enormous respect for him. His Social Darwinist popularizers were the ones she abhorred. She found Darwin's *Voyage of the Beagle* suffused with "love and freedom and human equality." She discerned a heartening correspondence between Darwin's sensitive attack on the mistreatment of both "primitive" and nineteenth-century black peoples and his discovery of the "mystery and meanings of the humblest forms of life . . . from the stripes on the wing of the bird and the life and motion of the worm." Schreiner, *Thoughts*, 351–53.
5. Ibid., 378, 296–97, 357; Schreiner, *Woman and Labor*, 298.
6. Harris, *Rise of Anthropological Theory*, 81; Nancy Stepan, *The Idea of Race*, xviii: "The result was to give a mental abstraction independent reality, to make real or 'reify' the idea of racial type when the type was actually a social construct."
7. For the impact of social and political ideology upon scientific discussion of race and gender, see Douglas Lorimer, *Colour, Class, and the Victorians* (Leicester: Leicester University Press, 1978), and Lorimer, "Theoretical Racism and Late Victorian Anthropology, 1870–1900," *Victorian Studies* 31, 1 (Spring 1988), 405–30. See also Janet Sayers, *Biological Politics: Feminist and Anti-feminist Perspectives* (London: Tavistock, 1982), 84–97; Ronald Rainger, "Race, Politics, and Science: The Anthropological Society of London in the 1860s," *Victorian Studies* 22, 1 (August 1978): 51–70; Ruth Bleier, *Science and Gender: A Critique of Biology and Its Theories of Gender* (New York: Pergamon, 1984). Cynthia Russett, in *Scientific Construction of Womanhood*, asserts that the homogeneity of scientific attitudes on race and gender reflects late-nineteenth-century anxieties, a "tapestry of uncertainty" over the eclipse of Christianity, the rapidity of social and political transfor-

mations, and the unclarity of the boundaries between men and animals, matter and spirit.

8. OS to KP, November 11, 1890, Rive, *Schreiner: Letters,* 177–80. At one point, shortly after her return to South Africa in 1890, Schreiner's research went beyond reading and data gathering to developing her language skills so as to study "Bantu-speaking Africans."

9. Schreiner, *Mary Wollstonecraft,* 5.

10. Schreiner, *From Man to Man,* 198.

11. Schreiner, *Thoughts,* 394–98.

12. Schreiner, *From Man to Man,* 66, 94, 222.

13. Schreiner, *Thoughts,* 28–29. Schreiner's blend of sympathy and detachment can best be viewed in relation to current anthropological and linguistic distinctions between emic and etic cognition. Whereas etic understanding relates to the external, structural manifestations of group and individual behavior, emic understanding seeks to grasp the subjective significance of acts—motives, interests, conflicts, personality development. Accordingly, she declares, "the comprehension not merely of the vices and virtues of its people, but of the how and why of their existence, is possible to a man only with regard to a country that is more or less his own. The stranger sees the barren scene, but of the emotion which the barren mountain is capable of awakening in the man who lives under its shadow [the stranger] knows nothing. He marks the curious custom, but of the social condition which originated it, and the passions concerned in its maintenance, he understands absolutely nothing. . . . to Balzac nothing was easier than to paint the Paris boarding-house. All the united intellect and genius of Europe could not have painted it if the grimy respectability of those chairs and tables, the sordid narrowness of the faded human lives, had not eaten first into their own substance, emotionally." Schreiner, *Thoughts,* 29.

14. Cynthia Eagle Russett, *Darwin in America* (San Francisco: W. H. Freeman, 1976).

15. Schreiner, *African Farm,* 87; Schreiner, *From Man to Man,* 192.

16. Schreiner, *From Man to Man,* 185, 187.

17. Ibid., 189–90, 197, 192–93.

18. Turner, *Between Science and Religion,* 249; Russett, *Darwin in America,* 105–14. Is it pure coincidence that the prototype of the "new man" in *From Man to Man* has the surname Drummond?

19. Schreiner, *Dawn,* 15, 34. Segments of Schreiner's unfinished manuscript appear in Schreiner, *Stories, Dreams, and Allegories* (London: Unwin, 1924), 159–72, and earlier in *The Nation and Athenaeum* (London), March 26, 1921; *From Man to Man,* 265; *Woman and Labor,* 290.

20. Schreiner, *From Man to Man,* 194.

21. Schreiner, *Dawn.* See further discussion in Chapter 7 on Schreiner's pacifism.

22. Schreiner, *From Man to Man,* 198–99; Schreiner, *Thoughts,* 365.

23. Schreiner, *Woman and Labor,* 240.

24. Schreiner, *From Man to Man*, 199.

25. Hamilton Cravens, *The Triumph of Evolution* (Philadelphia: University of Pennsylvania Press, 1978), 77. Between 1900 and 1920, at least 600 books and articles published in England and America proclaimed instinct theory; most of these publications after 1908 cited the writing of the English physician, William McDougall, *An Introduction to Social Psychology* (1908).

26. Russett, *Darwin in America*, 102–11.

27. Schreiner, *Woman and Labor*, 36, 219.

28. Schreiner, *From Man to Man*, 195–96,198–99, 224; Schreiner, *Woman and Labor*, 42–43, 58, 69.

29. Schreiner, *From Man to Man*, 275.

30. Schreiner, *Thoughts*, 257, 376.

31. Schreiner, *African Farm*, 262.

32. Ellis advocated attempts to persuade the biologically unfit to be sterilized in the interest of human progress; he became a founding member of the Eugenics Society in 1907. Pearson, by the early twentieth century, marshaled eugenic arguments to justify Britain's imperial enterprises and to promote state-rewarded motherhood for fit women. See Grosskurth, *Havelock Ellis*, 410, and Lorna Duffin, "Prisoners of Progress: Women and Evolution," in Lorna Duffin and Sara Delamont, eds., *The Nineteenth-Century Woman* (London: Croom Helm, 1978), 78–87. See also Bernard J. Norton, *Karl Pearson and the Galtonian Tradition* (Ph.D. diss., University College, 1978).

33. Schreiner, *Woman and Labor*, 107–8. See also Charlotte Perkins Gilman, *Woman and Economics* (1898; rpt., New York, 1966). Elements of Lamarckianism influenced Darwin's belief that a trained woman would breed mentally superior offspring. Russett, *Scientific Construction of Womanhood*, 11.

34. Schreiner, *Thoughts*, 272; Schreiner, *Woman and Labor*, 107–10.

35. The ways in which the leading nineteenth-century anthropologists affirmed the assumption of European cultural superiority, plotting different races at different points on a hierarchical, linear, and progressive time frame, are discussed by, among others, George W. Stocking, Jr., *Race, Culture, and Evolution: Essays in the History of Anthropology* (New York: Free Press, 1968); J. W. Burrow, *Evolution and Society: A Study in Victorian Social Theory* (Cambridge: Cambridge University Press, 1970); Philip Abrams, *The Origins of British Sociology, 1834–1914* (Chicago: University of Chicago Press, 1968).

36. Schreiner, *From Man to Man*, 182.

37. Schreiner, *Thoughts*, 20–51, and *From Man to Man*, 177–82, 409–10, 414.

38. Schreiner, *From Man to Man*, 177–79.

39. Ibid., 181.

40. Ibid., 172–73.

41. Schreiner, *Thoughts*, 19, 23.

42. Schreiner, *African Farm*, 247, 239; Schreiner, *From Man to Man*, 344.

43. Schreiner, *From Man to Man,* 130, 132, and *Woman and Labor,* 167.
44. Schreiner, *Thoughts,* 74, 75–76, 92, 105.
45. I will employ Schreiner's term *half-caste* despite its erroneous and negative connotations and its implication that Africans constituted a separate species. Schreiner's use of the term exemplifies her dependence on racist Victorian language.
46. Schreiner, *Thoughts,* 128–32.
47. Ibid., 137.
48. Ibid., 138.
49. Leonard Thompson, in *The Political Mythology of Apartheid* (New Haven: Yale University Press, 1988), viii, observes that anyone who writes about South Africa enters a "terminological minefield." The scholar must decide whether to follow modern usage or the language of the documents and how to make sense of the confusing meanings of the labels, such as "coloured," "black," "white," since each term encompasses a diversity of ethnic groups. Whites carelessly call the majority of blacks "natives," "Kaffirs," "Africans," "blacks," "Bantus."
50. Schreiner, *Thoughts,* 105–9, 24, 109–12, 116, and *Woman and Labor,* 5–6, 246. Schreiner often referred to blacks as "Kaffirs," a designation that, despite her neutral intent, bore insulting connotations for blacks.
51. Christine Bolt, *The Anti-slavery Movement and Reconstruction* (Oxford: Oxford University Press, 1969), 131–53.
52. Schreiner, *From Man to Man,* 417.
53. Schreiner, *Woman and Labor,* 221–23.
54. Darwin, *The Variation of Animals and Plants under Domestication,* vol. 2. See Peter J. Vorzimmer, *Charles Darwin: The Years of Controversy* (Philadelphia: Temple University Press, 1970), 35–37.
55. Schreiner, *Thoughts,* 133–34.
56. Ibid., 137–38, 139.
57. Ibid., 134, 139.
58. Schreiner, *Woman and Labor,* 261–62.
59. Schreiner, *Thoughts,* 385–86.
60. Ibid., 386. See also OS to J. C. Smuts, July 1, 1896, Rive, *Schreiner: Letters,* 286–87. Here Schreiner alleges that racial equality will make interracial mating less likely but that when it happens it will be as a result of great love.
61. Schreiner never used the term *gender.* Although she would likely accept the current distinction between *sex* as a biological designation and *gender* as culturally constructed male and female identity, neither she nor any of her contemporaries resorted to this fruitful linguistic strategy. I will use *gender* when I think it conforms to Schreiner's intent. For a lucid set of definitions of contemporary feminist usage of these terms, see Gerda Lerner, *The Creation of Patriarchy* (Oxford: Oxford University Press, 1986), App., "Definitions," 238: "*Sex* . . . Women are a separate

group due to their biological distinctiveness. . . . *Gender* . . . the cultural definition of behavior defined as appropriate to the sexes in a given society at a given time . . . a set of cultural roles. . . . *Sex-gender system* . . . term . . . introduced by the anthropologist Gayle Rubin . . . refers to the institutionalized system which allots resources, property, and privileges to persons according to culturally defined gender roles." See, too, Gayle Rubin, "The Traffic in Women: Notes on the 'Political Economy' of Sex," in Rayna Reiter, ed., *Toward an Anthropology of Women* (New York: Monthly Review, 1975).

62. For a thorough discussion of nineteenth-century scientific construction of gender, see Russett, *Scientific Construction of Womanhood.* Darwin did not hesitate to invoke the evidence of Karl Vogt, whose widely read *Lectures on Man* (English trans., 1864) enlisted brain weight measurements to validate male superiority. For Darwin, mental powers and disposition were linked to secondary sex characteristics. See full discussion in Susan Sleuth Mosedale, "Science Corrupted: Victorian Biologists Consider 'The Woman Question,'" *Journal of the History of Biology* 2, 1 (Spring 1978): 1–55, esp. 6–9. Herbert Spencer argued in *The Study of Sociology* (1871–72) that gender differences originated in "a somewhat earlier arrest of individual evolution in women than in men, necessitated by the reservation of vital power to meet the cost of reproduction." Employing the popular Helmholtz law of the conservation of energy, Spencer deduced that female energy spent in reproduction reduced women's mental powers. The most formidable and influential late-Victorian study on sex differences was that by two illustrious biologists, Patrick Geddes and J. Arthur Thomson, *The Evolution of Sex* (1889). The authors traced sex differences to basic cell metabolism, concluding that male cells are "katabolic" (actively spend energy) whereas female cells are "anabolic" (conserve energy, maintain stability, and support new life). This fundamental dualism could spawn infinite variation in human life but undergirded conventional belief in male assertiveness, courage, rationality, and creative restlessness in contrast to female intuitiveness, responsiveness, and passivity. Schreiner, though her ideas differed markedly from Geddes and Thomson, agreed with Ellis, who in late 1889 had sent her a copy of their book, that "The sex book is good." OS to HE, December 8, 1889, SCCS *Letters*, 172–73. See also Jill Ker Conway's discussion of Geddes and Thomson in "Stereotypes of Femininity in a Theory of Sexual Evolution," in Martha Vicinus, ed., *Suffer and Be Still: Women in the Victorian Age* (Bloomington: Indiana University Press, 1972), 140–54.

63. Schreiner, *Woman and Labor,* 4, 192–94.

64. Ibid., 192. See also Schreiner, *Mary Wollstonecraft,* 6, and *African Farm,* 214.

65. Schreiner, *Woman and Labor,* 194–95.

66. Schreiner, *Mary Wollstonecraft,* 7.

67. Schreiner, *Woman and Labor,* 164.

68. Ibid., 188.

69. Ibid., 196.

70. OS to KP, February 5, 1888, May 21, 1886, Rive, *Schreiner: Letters*, 135, 80; OS to HE, May 1912, SCCS *Letters*, 307.

71. Schreiner, *Woman and Labor*, 179.

72. OS to HE, July 16, 1884, SCCS *Letters*, 31–32.

73. OS to KP, June 10, 12, 16, 1886, Rive, *Schreiner: Letters*, 81–84.

74. Schreiner, *Thoughts*, 271. Among Schreiner's contemporaries who asserted women as standard bearers of the human race were Jane Hume Clapperton, *Scientific Meliorism* (1885), J. B. Haycroft, *Darwinism and Race Progress* (1895), Eliza Burt Gamble, *The Evolution of Woman* (1894), Frances Swiney, *The Cosmic Progression* (1906), Rhoda Broughton, *A Beginner* (1894).

75. Schreiner, *Woman and Labor*, 110, 76.

76. Ibid., 86, 110, 130–32.

77. Ibid., 133–34.

78. Ibid., 219, 224.

79. Ibid., 8, 159. See also Schreiner, *Thoughts*, 209–10.

80. Schreiner, *Woman and Labor*, 250. See also Schreiner, *Thoughts*, 205.

81. Schreiner, *Thoughts*, 206–7.

82. Ibid., 209. See also, *From Man to Man*, 195.

83. Schreiner, *Mary Wollstonecraft*, 8–9.

84. Rayna Reiter, ed., *Toward an Anthropology of Women* (New York: Monthly Review, 1975); Peggy Reeves Sanday, *Female Power and Male Dominance: On the Origins of Sexual Inequality* (Cambridge: Cambridge University Press, 1981); Nancy Tanner and Adrienne Zihlman, "Women in Evolution, Part I: Innovation and Selection in Human Origins," *Signs* 1, 3 (Spring 1976): 585–608, and "Women in Evolution, Part II: Subsistence and Social Organization among Early Hominids," ibid., 4, 1 (Autumn 1978): 4–20.

85. Schreiner, *From Man to Man*, 164–65. See also Schreiner, *Woman and Labor*, 86–90. Schreiner likened the fragility and evanescence of Greek culture to "a spray of shrub, plucked and placed in a vase of water in a hot-house." Bloom profusely as it might for a few days, it could never last or propagate itself "when it was without ground and had no root."

86. Schreiner, *From Man to Man*, 164–65.

87. Schreiner, *Thoughts*, 268–69, 329–30, and *Woman and Labor*, 46–47, 150–51.

88. Schreiner, *Thoughts*, 329–30.

89. Ibid., 175–76. Consider this cumbersome but meaty explanation: "prevented by their isolated position from any companionship with those of their own age beyond the limits of their family, and shut off from those sports and amusements which in cities and even small societies . . . satisfy the needs of youth . . . and render the celibacy of early youth not only endurable, but often make those years the most joyful of life: and shut out entirely . . . from all those intellectual enjoyments which are independent of actual society . . . a delight which, until under the pressure of

overpowering personal affection renders some men and women to give up their celibate life, fearing they shall be robbed of it! Devoid of all this, the life of the African Boer, whether man or woman, who has attained puberty, becomes inexpressively empty, and probably physically and mentally unhealthy, if they remain single."

90. Ibid., 210.
91. Schreiner, *Woman and Labor*, 5–6.
92. Ibid., 141, 146.
93. Ibid., 274, 284.

Chapter 4

1. W. K. Hancock, *Smuts: The Sanguine Years, 1870–1919* (Cambridge: Cambridge University Press, 1962), 1:59–60.
2. Quoted in Albie Sachs, *Justice in South Africa* (Berkeley: University of California Press, 1973), 136.
3. H. W. Massingham, ed., *H.W.M: A Selection from the Writings of H. W. Massingham* (London: J. Cape, 1925), 181–82. See also Frederic Whyte, *The Life of W. T. Stead* (Boston: Houghton Mifflin, 1927), 2:25–27, 194–95; Alan Paton, *Towards the Mountain: An Autobiography* (New York: Scribner, 1980). Gandhi, *Satyagraha in South Africa*, 192.
4. Notable exceptions are: Mary Benson, *The African Patriots: The Story of the African National Congress of South Africa* (London: Faber and Faber, 1963). Benson, in her account of the development of the African National Congress, acclaimed Schreiner's "astonishing foresight" (21) in envisaging the consequences of a South Africa where white men had dispossessed black Africans of their land, forced them into racial compounds and slums, and denied them citizenship. Leonard Thompson, in his searching analysis of the unification movement in South Africa, praises Schreiner's political arguments for a federal and democratic constitution as "perhaps the most original and penetrating statement of the case for federalism." Thompson, *The Unification of South Africa, 1902–1910* (Oxford: Oxford University Press, 1960), 108. See also Willan, *Sol Plaatje;* Phyllis Lewsen, *J. X. Merriman: Paradoxical South African Statesman* (New Haven: Yale University Press, 1982), 183–84; Rodney Davenport, "Olive Schreiner and South African Politics," in Malvern Van Wyk Smith and Don Maclennan, eds., *Olive Schreiner and After* (Cape Town: David Philip, 1983), 93–107.
5. Typical of the utter neglect of Schreiner writing and activity are Bernard Porter, *Critics of Empire* (London: St. Martin's Press, 1968), and Richard Koebner and Helmut Dan Schmidt, *Imperialism: The Story and Significance of a Political Word, 1840–1960* (Cambridge: Cambridge University Press, 1964). The only reference to Schreiner in Stephen Koss, ed., *The Pro-Boers: The Anatomy of an Anti-war Movement* (Chicago: University of Chicago Press, 1973), is his inclusion of the

London Daily News account (September 19, 1901) of Schreiner's internment under martial law during the Anglo–Boer War. No mention of Schreiner appears in Arthur Davy, *The British Pro-Boers, 1877–1902* (Cape Town: Tafelberg, 1978). Byron Farwell cites Schreiner in passing fashion as "one of the most fervent pro-Boer writers in the Empire" in *The Great Anglo–Boer War* (New York: Harper and Row, 1976), 156. Thomas Pakenham, in his widely acclaimed *The Boer War* (New York: Random House, 1979), fails to include her at all.

6. Nadine Gordimer, "'The Prison-House of Colonialism': Review of Ruth First and Ann Scott's *Olive Schreiner,*" *Times Literary Supplement* (London), August 15, 1980, is characteristic. Recent exceptions are the discussion by Phyllis Lewsen, "Olive Schreiner's Political Theories and Pamphlets" in Clayton, *Olive Schreiner,* 212–22. So, too, First and Scott in their otherwise incisive account of Schreiner's racial politics provide an ahistorical critique of the limits to her antiracism. They simplify her views on the South African Boers and mute the sharp edges of her attack on British imperialism and white racism.

7. It is telling that the Afro-American philosopher Howard Thurman praises Schreiner for her progressive racial views. As a South African white woman, she was, he claims, unique in not trying to Christianize blacks and in not loving the African for Christ's sake. Thurman is inspired by the depth of her understanding of oppression, which he traces to her experience of marginalization as a woman and to her compassionate radicalism. Howard Thurman, *A Track to the Water's Edge: The Olive Schreiner Reader* (New York: Harper and Row, 1973), xxvi.

8. I will refer to "Africans" and "blacks" interchangeably, recognizing that "blacks" in Africa include Asians and offspring of mating between whites and blacks. Schreiner's usage was inconsistent and rooted in nineteenth-century vocabulary (see Chapter 3).

9. Edward Carpenter, quoted in Koss, ed., *The Pro-Boers,* 55–57, from Carpenter's pamphlet for the Labour Press, Manchester, January 1, 1900.

10. Schreiner, *Thoughts,* 343, 379.

11. Ibid., 355, and Schreiner, *South African Question,* 113. Schreiner may have taken this image from Darwin's *Origin of Species,* where the tree of life, not specifically named as the banyan tree, appears in an extended metaphor.

12. Schreiner, *Thoughts,* 379–83, and *South African Question,* 20, 113.

13. Schreiner, *Thoughts,* 72.

14. Schreiner, *Thoughts,* 333, and *South African Question,* 113.

15. Schreiner, *Thoughts,* 254, 372, 375, 378, 383, 324.

16. Ibid., 324, 372–73.

17. Olive Schreiner, *Closer Union* (London: Fifield, 1909), 39–40.

18. Ibid., 374.

19. Schreiner, *From Man to Man,* 402. Obviously, people have memories they cherish and pass on, whereas trees do not; overstatement of inner colonization is easy.

Nonetheless, contemporary studies of colonization lend much credence to Schreiner's analysis.

20. Schreiner, "Letter on 'The Taal' (Afrikaans) in the 'Cape Times,' 10th May 1905," in SCCS *Letters*, App. E, 388–91.

21. Schreiner, *Thoughts*, 319. For additional references to these four figures, see *Thoughts*, 225–26; "The South African Nation," included in *Thoughts*, 380–81; and *South African Question*, 24–25, 492–93.

22. Schreiner, *Thoughts*, 226–27, 230–32, 234–35, and *South African Question*, 28–29.

23. Schreiner, *South African Question*, 23, and *Thoughts*, 226.

24. Schreiner, *South African Question*, 24, and *Thoughts*, 225, 235.

25. Many Britons misguidedly assumed that the Boers were tyrannical and retrogressive in denying the vote to the Uitlanders (i.e., the newcomers from foreign countries who had settled in Transvaal during the gold rush). Though rigidly restrictive, the franchise denial was not absolute, and in 1890 the Kruger government decreased the waiting period before a new immigrant could vote from fourteen to five years after the date of arrival. For the most part, the newcomers, who by the 1890s outnumbered the indigenous Boers, were transient. Lacking any intention to settle permanently in Transvaal, they were also exporting their wealth, investing little in the future development of the country. Further, many of the Uitlanders were opposed to the independence of Transvaal and campaigned for British control of the country. Under such circumstances, if Transvaal were to yield to British pressures to accord the franchise early to all newcomers, the survival and growth of Transvaal as an independent economic and political entity would be endangered. However, because some of these newcomers intended to remain permanently, Schreiner recommended that the franchise be available to them after a reasonable period of residency. This position, concurrently advocated by the Kruger government, was unacceptable to British leaders and citizens; and this impasse was the official precipitating cause of the devastating Anglo–Boer War.

26. Richard Price, *An Imperial War and the British Working Class* (London: Routledge and Kegan Paul, 1971), 236–37.

27. J. A. Hobson, *The War in South Africa* (1900; rpt., New York: Howard Fertig, 1969), chap. 15.

28. Schreiner, *South African Question*, 71, 72–73.

29. Pakenham, *The Boer War*, xxi, xiv; Thompson, *Political Mythology of Apartheid*, 28.

30. G. H. L. Le May, *British Supremacy in South Africa, 1899–1907* (Oxford: Oxford University Press [Clarendon Press], 1965); OS to W. P. Schreiner, June 11, 1899, in R. F. M. Immelman, "Olive Schreiner and her Brother W.P.," in Friedlander, *Until the Heart Changes*, 91–115.

31. The Social Democratic Federation in England assailed the Anglo–Boer War as

capitalist aggression in the interests of international millionaires. Hobson, in *War in South Africa*, dwelt at length upon the role of international mine owners and speculators in escalating tensions.

32. Schreiner, *Thoughts*, 310–11, 310.

33. Ibid., 312. In a thoughtful letter to Carpenter, October 8, 1894, Schreiner stated that economic equality was a requisite for positive race relations, and in order to redress years of blacks' dependence on whites it would be better still if the black man had more money than the white man. Rive, *Schreiner: Letters*, 242.

34. Schreiner, *Thoughts*, 313.

35. Ibid., 381.

36. Ibid., 294, 296–97, 317–18.

37. Ibid., 361.

38. Ibid., 361, 295.

39. Ibid., 302.

40. Richard Rive, in his foreword to *Thoughts on South Africa* (Johannesburg: Africana Book Society, 1976), accurately points up a danger in Schreiner's concessions to Boer kindness: They could be used to diminish anger at Dutch racist actions. Rive legitimately questions Schreiner's claim that Boers were slower than Britons in being roused to anger (xv). Among other examples of scholarly criticism of Schreiner's presentation of the Boers, see First and Scott, *Olive Schreiner*, 241–44. Schreiner was well aware of the need to combat Boer racial prejudice. She wrote J. X. Merriman, May 25, 1896, "but on the native question we have to fight the main body of them [Boers] to the death for the next 20 years." Rive, *Schreiner: Letters*, 278.

41. Schreiner, *Peter Halket*, 65, 66.

42. Schreiner, *Thoughts*, 307, 309.

43. Ibid., 347.

44. First and Scott, *Olive Schreiner*, 240.

45. The latest publication of *Trooper Peter Halket of Mashonaland* (Johannesburg: Donker, 1974), with introduction by Marion Friedmann, includes the frontispiece—which appeared only in 1897 printings of the novella—showing the hanging of black prisoners in Mashonaland during the chartered company's occupation. This photograph, viewed as inflammatory, was deleted from subsequent editions. The edition of the novella that I am citing, (Boston: Roberts Brothers, 1897), does include it. See Friedmann's account of the story of the frontispiece.

46. The range of scholarly response to the novella includes those who regard it as an inartistic polemic, e.g., Vineta Colby, *A Singular Anomaly* (New York: New York University Press, 1970), 86 ("a shrill propagandistic short novel"); Uys Krige, "Introduction: Olive Schreiner, Poet and Prophet," in Krige, ed., *Olive Schreiner: A Selection* (Cape Town: Oxford University Press, 1965), 5–6; Nadine Gordimer, "The English Novel in South Africa," *Winter School Conference 1959–60*: 16–21, esp. 17; as well as those, particularly more recent, critics who appraise the work

more positively, e.g., Stephen Gray, "'The Trooper at the Hanging Tree,'" *English in Africa* 2, 2 (September 1975), included in Clayton, *Olive Schreiner*, 198–208; Peter Wilhelm, "*Peter Halket*, Rhodes, and Colonialism," in ibid., 208–12; Rodney Davenport, "Olive Schreiner and South African Politics," Alan Paton, "*Trooper Peter Halket of Mashonaland*," and Arthur Ravenscraft, "Literature and Politics: Two Zimbabwean Novels," in Van Wyk Smith and Maclennan, *Olive Schreiner and After*, 104–5, 30–34, 46–47.

47. Schreiner, *Peter Halket*, 13, 40, 36, 37–38.

48. One politically influential person impressed by the novella was J. X. Merriman. Already a fan of Schreiner's writing who considered *African Farm* a work of genius, he declared the novella to be brave and pertinent. He and Schreiner engaged in a sporadic yet revelatory correspondence, in which both figures expressed their political views with depth and clarity. Lewsen, *J. X. Merriman*, 183–84.

49. OS to W. P. Schreiner, December 1896, Rive, *Schreiner: Letters*, 299–300.

50. Schreiner, *South African Question*, 120–21.

51. Ibid., 38.

52. Schreiner, *Thoughts*, 382. Clearly, Schreiner's image of the South African rose seems oblivious to the need for more than a merging of Boer and Briton. We must interpret her rhetoric in terms of her projected audience.

53. Pakenham, *The Boer War*, 607–8: Among the dead, 65,693 imperial and 82,742 colonial soldiers, 20,300 Dutch soldiers. An unknown number of African black soldiers were impressed into service by both sides, unknown numbers of additional noncombatants killed. The cost in horses, mules, and donkeys exceeded 400,000, and several million cattle, horses, and sheep were slain or appropriated. Dutch farms and homes were systematically burned down; roughly thirty thousand farmsteads were destroyed and about twenty villages. See T. R. H. Davenport, *The Afrikaner Bond: The History of a South African Political Party, 1880–1911* (Cape Town: Oxford University Press, 1966), 140. Among the most appalling dimensions of the war was the locking of several hundred thousand Boer and black men, women, and children into concentration camps. Herded into cramped, unsanitary surroundings, lacking medical supervision and denied fresh meat and vegetables, the inmates fell victim to typhoid fever and other epidemics. In October 1901 alone there were "2,156 deaths among 111,619 whites; 698 deaths among 43,780 colored people." Pakenham, *The Boer War*, 548. Official estimates vary as to the number who died in the camps; the usual figure is twenty to thirty thousand, though the unofficial deaths, especially of African blacks, were undoubtedly much higher. Pakenham, *The Boer War*, 607; Davenport, *The Afrikaner Bond*, 142, 146. It is noteworthy that an Englishwoman, Emily Hobhouse, was responsible for exposing the conditions of the concentration camps. Hobhouse and Schreiner were active correspondents.

54. Schreiner, *Thoughts*, 281, 20, 201.

55. OS to Mrs. Francis Smith, October 22, 1910, SCCS *Letters*, 295–96.

56. Schreiner, *South African Question*, 111, 106–7, and *Thoughts*, 19–20, 375.
57. Olive Schreiner, "Speech (in the form of a letter) on the Boer War at the Somerset East Women's Meeting, 12th October, 1900," SCCS *Letters*, App. C, 378–85, esp. 380.
58. Schreiner, *Thoughts*, Note A, "The South African Nation," 375–76.
59. Schreiner, "Eighteen-Ninety-Nine," in *Stories, Dreams, and Allegories*, 11.
60. Ibid., 58.
61. Schreiner, "Seeds a-Growing," in *Stories, Dreams, and Allegories*, 142.
62. OS to HE, December 1909, SCCS *Letters*, 365–66; OS to W. P. Schreiner, February 12, 1909, in Immelman, "Olive Schreiner," in Friedlander, *Until the Heart Changes*, 109.
63. Schreiner, *Closer Union*, 9.
64. Schreiner, *Thoughts*, "The South African Nation," 375.
65. Schreiner, *Closer Union*, 10–13.
66. Ibid., 35, 28, 26.
67. Schreiner, *Thoughts*, 52, 59–60.
68. Ibid., 61.
69. Schreiner, *Closer Union*, 18: "I believe that any attempt to base our national life on distinctions of race and colour, as such, will, after the lapse of many years, prove fatal to us."
70. Ibid., 25; Schreiner, *Thoughts*, "The South African Nation," 379.
71. Schreiner, *Closer Union*, 43–44.
72. Ibid., 49, 50–53: "If, blinded by the gain of the moment, we see nothing in our dark man but a vast engine of labour; if to us he is not man, but only a tool; if dispossessed entirely of the land for which he now shows that large aptitude for peasant proprietorship . . . if we force him permanently in his millions into the locations and compounds and slums of our cities, obtaining his labour cheaper . . . if, uninstructed in the highest forms of labour, without the rights of citizenship, his own social organisation broken up, without our having aided him to participate in our own; . . . then I would rather draw a veil over the future of this land. . . . One dissatisfied man or woman who feel themselves [*sic*] wronged is a point of weakness in a community; but when this condition animates the vast majority of the inhabitants of a State, there is a crack down the entire height of the social structure. . . . It is ordained by the laws of human life that a Nemesis should follow the subjection and use, purely for purposes of their own, of any race by another. . . . In the end the subjected people write their features on the face of the conquerors."
73. Ibid., 54.
74. Davenport, *The Afrikaner Bond*, 83: Until the Registration Act of 1887 and the Franchise and Ballot Act of 1887, African blacks numbered almost a quarter of the Cape electorate. The passage of these two acts substantially raised the property qualification for voting and diminished the rate of increase in black voting. In the

1890s roughly half the adult black male population of the Cape could vote, constituting about 15 percent of the total electorate.

75. OS to W. P. Schreiner, February 12, 1909, in Immelman, "Olive Schreiner," in Friedlander, *Until the Heart Changes,* 109.

76. Schreiner, *Closer Union,* 15.

77. Ibid., 21, 22, 24.

78. Ibid., 23, 24.

79. Ibid., 57–58, 59. Evidently unwilling to introduce into her remarks ideas that might thoroughly alienate possible converts to her constitutional proposals, Schreiner did not call for female leadership of the federal government.

80. Ibid., 61.

81. OS to W. P. Schreiner, November 1907, in Immelman, "Olive Schreiner," in Friedlander, *Until the Heart Changes,* 103.

82. OS to W. P. Schreiner, July 16, 1909, ibid., 112. A person with political instincts, Schreiner explained, grasped the ulterior motives behind a handshake or a promise of a vote, sensed the way masses of people were moving and would move, and charted a course of political action accordingly. She herself was capable of assessing the political subtexts of politicians' behaviors: for example, she doubted the sincerity of Jan Hofmeyr's apparent support of a federal system. Though he wrote her praising *Closer Union,* she asked her brother, "Do you think he means what he says? I have always looked at his professing to favour Federation as a *blind,* to make the English think the Boers were not united in wanting unification. Isn't it strange that the English cant [*sic*] see that." OS to W. P. Schreiner, December 28, 1908, ibid., 108.

83. OS to W. P. Schreiner, November 1907, ibid., 103–4.

84. The Constitution of 1910 united South Africa under a single government, sovereign in domestic affairs but tied to England in external matters linked to questions of war and peace. South Africa did not become a fully independent nation until 1961, when the Union of South Africa became the Republic of South Africa.

85. OS to W. P. Schreiner, December 28, 1908, in Immelman, "Olive Schreiner," in Friedlander, *Until the Heart Changes,* 108.

86. Clause 9 of Article 8. This clause not only foreshadowed the loss of the no-color-bar precedent in the Cape Colony but enabled leaders of Transvaal and the Orange River Colony (Orange Free State) to design their constitutions in 1906 and 1907 without provision for a black franchise. As Schreiner observed of the Boers, their postwar behavior reflected the common tendency of the underdog, especially once it gains power, to oppress others. OS to Carpenter, April 29, 1913, SCCS *Letters,* 324–25.

87. OS to SCCS, May 9, 1906, ibid., 253–54; February 1905, ibid., 251–52; December 18, 1906, ibid., 259–62.

88. OS to Carpenter, October 26, 1905, n.d. 1906, February 1909, CC; OS to Mrs. Rhys Davids, April 12, 1910, SCCS *Letters*, 292.

89. OS to Carpenter, April 25, 1911, CC.

90. OS to W. P. Schreiner, January 23, 1913, in Richard Rive, "In Search of Olive Schreiner, Part III," *Week-End Argus* (Cape Town), June 16, 1973. See also OS to W. P. Schreiner, May 25, 1911, ibid.: "I am so distressed about the black peril. Black peril!—It's a white peril that hangs over every black man."

91. OS to W. P. Schreiner, May 7, 1909, in Immelman, "Olive Schreiner," in Friedlander, *Until the Heart Changes*, 111.

92. OS to W. P. Schreiner, June 24, 1905, ibid., 102.

93. OS to W. P. Schreiner, August 30, 1909, ibid., 114.

94. Schreiner, *From Man to Man*, 419.

95. OS to Carpenter, February, 1909, CC. In the 1880s and 1890s South African black political leaders urged their people to seek education rather than political power. The extent of their political activism was reflected in the work of Tengo Jabavu, a good friend of Schreiner's, who launched the Native Electoral Association and in 1884 a newspaper, *Imvo Zabantsundu*. In 1908 Jabavu founded the Cape Native Convention. The rival organization, under the leadership of Pixley ka I. Seme, was the South African Native Congress, established in 1902, which planned the Native Congress of 1909 and the South African Native National Congress of 1912. Neither political association was in touch with other black movements, which ranged from the Zulu Rebellion of 1906 to Ethiopianism, a black autonomous religious movement, which also protested the racist policies of the postwar years.

Chapter 5

1. Constance G. Lytton, *Prisons and Prisoners: Experience of a Suffragette* (1914; rpt., West Yorkshire: E. P. Publishing, 1976), 157. See, too, among many testimonies, those by Vera Brittain, C. P. Gilman, Carrie Chapman Catt, Aletta Jacobs, and Abigail Duniway. Alice Clark's groundbreaking work in women's history, *The Working Life of Women in the Seventeenth Century*, first appearing in 1919, owed its origins to *Woman and Labour*. In her preface to the London, 1968, edition of her book, Clark testified that Schreiner was the first to draw the attention of feminists "to the difference between reality and the commonly received generalizations as to women's productive capacity."

2. Only in her correspondence did Schreiner comment upon personal reproductive experience and the physiology of her own erotic experience, e.g., OS to KP, June 10, 12, 1886, Rive, *Schreiner: Letters*, 81, 82; OS to HE, July 16, 1884, SCCS *Letters*, 31–32.

3. Schreiner, *Woman and Labor*, 13.

4. Ibid., 14–20.

5. The term *feminism* does not appear in the OED prior to its Supplement in 1933,

and then only as a rare equivalent to "womanism" (362–63). According to Jane Rendall, in *The Origins of Modern Feminism: Women in Britain, France, and the United States, 1780–1860* (New York: Schocken Books, 1984), the first recorded use of the term in English, derived from the French, occurred in 1894 and did not carry its modern meaning. Unfortunately, we have for England and South Africa no comparable study to Nancy F. Cott's account of the evolution of the term in America. See Cott, *The Grounding of Modern Feminism* (New Haven: Yale University Press, 1987).

6. Susan Kingsley Kent, in her recent study of turn-of-the-century feminist discourse, *Sex and Suffrage in Britain, 1860–1914* (Princeton, NJ: Princeton University Press, 1987), 3, 5, 7, 13, has significantly altered scholarly conclusions about the moderate feminism of British suffragists. Her study, limited to intellectual spokeswomen for the suffrage movement, highlights the zeal even of moderates to transform gender spheres, roles, and relationships.

7. Ibid., 85, 97, 105–7, 144, 161.

8. We first learn of Schreiner's reverence for Wollstonecraft when she writes to Karl Pearson about her undertaking an introduction to a projected new edition of *A Vindication of the Rights of Women*. Evidently she had glanced at the work before but never read it until requested to prepare that introduction. See OS to KP, October 26, 1886, Rive, *Schreiner: Letters*, 111. Her most emphatic statement of respect for Mary Wollstonecraft appears in a letter to Pearson, in which she calls Wollstonecraft "the greatest of English women because she saw a hundred years ago with regard to sex and sex relationships what a few see today, and what the world will see in three hundred years' time." OS to KP, May 12, 1886, ibid., 78. For a cogent discussion of Schreiner's relation to Wollstonecraft and Mill, see Cherry Clayton, "Olive Schreiner and Feminism," in Gardner, *Publisher/Writer/Reader*.

9. Schreiner, *African Farm*, 182.

10. Ibid., 178.

11. Schreiner, *Undine*, 137–38.

12. Ibid., 142. Not surprisingly, Schreiner responded with enthusiasm when, years after writing *Undine*, she read Ibsen's *Doll's House*.

13. Schreiner, *Woman and Labor*, 189.

14. Edward Carpenter, *Love's Coming of Age* (Manchester: Labour Press, 1896), 64–65; note that these were positive traits for Carpenter. For Ellis, see Havelock Ellis, *Man and Woman: A Study of Human Secondary Sexual Characteristics* (London: Walter Scott, 1894), *Studies in the Psychology of Sex*, vol. 1 (1899; rpt., Philadelphia: F. A. Davis, 1900), pt. 2, 24, 69, and *Essays in Wartime* (London: Constable, 1916), 103. See also Rowbotham and Weeks, *Socialism and the New Life*, 112, 169.

15. Schreiner, *African Farm*, 183.

16. Ibid., 188.

17. Ibid., 186.

18. Schreiner, *Undine*, 151, 155, 157–58.
19. OS to Alys Pearsall Smith, July 2, 1888, quoted in Hobman, *Olive Schreiner*, 43–44. I am indebted to my graduate student Karen Smith for a copy of this and other Schreiner letters to Alys Pearsall Smith held at the Fawcett Library, City of London Polytechnic, London.
20. Schreiner, *African Farm*, 306; Schreiner, *Thoughts*, 193.
21. Schreiner, *Woman and Labor*, 293.
22. Schreiner, *From Man to Man*, 275, 250.
23. Ibid., 269. Although Schreiner alleged that male aggression is not innate and that many women lack nurturant impulses, until the outbreak of World War I she attributed a greater propensity to life preserving to women as a result of both biology and cultural experience. See related discussion in Chapters 3 and 7.
24. Ibid., 270, 273–74.
25. Schreiner, *African Farm*, 232.
26. Schreiner, *From Man to Man*, 62. Simply substitute masculine names and, through the resulting social oddity, the gender-distinct character of the physical and emotional intimacy between the two women is all the more marked.
27. Schreiner had considered two alternate endings. According to Cronwright, she planned to have Drummond find Bertie in a brothel dying of venereal disease. Rebekah would take Bertie home and lavish her with love and the finest medical attention to no avail. Meanwhile, Rebekah and Drummond's love would deepen, but, perhaps because both were married and Rebekah the woman she is, a more intimate relationship would be impossible. They would part, and Rebekah, continuing her separation from her husband, would live alone with her sons and Sartje at her Matjesfontein cottage. Never a social activist, Rebekah's nobility would emerge at the end as stoic and brave individualism. SCCS *Life*, 462–64. Schreiner confided to Karl Pearson a very different ending, however. An English traveler, presumably Drummond, would leave Rebekah for refusing to divorce Frank. It would be Rebekah who then finds Bertie dying from venereal disease. When Frank chides Rebekah for openly burying Bertie, a prostitute, Rebekah would declare that for the past fourteen years she too has been a prostitute. Interspersed among these developments would be Rebekah's reflections on a future time of sexually expressive and reciprocal love. OS to KP, July 19, 1886, Rive, *Schreiner: Letters*, 91–95.
28. Schreiner, *African Farm*, 290. Transvestism was a common device in late-Victorian fiction. See, e.g., discussion of the appearance of Rochester in a gypsy costume in Charlotte Brontë's *Jane Eyre*, discussed in Sandra M. Gilbert and Susan Gubar, *The Madwoman in the Attic: The Woman Writer and the Nineteenth-Century Literary Imagination* (New Haven: Yale University Press, 1979), 353–55; John R. Reed, *Victorian Conventions* (Athens: Ohio University Press, 1975), chap. 13, "Disguise."
29. Schreiner, *Woman and Labor*, 57–59, 64–65. Margaret Sanger, *An Autobiography* (New York: Dover, 1971), 140. Many leading British feminists opposed birth

control, e.g., Millicent Fawcett and Elizabeth Blackwell. They represented the prevalent view that contraceptives would accord men greater sexual license. See Kent, *Sex and Suffrage*, 105.

30. Schreiner, *Woman and Labor*, 62, 90–91.

31. Ibid., 81. This view received its first forceful articulation in William Thompson, *Appeal of One Half of the Human Race*, London, 1825. For late nineteenth century expressions of this argument, see Kent, *Sex and Suffrage*, 69, 91.

32. Schreiner, *Woman and Labor*, 252, 251.

33. Ibid., 116, 45.

34. Ibid., 98.

35. Ibid., 16–17, 208.

36. OS to HE, October 24, 1884, HRC; also see OS to KP, July 19, 1885, Rive, *Schreiner: Letters*, 65–66. OS to HE, October 29, 1884, HRC.

37. Schreiner, *Woman and Labor*, 255.

38. Ibid., 114–15, 119–20, 169, 184, 201–2.

39. Linda Dowling, "The Decadent and the New Woman in the 1890s," *Nineteenth Century Fiction* 33 (March 1979): 434–53, 438–49.

40. A. R. Cunningham, "The 'New Woman Fiction' of the 1890s," *Victorian Studies* 17 (1973): 177–86.

41. Schreiner, *Woman and Labor*, 19.

42. Ibid., 22, 271.

43. OS to HE, March 1886, HRC.

44. Schreiner, *Woman and Labor*, 265, 91–92, 147–49.

45. Schreiner, *Thoughts*, 200–1.

46. Schreiner, *Woman and Labor*, 244.

47. Ibid., 267, 17.

48. Schreiner, *From Man to Man*, 455, 444.

49. Ibid., 460, 459, 439.

50. Schreiner, *African Farm*, 176.

51. Ibid., 69.

52. Ibid., 211, 12–13, 289.

53. Ibid., 191.

54. Ibid., 289, 214.

55. Schreiner, *From Man to Man*, 217, 277, 201.

56. Ibid., 220.

57. Ibid., 419.

58. Ibid., 18, 22–26.

59. Ibid., 396, e.g., the daughter of a robber baron who, in Rebekah's gender reversal of the more usual fairy tale rescue pattern, steals her father's keys so as to free prisoners from a dungeon where they are being starved to death. She leads them through a secret gate in the castle walls to the path through the woods by which they might escape.

60. Ibid., 420.

61. Ibid., 263.

62. Schreiner, "Three Dreams in a Desert," in *Dreams*, 66; Schreiner, *From Man to Man*, 202–3.

63. Kathleen Blake, in *Love and the Woman Question in Victorian Literature: The Art of Self-postponement* (Sussex: Harvester Press, 1983), faults Schreiner for her readiness to diminish and objectify women through her use of words such as *little* to describe women's anatomical features. I think Blake overly conflates Schreiner's views with those of her leading female characters, but, more crucially, *little* is not a pejorative word for Schreiner. She relished the seeming irony that though she, like many women, was little, she possessed a large mind and heart. Not surprisingly, she took pleasure in presenting that juxtaposition in her fiction.

64. Schreiner, *Woman and Labor*, 289.

65. Ibid., 258, 272.

66. Ibid., 294.

67. Ibid., 20, 21. Kent, in *Sex and Suffrage*, 218, properly situates Olive Schreiner in "the Centre" of the early-twentieth-century debate over female eroticism. Along with Billington-Grieg, Maude Royden, and Wolstenholme-Elmy, Schreiner applauded female sexual desire and pleasure but demanded its integration with spiritual and emotional fulfillment and its foundation in economic, political, and social equality and independence.

68. OS to W. T. Stead, ca. July 1890, ca. April 1896, SCCS *Letters*, 220–21, 193.

69. A notable example is her discussion with Pearson of the impact of pregnancy on erotic passion. She cites a "large mass of evidence" she collected from married women and medical men to verify women's continued erotic desire during pregnancy. She added that her brother Fred and his wife's erotic passions did not ebb because of pregnancy, and "they gratified it." OS to KP, June 10, 1886, June 12, 1886, Rive, *Schreiner: Letters*, 81, 82.

70. OS to KP, July 2, 6, 1886, ibid., 85–87, 87–90.

71. Schreiner, *Woman and Labor*, 242, 242–43, 238–39, 242–45, 258. See also Schreiner, *African Farm*, 189–90.

72. OS to HE, July 7, 1885, SCCS *Letters*, 75–76. See also OS to Carpenter, October 8, 1894, CC. For her contrasting position, see her letter to KP, October 11, 1885, Rive, *Schreiner: Letters*, 67–68.

73. OS to KP, January 25, 1887, Rive, *Schreiner: Letters*, 119.

74. Schreiner, *Woman and Labor*, 84; OS to Mrs. Francis Smith, May 14, 1904, SCCS *Letters*, 245–47.

75. Weeks, *Sex, Politics, and Society*, chap. 6, "The Construction of Homosexuality." Together with Carpenter and Ellis, who did exceed Schreiner in their positive defense of homosexuality, Schreiner and all others in the Victorian and Edwardian vanguard stopped far from gay advocates little more than half a century later, who

would consider homosexuals as another group of social outcasts for whose interests political action was imperative.

76. Schreiner, *Woman and Labor,* 19.

77. Ibid., 271; OS to W. T. Stead, January 10, 1895, and ca. 1896, SCCS *Letters,* 217, 220; OS to HE, August 19, 1885, ibid., 79.

78. OS to KP, August 10, 1885, Pearson Collection; OS to HE, August 2, 1884, Rive, *Schreiner: Letters,* 49–50; OS to KP, October 4, 1885, July 13, 1886, ibid., 55–58, 95–96. Also see Grosskurth, *Havelock Ellis,* 90.

79. Havelock Ellis, *Studies in the Psychology of Sex, Vol. 1* II (1899) Appendix B "The Development of the Sexual Instinct," Case History IX (Philadelphia: F. A. Davis, 1928), Meintjes, *Olive Schreiner,* 73; Grosskurth, *Havelock Ellis,* 94.

80. Schreiner, *Woman and Labor,* 20. See also Carpenter, *Love's Coming of Age,* 179–81.

81. Schreiner, *From Man to Man,* 221.

82. Feminist writers a generation younger than Schreiner treated topics such as menstruation in such early-twentieth-century periodicals as *The Freewoman* and *The New Freewoman.* These writers, however, were not representative of most feminist authors. Kent, *Sex and Suffrage,* 216–17.

83. Carroll Smith Rosenberg, "The New Woman as Androgyne: Social Disorder and Gender Crisis, 1870–1936," in her *Disorderly Conduct: Visions of Gender in Victorian America* (Oxford: Oxford University Press, 1985), 245–96.

84. Barbara Taylor, *Eve and the New Jerusalem* (New York: Pantheon Books, 1983); Dolores Hayden, *The Grand Domestic Revolution* (Cambridge, MA: MIT Press, 1981); Dora Marsden, editor of *The Freewoman,* a weekly feminist review (November 1911–May 1912), claimed that Schreiner thought housewives who stayed at home should receive an equal share of the wages of their husbands. *The Freewoman,* February 8, 1912. I can find no supporting evidence for Marsden's assertion.

85. OS to Betty Molteno, October 11, 1896, Rive, *Schreiner: Letters,* 291.

86. Olive Schreiner, "Letter to a Women's Meeting, held in London in July 1918, in Commemoration of John Stuart Mill; sent to Miss Emily Hobhouse for the Purpose and read by her at the Meeting," SCCS *Letters,* App. J, 402; and OS to Carpenter, January 16, 1914, CC.

87. In fact, Schreiner and Fred Bramley were the only eminent people who supported Sylvia Pankhurst's East London Federation in its protest of the age provision and continued to campaign for full adult suffrage. See E. Sylvia Pankhurst, *The Suffragette Movement* (London: Virago, 1984), 389, 604.

88. Kent, *Sex and Suffrage,* 11–14; OS to Mrs. Francis Smith, June 27, 1908, SCCS *Letters,* 280–81.

89. OS to Mrs. Francis Smith, July 1912, SCCS Letters, 309–10. Curiously, Schreiner's interest in dress reform is rarely expressed in her extant public writing. Like her character Rebekah, Schreiner refused to wear corsets. She also adopted sim-

ple, loose-fitting clothes for mountain climbing, horseback riding, and daily life in general. Treasuring a pair of sandals Edward Carpenter made for her, she told him that she would happily assist any movement for simple and light dress. (On occasion and in private, she indulged in nudity.) OS to Carpenter, May 17, 1894, CC.

90. OS to SCCS, February 18, 1912, SCCS *Letters*, 304.

91. Schreiner rarely discussed rape, wife beating, and other forms of physical abuse, which absorbed the attention of many of her feminist peers in England. Kent, *Sex and Suffrage*, chaps. 3 and 4.

92. OS to Mrs. Francis Smith, November 5, 1910, SCCS *Letters*, 291.

93. Ibid., and to Mrs. Francis Smith, August 12, 1912, ibid., 313–14; to Mrs. Francis Smith, August 27, 1912, and to Emily Hobhouse, June 4, 1913, ibid., 315–18, 327. When Mrs. Griffiths, one of the South African members of the Women's Enfranchisement League, was imprisoned for militant activity, Schreiner took pride in her courage. Schreiner particularly admired the resolute militance of Constance Lytton. Sentenced to her fourth imprisonment after breaking windows with hammers and stones, Lytton expressed gratitude for the comfort and support that Schreiner, Adela Smith, and two other friends offered her. First and Scott, *Olive Schreiner*, 261; Lytton, *Prisons and Prisoners*, 328.

94. Schreiner, "Three Dreams in a Desert," in *Dreams*, 59.

95. OS to Mrs. J. H. Philpot, March 17, 1889, SCCS *Letters*, 157.

96. Schreiner, *Woman and Labor*, 138–42, 136–37, 130.

97. Schreiner, "Three Dreams in a Desert," in *Dreams*, 66–68.

98. Schreiner, "Life's Gifts," in *Dreams*, 97.

99. Schreiner, *Woman and Labor*, 297–98.

Chapter 6

1. Leonard Woolf, *Beginning Again: An Autobiography of the Years 1911 to 1918* (New York: Harcourt, Brace and World, 1964), 57.

2. Schreiner Journal, June 29, 1888, SCCS *Life*, 180.

3. OS to HE, April 8, 1884, SCCS *Letters*, 14–15.

4. OS to HE, November 2, 1887, ibid., 122.

5. Olive Schreiner, "Letter read at a Johannesburg Shop Assistants' demonstration, probably early in 1905," ibid., App. D, 386–87.

6. OS to Carpenter, 1887, CC.

7. Schreiner, *Woman and Labor*, 120.

8. Schreiner, *Thoughts*, 273, 262, 353.

9. Schreiner, *Woman and Labor*, 100.

10. Schreiner, *Thoughts*, 267.

11. Ibid., 359.

12. Ibid., 275. See discussion of Schreiner's attitude toward Jews in Chapters 2 and 3.

13. Schreiner, *Undine*, 102, 104, 313.

14. Schreiner, *African Farm*, 266, 255–56.
15. Schreiner, *From Man to Man*, 310–11.
16. Ibid., 334–45.
17. Ibid., 173.
18. Ibid., 280, 47.
19. Schreiner, "The Sunlight Lay across My Bed," in *Dreams*, 121.
20. OS to Mrs. Cawood, October 3, 1883, SCCS *Letters*, 10.
21. OS to W. P. Schreiner, May 12, 1912, Clayton, *Olive Schreiner*, 128.
22. OS to KP, November 6, 1885, 147, Pearson Collection.
23. OS to SCCS, March 25, 1908, SCCS *Letters*, 296.
24. Schreiner, *From Man to Man*, 167–70.
25. Schreiner, *Thoughts*, 113.
26. Schreiner somewhat recognized her shortcoming and wrote of the need for a scientific socialism. OS to Carpenter, 1887, CC.
27. Stephen Yeo, "A New Life: The Religion of Socialism in Britain, 1883–1896," *History Workshop* 4 (Autumn 1977): 5–56, esp. 31. The promise and plasticity of 1880s socialism derives, according to Yeo, from its independence of particular party machinery, from electioneering and money raising. It had not yet become the ideology of social engineers and experts, for liberals and conservatives had not yet incorporated welfare legislation into their platforms. Stanley Pierson, in *Marxism and the Origins of British Socialism: The Struggle for a New Consciousness* (Ithaca, NY: Cornell University Press, 1973), 250–51, points out how the Conservative triumph in the election of 1895, coupled with the death of a number of key socialist pioneers, thwarted socialist growth and evoked disillusionment. A disillusioned Schreiner would reflect upon the decade of the 1880s, "no one who did not *live* through it can ever know the joy, and hope, and passion of enthusiasm with which we worked. . . . It was a brilliant sunrise, without which there could not have been any day." OS to SCCS, May 8, 1908, SCCS *Letters*, 278–79.
28. Yeo, "A New Life," 6–7, 12; Pierson, *Marxism*, 72, 140, 214; Willard Wolfe, *From Radicalism to Socialism: Men and Ideas in the Formation of Fabian Socialist Doctrines, 1881–1889* (New Haven: Yale University Press, 1975), 2–13, 157.
29. Pierson, *Marxism*, 104.
30. OS to HE, May 2, 1884, SCCS *Letters*, 171. Schreiner's impact on Carpenter's socialist friends was considerable. See Katherine Conway Glasier to D. L. Hobman, quoted in Hobman, *Olive Schreiner*, 91; Stephen Winsten, *Salt and His Circle* (London: Hutchinson, 1951). Schreiner's socialist education benefited from visits to John and Mary Brown. In her biography of the remarkable working-class socialist Selina Cooper, Jill Liddington, in *The Life and Times of a Respectable Rebel: Selina Cooper, 1864–1946* (London: Virago, 1984), 56–58, discusses the circle of working-class men and women who met at the Browns' home and conversed with Schreiner.
31. Sheila Rowbotham, "In Search of Carpenter," *History Workshop* 3 (Spring 1977):

122–24; Emile Delavenay, *D. H. Lawrence and Edward Carpenter: A Study in Edwardian Transition* (New York: Taplinger, 1971), 11, 19; Pierson, *Marxism*, 72, 89; Hobman, *Olive Schreiner*, 95; Lawrence Thompson, *The Enthusiasts* (London: Victor Gollancz, 1971), 66, 69; First and Scott, *Olive Schreiner*, 180; Jill Liddington and Jill Norris, *One Hand Tied behind Us: The Rise of the Woman's Suffrage Movement* (London: Virago, 1978), 118, 130, 133.

32. Edward Carpenter, *Toward Democracy* (1883; rpt., New York: Mitchell Kennerley, 1922), 372, 25; see also 6, 11, 27, 374.

33. Since William Morris was a leading exponent of the importance of integrating manual and mental labor, it is curious that Schreiner never mentions Morris in her writing. On the other hand, she was familiar with Ruskin's writing. Though she did not specify what of Ruskin she read, she referred to his social and artistic ideas in various of her letters, e.g., OS to SCCS, March 25, 1908, and OS to HE, June 12, 1890, SCCS *Letters*, 276, 188–90. It should be added that another who sought to discover ways of life that combined manual and intellectual work was Havelock Ellis. One of the primary appeals of the Fellowship of the New Life, which spawned diverse socialist groups in the mideighties, was its plan for a commune where such a combination would be essential. OS to HE, May 2, 1884, ibid., 17–18; OS to HE, October 17, 1884, HRC.

34. Schreiner, *Thoughts*, 273.

35. Yeo, "A New Life," 13.

36. John Stuart Mill, *Utilitarianism* (London: Everyman, 1910), 15, 30, 48.

37. Yeo, "A New Life," 14–16; Pierson, *Marxism*, 144.

38. Wolfe, *Radicalism to Socialism*, 33–34.

39. Kapp, *Eleanor Marx*, 2:413.

40. Wolfe, *Radicalism to Socialism*, 20, 24–30, 33–34.

41. Karl Pearson, "Socialism: In Theory and Practise," in Pearson, *Ethic of Freethought*, 330–54.

42. Ibid. See also Karl Pearson, *The Chances of Death and Other Studies in Evolution* (London: Edward Arnold, 1897), chap. 7, "Woman and Labour."

43. Minute Book, Men and Women's Club, December 14, 1885, 163–64, Pearson Collection. Schreiner was otherwise approving of Bebel's *Women and Socialism* (English trans., 1885), happily loaning her copy to friends. OS to HE, August 25, 1885, SCCS *Letters*, 80.

44. " 'Sex and Socialism' . . . expresses most *exactly* my views on the subject, except with regard to the state supporting the childbearing woman etc." OS to Carpenter, April 11, 1887, CC. See Pearson, "Socialism: In Theory and Practise" and "Woman and Socialism," in *Ethic of Freethought*.

45. OS to HE, late 1919, SCCS *Letters*, 363.

46. Yeo, "A New Life," 16, 27.

47. Schreiner, *From Man to Man*, 166, 170.

48. OS to SCCS, May 8, 1908, SCCS *Letters*, 278.

49. Schreiner, *From Man to Man*, 170.
50. Ibid., 163; Schreiner, *Thoughts*, 323–34.
51. Schreiner, *Thoughts*, 359.
52. H. J. Simons and R. E. Simons, *Class and Colour in South Africa: 1850–1950* (London: International Defense and Aid Fund for South Africa, 1983), 79.
53. Schreiner, *Thoughts*, 310–15; Schreiner, "Letter read at Johannesburg Shop Assistants' demonstration, 1905"; Schreiner, *Closer Union*, 45, 50–55; OS to W. P. Schreiner, April 24, 1909, in Immelman, "Olive Schreiner," in Friedlander, *Until the Heart Changes*, 110.
54. Schreiner, "Letter read at Johannesburg Shop Assistants' demonstration, 1905." For a fictional version of the same advice, see Schreiner, *Peter Halket*, 79. See, too, her letter to Betty Molteno, March 1898, in which she calls upon Boers, Britons, and Africans to combine against capitalism, "the common enemy." Rive, *Schreiner: Letters*, 326.
55. Schreiner, *Peter Halket*, 40.
56. OS to HE, May 2, 1884, SCCS *Letters*, 17–19.
57. Schreiner, "Letter read at Johannesburg Shop Assistants' demonstration, 1905."
58. Schreiner, "The Sunlight Lay across My Bed," in *Dreams*, 150.
59. Schreiner, *Woman and Labor*, 121.
60. Schreiner, *Thoughts*, 215.
61. Schreiner, *Woman and Labor*, 122–25.
62. Ibid., 125.
63. Ibid., 114–20, 123.
64. Mari Jo Buhle, *Women and American Socialism, 1870–1929* (Urbana: University of Illinois Press, 1981), 147–53, 305–13; Charles Sowerwine, "The Socialist Women's Movement from 1850 to 1940," in Renate Bridenthal, Claudia Koonz, and Susan Stuard, eds., *Becoming Visible: Women in European History* (Boston: Houghton Mifflin, 1987), 399–426.
65. Liddington and Norris, *One Hand Tied behind Us*, chaps. 7 and 8; and 148–51, 216–17, 232.
66. Ibid., 44, 185. See also Rowbotham, *Hidden from History* (New York: Random House, 1974), 92, 95.
67. Liddington and Norris, *One Hand*, 181.
68. Schreiner, "Letter read at Johannesburg Shop Assistants' demonstration, 1905."
69. Ibid.; and Schreiner, *Woman and Labor*, 123.
70. OS to W. P. Schreiner, May 8, 1908, in Immelman, "Olive Schreiner," in Friedlander, *Until the Heart Changes*, 106.

Chapter 7

1. OS to Carpenter, October 1914, SCCS *Letters*, 340–41.
2. Midge Mackenzie, *Shoulder to Shoulder* (New York: Knopf, 1975), 290.

3. os to Mrs. Francis Smith, August 27, 1913, sccs *Letters*, 316; Olive Schreiner, "On 'Conscientious Objectors' contributed to the *Labour Leader*, London, 16th March 1916," ibid., App. H, 398–99. See, too, Schreiner's notes to Resolutions of the Hampstead Pacifist Society, England, in Hobman, *Olive Schreiner*, 163.

4. Schreiner did exert a formative impact on Vera Brittain, one of England's leading antiwar writers and speakers between the two world wars. Alan Bishop, " 'With suffering and through time': Olive Schreiner, Vera Brittain, and the Great War," in Smith and Maclennan, *Olive Schreiner And After*, 80–92. An equally prominent World War I pacifist and feminist, Maude Royden, considered Schreiner's antiwar writing as offering a compelling approach for women and warfare. A. Maude Royden, "War and the Women's Movement," in Charles Buxton, ed., *Toward a Lasting Settlement* (New York: Macmillan, 1916), 134.

5. Joyce Avrech Berkman, "Feminism, War, and Peace Politics: The Case of World War One," in Jean Bethke Elshtain and Sheila Tobias, eds., *Women, Militarism, and War* (New York: Rowan and Littlefield, forthcoming).

6. A growing body of scholarship underscores feminist issues and World War I. Among the more thought-provoking studies are: Margaret Randolph Higonnet et al., eds., *Behind the Lines: Gender and the Two World Wars* (New Haven: Yale University Press, 1987); Elshtain and Tobias, *Women, Militarism, and War;* Jo Vellacott, "Anti-war Suffragists," *History* 62 (October 1977): 411–25; Sandra Stanley Holton, *Feminism and Democracy: Women's Suffrage and Reform Politics in Britain, 1900–1918* (Cambridge: Cambridge University Press, 1986); Ruth Roach Pearson and Somer Brodribb, eds., *Women and Peace: Theoretical, Historical, and Practical Perspectives* (London: Croom Helm, forthcoming); Anne Wiltsher, *Most Dangerous Women: Feminist Peace Campaigners of the Great War* (London: Pandora Press, 1985); Jean Bethke Elshtain, *Women and War* (New York: Basic Books, 1987).

7. These published versions omit the lengthy analysis of the causes of war in the original, unrevised manuscript of *The Dawn of Civilization*. To date, no scholar has utilized her original manuscript in a published account of Schreiner's ideas on peace and war.

8. Schreiner, *Woman and Labor*, 179.

9. Ibid., 175–76.

10. Ibid., 183, 176.

11. Schreiner, *Dawn*, 1.

12. Ibid.

13. Ibid., 3, 4.

14. Ibid., 8–10.

15. Ibid., 11.

16. Ibid.

17. Ibid., 7, 8, 10.

18. Ibid.

19. Ibid., 14.
20. Ibid., 15.
21. Ibid., 15–16.
22. Ibid., 26–27.
23. Ibid., 38, 39.
24. Ibid., 47, 41, 43–44, 49.
25. Schreiner, *Woman and Labor,* 173, 159, and *Dawn,* 30–35.
26. Sandra Gilbert, "Soldier's Heart: Literary Men, Literary Women, and the Great War," *Signs* 8, 3 (1983): 422–50.
27. Olive Schreiner, "Who Knocks at the Door?" in *Stories, Dreams and Allegories,* 147–54, esp. 151.
28. Schreiner, *Dawn,* 34.
29. Ibid., 31–32, 33.
30. Ibid.
31. Ibid., 35.
32. Jane Lewis, "Beyond Suffrage, English Feminism during the 1920s," *The Maryland Historian* 4 (Spring 1975), passim.
33. Erik H. Erikson, "Inner and Outer Space: Reflections on Womanhood," in Robert Jay Lifton, ed., *The Woman in America* (Boston: Beacon Press, 1964), 1–26.
34. Among current leading proponents of this maternalist optimism, Sara Ruddick, whose ideas reveal the impact of contemporary feminist psychology, especially the writing of Nancy Chodorow, Jean Baker Miller, Dorothy Dinnerstein, and Carol Gilligan, offers the clearest articulation: Sara Ruddick, "Maternal Thinking," *Feminist Studies* 6, 2 (Summer 1980), and "Preservative Love and Military Destruction: Some Reflections on Mothering and Peace," in Joyce Trebilcot, ed., *Mothering: Essays in Feminist Theory* (Totowa, NJ: Rowan and Allanheld, 1984). In the same vein, two prominent anthropologists, Michelle Zimbalist Rosaldo and Jane Honnig Atkinson, stress male conditioning through the hunt and warfare to take lives, whereas women, as a result of child-nurturing responsibilities, are life givers. Rosaldo and Atkinson find men and women develop widely divergent symbolic concepts of their gender roles. Michelle Zimbalist Rosaldo and Jane Honnig Atkinson, "Man the Hunter and Woman," in Roy Willis, ed., *The Interpretation of Symbolism* (London: A.S.A. Studies, 1975). Though not all anthropologists concur, with the present decade yielding various studies of women as warriors as well as studies of folklore traditions and legends of antiquity that present women as life takers as well as life givers, the dominant premise is that women are peacemakers.
35. Despite the prevalent assumption today that women are peacefully inclined, historian Natalie Zemon Davis has elucidated how theories of female aversion to violence crumble under close historical scrutiny. In premodern Europe, Davis points out, multiple ideals of gender roles prevailed with regard to fighting. Just as numbers of men were disinclined to combat, so too numbers of women engaged

routinely in hunting and fighting and violent uprisings. Davis does acknowledge that fighting appeared as a masculine identity characteristic, whereas such was not the case for women. Nonetheless, for Davis, social arrangements, not gender, were the primary determinant of who could fight and in what ways. Davis, "Men, Women, and Violence: Some Reflections on Equality," *Smith College Alumnae Quarterly*, 68, 3 (April 1977): 12–15.

36. Lionel Tiger, *Men in Groups* (New York: Random House, 1969), 218, 224–26, 233.

37. Schreiner, *Dawn*, 17.

38. Interestingly, it was another woman, Caroline Playne, who popularized the psychological analysis of war in the 1920s and 1930s. Caroline Playne offered theories on collective violence in several of her pioneering studies of World War I: *The Prewar Mind in Britain* (London: Allen and Unwin, 1928), *Society in War, 1914–1916* (Boston: Houghton Mifflin, 1931), and *Britain Holds On, 1917, 1918* (London: Allen and Unwin, 1937).

39. Olive Schreiner, Message, read by Emmeline Pethick-Lawrence, Carnegie Hall, New York, October 31, 1914, in Mackenzie, *Shoulder to Shoulder*, 299; OS to Emily Hobhouse, March 1915, SCCS *Letters*, 347–48.

40. OS to HE, August 21, 1914, SCCS *Letters*, 338.

41. OS to HE, August 27, 1915, ibid., 353–54.

42. OS to HE, August 1915, HRC.

43. OS to HE, December 1919, SCCS *Letters*, 365–66.

44. Mary Chamberlain, quoting Schreiner, in "Women after the War," *Survey*, August 14, 1915, 452.

45. Ibid.

46. OS to Mrs. Francis Smith, late 1919, SCCS *Letters*, 36.

47. Schreiner to Carpenter, October 1918, ibid., 340. See, too, Schreiner's remarks to Mary Chamberlain in "Women after the War," 450–52, in which she forecast that the war would weaken women's position in society.

48. OS to HE, December 1919, SCCS *Letters*, 365–66.

49. Schreiner, "Who Knocks at the Door?" in *Stories, Dreams, and Allegories*, 147.

50. Schreiner, *Dawn*, 37.

51. Ibid., 16, 4.

52. Ibid., 1.

53. Schreiner, *Woman and Labor*, 182–83.

54. Even Schreiner's lifelong ambivalence toward the virtue of suffering oneself rather than inflicting injury on another was not a sign of the tugs exclusively of Christian values. A prizing of self-sacrifice appeared in classic Greek and Indian thought, voiced by Socrates, Plato, and Buddha. Indeed, the Stoics viewed peace as a state of coherence and connection; the Greek word for peace was *eirene*, meaning "linkage." See Roland Bainton, *Christian Attitudes toward War and Peace* (New York: Abingdon, 1960), 17–18.

55. Olive Schreiner, "On 'Conscientious Objectors' contributed to the *Labour Leader,* London, 16th March 1916," SCCS *Letters,* App. H, 398–99.

56. Ibid.

57. Schreiner, "Who Knocks at the Door?" in *Stories, Dreams, and Allegories,* 152.

58. Schreiner, *Dawn,* 13.

59. OS to Emily Hobhouse, London, 1914(?), SCCS *Letters,* 341–42.

60. Schreiner, *From Man to Man,* 174.

61. OS to Mrs. Pethick-Lawrence, London, 1914(?), SCCS *Letters,* 345–46.

62. Olive Schreiner, "Letter to a Peace Meeting, held in London about March, 1916, under the Auspices of the 'Union of Democratic Control,'" SCCS *Letters,* App. I, 400–1.

63. Ibid., 400.

64. OS to Emily Hobhouse, London, 1915, SCCS *Letters,* 347.

65. Schreiner, "Letter to a Peace Meeting," SCCS *Letters,* 401.

66. OS to Mrs. Francis Smith, April 1915, and to HE, April 16, 1915, ibid., 349, 349–50.

67. Vellacott Newberry, "Anti-war Suffragists," 419.

68. Joyce Avrech Berkman, "Transformations in Pacifist Consciousness in England, 1914–1939," in Warren Wagar, ed., *The Secular Mind: Transformations of Faith in Modern Europe* (New York: Holmes and Meier, 1982), 142–68; Joyce Avrech Berkman, "Eric Gill," "Aldous Huxley," and "Olive Schreiner," in Harold Josephson, ed., *Biographical Dictionary of Modern Peace Leaders* (Westport, CT: Greenwood Press, 1985).

Chapter 8

1. For the response of prominent Victorian intellectuals and literary critics, such as William Lecky, George Meredith, and Arthur Symons, see SCCS *Life,* 212, 153–54, 184–90. William Lecky deemed *African Farm* one of the finest novels in the English language; Sir Charles Dilke went further and, after claiming it the greatest novel in the English language by a female writer, went on to declare it "the greatest novel [I] had ever read—greater than Bunyan's *Pilgrim's Progress.*" Frank Harris quoting Charles Dilke, cited in SCCS *Life,* 212. See, for John Galsworthy, H. V. Marrot, *Life and Letters of John Galsworthy* (New York: Scribner, 1936); Cazamian, *Le roman et les idées,* 3:351; for Havelock Ellis, *My Life,* 184; for Rudyard Kipling, Angus Wilson, *The Strange Ride of Rudyard Kipling* (New York: Viking Press, 1977), 277; for Edward Carpenter, *My Days and Dreams* (London: Allen and Unwin, 1916); for D. H. Lawrence and George Moore, Christopher Heywood, "Olive Schreiner's Influence on George Moore and D. H. Lawrence," in *Aspects of South African Literature* (London: Heinemann, 1976); for George Bernard Shaw, Gregg, *Memories of Schreiner,* 23; for Stephen

Crane, Carlin T. Kindilien, "Stephen Crane and the 'Savage Philosophy' of Olive Schreiner," *Studies in English* 3, 2 (Summer 1957). Well-known British writer of fiction, pacifist and feminist tracts, Vera Brittain, whose youth overlapped Schreiner's later years, recorded her intellectual debt to *African Farm*—"a great book . . . plays the part of a Bible with me"—in *Diary: Chronicle of Youth,* 68, 162, cited by Rita Kissen in her Ph.D. dissertation, *Vera Brittain: Writing a Life,* 9, University of Massachusetts at Amherst, 1986; in South Africa, Cecil Rhodes and General J. C. Smuts revered *African Farm;* for Rhodes, see sccs *Life,* 212–13; for Smuts, Introduction by Smuts to Buchanan-Gould, *Not without Honour.*

2. "A Felt Hat Worker," in Margaret Llewelyn Davies, ed., *Life as We Have Known It: By Co-operative Working Women* (1931; rpt., New York: W. W. Norton, 1975), 101, and Angela James and Mina Hills, eds., *Mrs. John Brown, 1847–1935* (London: John Murray, 1937), 189. Anon., *Church Quarterly Review* (London) 29 (January 1890), from "Three Controversial Novels," included in Clayton, *Olive Schreiner,* 74–75.

3. Among others, see: Colby, *Singular Anomaly,* 72–73, 62–63; Hugh Walpole, "The Permanent Elements in Olive Schreiner's Fiction," review of *From Man to Man, New York Herald Tribune,* May 1, 1927; Virginia Woolf, "Olive Schreiner," review of *The Letters of Olive Schreiner, New Republic* (London) 42 (March 18, 1925).

4. Alexander, "Olive Schreiner." See, among others, Krige, *Olive Schreiner,* 26–28; Geoffrey Haresnape, "The *Voorslag* Movement and Olive Schreiner," in Smith and Maclennan, *Olive Schreiner and After,* 108–15; Isak Dinesen, Introduction to *The Story of an African Farm* (New York: Paul Hogarth, 1961), v.

5. Gordimer, "English Novel in South Africa," 16–21, esp. 20–21, which highly praises *African Farm,* must be contrasted with her less favorable appraisal in " 'Prison-House of Colonialism.' " Doris Lessing, "Afterword to *The Story of an African Farm* by Olive Schreiner," in Lessing, *A Small Personal Voice* (New York: Knopf, 1974), 97–120. See Victoria Middleton, "Doris Lessing's 'Debt' to Olive Schreiner," in Carey Kaplan and Ellen Cronan Rose, eds., *Doris Lessing: The Alchemy of Survival* (Athens: Ohio University Press: 1988), 135–48. Stephen Gray, *South African Literature: An Introduction* (New York: Harper and Row, 1979); Gray also praises Schreiner's treatment of social and philosophical paradoxes as "broad and breathtaking" (143).

6. Liz Stanley, "Olive Schreiner: New Women, FreeWomen, All Women," in Dale Spender, ed., *Feminist Theorists* (New York: Pantheon Books, 1983), 240–41; Elaine Showalter, *A Literature of Their Own: British Women Novelists from Bronte to Lessing* (Princeton, NJ: Princeton University Press, 1977), 196–203. See Cherry Clayton, Introduction, and "Olive Schreiner, Child of Queen Victoria: *Stories, Dreams, and Allegories,* " in Clayton, *Olive Schreiner.* See also Gray, *South African Literature,* 134–36.

7. Among a multitude of references to her revising labors, see OS to HE, March 28, April 21, November 21, 1884, SCCS Letters, 14, 15, 46; OS to SCCS, April 1893, SCCS Life, 251; Schreiner Journal, June 4, 1902, SCCS Life, 347–48. The only contrary evidence appears in a letter to Edward Carpenter, January 31, 1889, in which she denies reworking her fiction, Rive, Schreiner: Letters, 148.

8. Schreiner, From Man to Man, 447.

9. Ibid.; OS to SCCS, February 23, 1894, SCCS Life, 246; OS to HE, January 12, 1890, April 9, 1885, SCCS Letters, 188–90, 69; Arthur Symons interview of Schreiner, SCCS Life, 184–90; OS to Betty Molteno, January 9, 1885, cited in First and Scott, Olive Schreiner, 226.

10. Schreiner, "A Dream of Wild Bees" in Dreams, 74; Schreiner, From Man to Man, 220, 202–3.

11. OS to HE, June 12, 1890, SCCS Letters, 188–90. See OS to Ettie Schreiner, Christmas Eve, 1902, unpublished, loaned to Vera Buchanan-Gould, Not without Honour, 159–60.

12. Schreiner, From Man to Man, 448; OS to HE, June 12, 1890, SCCS Letters, 188–90.

13. See discussion in Chapter 2 of Schreiner's mystic experiences. Charles T. Tart has proposed that the image of light for inspiration may well be an empirical, sensory experience, common to all individuals who experience "perceptual expansion"; it may be the sensory response to the energy that is liberated with experiences of the merging of self with others. Tart, Altered States of Consciousness (New York: Doubleday, 1972).

14. Henri F. Ellenberger, The Discovery of the Unconscious (New York: Basic Books, 1970), 302–3; See also James Engell, The Creative Imagination (Cambridge, MA: Harvard University Press, 1981); René Wellek, A History of Modern Criticism, 1750–1950, vol. 2, The Romantic Age (New Haven: Yale University Press, 1955); OS to KP, July 2, 6, 7, 1886, Rive, Schreiner: Letters, 85–95. Schreiner claimed that joy in creative activity was felt viscerally and erotically and that it was this joy in the artistic action itself that defined aesthetic. See also Delavenay, Lawrence and Carpenter, 123.

15. OS to HE, May 26, 1889, SCCS Letters, 164.

16. Grosskurth, Havelock Ellis, 114–15, 165–67.

17. OS to HE, August 11, 1890, SCCS Letters, 194–95.

18. Symons interview of Schreiner, SCCS Life, 184–90; Schreiner, From Man to Man, 450–51.

19. OS to W. T. Stead, June 19, 1892, SCCS Letters, 207–8; OS to HE, December 28, 1884, ibid., 52–53.

20. Schreiner, From Man to Man, 449; SCCS Life, 69; OS to SCCS, May 26, 1898, SCCS Letters, 303–4.

21. SCCS Life, 165, 188, 184, 190, 246; see also OS to HE, April 9, October 5, 1885, SCCS Letters, 69, 83, and to Mrs. J. H. Philpot, February 18, 1888, ibid., 132.

22. OS to HE, March 27, December 22, 1886, SCCS *Letters,* 112, 123, and to Mrs. J. H. Philpot, November 7, 1886, ibid., 125.

23. OS to HE, August 7, 1884, ibid., 38; OS to Carpenter, April 28, 1911, CC.

24. OS to HE, April 11, 1885, SCCS *Letters,* 161–62.

25. OS to HE, August 7, 1884, ibid., 38.

26. Schreiner, *From Man to Man,* 452; OS to HE, April 10, 1888, February 14, 1889, SCCS *Letters,* 134, 155; OS to HE, April 5, 1889, ibid., 160. See also to Carpenter, January 28, 1888—"I write for myself and to myself. This is the secret of my work as an artist"—CC.

27. OS to SCCS, October 18, 1898, SCCS *Letters,* 225; Schreiner, *From Man to Man,* 453; SCCS *Life,* 251.

28. Schreiner, *Thoughts,* 27, 30.

29. OS to Carpenter, January 28, 1888, CC; OS to HE, May 23, 1890, SCCS *Letters,* 187–88. Schreiner expanded the blood image in an allegory, "The Artist's Secret," in *Dreams,* 103–5, which concerns an artist whose pictures glow with an incomparable red pigment that other artists try in vain to emulate. The envied artist's paintings become "redder and redder," but at the same time he grows "whiter and whiter." Eventually he dies. Other artists look in his pots and crucibles for his red pigments but find nothing. When they prepare him for burial, they notice the mark of a wound above his left breast, "an old, old wound, that must have been there all his life, for the edges were old and hardened." The story concludes consolingly, for though the other artists never discover the source of the red color and in time the dead man is forgotten "the work lived" (104).

30. OS to HE, March 28, April 21, 1884, March 29, 1885, July 1890, SCCS *Letters,* 14, 16, 192, 66. See also SCCS *Life,* 131, 153, 339, 347, 349.

31. OS to HE, April 8, 1886, SCCS *Letters,* 97; Schreiner, *African Farm,* 158.

32. OS to HE, July 12, 1884, SCCS *Letters,* 28–29; OS to HE, April 2, 1885, ibid., 68.

33. OS to HE, November 21, December 9, 1884, ibid., 46, 49. In Schreiner's multifaceted discussion of craft, she described her use of "buffer scenes," in order to elevate or lower her literary tone and enhance emotional dynamic: OS to HE, April 12, 1886, ibid., 97–98. Another device she utilized was the "stroke oblique." According to Cronwright, Schreiner intended to execute such a stroke in her conclusion of *From Man to Man.* She planned to have the malicious Mrs. Drummond, whose gossip contributed to Bertie's tragic fate, present at Bertie's deathbed, and when Rebekah asked Bertie whether she wished those present to pray for her, Bertie would reply, "'Let Mrs. Drummond pray . . . she is a Christian.'" See note by Cronwright in *From Man to Man,* 462.

34. Ridley Beeton, "The Signals of Great Art? A Manuscript of Olive Schreiner's Unfinished Novel," *Stanpunte* (Cape Town) 145 (February 1980): 4–13. Because the transcribing of revisions in legible form for a publisher was particularly tedious for Schreiner, whose handwriting was frequently illegible, she occasion-

ally entrusted final editing responsibility to others. For example, in a letter dated November 9, 1890, she asked Ellis, who held an original and corrected version of her allegories "In a Ruined Chapel" and "The Sunlight Lay across My Bed," to publish her full collection of *Dreams* but added, *"Please revise carefully."* SCCS *Letters*, 198. Ellis's task involved reviewing her manuscript for "legibility, spelling, words left out, etc." See also OS to HE, May 27, 1886, October 1, 1890, SCCS *Letters*, 100, 197.

35. OS to HE, February 25, 1884, SCCS *Letters*, 12. It remains unclear what she meant by "too much moralizing," since all of her writing is saturated with plentiful moral reflection. She might have been referring specifically to her didactic use of her narrator, a practice she eschewed in her later fiction.

36. OS to HE, February 25, March 16, 1884, ibid., 12, 13.

37. George Levine, *The Realistic Imagination: English Fiction from Frankenstein to Lady Chatterley* (Chicago: University of Chicago Press, 1981), 271; SCCS *Life*, 184–90: Although Krige, in the Introduction to his edited *Olive Schreiner*, typifies those who view Blenkins as a caricature, note that other contemporary critics are divided as to the desirability of Schreiner's fleshing out all the novel's characters. Some argue that realist standards are inappropriate for this mixed symbolic-realistic novel. See Doris Lessing's defense of Schreiner's presentation of Bonaparte Blenkins in "Afterword to *The Story of an African Farm*," in Lessing, *Small Personal Voice*, 104. See also Carol E. Bastian's argument, in *A First Generation of Autobiographical Novelists: Olive Schreiner, William Hale White, Samuel Butler* (Ph.D. diss., Indiana University, 1975), 83–84., that the reader's vision is that of the farm children, for whom Blenkins is a grotesque, animated presence. So also Dan Jacobson, in his Introduction to *The Story of an African Farm*, 19, relishes Blenkins as a superb character invention. Schreiner sometimes referred to her approach as "classical" in the manner of Walter Bagehot: OS to HE, May 3, 1885, SCCS *Letters*, 72.

38. With regard to Shaw's characters, Schreiner announced, "You wouldn't care at any moment if the whole lot were drowned." Likewise, Ernest Pontifex, in Samuel Butler's *Way of All Flesh*, was not credible to her, too one-dimensional and unalloyed in his evil. Although Hardy did not evince these same failings as extensively, his characters, at least in *A Pair of Blue Eyes*, appeared shallow to Schreiner, because he too was writing from the outside, "fingering his characters with his hands, not pressing them up against him till he felt their hearts beat." Of course, she was familiar only with Hardy's early work. OS to HE, June 1911, and to SCCS, April 1917, SCCS *Letters*, 302, 356.

39. OS to Mrs. Francis Smith, November 20, 1910, and to HE, June 1911, ibid., 296, 302; Schreiner, *Thoughts*, 291; she cites, e.g., Balzac's verbal painting of "the grimy respectability" of Paris boardinghouse chairs and tables.

40. Schreiner, *African Farm*, iii.

41. Schreiner, *From Man to Man*, 161; Schreiner, *African Farm*, iv.
42. Schreiner, *From Man to Man*, 209; Schreiner, *African Farm*, 157.
43. Schreiner, *From Man to Man*, 164. See Dorrit Cohn, *Transparent Minds* (Princeton, NJ: Princeton University Press, 1978), on the historical literary context for nineteenth- and twentieth-century approaches to expressing characters' inner states. Unfortunately, Cohn overlooks the projection of inner dialogue onto external symbolic characters, a mode Schreiner effects in her allegories.
44. Schreiner, *From Man to Man*, 203.
45. Schreiner, *African Farm*, iii, iv; Elizabeth Ermath, *Realism and Consensus in the English Novel* (Princeton, NJ: Princeton University Press, 1983), 47–48: Ermath argues that realistic novels hold in tense balance the elements of form and formlessness. Although they assume an objective cosmic order, the characters' and narrators' perspectives are ultimately finite and cannot encompass that order completely.
46. Schreiner Journal, April 28, 1909, SCCS *Life*, 350, 189–90; OS to HE, August 11, 1890, SCCS *Letters*, 194.
47. OS to HE, February 1885, HRC; Schreiner, *African Farm*, 157; OS to HE, November 2, 1888, SCCS *Letters*, 144–45.
48. Gregg, *Memories of Schreiner*, 68; Virginia Woolf, "Olive Schreiner," 103.
49. OS to SCCS, February 2, 1901, January 11, 1911, February 16, 1904, SCCS *Letters*, 231, 298, 243; to Mrs. Francis Smith, May 5, 1910, ibid., 292–3; to HE, April 8, 1884, HRC. See also SCCS *Life*, 181. Throughout Schreiner's life George Sand was a particularly revered model. Such reverence for Sand was common among advanced women and feminist-minded men in Europe. In England, Sand assumed legendary proportions, inspiring Elizabeth Barrett Browning's sonnet "To George Sand: A Recognition," a sonnet Schreiner admired. Often citing *Elle et lui* as a work of genius, Schreiner valued Sand the woman as much as Sand the writer—"a colossal human soul," she called her: OS to SCCS, February 2, 1901, SCCS *Letters*, 231; to HE, February 23, 24, 1886, March 29, April 11, 1885, May 12, 1890, ibid., 93, 94, 66–67, 69–70, 185–86.
50. OS to Mrs. Francis Smith, September 10, 1906, SCCS *Letters*, 254–55.
51. In an amusing comparative ranking of some of these artists, Schreiner further underscored her reverence for Heine. She once mused that if someone showed her a lock of hair from Shakespeare she would stroke it; if it were Shelley's, she'd kiss it; but if it were Heine's, she would "carry it about with me wherever I went." OS to HE, April 21, 1884, ibid., 15–16; see also OS to Mrs. Francis Smith, September 1908, September 10, 1906, ibid., 282, 254–55. See also SCCS *Life*, 189.
52. OS to Mrs. Francis Smith, November 20, 1910, SCCS *Letters*, 296.
53. OS to HE, January 21, 1888, ibid., 129; to SCCS, December 5, 1906, ibid., 258; to HE, January 26, 1888, ibid., 129. After reading a number of French writers—

Daudet, Dumas, Balzac, Maupassant—she wrote John X. Merriman and Havelock Ellis that their fiction quickly became boring, since they tended to treat the same types of persons, the same circle of subjects, the same kind of lovemaking and marital relations. She found this writing wanting in range and complexity. OS to HE, November 9, 1903, in Clayton, *Olive Schreiner*, 120. She also detested the music of Wagner and never explained why. OS to HE, January 26, 1915, SCCS *Letters*, 346.

54. Schreiner, *From Man to Man*, 454–55; OS to Carpenter, January 28, 1888, CC. On one occasion Schreiner stated to Carpenter that she published in order to make money to help other people do their work.

55. Schreiner, *From Man to Man*, 455; OS to Sarah Ann Tooley, SCCS *Life*, 295–97; OS to SCCS, March 27, 1913, SCCS *Letters*, 323.

56. OS to Mrs. J. H. Philpot, March 17, 1889, SCCS *Letters*, 157; to HE, July 12, 1884, ibid., 28–29; to T. Fisher Unwin, September 26, 1892, ibid., 209. Schreiner Journal, January 29, 1888, SCCS *Life*, 180; OS to Emily Hobhouse, March 1913, SCCS *Letters*, 321.

57. OS to SCCS, February 25, 1907, SCCS *Letters*, 263–64.

58. OS to T. Fisher Unwin, September 26, 1892, ibid., 209.

59. OS to HE, April 5, 1889, ibid., 160–61.

60. Showalter, *Literature of Their Own*, 81.

61. OS to HE, May 12, 16, 1890, SCCS *Letters*, 185, 187; to J. T. Lloyd, December 1896, ibid., 223; to Erilda Cawood, June 16, 1890, ibid., 190; to W. T. Stead, July 12, 1890, ibid., 191; to HE, November 26, 1886, April 1–2, 1887, ibid., 105, 113.

62. Schreiner, *African Farm*, 312.

63. Jane Marcus, in "Olive Schreiner," 65, has ably defended Schreiner's recourse to allegorical dreams. She charges that the critics who are discomforted by allegory have been taught that irony is the sharpest tool for shaping dissent. "But irony is only the last resort of the defenseless intellectual, not the hapless black, woman or working class prophet."

64. The brief allegory "Seeds a-Growing," in *Dreams, Stories, and Allegories*, 142–44, is an exception. The narrator's dream serves only to soothe the disconsolate Schreiner during the Anglo–Boer War by assuring retribution for England's military aggression.

65. SCCS *Life*, 202–5.

66. Paul Piehler, *The Visionary Landscape: A Study in Medieval Allegory* (London, Edward Arnold, 1971), 115–16.

67. Olive Schreiner, "The Great Heart of England" in *Stories, Dreams, and Allegories*, 145.

68. Piehler, *Visionary Landscape*, 5, 19–20; Gray, "The Trooper at the Hanging Tree."

69. Schreiner, *African Farm*, 282, 311, 297.
70. As a life parallel, Willie Bertram's appearance at a crucial time in Schreiner's life was not fantasy, but Willie was much less mythic and omniscient, and at least he had a name and a history, however murky. SCCS *Life*, 80–84.
71. Schreiner, *African Farm*, 4, 128, 304, 303.
72. Schreiner, *From Man to Man*, 220–21, 202–3. See discussion in Chapter 5, herein.
73. Ibid., 26.
74. Ibid., 213–14.
75. According to Meyer Abrams, in *The Mirror and the Lamp: Romantic Theory and the Critical Tradition* (London: Oxford University Press, 1953), this imagery has roots in the philosophy of Cambridge Platonists, who were influenced strongly by Plotinus's theology of emanation.
76. Gillian Beer, *Darwin's Plots* (London: Routledge and Kegan Paul, 1983), 179.
77. Schreiner, *African Farm*, 290. The conventional opposition of light and dark continues to pervade writing in our own time, as evident in the perceptive literary criticism of Levine in *The Realistic Imagination*, 254, with its telling description of Victorian thought: "From the exhilaration and optimism of discovery and the beating back of the frontiers of superstitious darkness, through the struggles to reconcile some of the dark superstition with some of that luminous brightness, emerged some rather nervous, even gloomy visions."
78. Schreiner, *African Farm*, 27, 154.
79. Schreiner, "A Dream of Wild Bees," in *Dreams*, 80; Schreiner, "In a Ruined Chapel," ibid., 94; Schreiner, "The Sunlight Lay across My Bed," ibid., 159.
80. Schreiner, *African Farm*, 312. Oliver Elton contrasted Hardy and Eliot in words that could apply to Schreiner. Like Hardy, and unlike Eliot, Schreiner, for all her own and her characters' sufferings, was determined to enjoy life, "Its unashamed passion, its careless gaiety, the intoxication of sunshine." Elton cited in Gordon S. Haight, *A Century of George Eliot Criticism* (Boston: Houghton Mifflin, 1965), 192.
81. Of less significance, Schreiner noted the defects sunlight exposed, such as facial freckles and wrinkles disguised at night. *African Farm*, 5.
82. Schreiner, *Peter Halket*, 33; Schreiner, *African Farm*, 145.
83. Schreiner, *From Man to Man*, 423; Schreiner, *Peter Halket*, 59.
84. Schreiner, *African Farm*, 152, 10.
85. Schreiner, "In a Ruined Chapel," in *Dreams*, 89; Schreiner, *From Man to Man*, 259, 273.
86. Schreiner, *From Man to Man*, 145, 332. See Virginia Woolf's *Orlando* for identical imagery.
87. Schreiner, *From Man to Man*, 345–46, 377.
88. Schreiner, *African Farm*, 295, 296.

89. Schreiner, *From Man to Man,* 202. For a perceptive discussion of the oppressive qualities of rain in this novel, see Leonore Hoffmann, *A Delicate Balance: The Resolutions to Conflict of Women in the Fiction of Four Women Writers of the Victorian Period* (Ph.D. diss., Indiana Univeristy, 1974), chap. 5, "The Integrated Self: From Man to Man," 175–76, 178.

90. Schreiner, *From Man to Man,* 278.

91. Ibid., 360.

92. J. E. Cirlot, *A Dictionary of Symbols* (New York: Philosophical Library, 1971).

93. Schreiner, *Undine,* 352, 357.

94. Schreiner, *From Man to Man,* 439–40, 166.

95. As noted, Schreiner often invoked the verb *to paint* to refer to her writing. Among many references, see OS to HE, December 10, 1884, March 29, 1885, SCCS *Letters,* 49–50, 66; to Carpenter, July 4, 1911, ibid.; Schreiner, Preface to *African Farm;* Schreiner, *Thoughts,* chap. 1; OS to HE, April 10, 1886, SCCS *Letters,* 97. Eighteenth-century theorists of the imagination had frequently enlisted the painter as image for the psyche; and Herder viewed poets as trying to reproduce in their souls the image God painted on the huge illuminated canvas of nature. See Engell, *Creative Imagination,* 57, 219–21. Ermath notes how Victorian paintings were rich in narrative suggestiveness. The visual details on the canvas were tips of a historical iceberg, embodying the temporal depth of a lived sequence of events. Ermath, *Realism and Consensus,* 25–26. First and Scott, *Olive Schreiner,* 98, underscore the impact of popular Bible illustrations of the day on Schreiner's painting of early childhood spiritual experiences in *African Farm,* and Buchanan-Gould, *Not without Honour,* 35, observes how Schreiner's argumentation in her nonfiction followed Ruskin's and Gibbon's style of building up a series of graphic pictures.

96. Dinesen, Introduction to *Story of an African Farm,* viii. See Shelley's equation of the poetic imagination with the aeolian lyre in Abrams, *Mirror and Lamp,* 51. SCCS *Life,* 399; OS to SCCS, December 5, 1906, SCCS *Letters,* 258; to W. T. Stead, October 1895, ibid., 219.

97. See Schreiner, "Three Dreams in a Desert" in *Dreams,* 54–55; Schreiner, *African Farm,* 246, 23, 36, 37, 252; Schreiner, "In a Ruined Chapel," in *Dreams,* 85; Schreiner "Great Heart of England," in *Stories, Dreams, and Allegories,* 145; Schreiner, *From Man to Man,* 97–98; Schreiner, "The South African Nation," (1900), Note A in *Thoughts,* 379–80; Schreiner, *Woman and Labor,* 28–34.

98. Schreiner, "The Sunlight Lay across My Bed," in *Dreams,* 134; Schreiner, "The Lost Joy," in *Dreams,* 7. See also Schreiner, "Three Dreams in a Desert" and "Ruined Chapel," in *Dreams,* 132, 138–39, 37, 85–86, 91, 93.

99. OS to HE, March 20, 1913, SCCS *Letters,* 325–26. Significantly, Schreiner discriminated among Boer styles of diction. As A. E. Voss, in his close study of the language of *African Farm,* indicates, the speech of Tant' Sannie differed from that

of Piet Van der Velt, who in turn exhibited variations from Grana and the "transport-rider." As part of her carefully chosen diction, Schreiner incorporated South African turns of phrase that situated her novels in an unmistakable place and time and introduced fresh tones and rhythms. Voss, " 'Not a Word or a Sound in the World about Him That Is Not Modifying Him': Learning, Lore, and Language in *The Story of an African Farm*," in Clayton, *Olive Schreiner*, 170–80.

100. Schreiner, *From Man to Man*, 74.

SELECT BIBLIOGRAPHY

Bibliographies

Davis, Roslyn. *Olive Schreiner, 1920–1971*. Johannesburg: University of Witwatersrand, Department of Bibliography, 1972.

Verster, E. *Olive Emilie Albertina Schreiner*. Cape Town: University of Cape Town, School of Librarianship, 1946.

Manuscript Collections

Albany Library, 1820 Settlers Memorial Division, Grahamstown.
Cory Library, Rhodes University, Grahamstown.
Cradock Library, Municipality of Cradock.
Cullen Library, University of Witwatersrand, Johannesburg.
Fales Library, New York University, Elizabeth Robins Papers.
Fawcett Library, City of London Polytechnic, London.
Harry Ransom Humanities Research Center, University of Texas at Austin.
International Archives of the Women's Movement, Amsterdam.
J. W. Jagger Library, University of Cape Town, African and Special Collections.
National English Literary Museum and Documentation Centre, Grahamstown.
Sheffield City Libraries Archives Division, Edward Carpenter Collection.
South African Library, Cape Town, Special Collections.
Swarthmore College Peace Library, Jane Addams Collection.
University College Library, London, Karl Pearson Collection.

Published Letters

Cronwright Schreiner, Samuel Cron, ed. *The Letters of Olive Schreiner, 1876–1920*. London: Unwin, 1924.

Findlay, Joan, ed. *The Findlay Letters, 1806–1870*. Pretoria: L. Van Schaik, 1954.

Rive, Richard, ed. *Olive Schreiner: Letters*. Vol. 1, *1871–1899*. Oxford: Oxford University Press, 1988. (Vol. 2 forthcoming.)

Primary Works: Olive Schreiner

N. B. Reprint information follows data for original publication when reprints have been used for text citations.

The Story of an African Farm. Published originally under the pseudonym Ralph Iron. London: Chapman and Hall, 1883. Reprint. New York: A. L. Burt, Cornell Series, n.d.

Dreams. London: Unwin, 1890. Reprint. Boston: Little, Brown, 1916.

Dream Life and Real Life. London: Unwin, 1893. Reprint. Boston: Roberts Brothers, 1893.

The Political Situation. Coauthored with S. C. Cronwright Schreiner. London: Unwin, 1896. Reprint. Chicago, 1899.

Trooper Peter Halket of Mashonaland. London: Unwin, 1897. Reprint. Boston: Roberts Brothers, 1897.

An English South African's View of the Situation: Words in Season. London: Hodder and Stoughton, 1899. Also published as *The South African Question.* Chicago: Charles H. Segel, 1899.

A Letter on the Jew. Cape Town: Liberman, 1906.

Closer Union. London: Fifield, 1909.

Woman and Labour. London: Unwin, 1911. Reprint. *Woman and Labor.* New York: Frederick A. Stokes, 1911.

Thoughts on South Africa. London: Unwin, 1923. Reprint. New York: Frederick A. Stokes, 1923.

Stories, Dreams, and Allegories. London: Unwin, 1923. The 1924 edition adds excerpts from *The Dawn of Civilization.*

From Man to Man; or, Perhaps Only . . . London: Unwin, 1926. Reprint. New York: Harper and Brothers, 1927.

Undine. London: Benn, and New York: Harper and Brothers, 1929.

Anthologies

Barash, Carol. *An Olive Schreiner Reader.* London: Pandora, 1987.

Clayton, Cherry, ed. *Olive Schreiner.* Johannesburg: McGraw-Hill, 1983.

Krige, Uys, ed. *Olive Schreiner: A Selection.* Cape Town: Oxford University Press, 1968.

Nuttall, Neveille, ed. *The Silver Plume.* Johannesburg: A.P.B., 1956.

Purcell, Anna, ed. *Olive Schreiner's Thoughts about Women.* Cape Town: South African News, 1909.

Thurman, Howard, ed. *A Track to the Water's Edge: The Olive Schreiner Reader.* New York: Harper and Row, 1973.

Supplementary Primary Sources

Brittain, Vera. *Testament of Youth.* New York: Macmillan, 1937.

Carpenter, Edward. *Love's Coming of Age.* Manchester: Labour Press, 1896.

Bibliography

———. *My Days and Dreams*. London: Allen and Unwin, 1916.
———. *Toward Democracy*. New York: Mitchell Kennerley, 1922.
Ellis, Havelock. *Essays in Wartime*. London: Constable, 1916.
———. *Man and Woman*. London: Walter Scott, 1894.
———. *My Confessional: Questions of Our Day*. Boston: Houghton Mifflin, 1934.
———. *My Life: Autobiography of Havelock Ellis*. Boston: Houghton Mifflin, 1939.
———. *Studies in the Psychology of Sex*. Vol. 1. 1899. Reprint. Philadelphia: F. A. Davis, 1900.
Gandhi, Mohandas Karamchand. *Satyagraha in South Africa*. Translated from original in Gujarati by M. Desai. Madras: S. Ganesau, 1938.
Gilman, Charlotte Perkins. *The Living of Charlotte Perkins Gilman: An Autobiography*. New York: Harper and Row, 1975.
Gosse, Edmond. *Father and Son*. New York: Scribner, 1916.
Hancock, W. K., and Jean van der Poel, eds. *Selections from the Smuts Papers*. Vol. 1. Cambridge: Cambridge University Press, 1966.
Housman, Laurence. *The Unexpected Years*. London: J. Cape, 1937.
Lewsen, Phyllis, ed. *Correspondence of J. X. Merriman, 1890–1898*. Cape Town: Van Riebeck Society, 1966.
Lifton, Robert Jay, ed. *The Woman in America*. Boston: Beacon Press, 1964.
Lytton, Constance G. *Prisons and Prisoners: Experience of a Suffragette*. 1914. Reprint. West Yorkshire: E. P. Publishing, 1976.
Massingham, H. W., ed. *H.W.M: A Selection from the Writings of H. W. Massingham*. London: J. Cape, 1925.
Mill, John Stuart. *Utilitarianism*. London: Everyman, 1910.
Paton, Alan. *Toward The Mountain: An Autobiography*. New York: Scribner, 1980.
Pearson, Karl. *The Chances of Death and Other Studies in Evolution*. London: Edward Arnold, 1897.
———. *The Ethic of Freethought*. 1888. Reprint. London: Adam and Charles Black, 1901.
Sanger, Margaret. *An Autobiography*. New York: Dover, 1971.
Stanton, Elizabeth Cady. *The Original Feminist Attack on the Bible*. 1895 (*The Woman's Bible*). Reprint. New York, Arno Press, 1974.
Woolf, Leonard. *Beginning Again: An Autobiography of the Years 1911 to 1918*. New York: Harcourt, Brace and World, 1964.

Secondary Sources

Abrams, Meyer. *The Mirror and the Lamp: Romantic Theory and the Critical Tradition*. Oxford: Oxford University Press, 1953.
Abrams, Philip. *The Origins of British Sociology, 1834–1914*. Chicago: University of Chicago Press, 1968.
Alexander, Ruth. "Olive Schreiner: A Study of Her Amazing Personality." *Cape Times*, April 26, 1930.

Bainton, Roland. *Christian Attitudes toward War and Peace.* New York: Abingdon, 1960.

Bastian, Carol E. *A First Generation of Autobiographical Novelists: Olive Schreiner, William Hale White, Samuel Butler.* Ph.D. diss., Indiana University, 1975.

Baumer, Franklin L. *Religion and the Rise of Scepticism.* New York: Harcourt, Brace, 1960.

Beer, Gillian. *Darwin's Plots.* London: Routledge and Kegan Paul, 1983.

Beeton, Ridley. "In Search of Olive Schreiner in Texas." *Texas Quarterly* 17, 3 (Autumn 1974): 105–54.

———. "The Signals of Great Art? A Manuscript of Olive Schreiner's Unfinished Novel." *Stanpunte* (Cape Town) 145 (February 1980): 4–13.

Benson, Mary. *The African Patriots: The Story of the African National Congress of South Africa.* London: Faber and Faber, 1963.

Berkman, Joyce Avrech. "Eric Gill," "Aldous Huxley," and "Olive Schreiner." In Harold Josephson, ed., *Biographical Dictionary of Modern Peace Leaders.* Westport, CT: Greenwood Press, 1985.

———. "Feminism, War, and Peace Politics: The Case of World War One." In Jean Bethke Elshtain and Sheila Tobias, eds., *Women, Militarism, and War.* New York: Rowan and Littlefield, forthcoming.

———. "The Nurturant Fantasies of Olive Schreiner." *Frontiers* 2, 3 (1977).

———. "Transformations in Pacifist Consciousness in England, 1914–1939." In Warren Wagar, ed., *The Secular Mind: Transformations of Faith in Modern Europe.* New York: Holmes and Meier, 1982.

———. *Olive Schreiner: Feminism on the Frontier.* Montreal: Eden Press, 1979.

Blake, Kathleen. *Love and the Woman Question in Victorian Literature: The Art of Self-postponement.* Sussex: Harvester Press, 1983.

Bleier, Ruth. *Science and Gender: A Critique of Biology and Its Theories of Gender.* New York: Pergamon, 1984.

Bolt, Christine, *The Anti-slavery Movement and Reconstruction.* Oxford: Oxford University Press, 1969.

Bradley, Ian. *The Call to Seriousness: The Evangelical Impact on the Victorians.* New York: Macmillan, 1976.

Buchanan-Gould, Vera. *Not without Honour: The Life and Writings of Olive Schreiner.* London: Hutchinson, 1948.

Budd, Susan. "Reasons for Unbelief among Members of the Secular Movement in England, 1850–1950." *Past and Present* 36 (April 1967): 106–25.

Buhle, Mari Jo. *Women and American Socialism, 1870–1929.* Urbana: University of Illinois Press, 1981.

Burrow, J. W. *Evolution and Society: A Study in Victorian Social Theory.* Cambridge: Cambridge University Press, 1970.

Buxton, Charles, ed. *Toward A Lasting Settlement.* New York: Macmillan, 1916.

Bynum, Caroline Walker. *Jesus as Mother: Studies in the Spirituality of the High Middle Ages.* Berkeley: University of California Press, 1982.

Cazamian, Madeleine. *Le roman et les idées en Angleterre, 1860–1914.* Paris: Société d'Edition, 1955.

Chadwick, Owen. *The Victorian Church.* Vol. 11. Oxford: Oxford University Press, 1966–70.

Chamberlain, Mary. "Women after the War," *Survey,* August 14, 1915.

Chodorow, Nancy. *The Reproduction of Mothering: Psychoanalysis and the Sociology of Gender.* Berkeley, University of California Press, 1978.

Christ, Carol P., and Judith Plaskow, eds. *Womanspirit Rising.* San Francisco: Harper and Row, 1979.

Cirlot, J. E. *A Dictionary of Symbols.* New York: Philosophical Library, 1971.

Clayton, Cherry. "Olive Schreiner: Life into Fiction." *English in Africa* 12, 1 (May 1985).

Cobbe, Frances Power. *Darwinism in Morals and Other Essays.* Boston: George H. Ellis, 1885.

Cockshut, A. O. J. *The Unbelievers: Early Agnostic Thought, 1840–1890.* New York: New York University Press, 1966.

Cohn, Dorrit. *Transparent Minds.* Princeton, NJ: Princeton University Press, 1978.

Colby, Vineta. *A Singular Anomaly.* New York: New York University Press, 1970.

Cott, Nancy. *The Grounding of Modern Feminism.* New Haven: Yale University Press, 1987.

Cravens, Hamilton. *The Triumph of Evolution.* Philadelphia: University of Pennsylvania Press, 1978.

Cronwright Schreiner, Samuel Cron. *The Life of Olive Schreiner.* London: Unwin, 1924.

Cunningham, A. R. "The 'New Woman Fiction' of the 1890s." *Victorian Studies* 17 (1973): 177–86.

Cunningham, Valentine. *Everywhere Spoken Against: Dissent in the Victorian Novel.* Oxford: Oxford University Press (Clarendon Press), 1975.

———. "Mad Pilgrimings, Aimless Discontinuities, Painful Transitions, Faith and Doubt in Victorian Fiction." *Victorian Studies* 22, 3 (September 1979): 321–34.

Daly, Mary. *Gyn/Ecology: The Metaethics of Radical Feminism.* Boston: Beacon Press, 1978.

Davenport, T. R. H. *The Afrikaner Bond: The History of a South African Political Party, 1880–1911.* Cape Town: Oxford University Press, 1966.

Davies, Margaret Llewelyn, ed. *Life as We Have Known It: By Co-operative Working Women.* 1931. Reprint. New York: W. W. Norton, 1975.

Davis, Natalie Zemon, "Men, Women, and Violence: Some Reflections on Equality." *Smith College Alumnae Quarterly* 68, 3 (April 1977): 12–15.

Davy, Arthur. *The British Pro-Boers, 1877–1902.* Cape Town: Tafelberg, 1978.

Delavenay, Emile. *D. H. Lawrence and Edward Carpenter: A Study in Edwardian Transition.* New York: Taplinger, 1971.

Dilke, Charles Wentworth. *Problems of Greater Britain.* London: Macmillan, 1890.

Dowling, Linda. "The Decadent and the New Woman in the 1890s." *Nineteenth Century Fiction* 33 (March 1979): 434–53.

Draznin, Yaffa. "Did Victorian Medicine Crush Olive Schreiner's Creativity?" *Historian* (February 1985): 196–207.

Duffin, Lorna, and Sara Delamont, eds. *The Nineteenth-Century Woman.* London: Croom Helm, 1978.

Du Plessis, Rachel Blau. *Writing beyond the Ending: Narrative Strategies of Twentieth-Century Women Writers.* Bloomington: Indiana University Press, 1985.

Eliade, Mercea. *The Two and the One.* Chicago: University of Chicago Press, 1965.

Ellenberger, Henri F. *The Discovery of the Unconscious.* New York: Basic Books, 1970.

Elshtain, Jean Bethke. *Women and War.* New York: Basic Books, 1987.

Engle, Barbara Alpern. *Mothers and Daughters: Women of the Intelligentsia in Nineteenth-Century Russia.* Cambridge: Cambridge University Press, 1983.

Engell, James. *The Creative Imagination.* Cambridge, MA: Harvard University Press, 1981.

Ermath, Elizabeth. *Realism and Consensus in the English Novel.* Princeton, NJ: Princeton University Press, 1983.

Farwell, Byron. *The Great Anglo–Boer War.* New York: Harper and Row, 1976.

First, Ruth, and Ann Scott. *Olive Schreiner.* London: Andre Deutsch, 1980.

Foucault, Michel. *The History of Sexuality.* Vol. 1: *An Introduction.* London: Allen Lane, 1978.

Fradkin, Betty McGinnis. "Havelock Ellis and Olive Schreiner's 'Gregory Rose.'" *Texas Quarterly,* Fall 1978, 145–53.

———. "Olive Schreiner and Karl Pearson." *Quarterly Bulletin of the South African Library* 31, 4 (June 1977): 83–93.

Friedlander, Zelda, ed. *Until the Heart Changes: A Garland for Olive Schreiner.* Cape Town: Tafelberg, 1967.

Friedmann, Marion. *Olive Schreiner: A Study in Latent Meanings.* Johannesburg: Witwatersrand University Press, 1955.

Fromm, Erich. *Psychoanalysis and Religion.* New Haven: Yale University Press, 1958.

Gardner, Susan. "'No "Story," No Script, Only the Struggle': First and Scott's *Olive Schreiner.*" *Hecate* 7, 1 (1981): 40–61.

———, ed. *Publisher/Writer/Reader: Sociology of Southern African Literature.* Johannesburg: University of Witwatersrand, 1986.

Garrett, Peter K. *The Victorian Multiplot Novel: Studies in Dialogical Form.* New Haven: Yale University Press, 1980.

Gilbert, Sandra. "Soldier's Heart: Literary Men, Literary Women, and the Great War." *Signs* 8, 3 (1983): 422–50.

Gilbert, Sandra M., and Susan Gubar. *The Madwoman in the Attic: The Woman Writer and the Nineteenth-Century Literary Imagination.* New Haven: Yale University Press, 1979.

Gilman, Charlotte Perkins. "Woman and Labor." *Forerunner* 2, 7 (July 1911): 197–98.

Bibliography

Gordimer, Nadine. "The English Novel in South Africa." *Winter School Conference* 1959–60: 16–21. Sponsored by the 1820 Foundation in Grahamstown.

——. "'The Prison-House of Colonialism': Review of Ruth First and Ann Scott's *Olive Schreiner*." *Times Literary Supplement* (London), August 15, 1980.

Gray, Stephen. *Schreiner: A One-Woman Play.* Cape Town: David Philip, 1983.

——. *South African Literature: An Introduction.* New York: Harper and Row, 1979.

Gregg, Lyndall. *Memories of Olive Schreiner.* London: Chambers, 1957.

Grosskurth, Phyllis. *Havelock Ellis: A Biography.* New York: Knopf, 1980.

Grylls, David. *Guardians and Angels: Parents and Children in Nineteenth Century Literature.* London: Faber and Faber, 1978.

Haight, Gordon S. *A Century of George Eliot Criticism.* Boston: Houghton Mifflin, 1965.

Halfaer, Philip M. *The Psychology of Religious Doubt.* Boston: Beacon Press, 1972.

Hancock, W. K. *Smuts: The Sanguine Years, 1870–1919.* Cambridge: Cambridge University Press, 1962.

Harris, Marvin. *The Rise of Anthropological Theory.* New York: Crowell, 1968.

Hayden, Dolores. *The Grand Domestic Revolution.* Cambridge, MA: MIT Press, 1981.

Heywood, Christopher. "Olive Schreiner's Influence on George Moore and D. H. Lawrence." In *Aspects of South African Literature.* London: Heinemann, 1976.

——, ed. *Aspects of South African Literature.* London: Heinemann, 1976.

Higonnet, Margaret Randolph, Jane Jensen, Sonya Michel, and Margaret Collins Weitz, eds. *Behind the Lines: Gender and the Two World Wars.* New Haven: Yale University Press, 1987.

Hill, Mary A. *Charlotte Perkins Gilman: The Making of a Radical Feminist, 1860–1896.* Philadelphia: Temple University Press, 1979.

Hobman, D. L. *Olive Schreiner: Her Friends and Times.* London: Watts, 1955.

Hobson, J. A. *The War in South Africa.* 1900. Reprint. New York: Howard Fertig, 1969.

Hoffmann, Leonore. *A Delicate Balance: The Resolutions to Conflict of Women in the Fiction of Four Women Writers of the Victorian Period.* Ph.D. diss., Indiana University, 1974.

Holton, Sandra Stanley. *Feminism and Democracy: Women's Suffrage and Reform Politics in Britain, 1900–1918.* Cambridge: Cambridge University Press, 1986.

Houghton, Walter E. *The Victorian Frame of Mind, 1830–1870.* New Haven: Yale University Press, 1957.

James, Angela, and Mina Hills, eds. *Mrs. John Brown, 1847–1935.* London: John Murray, 1937.

James, William. *The Varieties of Religious Experience.* 1902. Reprint. New York: New American Library, 1958.

Jay, Nancy. "Gender and Dichotomy." *Feminist Studies* 7, 1 (Spring 1981): 38–56.

Kaplan, Carey, and Ellen Cronan Rose, eds. *Doris Lessing: The Alchemy of Survival.* Athens: Ohio University Press, 1988.

Kapp, Yvonne. *Eleanor Marx.* Vol. 2. London: Lawrence and Wishart, 1976.

Kent, Susan Kingsley. *Sex and Suffrage in Britain, 1860–1914*. Princeton, NJ: Princeton University Press, 1987.

Kindilien, Carlin T. "Stephen Crane and the 'Savage Philosophy' of Olive Schreiner." *Studies in English* 3, 2 (Summer 1957).

Kissen, Rita. *Vera Brittain: Writing a Life*. Ph.D. diss., University of Massachusetts at Amherst, 1986.

Koebner, Richard, and Helmut Dan Schmidt. *Imperialism: The Story and Significance of a Political Word, 1840–1960*. Cambridge: Cambridge University Press, 1964.

Koss, Stephen, ed. *The Pro-Boers: The Anatomy of an Anti-war Movement*. Chicago: University of Chicago Press, 1973.

Laski, Marghanita. *Ecstasy: A Study of Some Secular and Religious Experiences*. Bloomington: Indiana University Press, 1961.

Le May, G. H. L. *British Supremacy in South Africa, 1899–1907*. Oxford: Oxford University Press (Clarendon Press), 1965.

Lerner, Gerda. *The Creation of Patriarchy*. Oxford: Oxford University Press, 1986.

Lessing, Doris. *A Small Personal Voice*. New York: Knopf, 1974.

Levine, George. *The Realistic Imagination: English Fiction from Frankenstein to Lady Chatterley*. Chicago: University of Chicago Press, 1981.

Lewis, I. M. *Ecstatic Religion*. Middlesex: Penguin Books, 1971.

Lewis, Jane. "Beyond Suffrage: English Feminism during the 1920s." *Maryland Historian* 4 (Spring 1975).

Lewsen, Phyllis. *J. X. Merriman: Paradoxical South African Statesman*. New Haven: Yale University Press, 1982.

Liddington, Jill. *The Life and Times of a Respectable Rebel: Selina Cooper, 1864–1946*. London: Virago, 1984.

Liddington, Jill, and Jill Norris. *One Hand Tied behind Us: The Rise of the Women's Suffrage Movement*. London: Virago, 1978.

Lightman, Bernard. *The Origins of Agnosticism: Victorian Unbelief and the Limits of Knowledge*. Baltimore: Johns Hopkins University Press, 1987.

Lorimer, Douglas. *Colour, Class, and the Victorians*. Leicester: Leicester University Press, 1978.

——. "Theoretical Racism and Late Victorian Anthropology, 1870–1900." *Victorian Studies* 31, 1 (Spring 1988): 405–30.

Mackenzie, Midge. *Shoulder to Shoulder*. New York: Knopf, 1975.

Maison, Margaret. *Search Your Soul, Eustace: Victorian Religious Novels*. London: Sheed and Ward, 1961.

Marcus, Jane. "Olive Schreiner: Cartographer of the Spirit/A Review Article." *Minnesota Review*, Spring 1979, 58–66.

Marks, Sheila, and Anthony Atmore, eds. *Economy and Society in Pre-industrial South Africa*. London: Longman Group, 1980.

Marrot, H. V. *Life and Letters of John Galsworthy*. New York: Scribner, 1936.

Maslow, Abraham H. *Religions, Values, and Peak Experiences.* Columbus: Ohio State University Press, 1964.

Meintjes, Johannes. *Olive Schreiner: Portrait of a South African Woman.* Johannesburg: Keartland, 1965.

Moore, Doris Langley. *E. Nesbit: A Biography.* Philadelphia: Chilton, 1966.

Moore, James R. *The Post-Darwinian Controversies: A Study of the Protestant Struggle to Come to Terms with Darwin in Great Britain and America, 1870–1900.* Cambridge: Cambridge University Press, 1979.

Morantz-Sanchez, Regina Markell. *Sympathy and Science: Women Physicians in American Medicine.* Oxford: Oxford University Press, 1985.

Mosedale, Susan Sleuth. "Science Corrupted: Victorian Biologists Consider 'The Woman Question.' " *Journal of the History of Biology* 2, 1 (Spring 1978): 1–55.

Murphy, Howard R. "The Ethical Revolt against Orthodoxy in Early Victorian England." *American Historical Review* 60 (1955): 800–17.

Newton, Judith, and Nancy Hoffman. "Preface." *Feminist Studies* 14, 1 (Spring 1988).

Nord, Deborah Epstein. *The Apprenticeship of Beatrice Webb.* Amherst: University of Massachusetts Press, 1985.

Norton, Bernard J. *Karl Pearson and the Galtonian Tradition.* Ph.D. diss., University College, 1978.

Ochs, Carol. *Behind the Sex of God.* Boston: Beacon Press, 1977.

Olsen, Tillie. "Silences: When Writers Don't Write." In Susan Koppelman Cornillon, ed., *Images of Women in Fiction: Feminist Perspectives.* Bowling Green, OH: Bowling Green University Press, 1972.

Pakenham, Thomas. *The Boer War.* New York: Random House, 1979.

Pankhurst, E. Sylvia. *The Suffragette Movement.* London: Virago, 1984.

Parker, Kenneth, ed. *The South African Novel in English: Essays in Criticism and Society.* New York: Africana, 1978.

Pearson, Ruth Roach, and Somer Brodribb, eds. *Women and Peace: Theoretical, Historical and Practical Perspectives.* London: Croom Helm, forthcoming.

Petroff, Elizabeth Alvilda. *Consolation of the Blessed.* New York: Alta Gaia Society, 1979.

Piehler, Paul. *The Visionary Landscape: A Study in Medieval Allegory.* London: Edward Arnold, 1971.

Pierson, Stanley. *Marxism and the Origins of British Socialism: The Struggle for a New Consciousness.* Ithaca, NY: Cornell University Press, 1973.

Plomer, William. *Cecil Rhodes.* London: Peter Davies, 1933.

Porter, Bernard. *Critics of Empire.* London: St. Martin's Press, 1968.

Postlethwaite, Diane. *Making It Whole: A Victorian Circle and the Shape of Their World.* Columbus: Ohio State University Press, 1984.

Pratt, Annis. *Archetypal Patterns in Women's Fiction.* Bloomington: Indiana University Press, 1981.

Price, Richard. *An Imperial War and the British Working Class.* London: Routledge and Kegan Paul, 1971.

Rainger, Ronald. "Race, Politics, and Science: The Anthropological Society of London in the 1860s." *Victorian Studies* 22, 1 (August 1978): 51–70.

Reed, John R. *Victorian Conventions*. Athens: Ohio University Press, 1975.

Rendall, Jane. *The Origins of Modern Feminism: Women in Britain, France, and the United States, 1780–1860*. New York: Schocken Books, 1894.

Renier, Olive. *Before the Bonfire*. Warwickshire: P. Drinkwater, 1984.

Rive, Richard. "An Infinite Compassion: A Critical Comparison of Olive Schreiner's Novels." *Contrast* (Cape Town) 29 (October 1972).

———. "In Search of Olive Schreiner, Part III." *Week-End Argus* (Cape Town), June 16, 1973.

———. "New Light on Olive Schreiner." *Contrast* (Cape Town) 32 (November 1973).

———. "Prophetess of Doom." *Week-End Argus* (Cape Town), June 2, 1973.

Rose, Jonathan. *The Edwardian Temperament*. Athens: Ohio University Press, 1986.

Rosenberg, Carroll Smith. *Disorderly Conduct: Visions of Gender in Victorian America*. Oxford: Oxford University Press, 1985.

Rowbotham, Sheila. *Hidden From History: Rediscovering Women in History from the 17th Century to the Present*. New York: Random House, 1974.

———. "In Search of Carpenter." *History Workshop* 3 (Spring 1977): 122–24.

Rowbotham, Sheila, and Jeffrey Weeks. *Socialism and the New Life: The Personal and Sexual Politics of Edward Carpenter and Havelock Ellis*. London: Pluto Press, 1977.

Rowell, Peter. *Hell and the Victorians*. Oxford: Oxford University Press (Clarendon Press), 1971.

Rubin, Gayle. "The Traffic in Women: Notes on the 'Political Economy' of Sex." In Rayna Reiter, ed., *Toward an Anthropology of Women*. New York: Monthly Review. 1975.

Ruddick, Sara. "Maternal Thinking." *Feminist Studies* 6, 2 (Summer 1980).

———. "Preservative Love and Military Destruction: Some Reflections on Mothering and Peace." In Joyce Trebilcot, ed., *Mothering: Essays in Feminist Theory*. Totowa, NJ: Rowan and Allanheld, 1984.

Russett, Cynthia Eagle. *Darwin in America: The Intellectual Response, 1865–1912*. San Francisco: W. H. Freeman, 1976.

———. *The Scientific Construction of Womanhood in the Late Nineteenth Century*. Cambridge, MA: Harvard University Press, forthcoming.

Sachs, Albie. *Justice in South Africa*. Berkeley: University of California Press, 1973.

Sanday, Peggy Reeves. *Female Power and Male Dominance: On the Origins of Sexual Inequality*. Cambridge: Cambridge University Press, 1981.

Sayers, Janet. *Biological Politics: Feminist and Anti-feminist Perspectives*. London: Tavistock, 1982.

Showalter, Elaine. *A Literature of Their Own: British Women Novelists from Bronte to Lessing*. Princeton, NJ: Princeton University Press, 1977.

Simons, H. J., and R. E. Simons. *Class and Colour in South Africa, 1850–1950*. London: International Defense and Aid Fund for South Africa, 1983.

Singer, June. *Androgyny: Toward a New Theory of Sexuality.* New York: Doubleday (Anchor Books), 1977.

Smith, Malvern van Wyk, and Don Maclennan, eds. *Olive Schreiner and After.* Cape Town: David Philip, 1983.

Sowder, William J. *Emerson's Impact on the British Isles and Canada.* Charlottesville: University of Virginia Press, 1966.

Sowerwine, Charles. "The Socialist Women's Movement from 1850 to 1940." In Renate Bridenthal, Claudia Koonz, and Susan Stuard, eds., *Becoming Visible: Women in European History.* Boston: Houghton Mifflin, 1987.

Spender, Dale, ed. *Feminist Theorists.* New York, Pantheon Books, 1983.

Stepan, Nancy. *The Idea of Race in Science: Great Britain, 1800–1960.* Hamden, CT: Archon Books, 1982.

Stites, Richard. *The Women's Liberation Movement in Russia: Feminism, Nihilism, and Bolshevism, 1860–1930.* Princeton, NJ: Princeton University Press, 1978.

Stocking, George W., Jr. *Race, Culture, and Evolution: Essays in the History of Anthropology.* New York: Free Press, 1968.

Strunk, Robert C., and Joyce Walker Boyd. "The Student with Asthma." *Today's Education: Journal of the National Education Association* 69, 4 (November–December 1980): 64–68.

Symondson, Anthony, ed. *The Victorian Crisis of Faith.* London: Society for Promoting Christian Knowledge, 1970.

Tanner, Nancy, and Adrienne Zihlman. "Women in Evolution, Part I: Innovation and Selection in Human Origins." *Signs* 1, 3 (Spring 1976): 585–608.

———. "Women in Evolution, Part II: Subsistence and Social Organization among Early Hominids." *Signs* 4, 1 (Autumn 1978): 4–20.

Tart, Charles T. *Altered States of Consciousness.* New York: Doubleday, 1972.

Taylor, Barbara. *Eve and the New Jerusalem.* New York: Pantheon Books, 1983.

Thompson, E. P. *William Morris: Romantic to Revolutionary.* New York: Pantheon Books, 1955.

Thompson, Lawrence. *The Enthusiasts.* London: Victor Gollancz, 1971.

Thompson, Leonard. *The Political Mythology of Apartheid.* New Haven: Yale University Press, 1988.

———. *The Unification of South Africa, 1902–1910.* Oxford: Oxford University Press, 1960.

Tiger, Lionel. *Men in Groups.* New York: Random House, 1969.

Turner, Frank. *Between Science and Religion.* New Haven: Yale University Press, 1974.

Vellacott Newberry, Jo. "Anti-war Suffragists." *History* 62 (October 1977): 411–25.

Vicinus, Martha, ed. *Suffer and Be Still: Women in the Victorian Age.* Bloomington: Indiana University Press, 1972.

———, ed. *A Widening Sphere: Changing Roles of Victorian Women.* Bloomington: Indiana University Press, 1977.

Vorzimmer, Peter J. *Charles Darwin: The Years of Controversy*. Philadelphia: Temple University Press, 1970.

Walkowitz, Judith R. "Science, Feminism, and Romance: The Men and Women's Club, 1885–1889." *History Workshop* 21 (Spring 1986): 37–59.

Weeks, Jeffrey. *Sex, Politics, and Society: The Regulation of Sexuality since 1800*. London: Longman, 1981.

Wellek, René. *A History of Modern Criticism, 1750–1950*. Vol. 2: *The Romantic Age*. New Haven: Yale University Press, 1955.

Whyte, Frederic. *The Life of W. T. Stead*. Boston: Houghton Mifflin, 1927.

Willan, Brian. *Sol Plaatje: South African Nationalist (1876–1932)*. Berkeley: University of California Press, 1984.

Willis, Roy, ed. *The Interpretation of Symbolism*. London: A.S.A. Studies, 1975.

Wilson, Angus. *The Strange Ride of Rudyard Kipling*. New York: Viking Press, 1977.

Wiltsher, Anne. *Most Dangerous Women: Feminist Peace Campaigners of the Great War*. London: Pandora Press, 1985.

Winkler, Barbara Scott. "Victorian Daughters: The Lives and Feminism of Charlotte Perkins Gilman and Olive Schreiner." *University of Michigan Occasional Papers in Women's Studies* 13.

Winsten, Stephen. *Salt and His Circle*. London: Hutchinson, 1951.

Wolfe, Willard. *From Radicalism to Socialism: Men and Ideas in the Formation of Fabian Socialist Doctrines, 1881–1889*. New Haven: Yale University Press, 1975.

Woolf, Virginia. "Olive Schreiner." *New Republic* 42 (March 1925).

Yeo, Stephen. "A New Life: The Religion of Socialism in Britain, 1883–1896." *History Workshop* 4 (Autumn 1977): 5–56.

INDEX